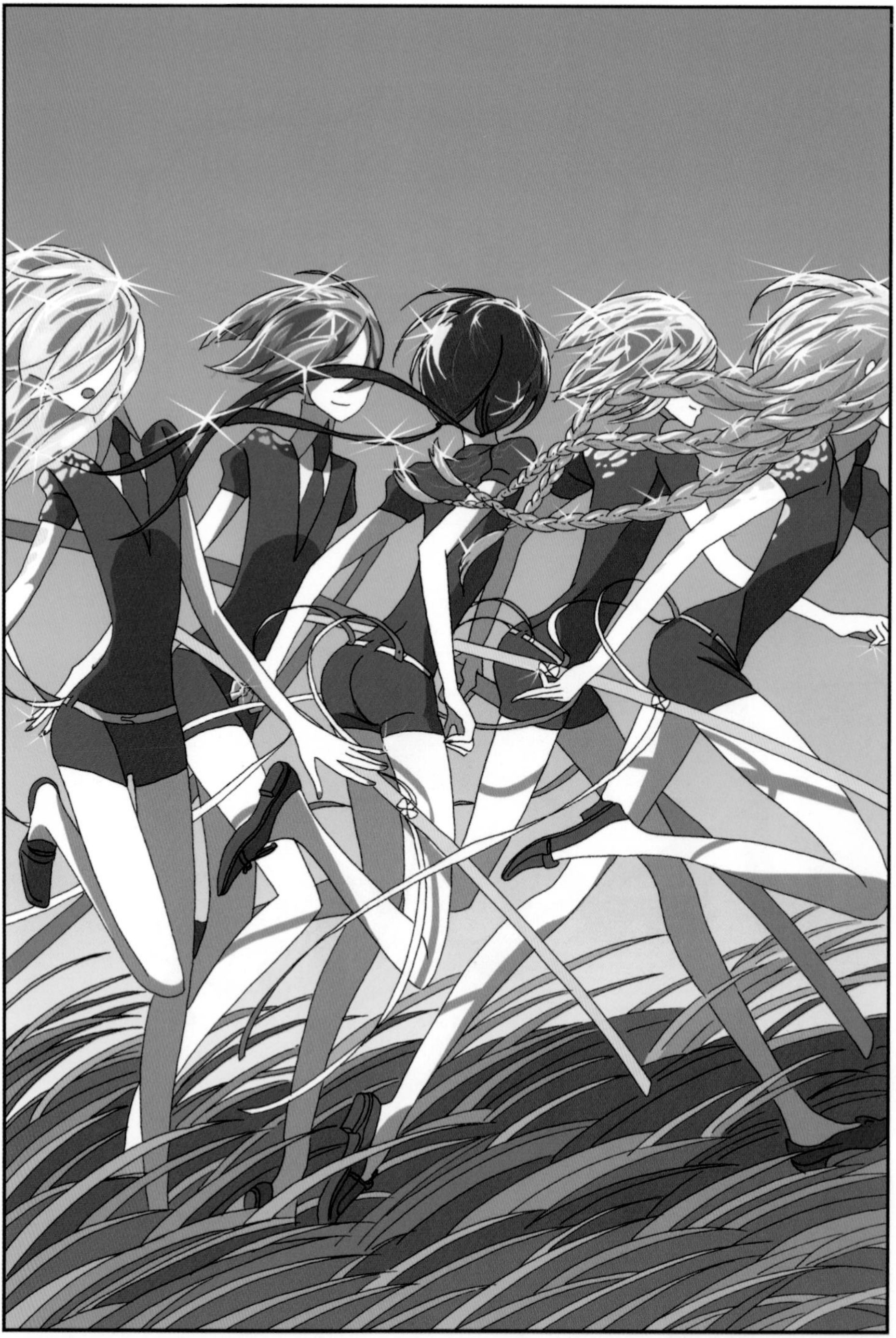

LAND OF THE LUSTROUS

1

HARUKO ICHIKAWA

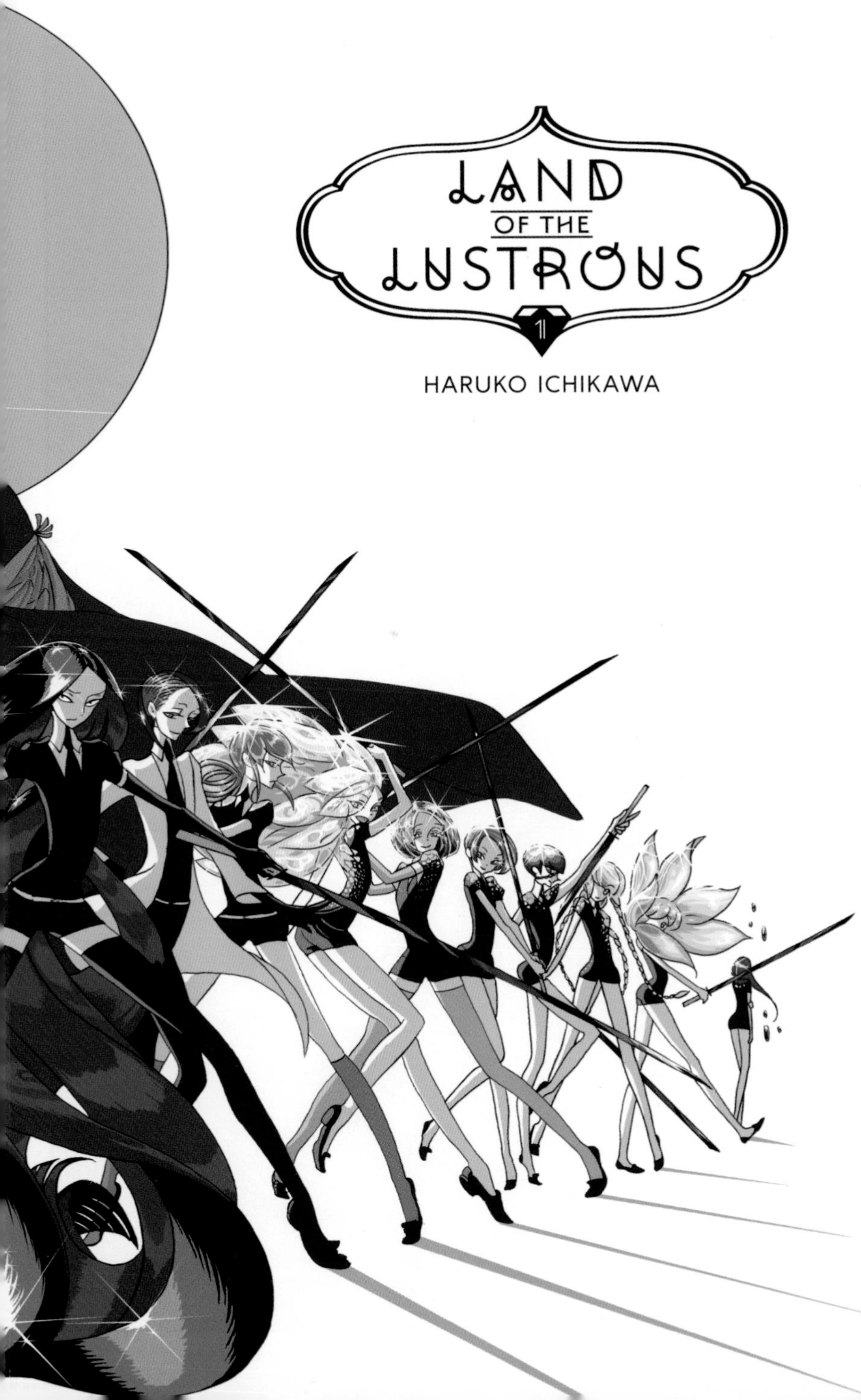

CONTENTS

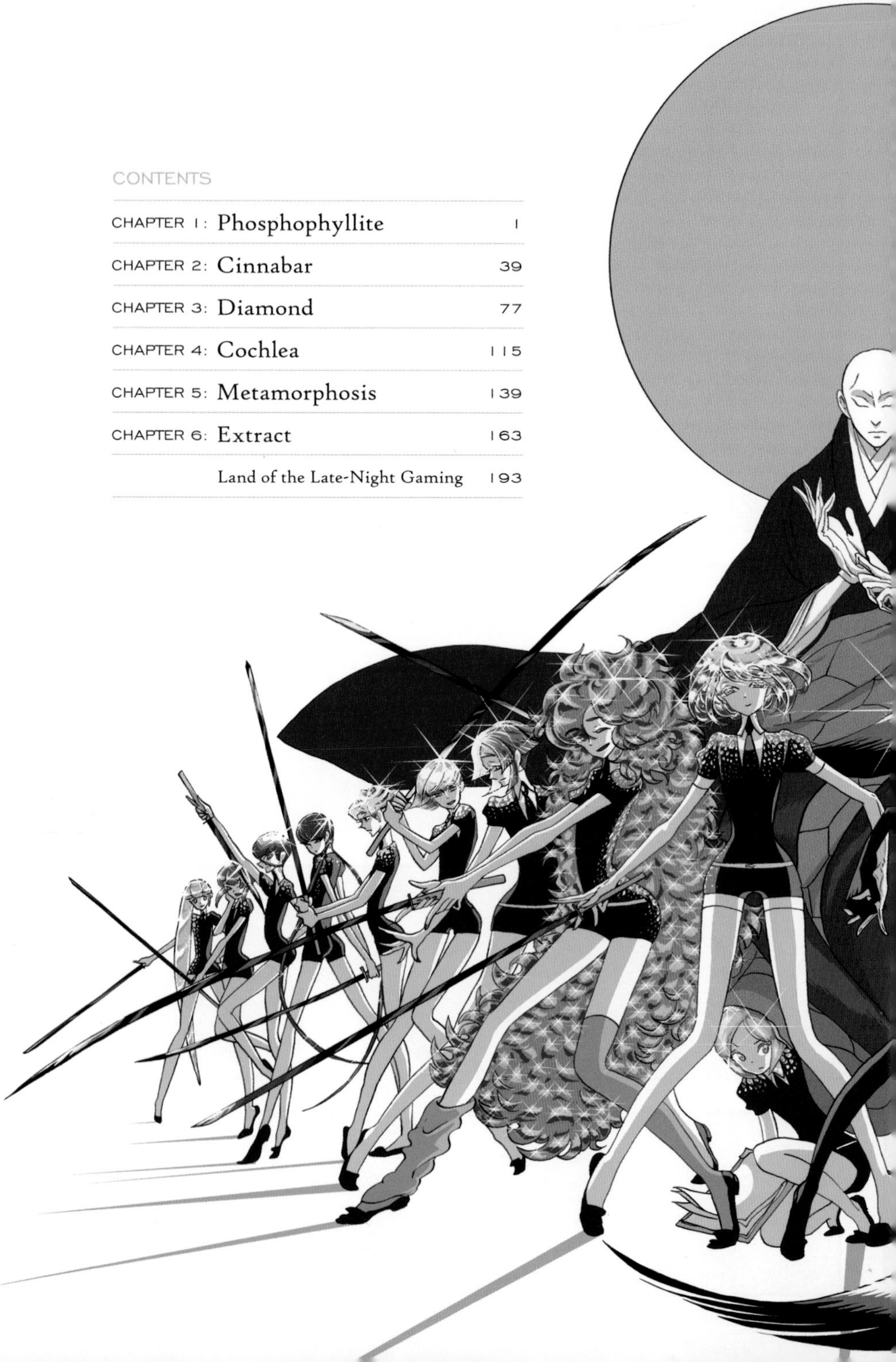

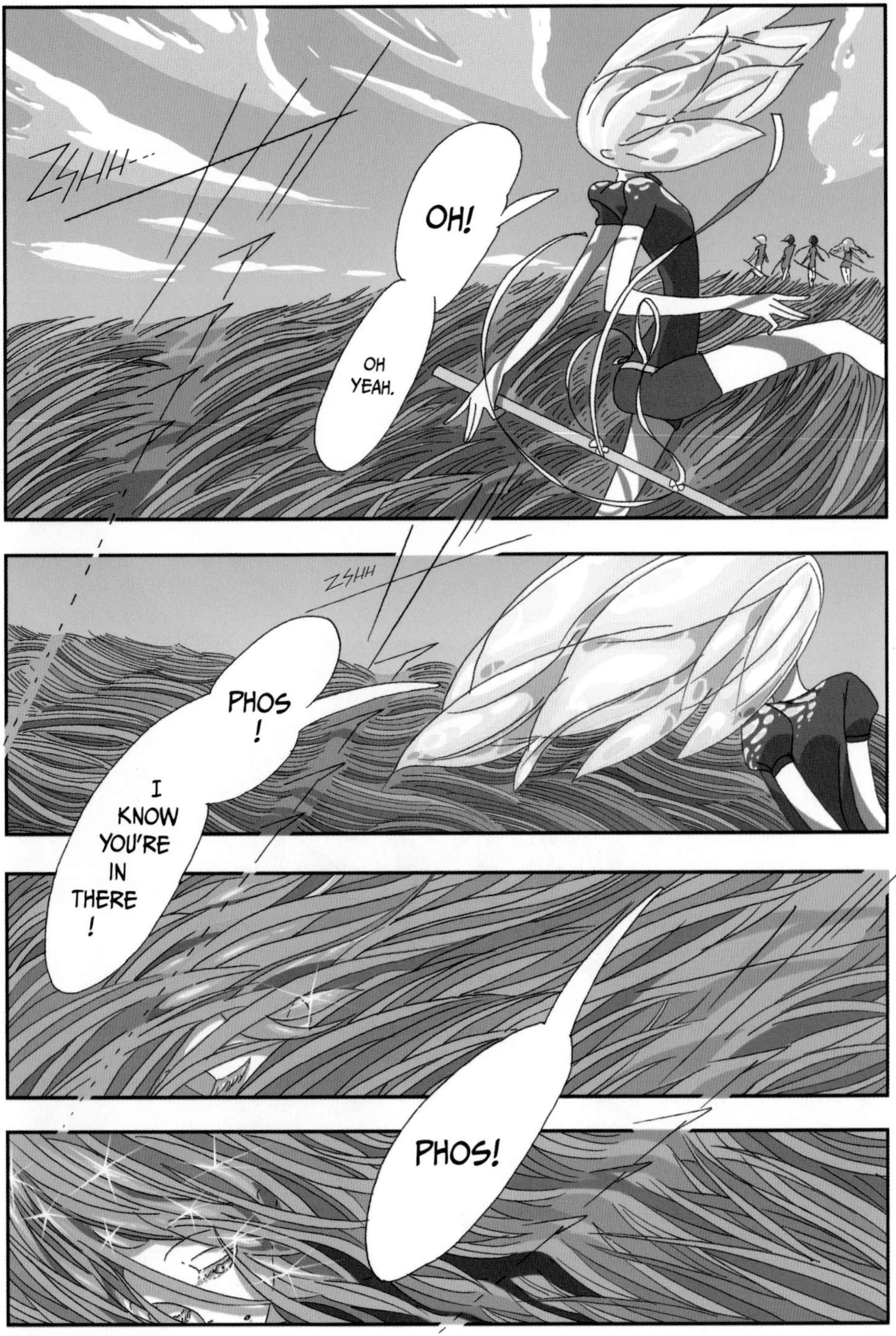
ZSHH-...
OH!
OH YEAH.
ZSHH
PHOS!
I KNOW YOU'RE IN THERE!
PHOS!

[redacted]

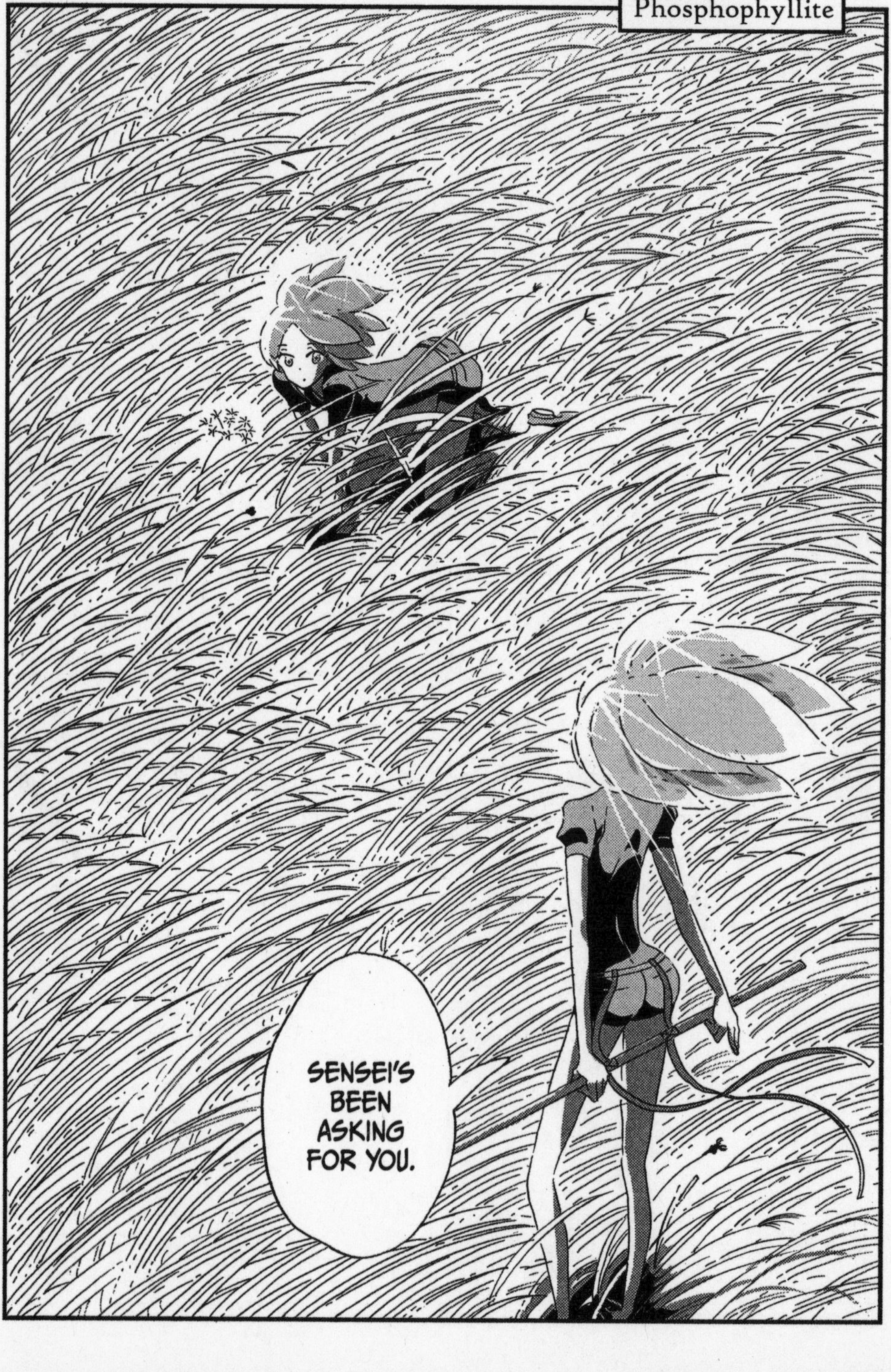
Phosphophyllite
SENSEI'S BEEN ASKING FOR YOU.

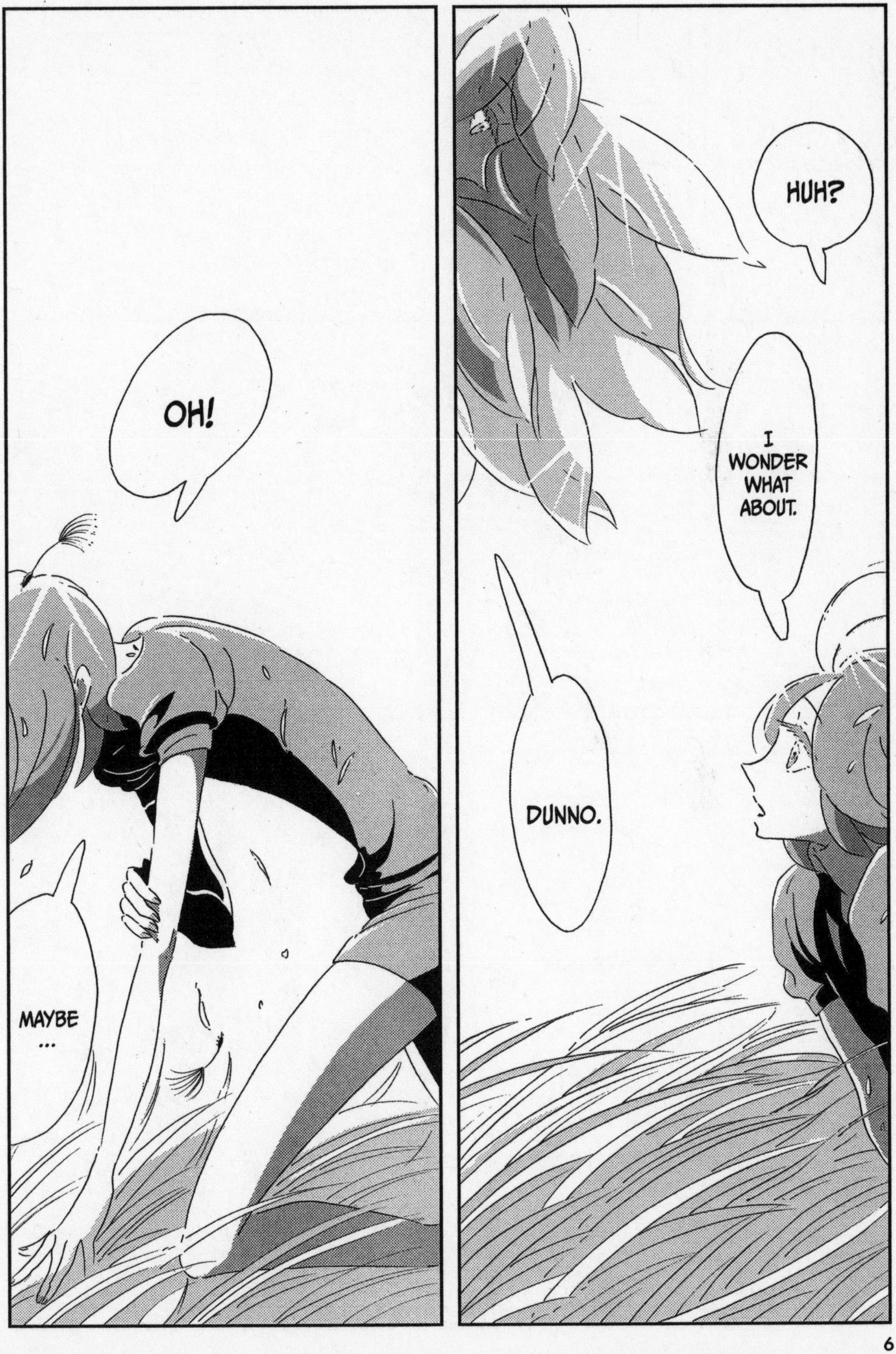
HUH?
I WONDER WHAT ABOUT.
DUNNO.
OH!
MAYBE ...

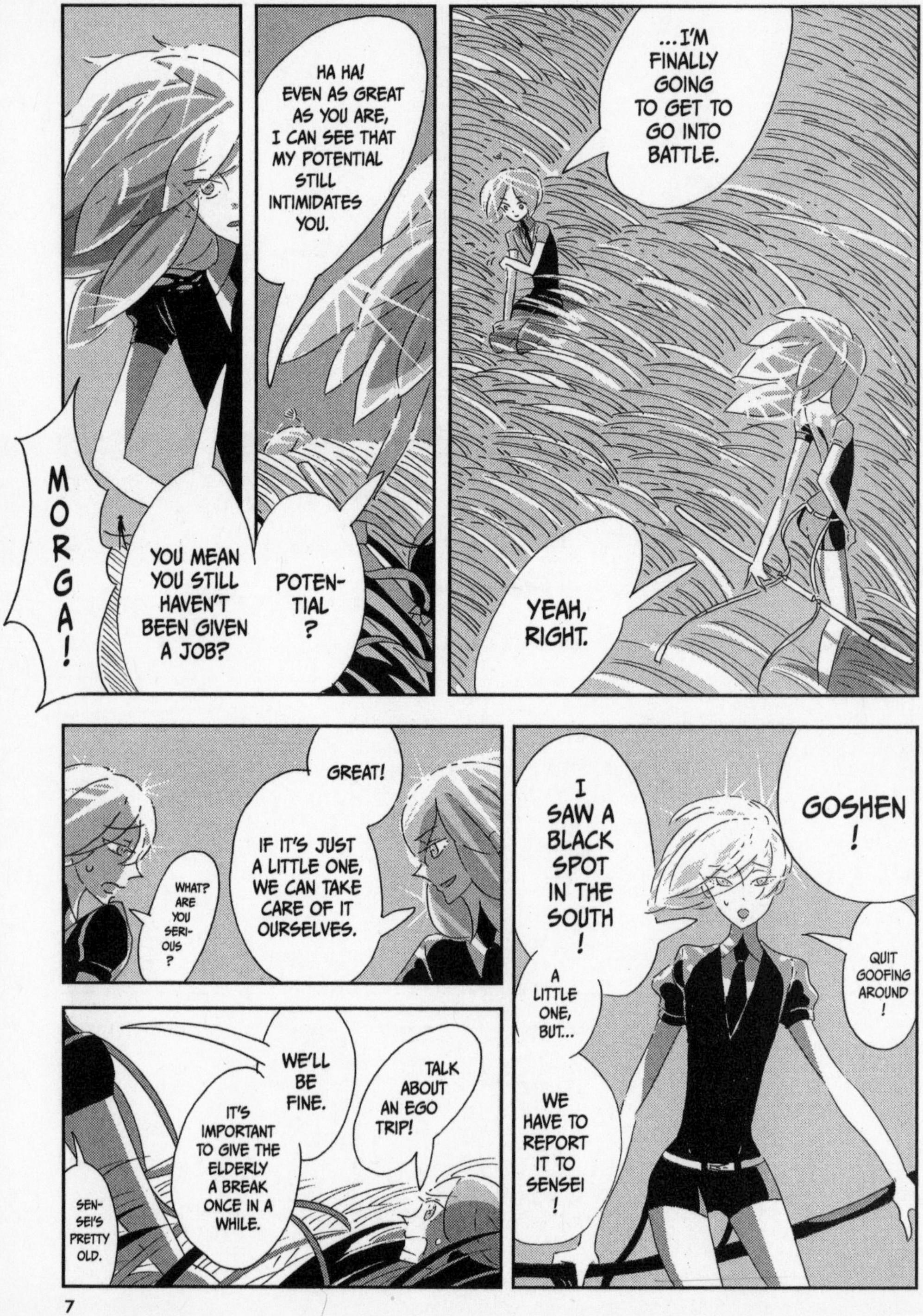
...I'M FINALLY GOING TO GET TO GO INTO BATTLE.
YEAH, RIGHT.
HA HA! EVEN AS GREAT AS YOU ARE, I CAN SEE THAT MY POTENTIAL STILL INTIMIDATES YOU.
POTEN-TIAL?
YOU MEAN YOU STILL HAVEN'T BEEN GIVEN A JOB?
MORGA!
GOSHEN!
I SAW A BLACK SPOT IN THE SOUTH!
QUIT GOOFING AROUND!
A LITTLE ONE, BUT...
WE HAVE TO REPORT IT TO SENSEI!
GREAT!
IF IT'S JUST A LITTLE ONE, WE CAN TAKE CARE OF IT OURSELVES.
WHAT? ARE YOU SERI-OUS?
WE'LL BE FINE.
TALK ABOUT AN EGO TRIP!
IT'S IMPORTANT TO GIVE THE ELDERLY A BREAK ONCE IN A WHILE.
SEN-SEI'S PRETTY OLD.

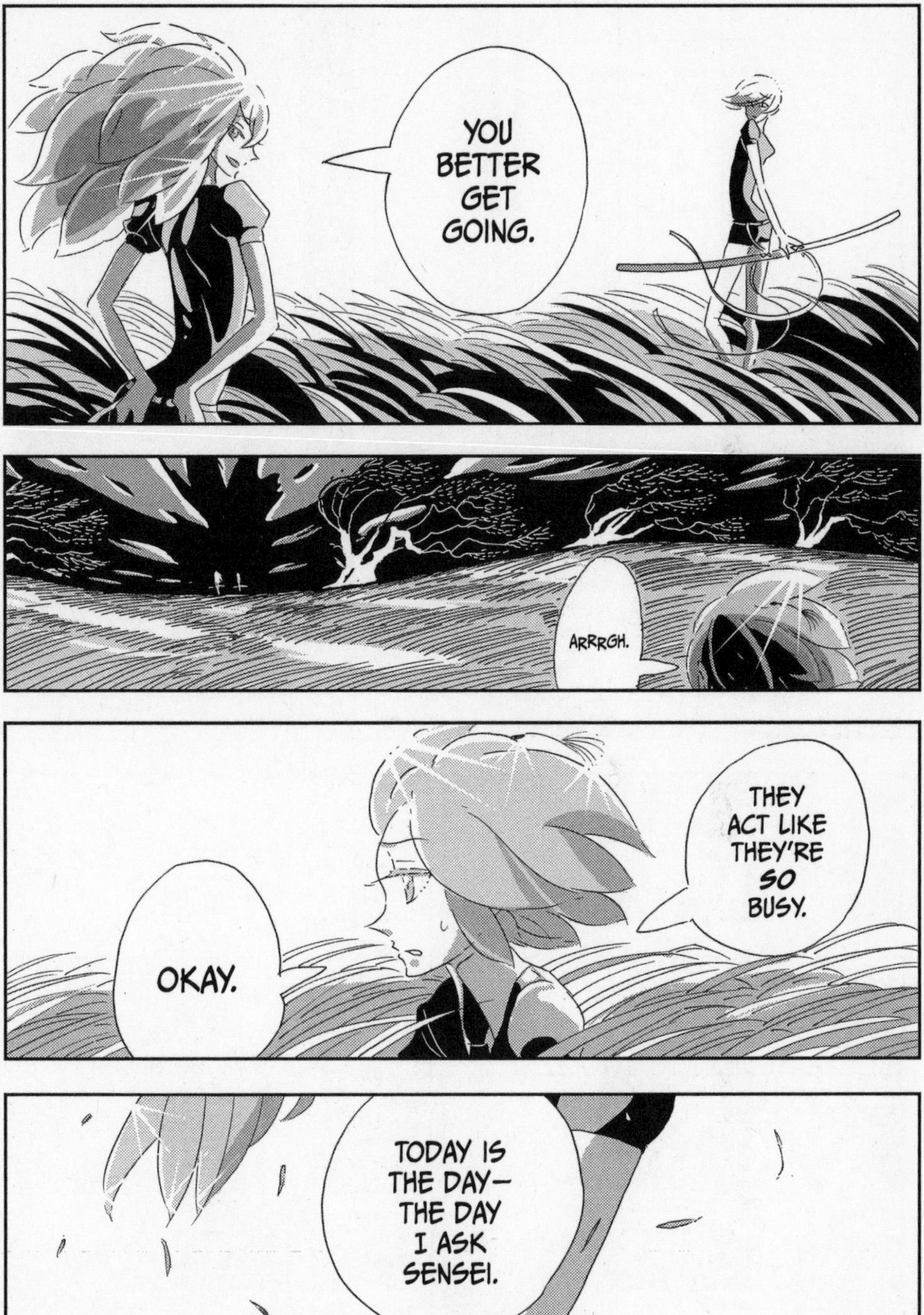
YOU BETTER GET GOING.
ARRRGH.
THEY ACT LIKE THEY'RE *SO* BUSY.
OKAY.
TODAY IS THE DAY—THE DAY I ASK SENSEI.

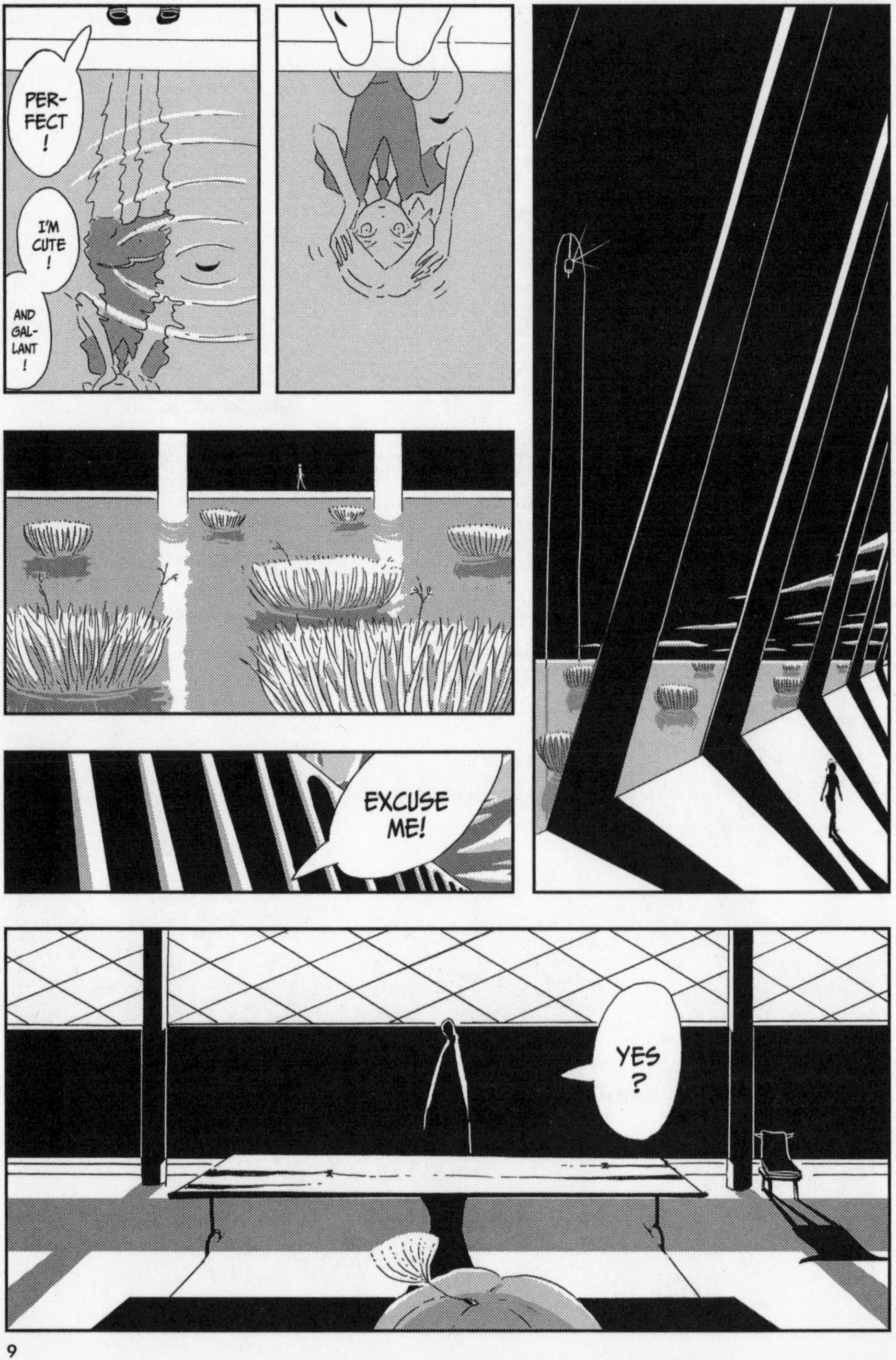
PER-FECT!
I'M CUTE!
AND GAL-LANT!
EXCUSE ME!
YES?

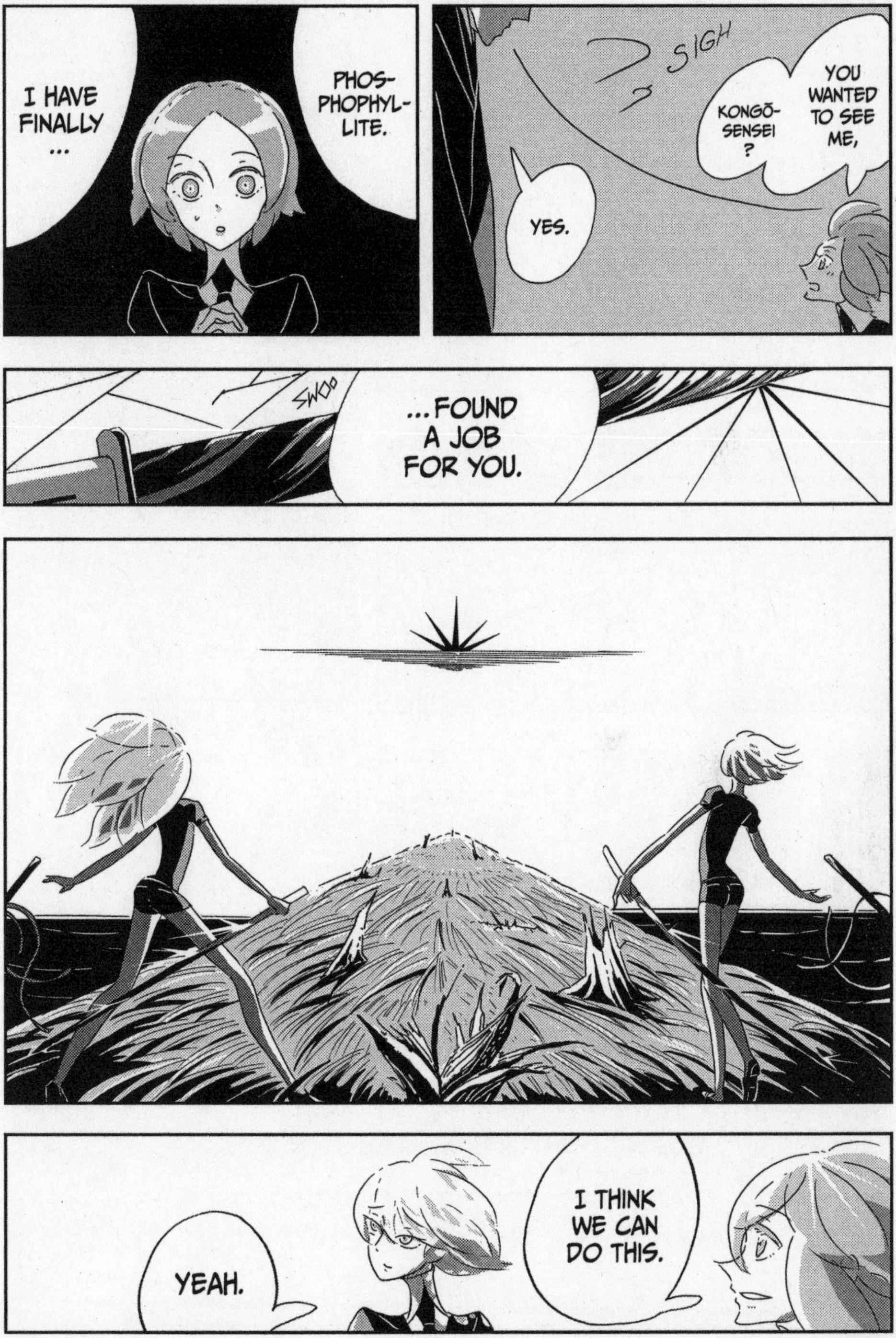
YOU WANTED TO SEE ME, KONGŌ-SENSEI?
SIGH
YES.
PHOS-PHOPHYL-LITE.
I HAVE FINALLY ...
SWOO
...FOUND A JOB FOR YOU.
I THINK WE CAN DO THIS.
YEAH.

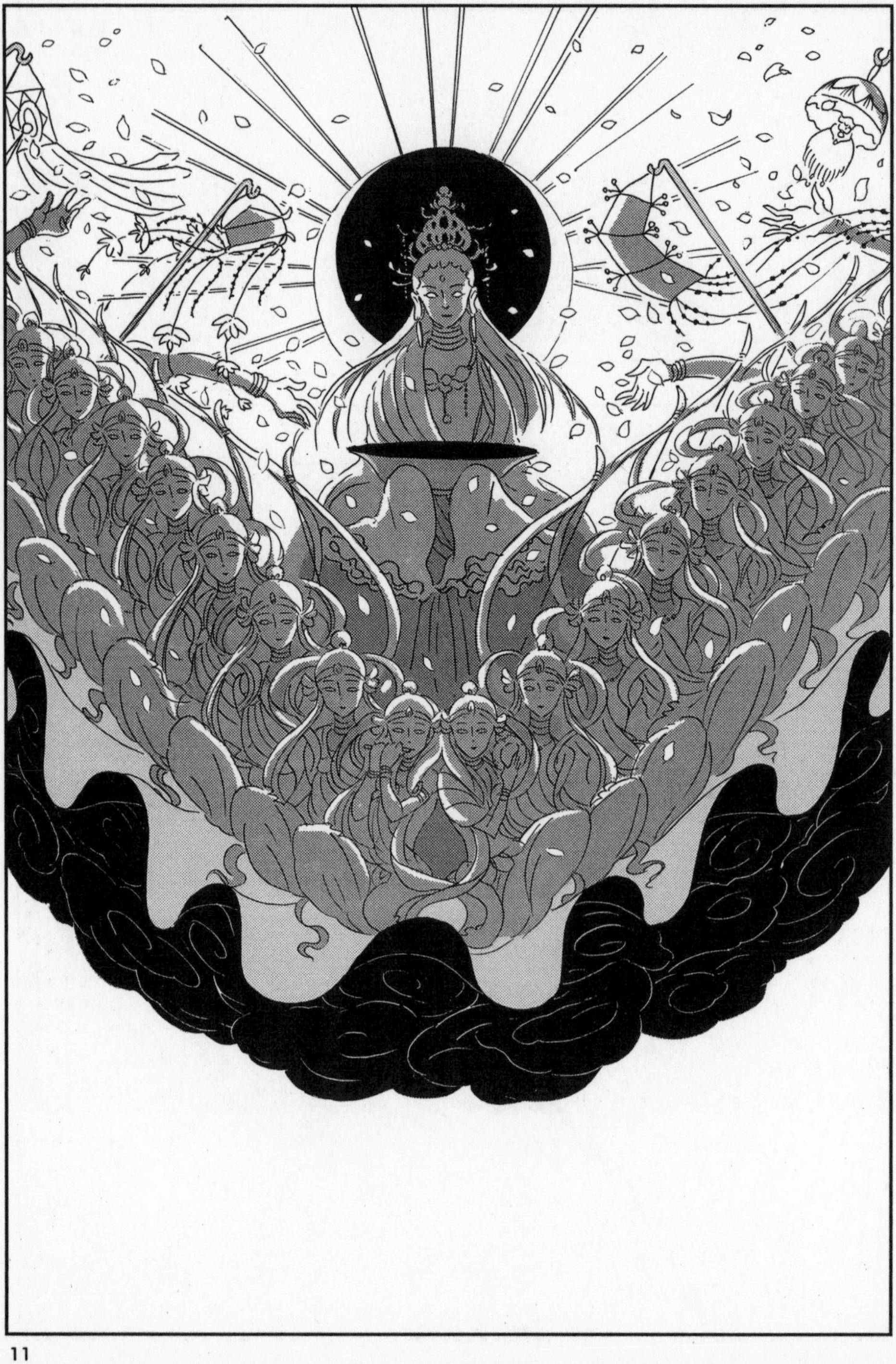

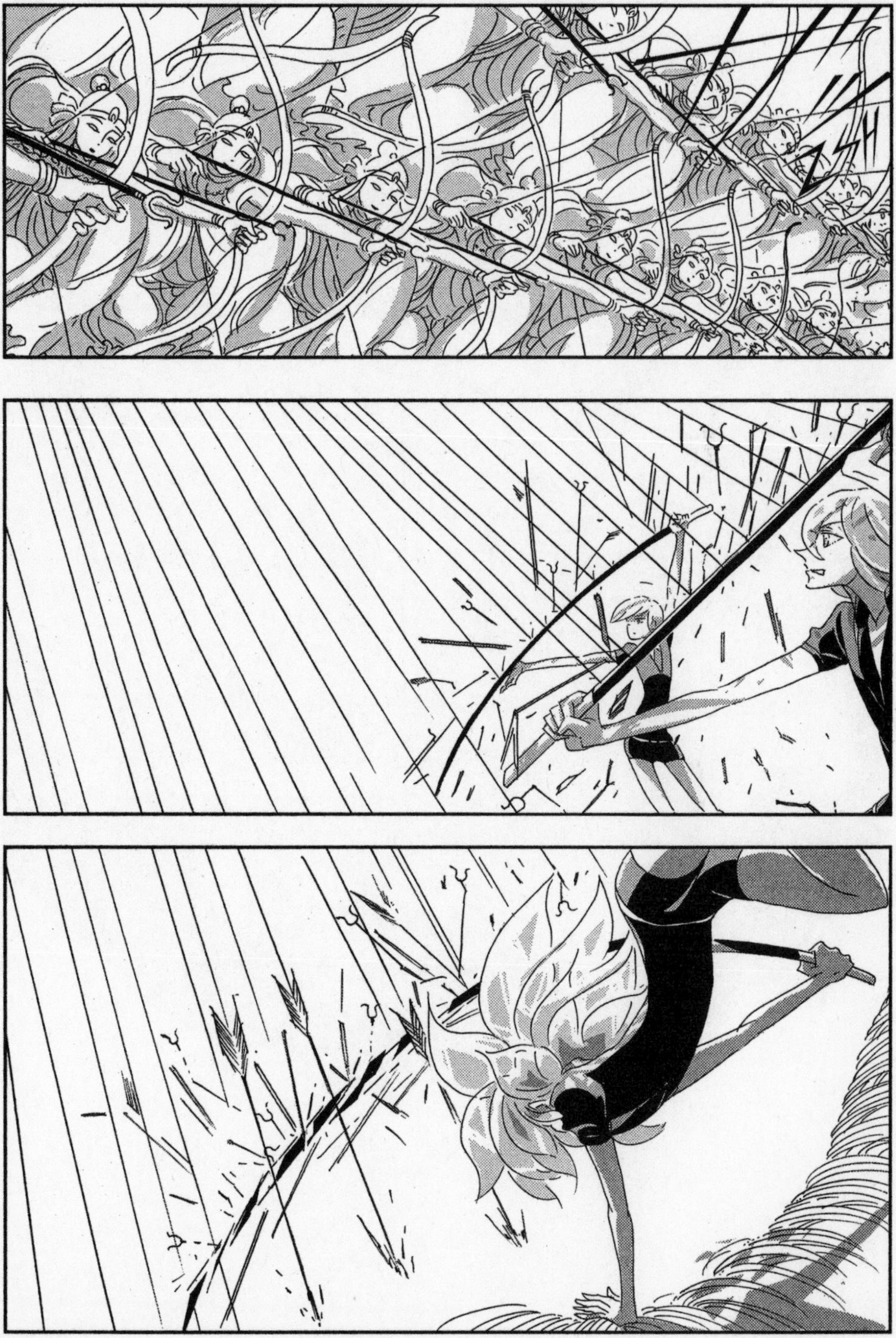
ZSH

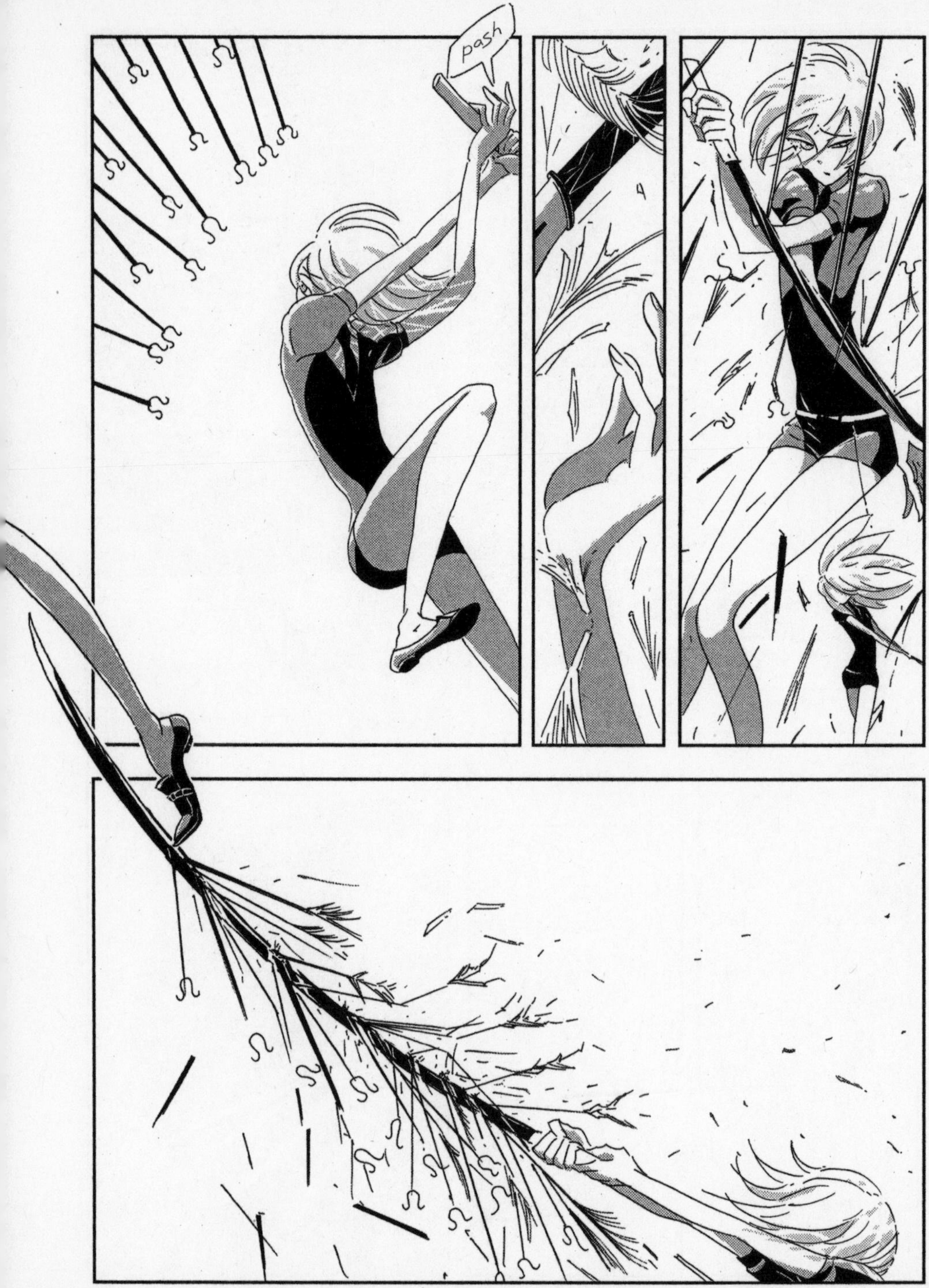
pash

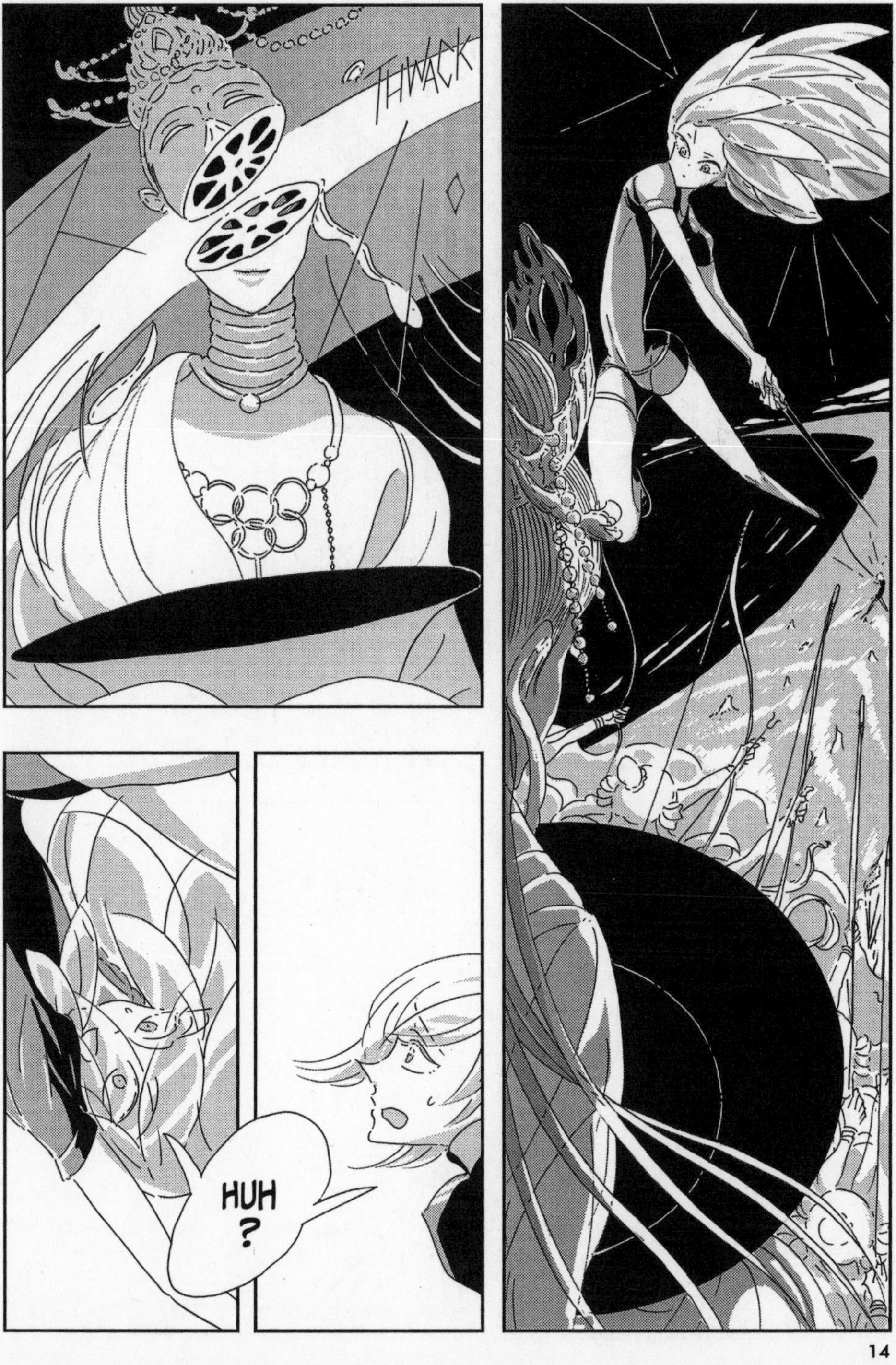
THWACK
HUH ?

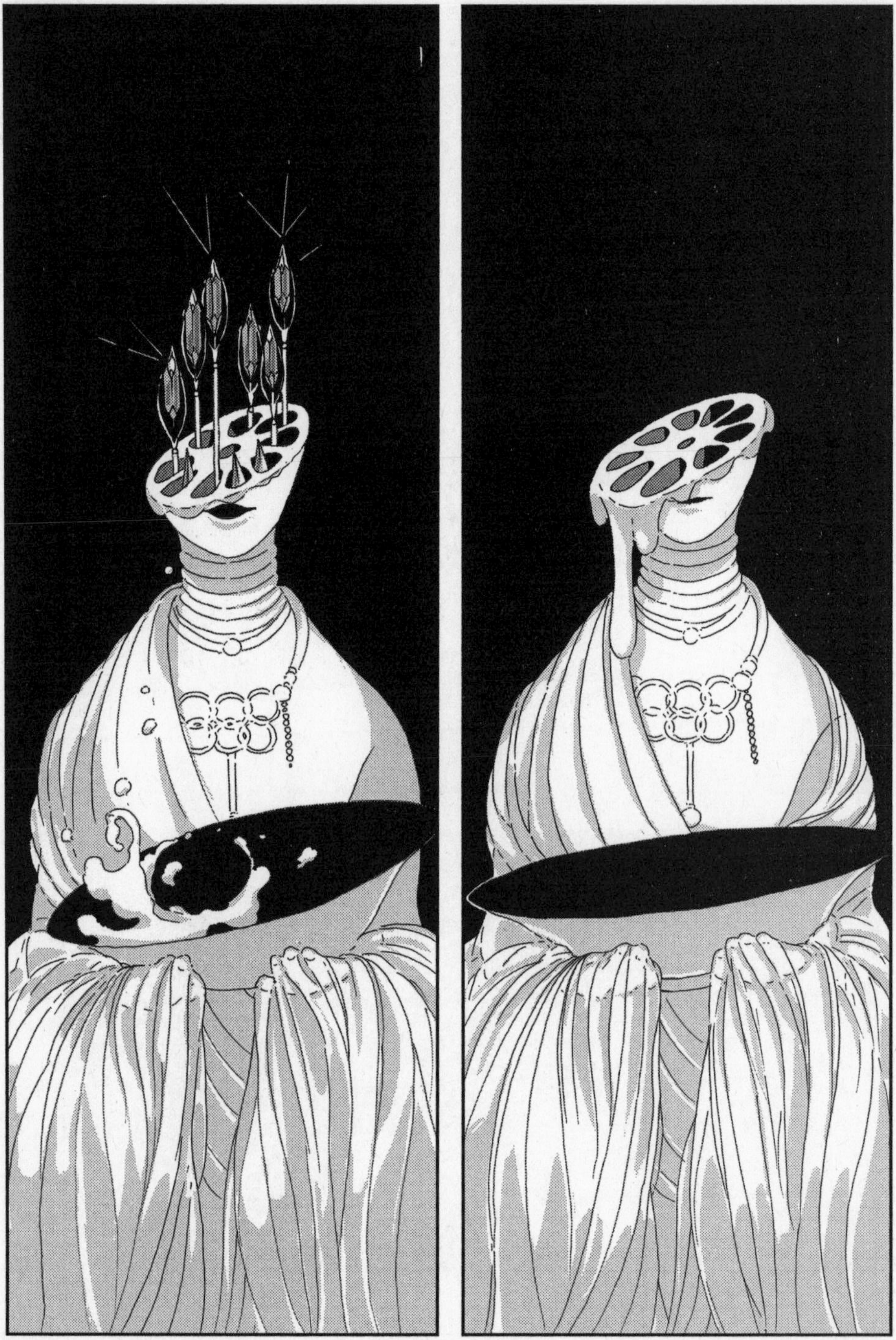

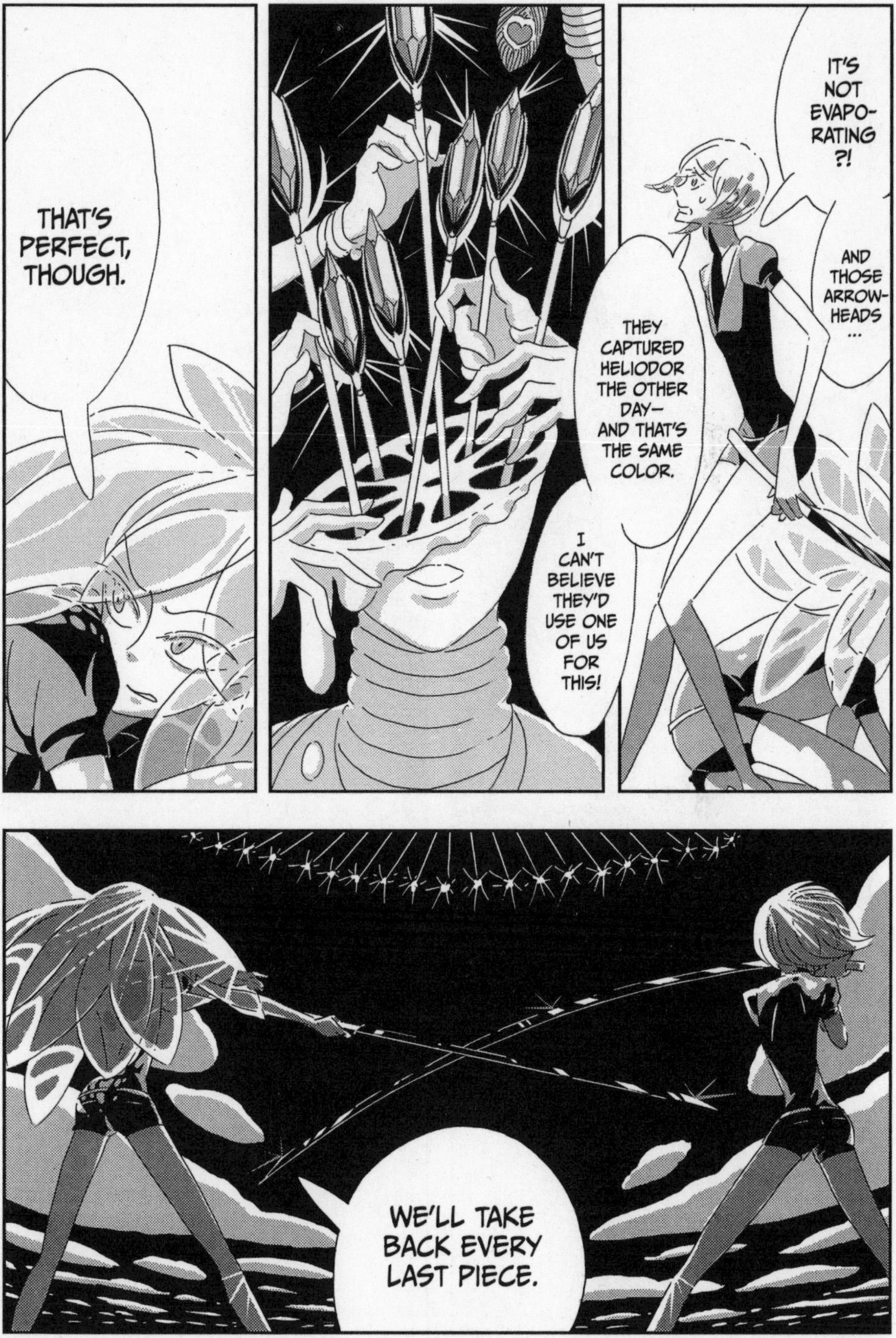
IT'S NOT EVAPO-RATING ?!
AND THOSE ARROW-HEADS ...
THEY CAPTURED HELIODOR THE OTHER DAY— AND THAT'S THE SAME COLOR.
I CAN'T BELIEVE THEY'D USE ONE OF US FOR THIS!
THAT'S PERFECT, THOUGH.
WE'LL TAKE BACK EVERY LAST PIECE.

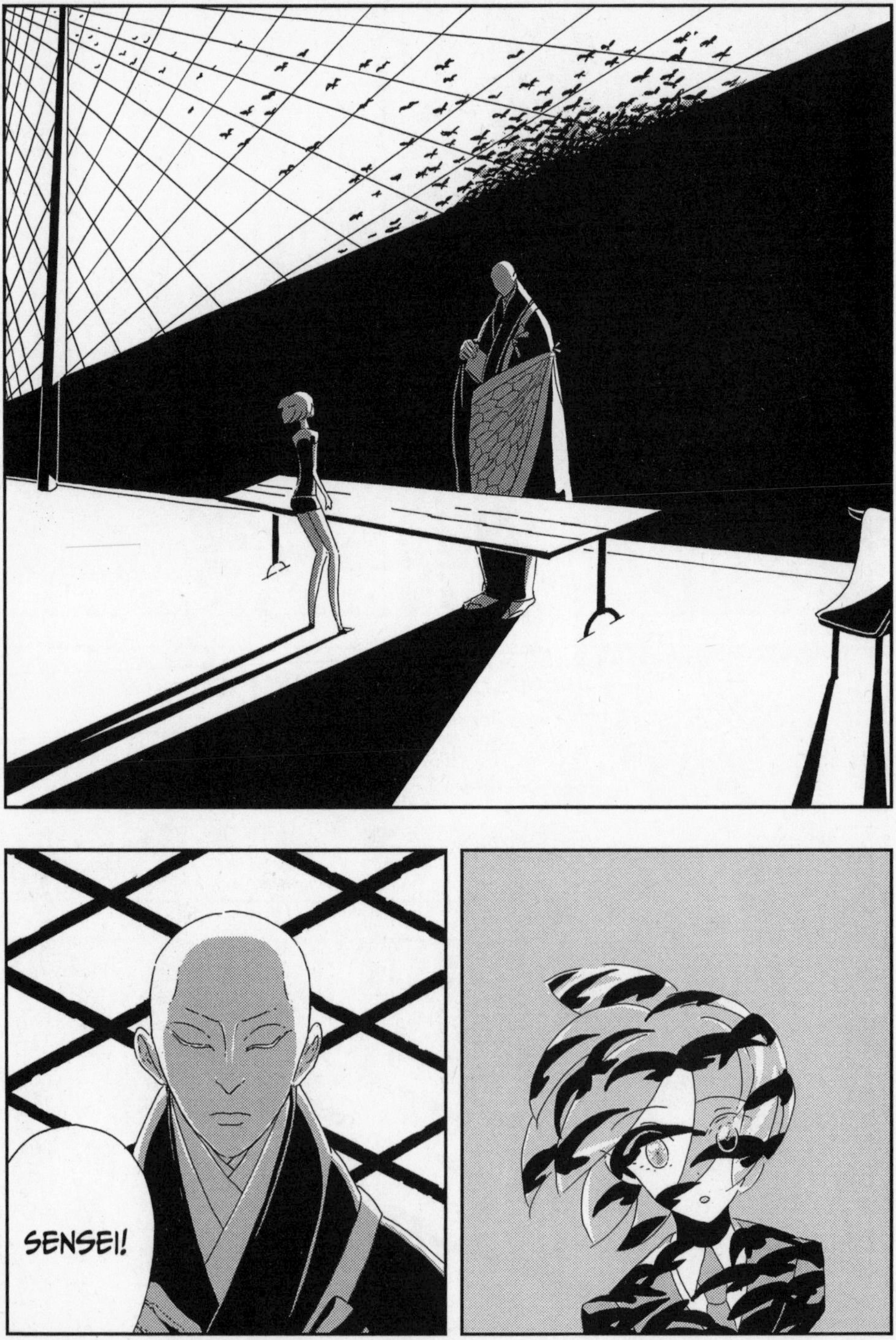
SENSEI!

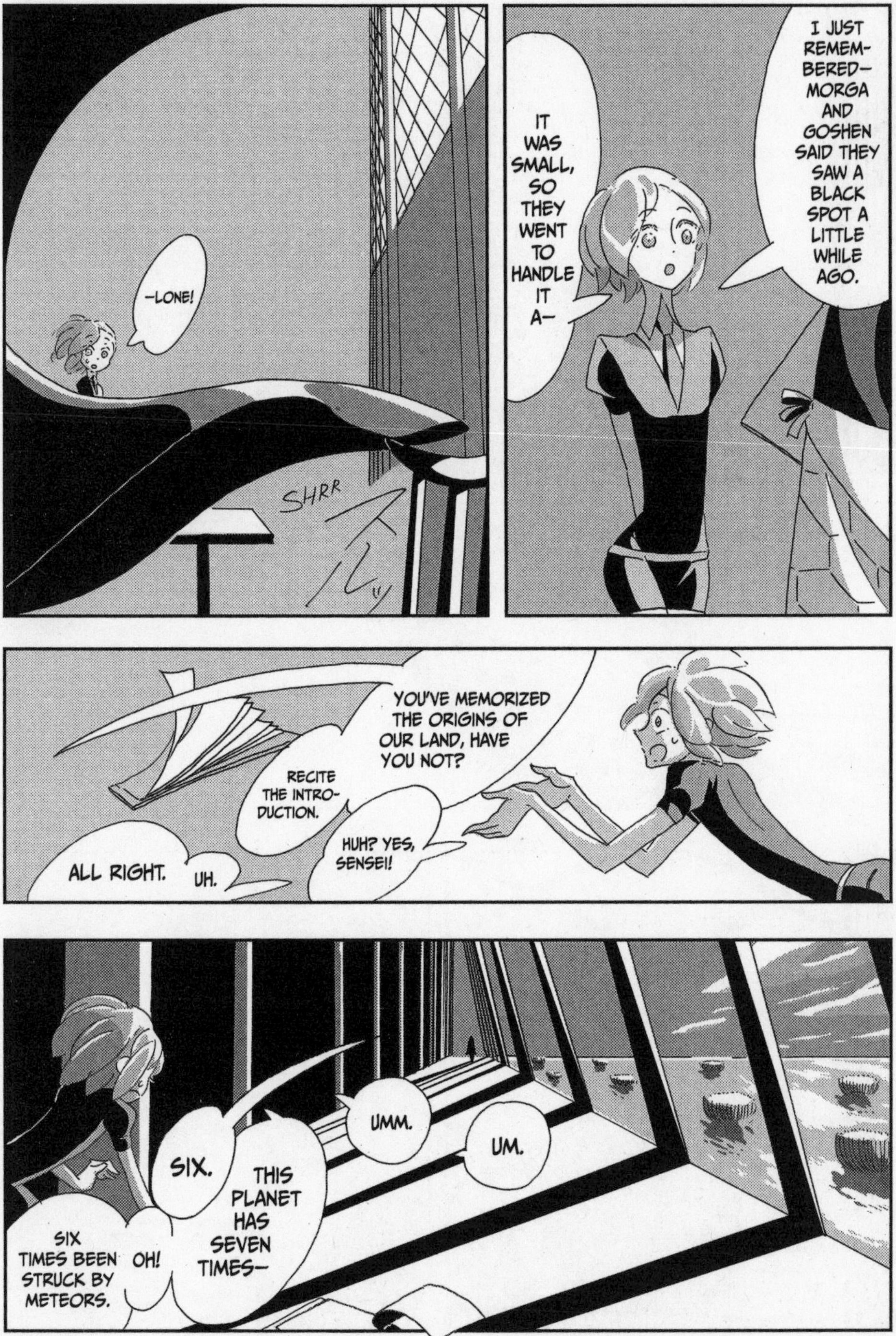
I JUST REMEMBERED—MORGA AND GOSHEN SAID THEY SAW A BLACK SPOT A LITTLE WHILE AGO.
IT WAS SMALL, SO THEY WENT TO HANDLE IT A—
—LONE!
SHRR
YOU'VE MEMORIZED THE ORIGINS OF OUR LAND, HAVE YOU NOT?
RECITE THE INTRODUCTION.
HUH? YES, SENSEI!
UH.
ALL RIGHT.
UMM.
UM.
THIS PLANET HAS SEVEN TIMES—
SIX.
OH!
SIX TIMES BEEN STRUCK BY METEORS.

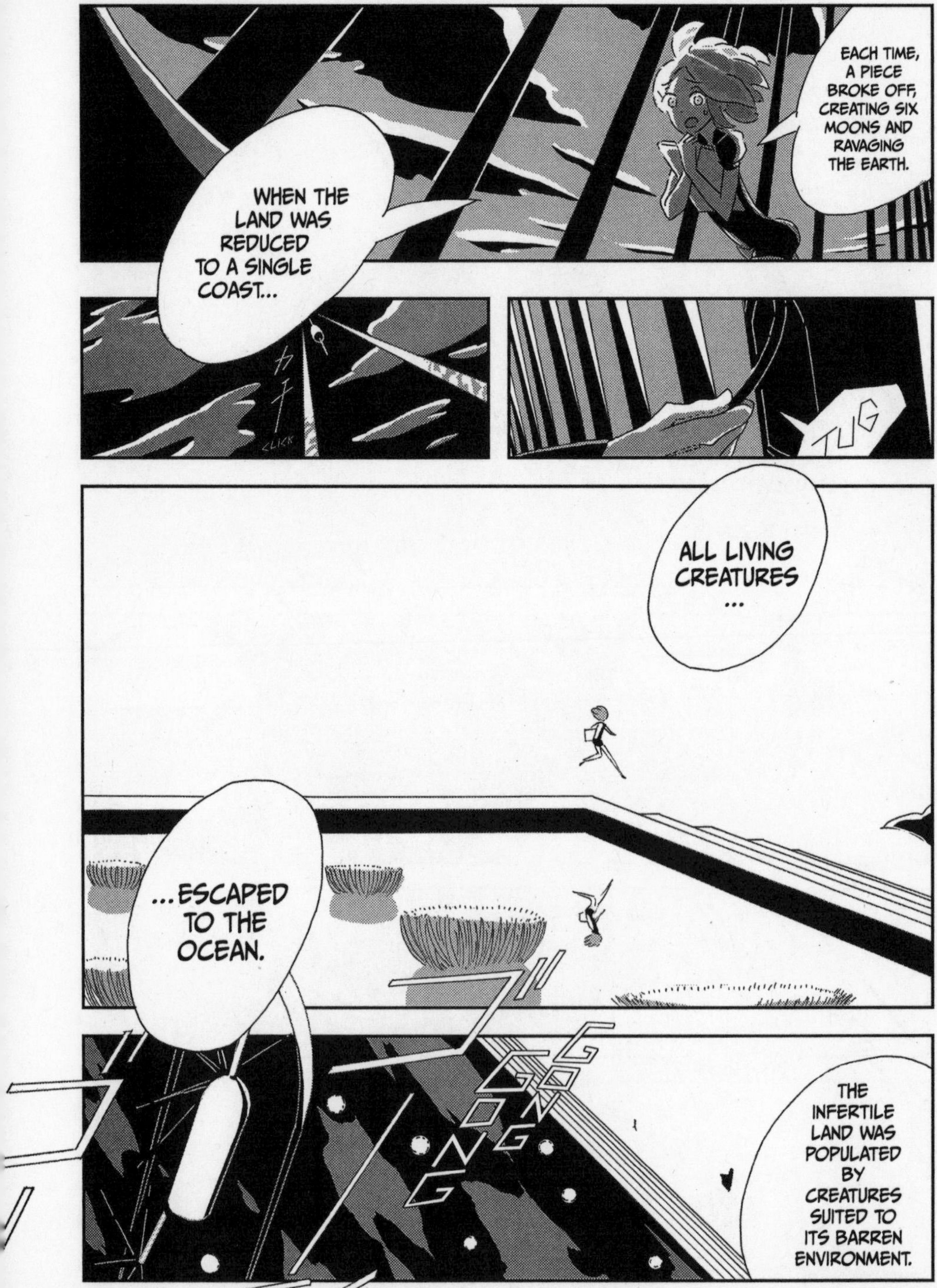
EACH TIME, A PIECE BROKE OFF, CREATING SIX MOONS AND RAVAGING THE EARTH.
WHEN THE LAND WAS REDUCED TO A SINGLE COAST...
TUG
カチ
CLICK
ALL LIVING CREATURES ...
...ESCAPED TO THE OCEAN.
GONG GONG
THE INFERTILE LAND WAS POPULATED BY CREATURES SUITED TO ITS BARREN ENVIRONMENT.

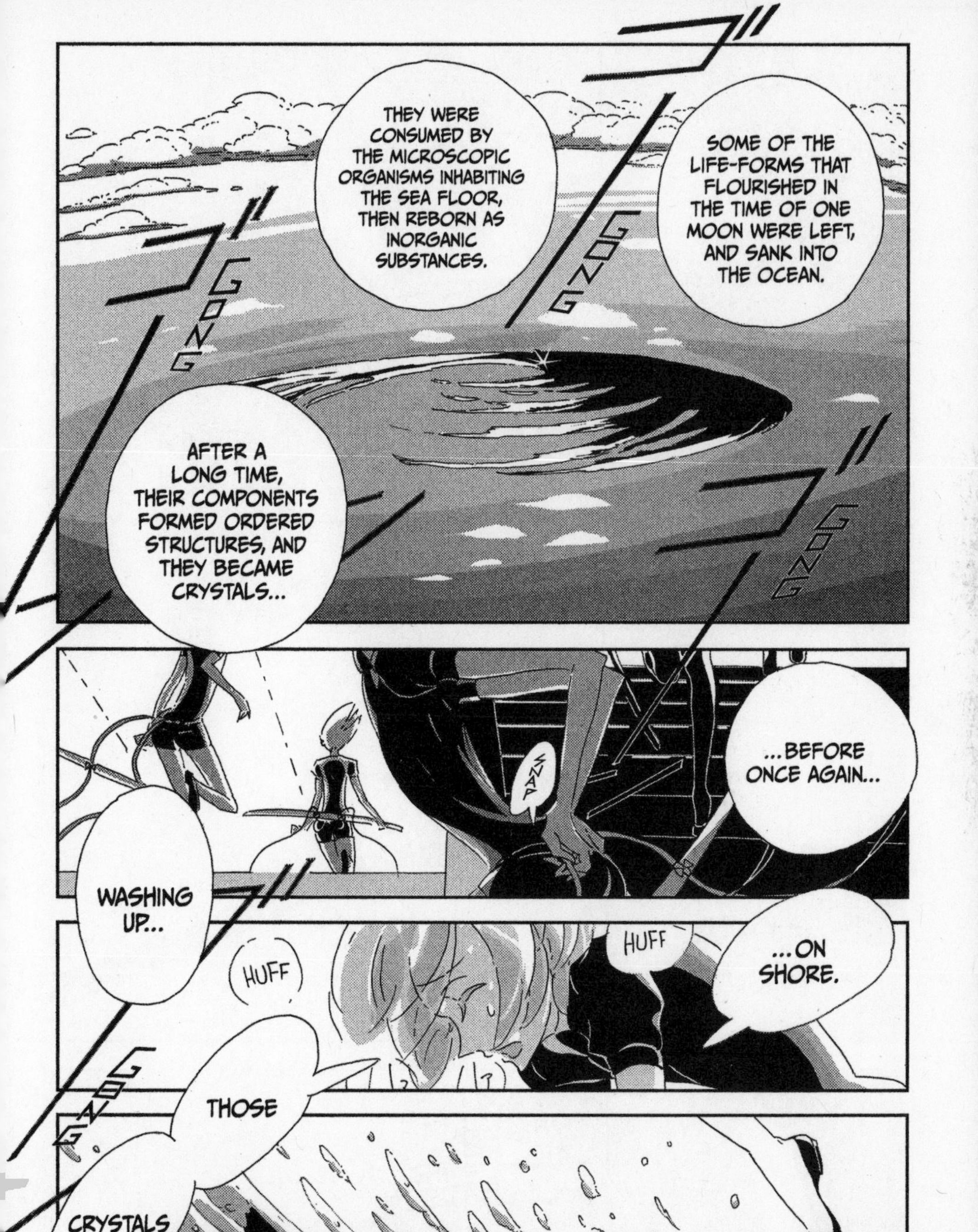

SOME OF THE LIFE-FORMS THAT FLOURISHED IN THE TIME OF ONE MOON WERE LEFT, AND SANK INTO THE OCEAN.
THEY WERE CONSUMED BY THE MICROSCOPIC ORGANISMS INHABITING THE SEA FLOOR, THEN REBORN AS INORGANIC SUBSTANCES.
GONG
GONG
AFTER A LONG TIME, THEIR COMPONENTS FORMED ORDERED STRUCTURES, AND THEY BECAME CRYSTALS...
GONG
...BEFORE ONCE AGAIN...
SNAP
WASHING UP...
HUFF
HUFF
...ON SHORE.
GONG
THOSE
CRYSTALS

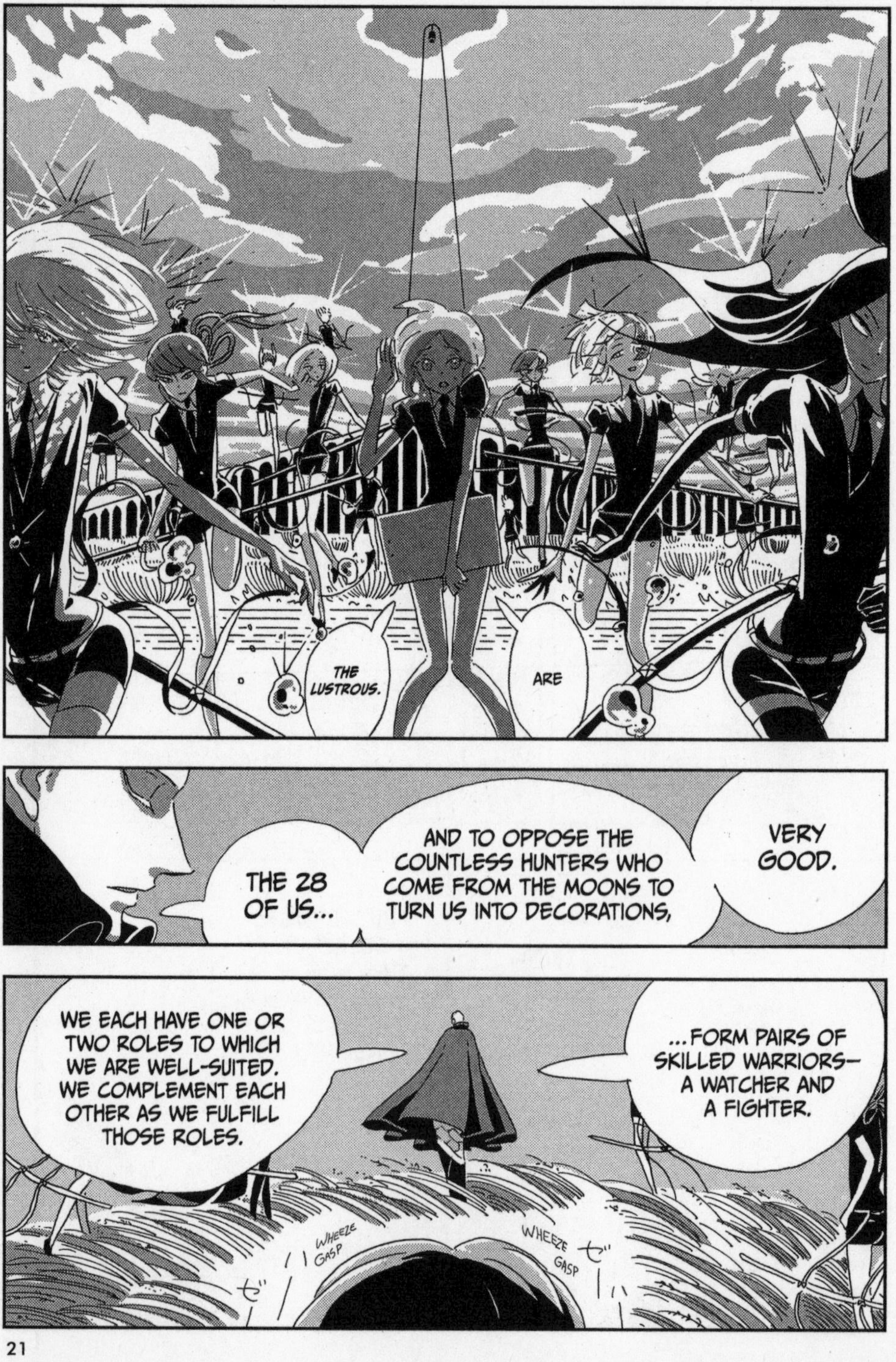
ARE
THE LUSTROUS.
VERY GOOD.
AND TO OPPOSE THE COUNTLESS HUNTERS WHO COME FROM THE MOONS TO TURN US INTO DECORATIONS,
THE 28 OF US...
...FORM PAIRS OF SKILLED WARRIORS— A WATCHER AND A FIGHTER.
WE EACH HAVE ONE OR TWO ROLES TO WHICH WE ARE WELL-SUITED. WE COMPLEMENT EACH OTHER AS WE FULFILL THOSE ROLES.
WHEEZE GASP
WHEEZE GASP

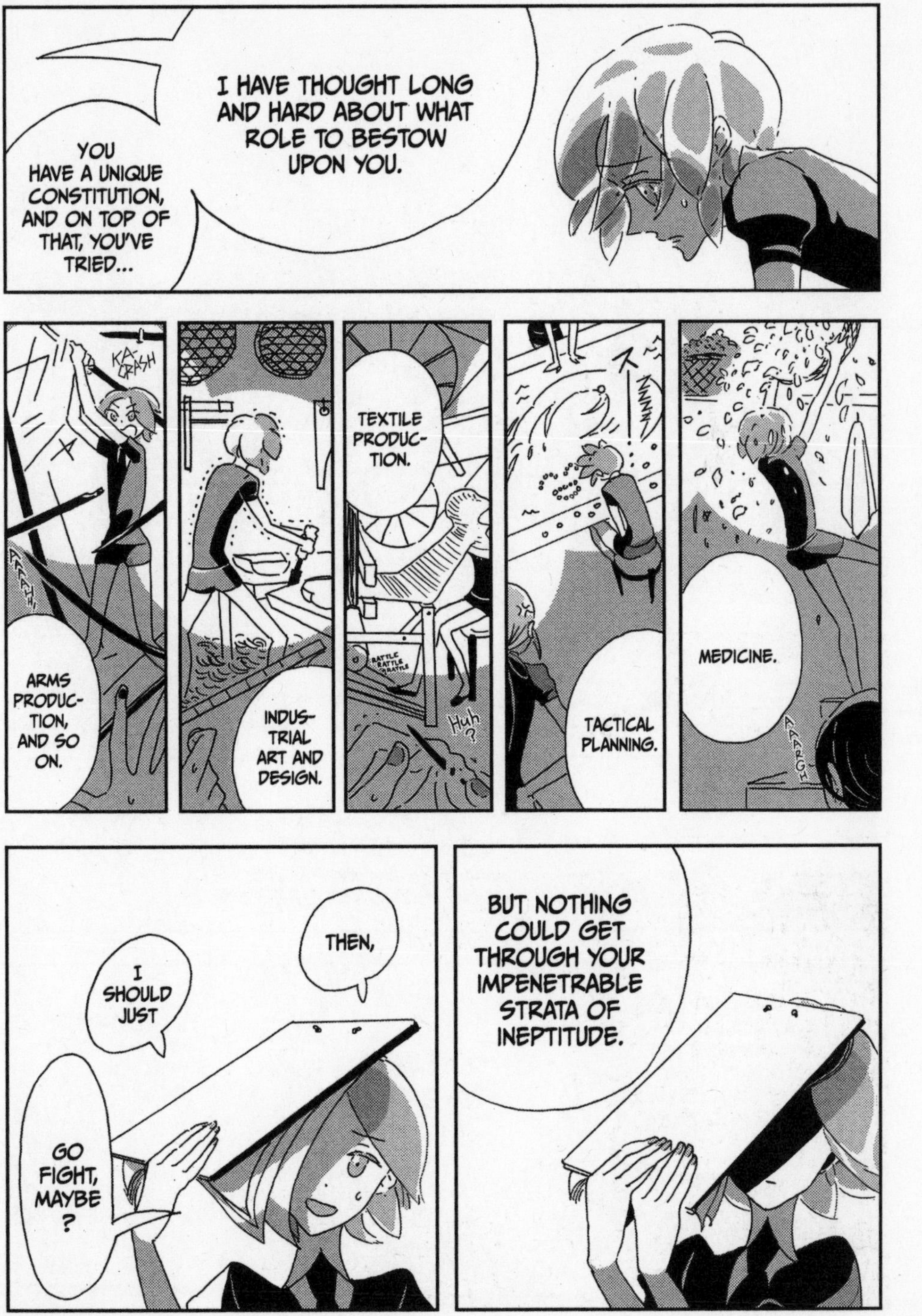
I HAVE THOUGHT LONG AND HARD ABOUT WHAT ROLE TO BESTOW UPON YOU.
YOU HAVE A UNIQUE CONSTITUTION, AND ON TOP OF THAT, YOU'VE TRIED...
MEDICINE.
AAARGH
TACTICAL PLANNING.
TEXTILE PRODUCTION.
RATTLE RATTLE RATTLE
Huh?
INDUSTRIAL ART AND DESIGN.
KA-CRASH
ARMS PRODUCTION, AND SO ON.
BUT NOTHING COULD GET THROUGH YOUR IMPENETRABLE STRATA OF INEPTITUDE.
THEN,
I SHOULD JUST
GO FIGHT, MAYBE?

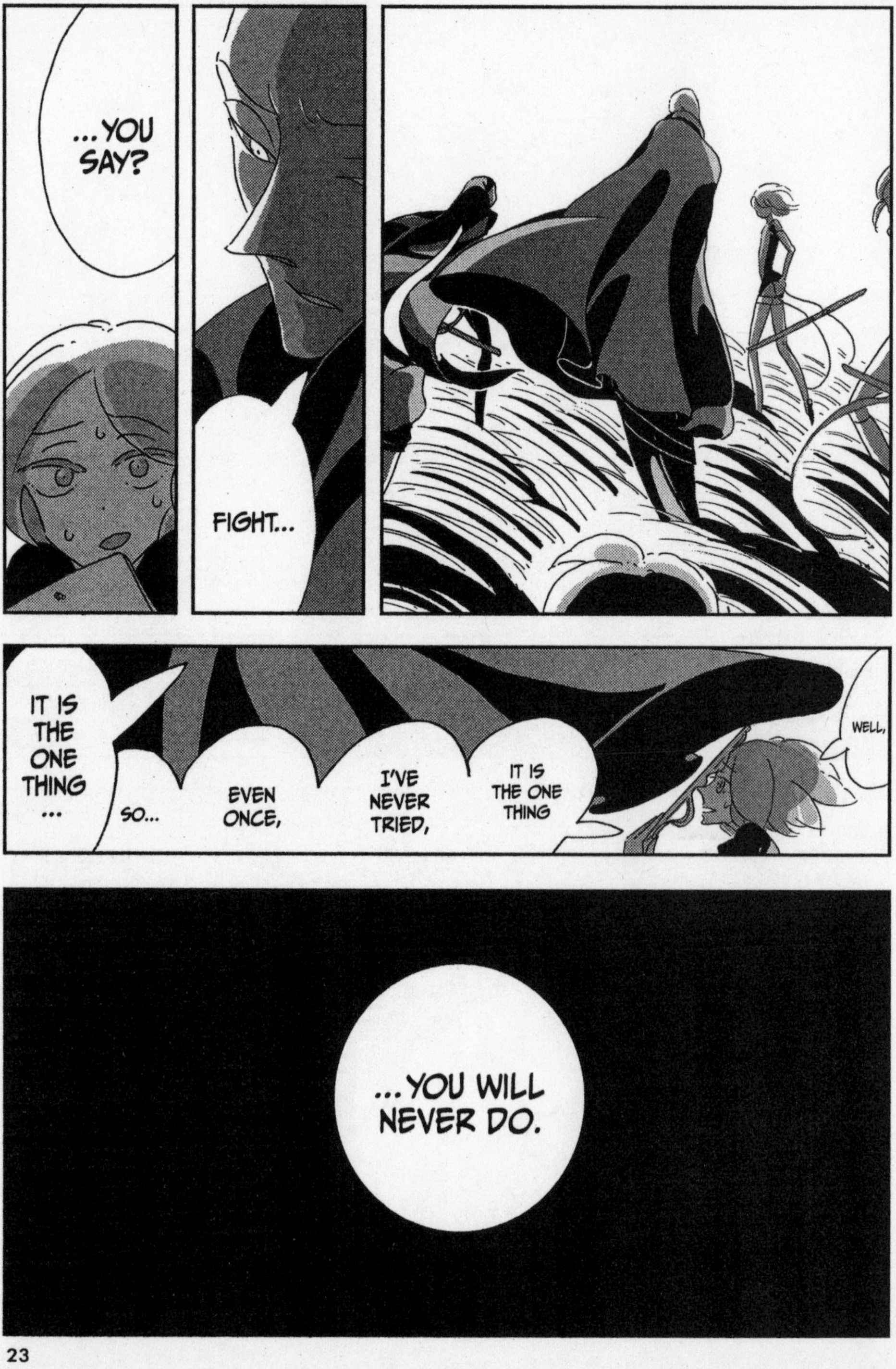
FIGHT...
...YOU SAY?
WELL,
IT IS THE ONE THING
I'VE NEVER TRIED,
EVEN ONCE,
SO...
IT IS THE ONE THING ...
...YOU WILL NEVER DO.

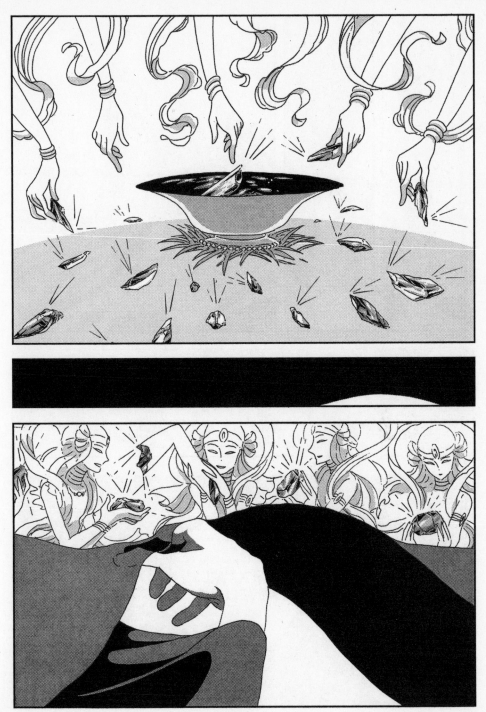

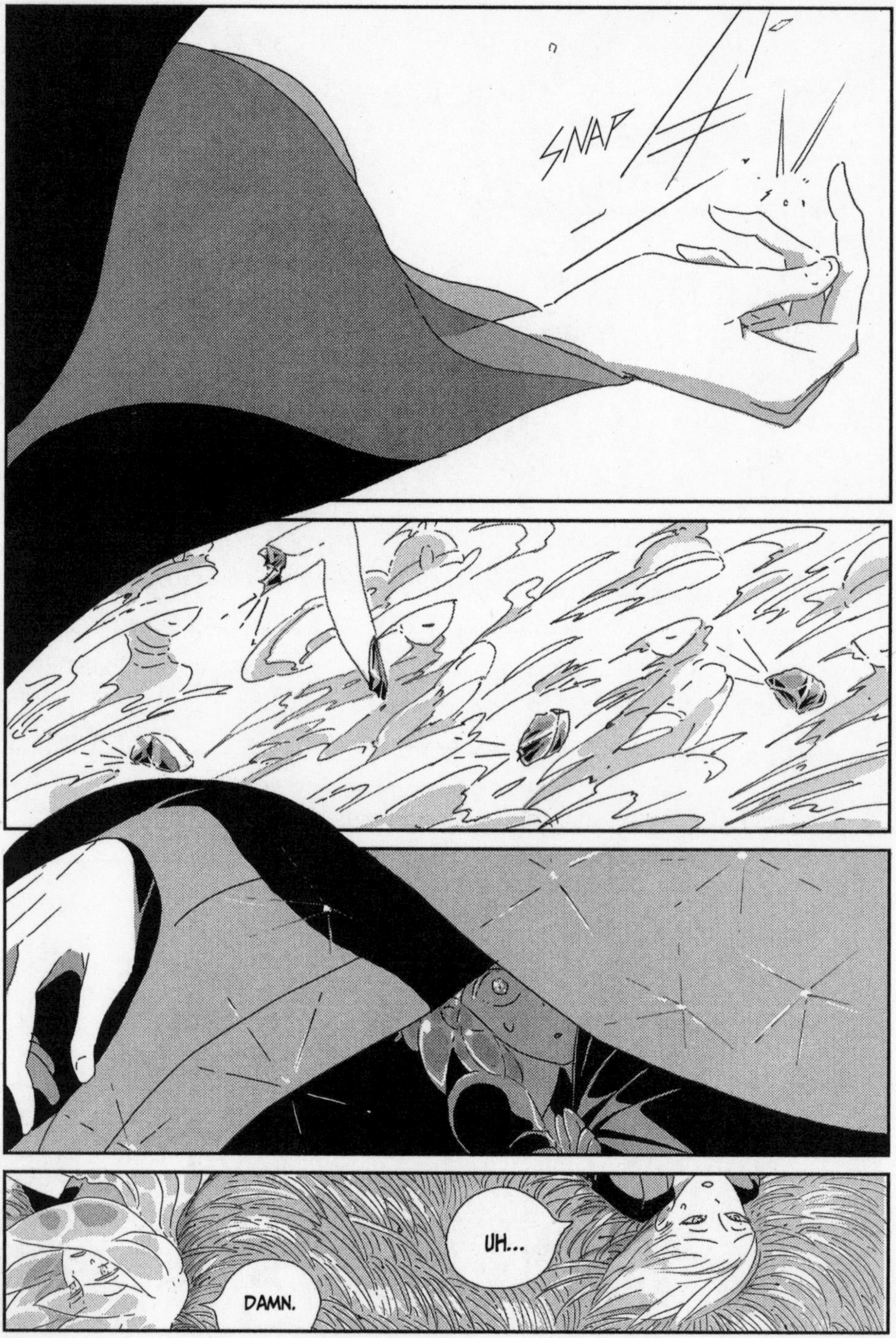
SNAP
UH...
DAMN.

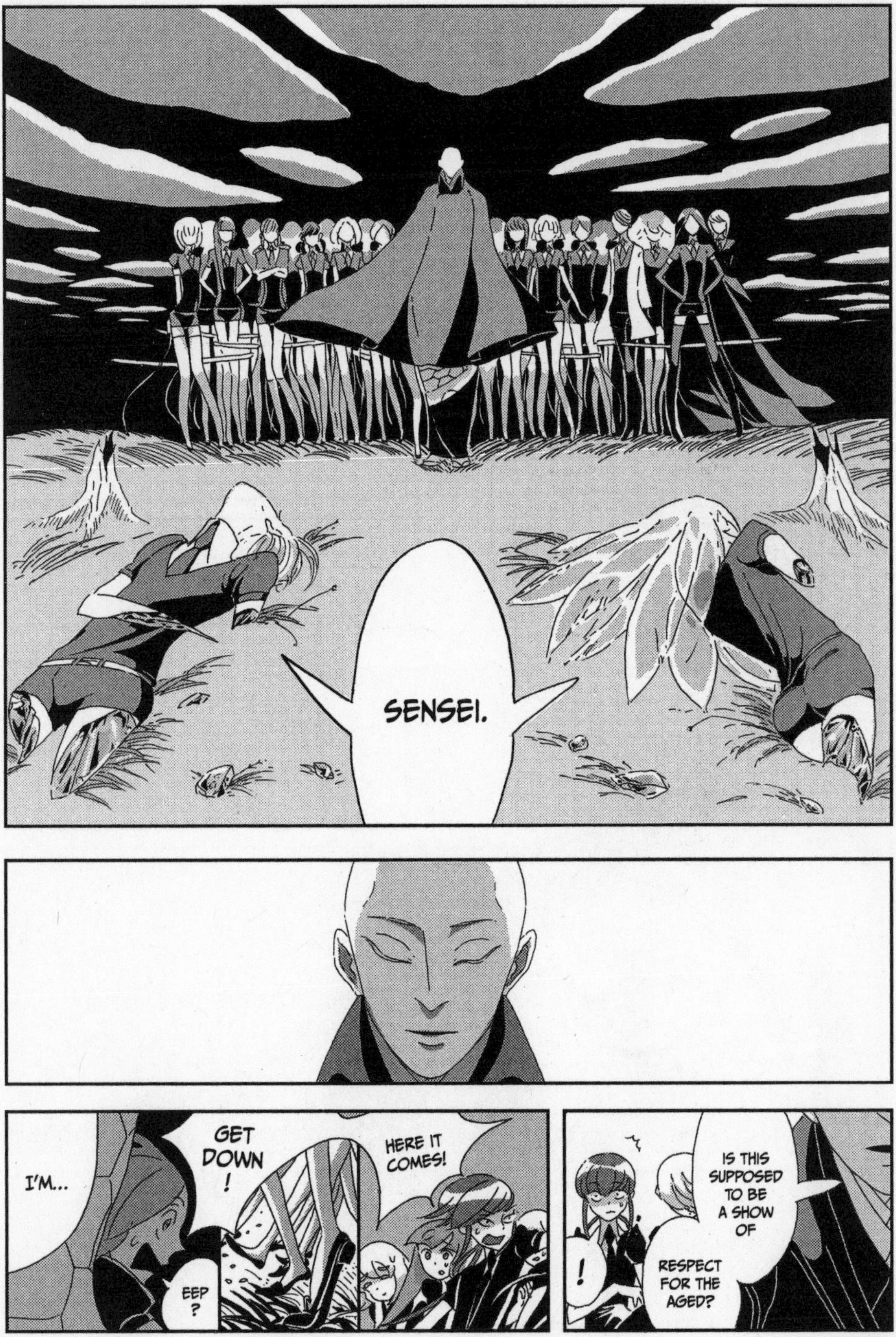
SENSEI.
IS THIS SUPPOSED TO BE A SHOW OF
!
RESPECT FOR THE AGED?
HERE IT COMES!
GET DOWN!
I'M...
EEP?

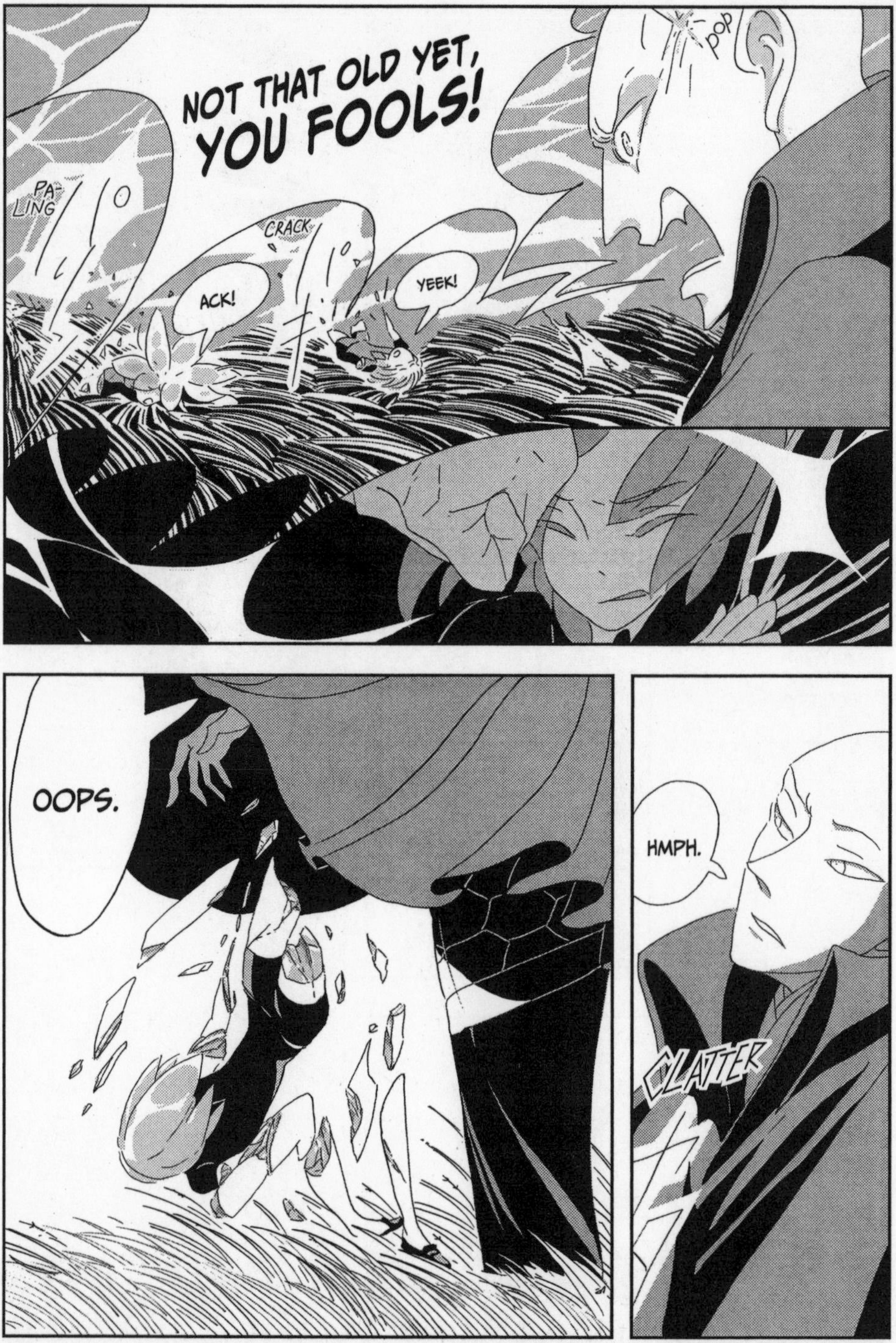
POP
NOT THAT OLD YET, YOU FOOLS!
YEEK!
CRACK
ACK!
PA-LING
HMPH.
CLATTER
OOPS.

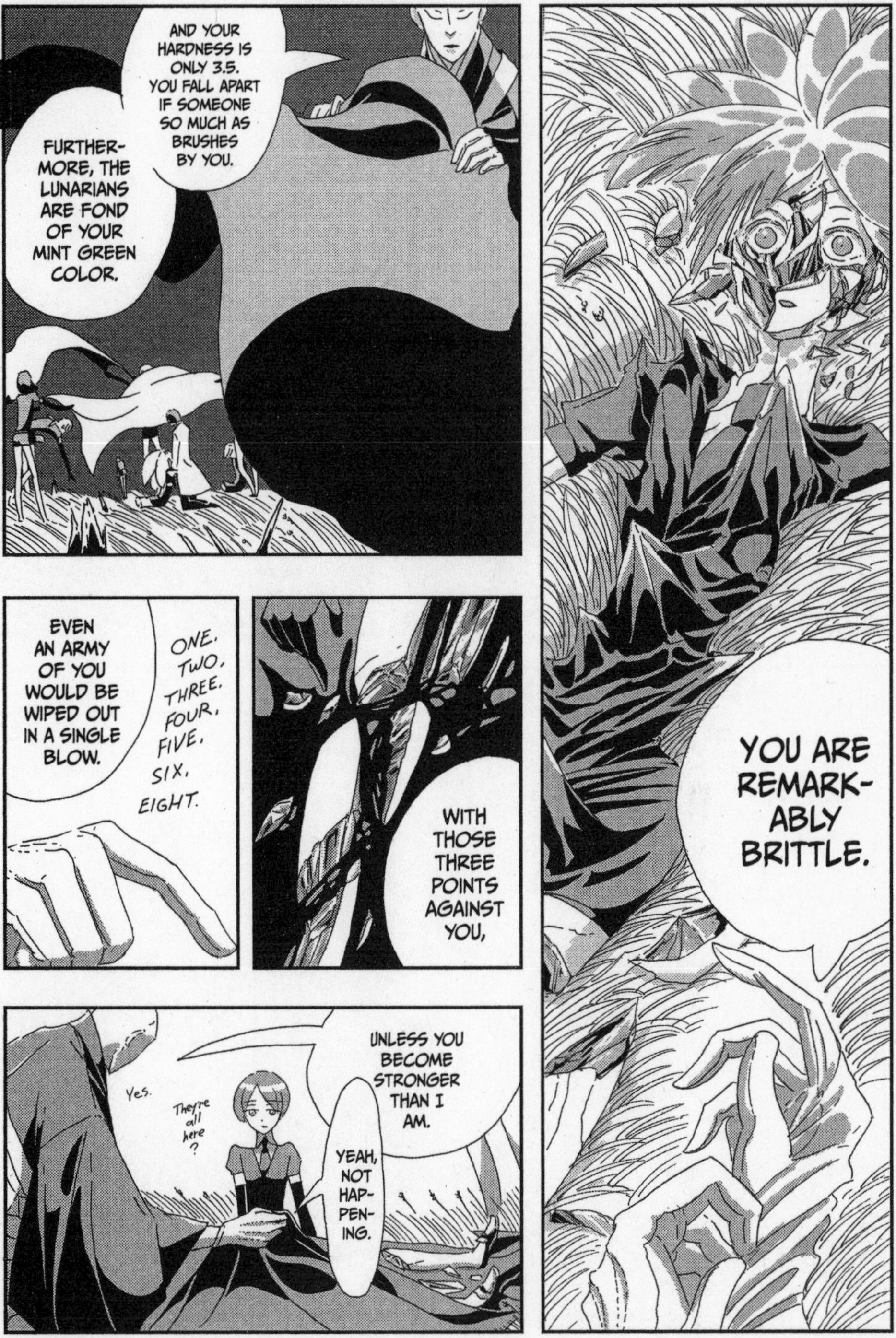
YOU ARE REMARKABLY BRITTLE.
AND YOUR HARDNESS IS ONLY 3.5. YOU FALL APART IF SOMEONE SO MUCH AS BRUSHES BY YOU.
FURTHERMORE, THE LUNARIANS ARE FOND OF YOUR MINT GREEN COLOR.
WITH THOSE THREE POINTS AGAINST YOU,
EVEN AN ARMY OF YOU WOULD BE WIPED OUT IN A SINGLE BLOW.
ONE. TWO. THREE. FOUR. FIVE. SIX. EIGHT.
UNLESS YOU BECOME STRONGER THAN I AM.
YEAH, NOT HAPPENING.
They're all here?
Yes.

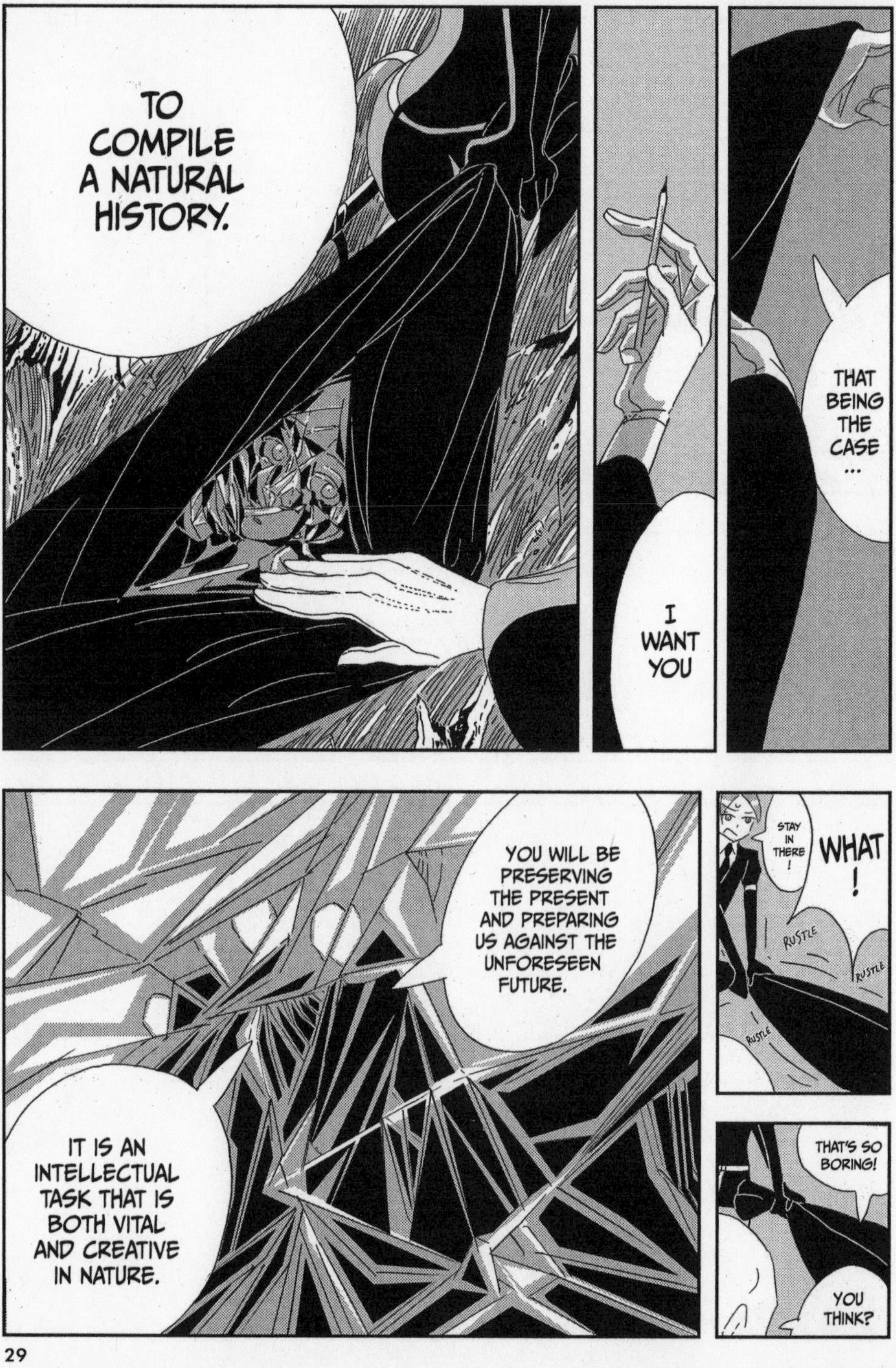
THAT BEING THE CASE ...
I WANT YOU
TO COMPILE A NATURAL HISTORY.
WHAT!
STAY IN THERE!
RUSTLE
RUSTLE
RUSTLE
THAT'S SO BORING!
YOU THINK?
YOU WILL BE PRESERVING THE PRESENT AND PREPARING US AGAINST THE UNFORESEEN FUTURE.
IT IS AN INTELLECTUAL TASK THAT IS BOTH VITAL AND CREATIVE IN NATURE.

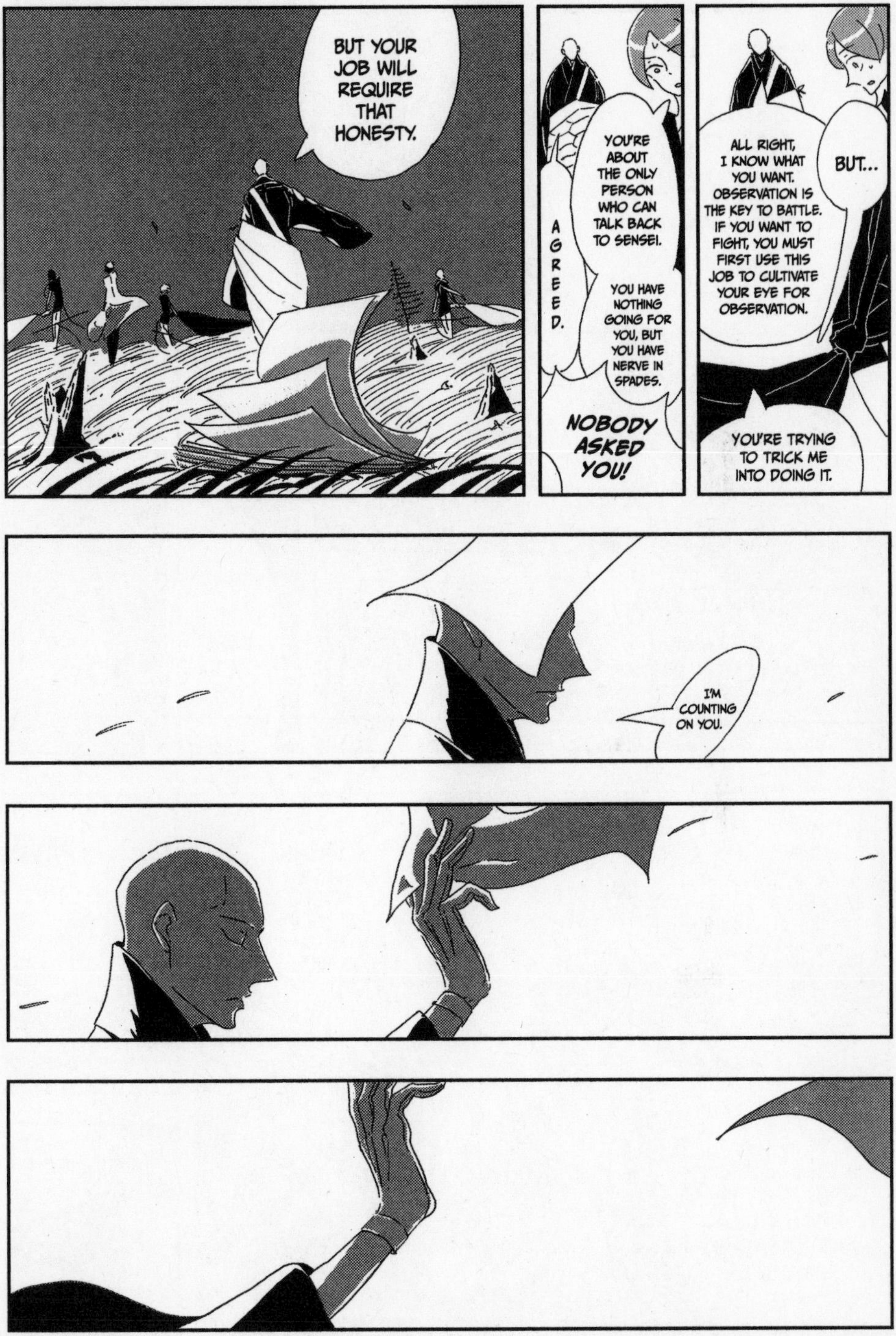
BUT...
ALL RIGHT, I KNOW WHAT YOU WANT. OBSERVATION IS THE KEY TO BATTLE. IF YOU WANT TO FIGHT, YOU MUST FIRST USE THIS JOB TO CULTIVATE YOUR EYE FOR OBSERVATION.
YOU'RE TRYING TO TRICK ME INTO DOING IT.
YOU'RE ABOUT THE ONLY PERSON WHO CAN TALK BACK TO SENSEI.
AGREED.
YOU HAVE NOTHING GOING FOR YOU, BUT YOU HAVE NERVE IN SPADES.
NOBODY ASKED YOU!
BUT YOUR JOB WILL REQUIRE THAT HONESTY.
I'M COUNTING ON YOU.

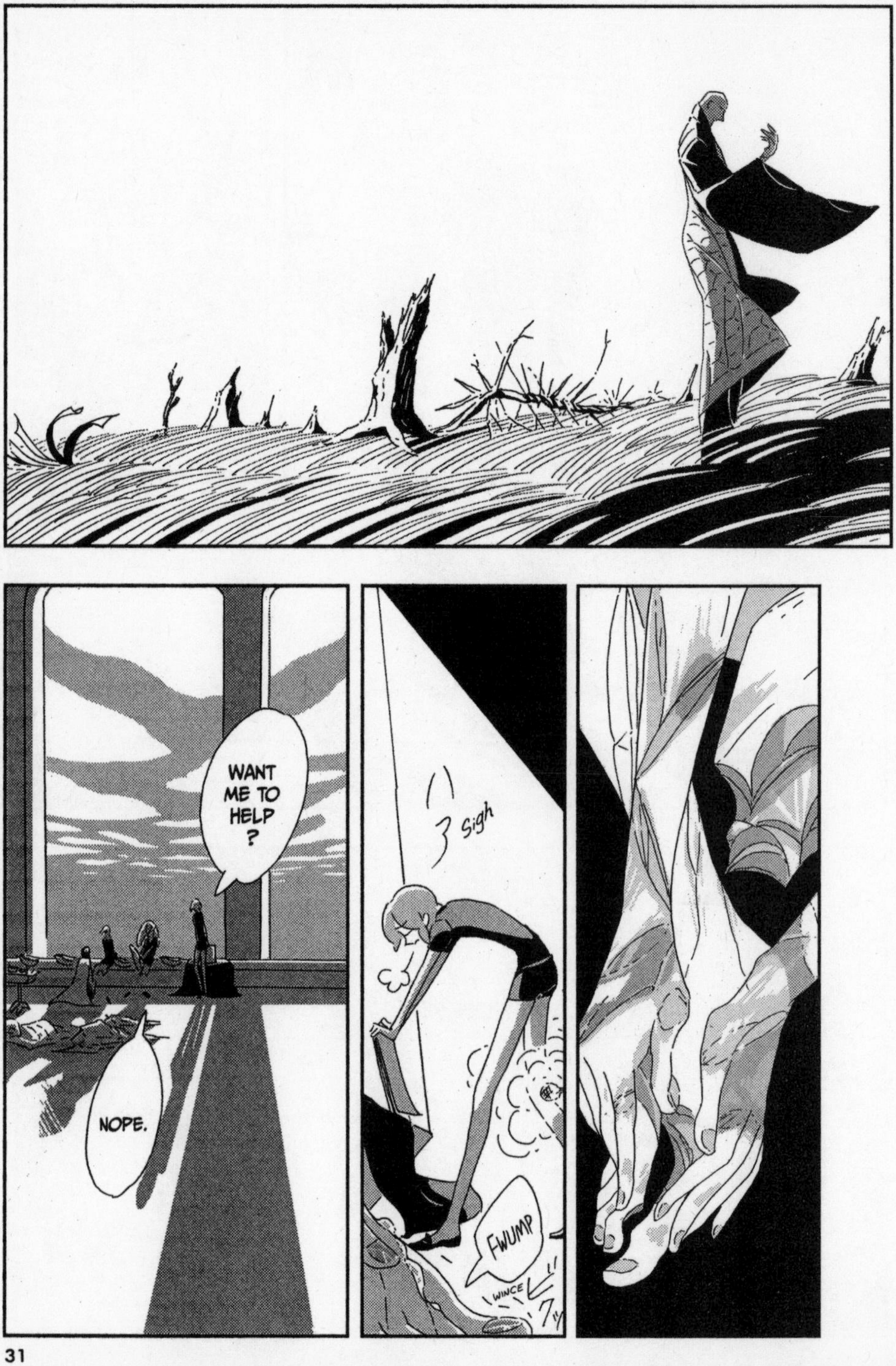
Sigh
FWUMP
WINCE
WANT ME TO HELP?
NOPE.

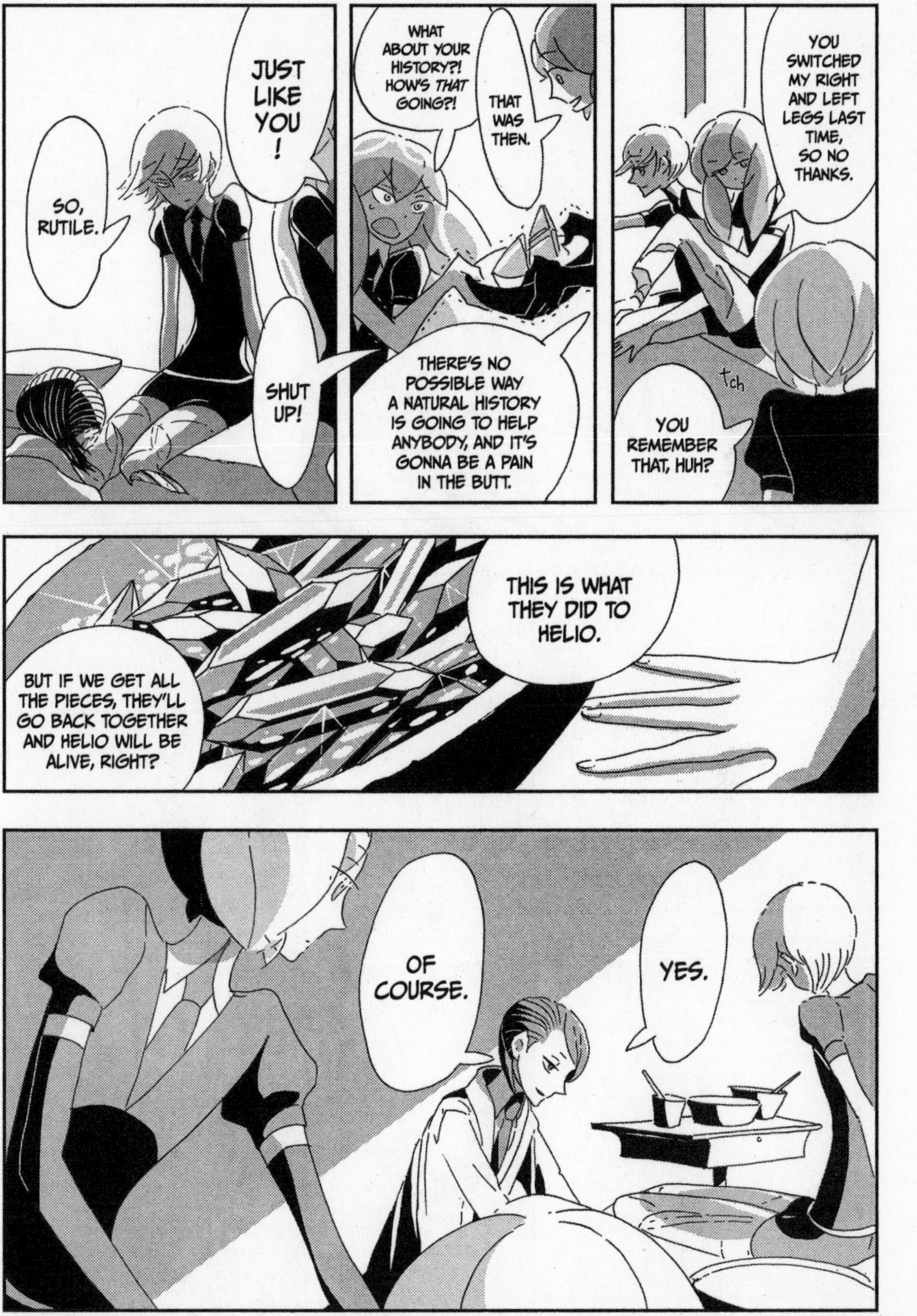

YOU SWITCHED MY RIGHT AND LEFT LEGS LAST TIME, SO NO THANKS.
tch
YOU REMEMBER THAT, HUH?
THAT WAS THEN.
WHAT ABOUT YOUR HISTORY?! HOW'S *THAT* GOING?!
THERE'S NO POSSIBLE WAY A NATURAL HISTORY IS GOING TO HELP ANYBODY, AND IT'S GONNA BE A PAIN IN THE BUTT.
JUST LIKE YOU!
SHUT UP!
SO, RUTILE.
THIS IS WHAT THEY DID TO HELIO.
BUT IF WE GET ALL THE PIECES, THEY'LL GO BACK TOGETHER AND HELIO WILL BE ALIVE, RIGHT?
YES.
OF COURSE.

*Material trapped inside a mineral during formation.

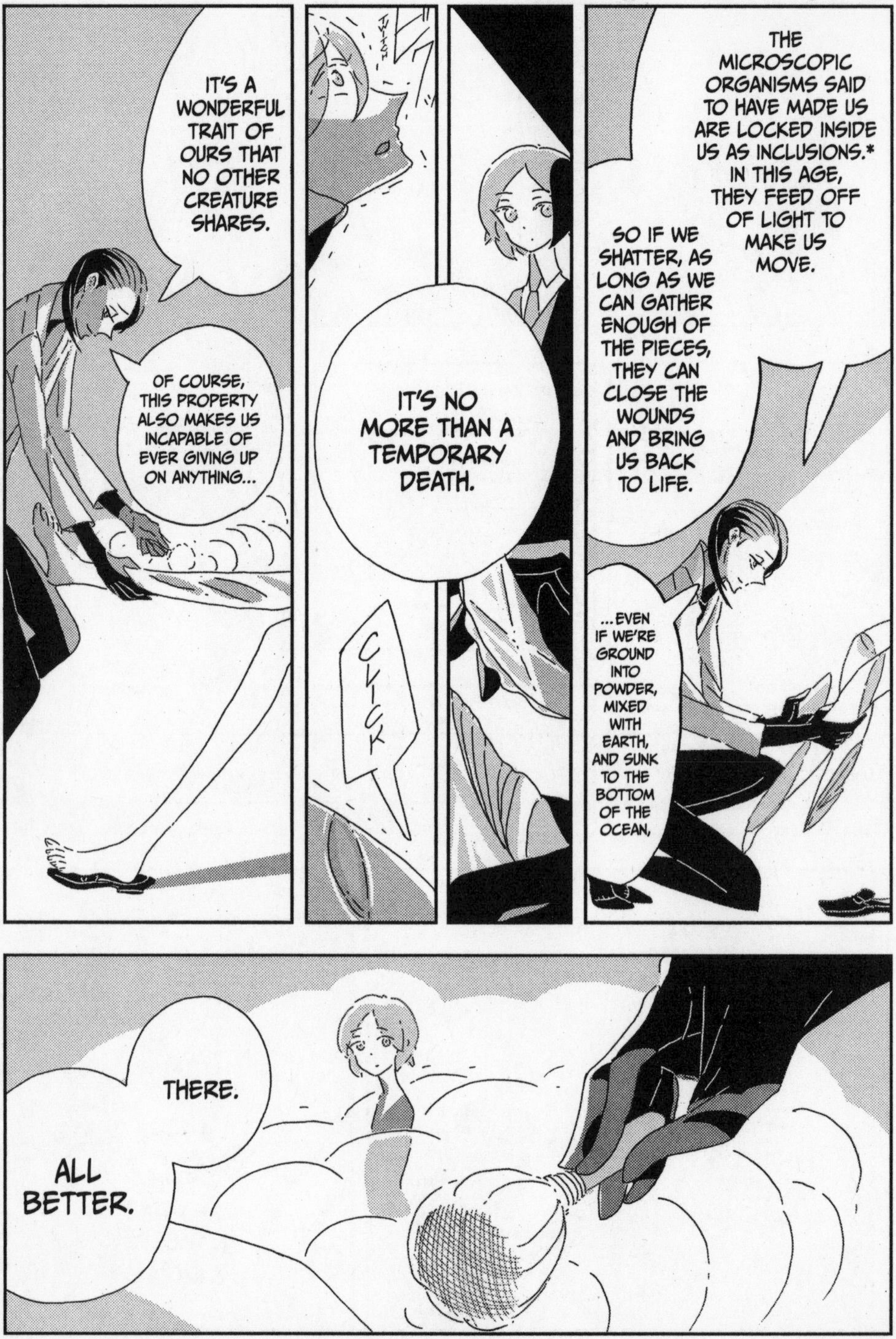
THE MICROSCOPIC ORGANISMS SAID TO HAVE MADE US ARE LOCKED INSIDE US AS INCLUSIONS.* IN THIS AGE, THEY FEED OFF OF LIGHT TO MAKE US MOVE.
SO IF WE SHATTER, AS LONG AS WE CAN GATHER ENOUGH OF THE PIECES, THEY CAN CLOSE THE WOUNDS AND BRING US BACK TO LIFE.
...EVEN IF WE'RE GROUND INTO POWDER, MIXED WITH EARTH, AND SUNK TO THE BOTTOM OF THE OCEAN,
IT'S NO MORE THAN A TEMPORARY DEATH.
TWITCH
CLICK
IT'S A WONDERFUL TRAIT OF OURS THAT NO OTHER CREATURE SHARES.
OF COURSE, THIS PROPERTY ALSO MAKES US INCAPABLE OF EVER GIVING UP ON ANYTHING...
THERE.
ALL BETTER.

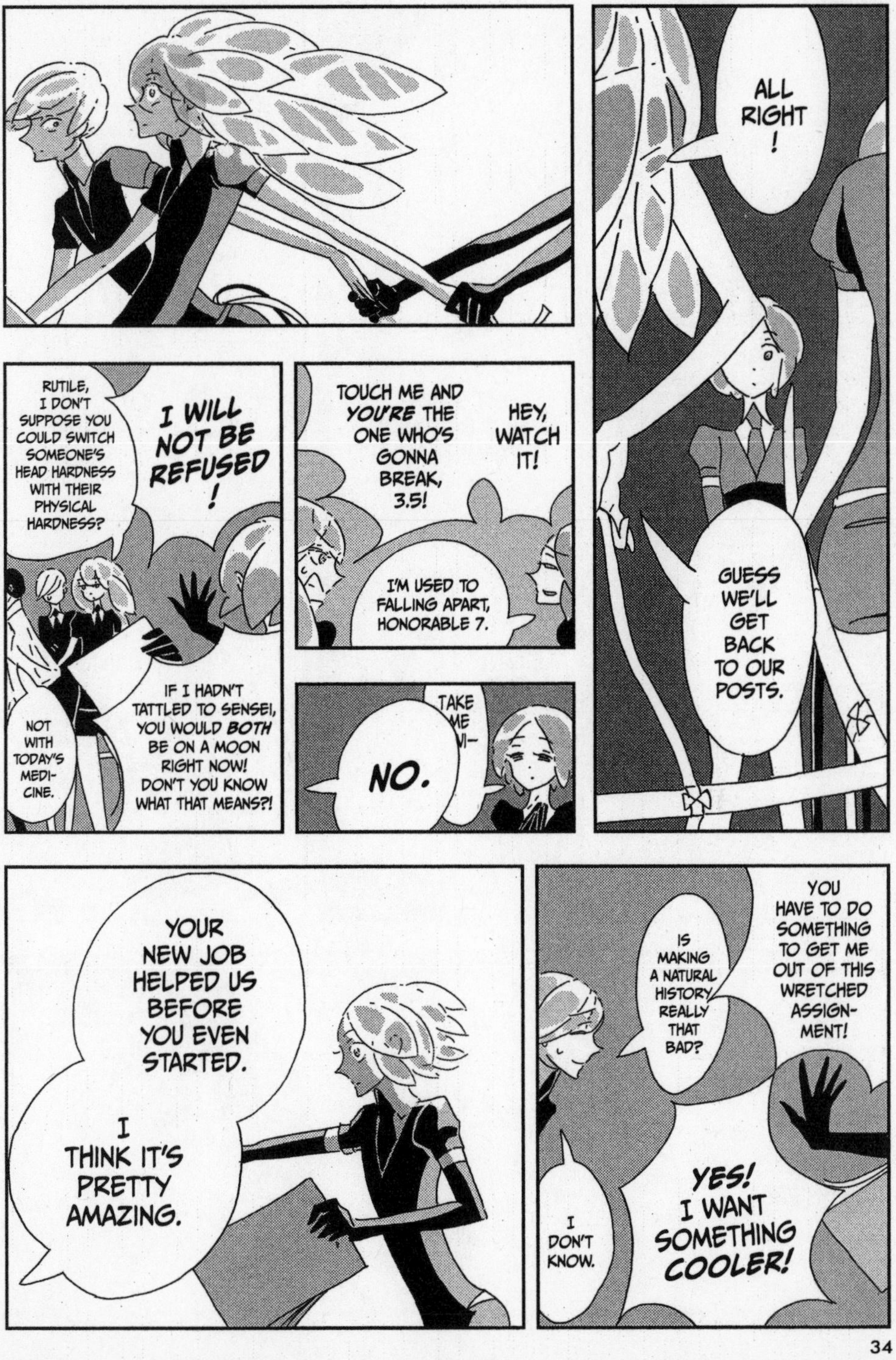
ALL RIGHT!
GUESS WE'LL GET BACK TO OUR POSTS.
HEY, WATCH IT!
TOUCH ME AND *YOU'RE* THE ONE WHO'S GONNA BREAK, 3.5!
I'M USED TO FALLING APART, HONORABLE 7.
TAKE ME WI–
NO.
I WILL NOT BE REFUSED!
RUTILE, I DON'T SUPPOSE YOU COULD SWITCH SOMEONE'S HEAD HARDNESS WITH THEIR PHYSICAL HARDNESS?
IF I HADN'T TATTLED TO SENSEI, YOU WOULD *BOTH* BE ON A MOON RIGHT NOW! DON'T YOU KNOW WHAT THAT MEANS?!
NOT WITH TODAY'S MEDICINE.
YOU HAVE TO DO SOMETHING TO GET ME OUT OF THIS WRETCHED ASSIGNMENT!
IS MAKING A NATURAL HISTORY REALLY THAT BAD?
YES! I WANT SOMETHING *COOLER!*
I DON'T KNOW.
YOUR NEW JOB HELPED US BEFORE YOU EVEN STARTED.
I THINK IT'S PRETTY AMAZING.

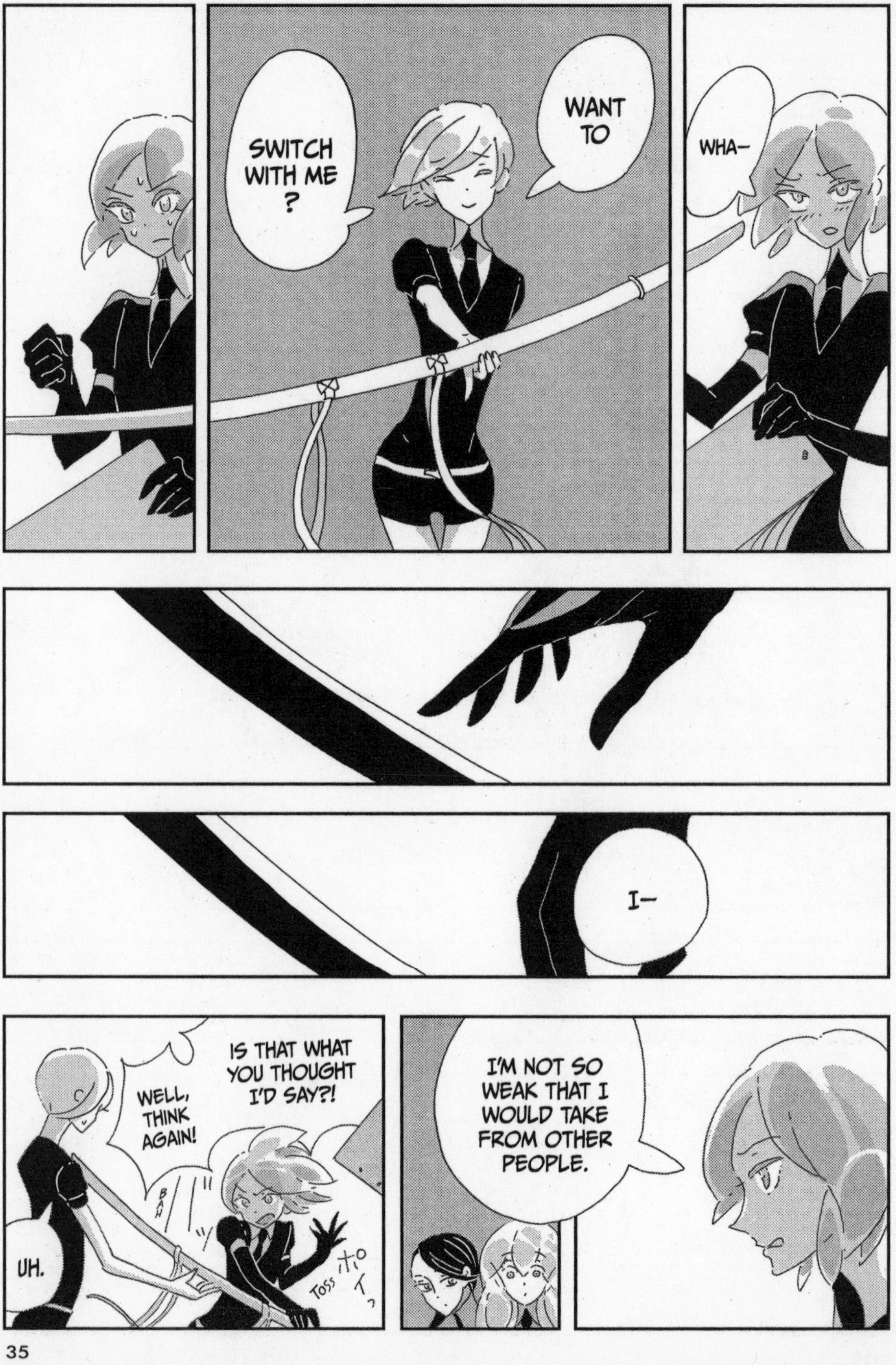
WHA–
WANT TO
SWITCH WITH ME ?
I–
I'M NOT SO WEAK THAT I WOULD TAKE FROM OTHER PEOPLE.
IS THAT WHAT YOU THOUGHT I'D SAY?!
WELL, THINK AGAIN!
BAH
TOSS
ポイッ
UH.

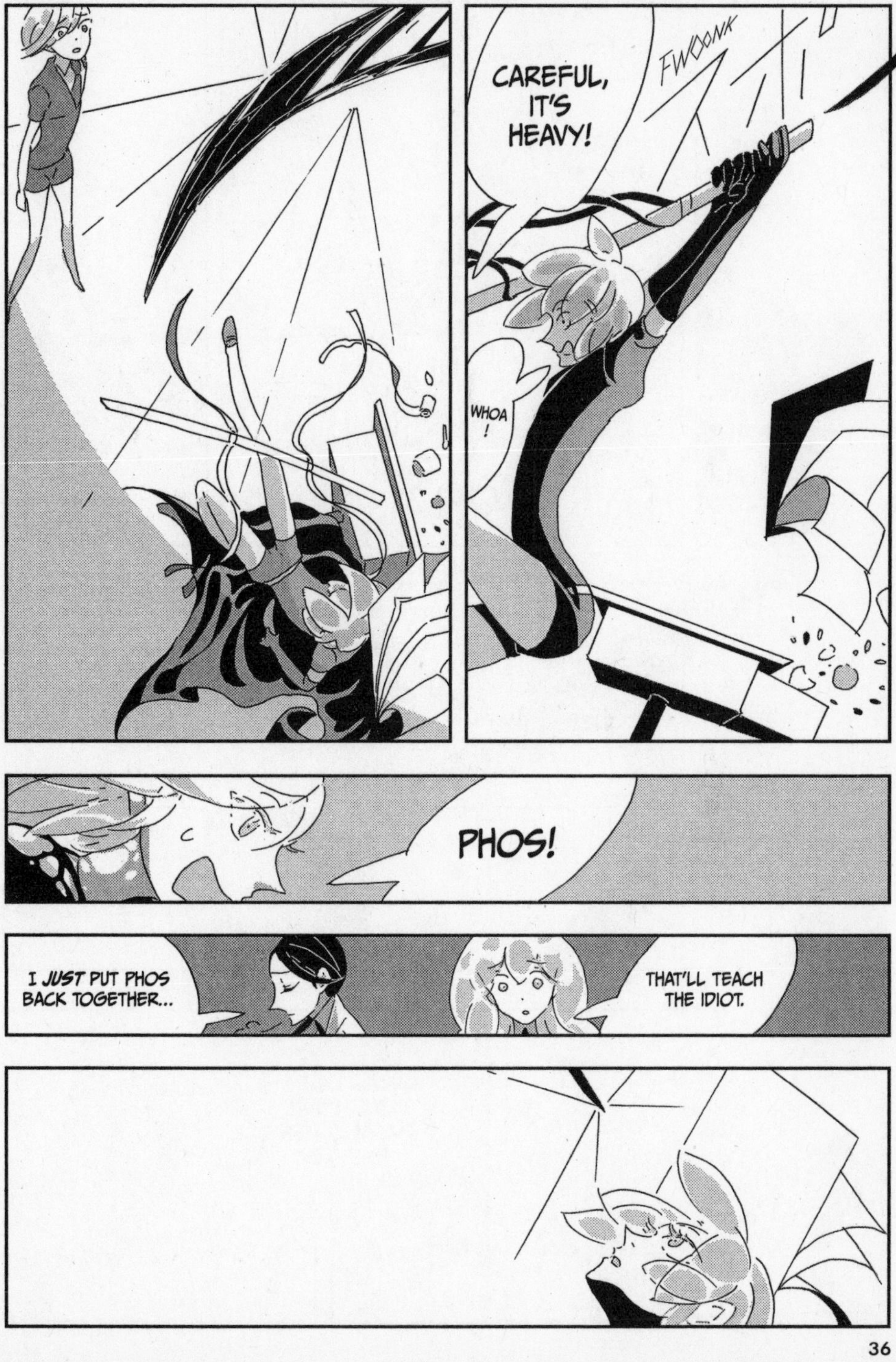
CAREFUL, IT'S HEAVY!
FWOONK
WHOA!
PHOS!
THAT'LL TEACH THE IDIOT.
I JUST PUT PHOS BACK TOGETHER...

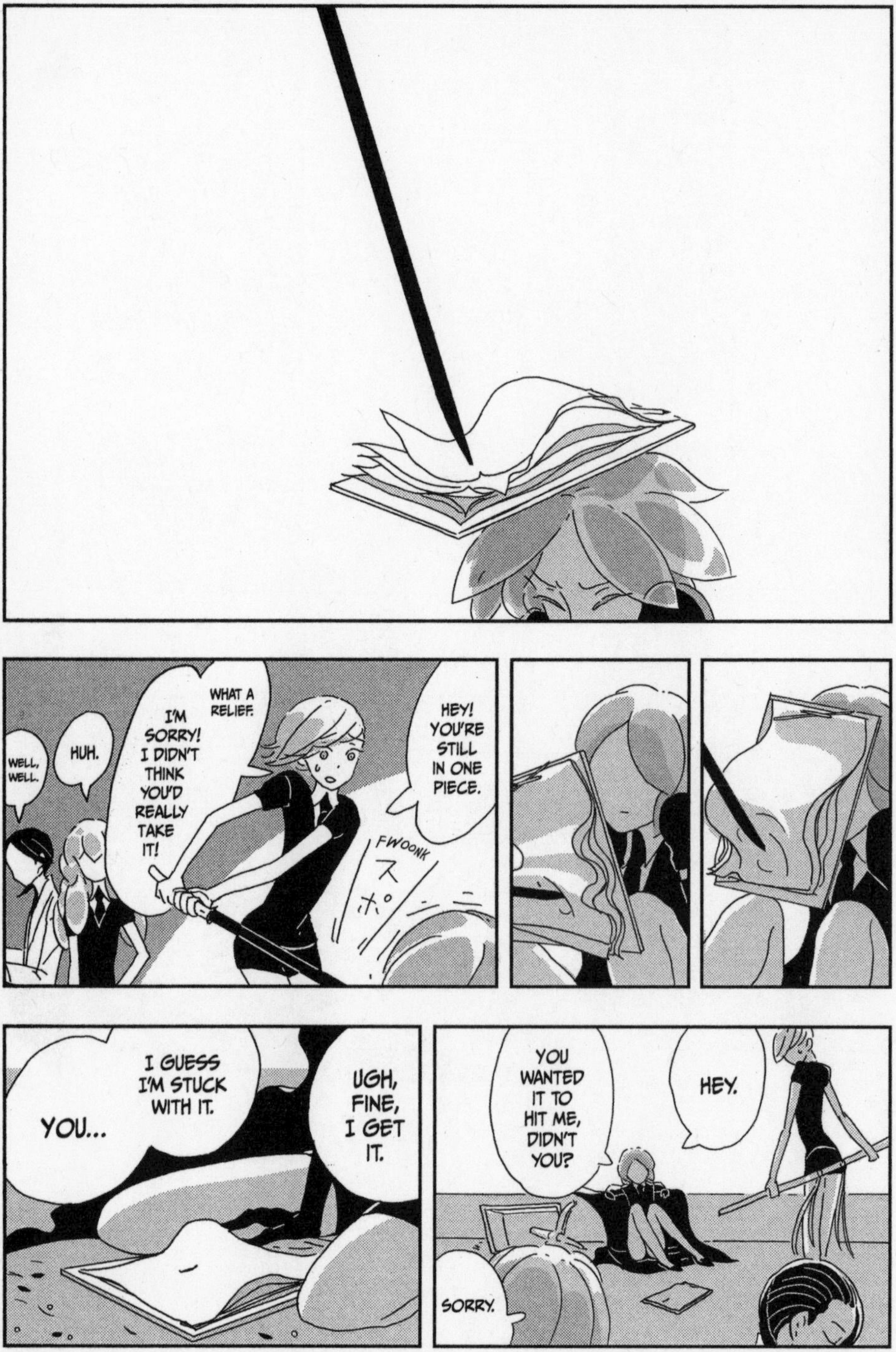
HEY! YOU'RE STILL IN ONE PIECE.
FWOONK
スポ
WHAT A RELIEF.
I'M SORRY! I DIDN'T THINK YOU'D REALLY TAKE IT!
HUH.
WELL, WELL.
HEY.
YOU WANTED IT TO HIT ME, DIDN'T YOU?
SORRY.
UGH, FINE, I GET IT.
I GUESS I'M STUCK WITH IT.
YOU...

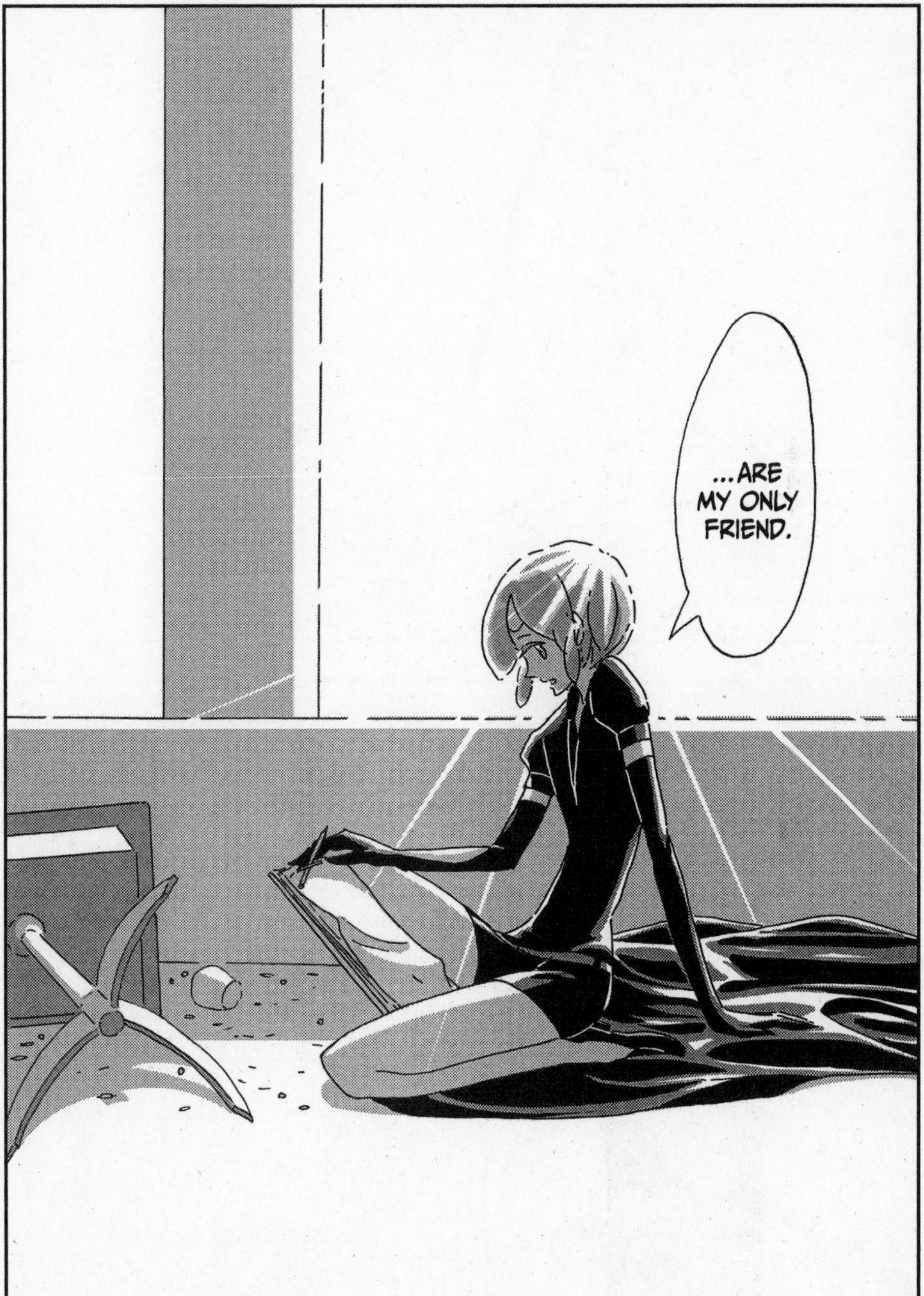
...ARE MY ONLY FRIEND.

CHAPTER 1: Phosphophyllite END

CHAPTER 2:

Cinnabar

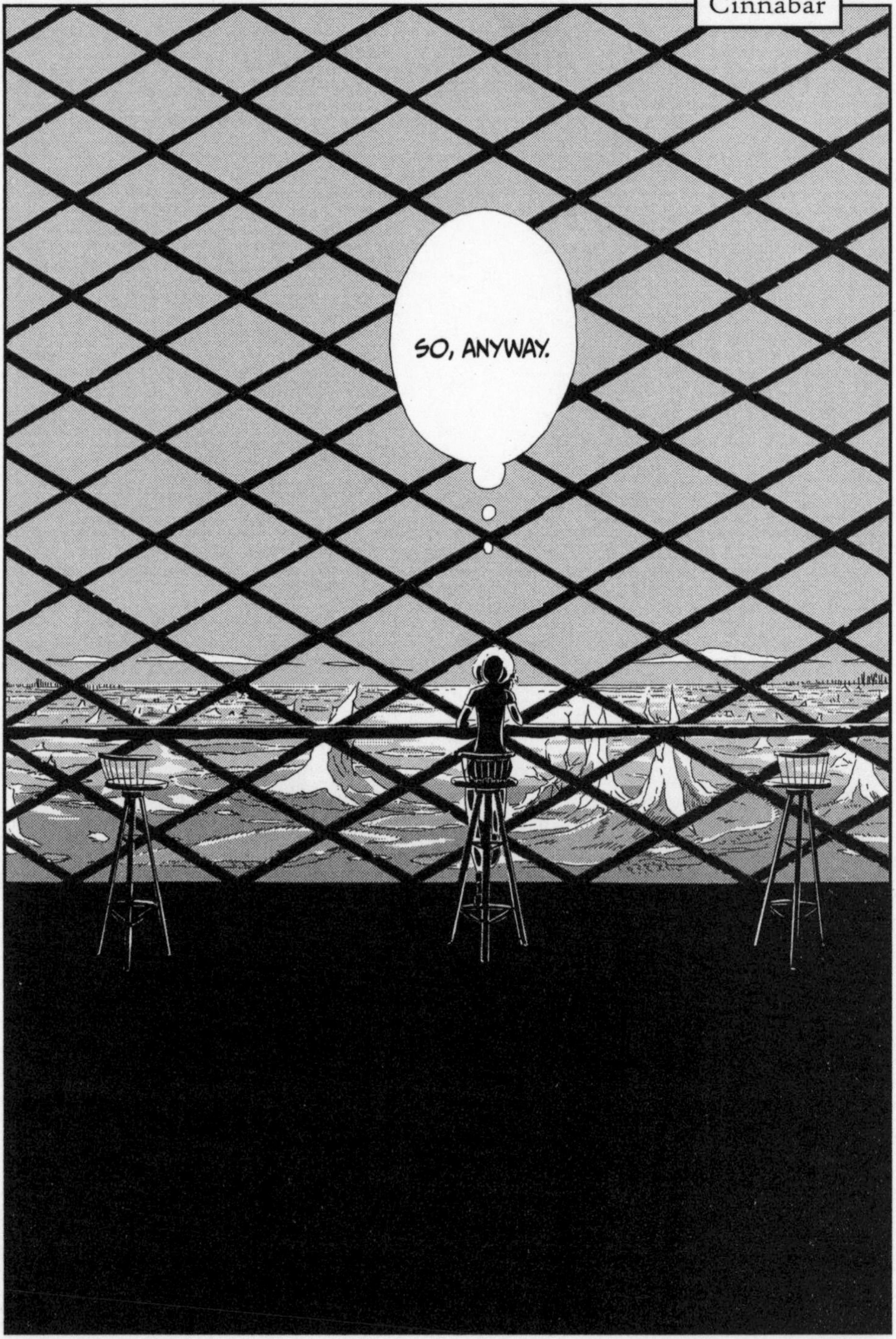
SO, ANYWAY.

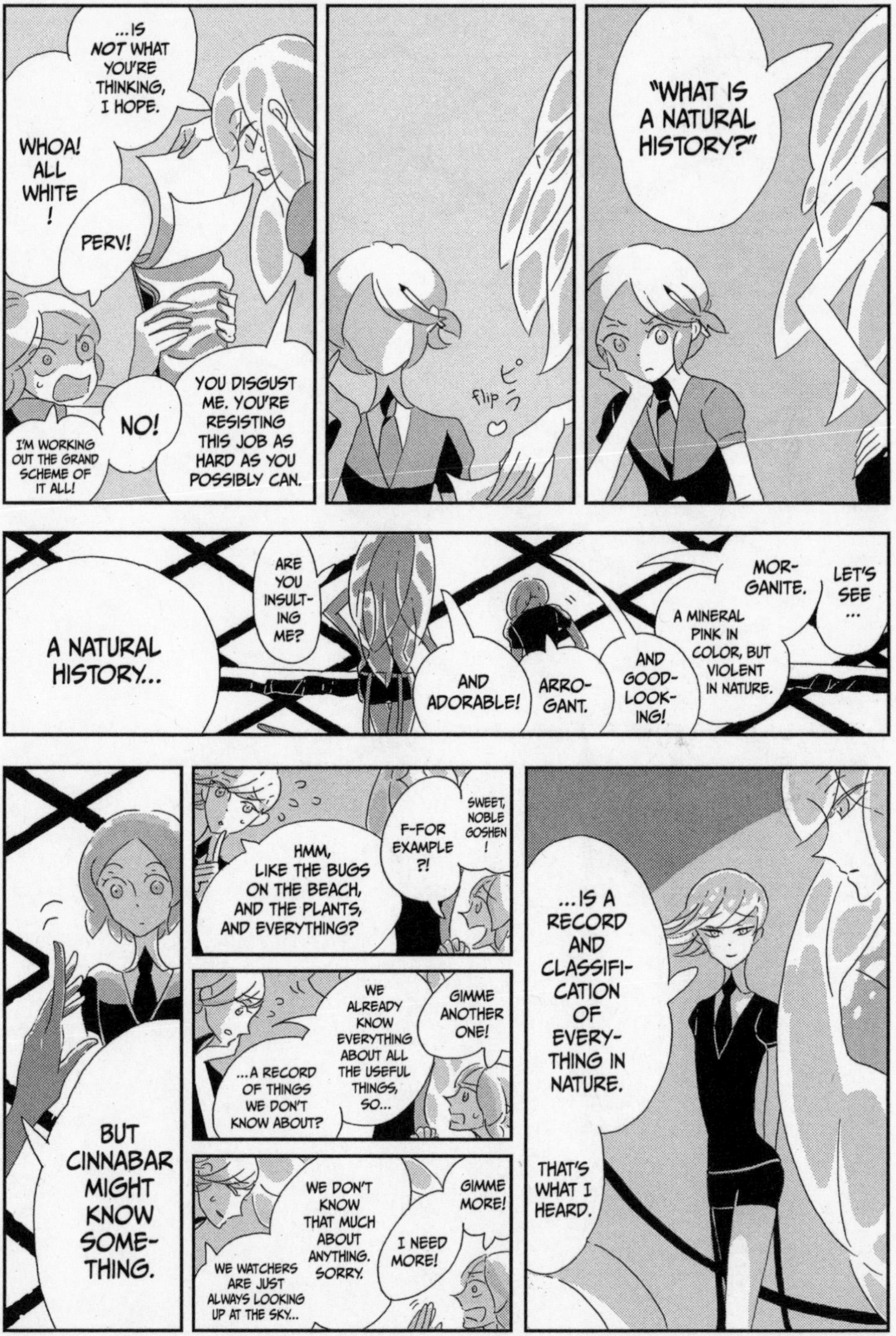
"WHAT IS A NATURAL HISTORY?"
ピラ flip
...IS NOT WHAT YOU'RE THINKING, I HOPE.
WHOA! ALL WHITE!
PERV!
YOU DISGUST ME. YOU'RE RESISTING THIS JOB AS HARD AS YOU POSSIBLY CAN.
NO!
I'M WORKING OUT THE GRAND SCHEME OF IT ALL!
LET'S SEE...
MOR-GANITE.
A MINERAL PINK IN COLOR, BUT VIOLENT IN NATURE.
AND GOOD-LOOK-ING!
ARRO-GANT.
AND ADORABLE!
ARE YOU INSULT-ING ME?
A NATURAL HISTORY...
...IS A RECORD AND CLASSIFI-CATION OF EVERY-THING IN NATURE.
THAT'S WHAT I HEARD.
SWEET, NOBLE GOSHEN!
F-FOR EXAMPLE?!
HMM, LIKE THE BUGS ON THE BEACH, AND THE PLANTS, AND EVERYTHING?
GIMME ANOTHER ONE!
WE ALREADY KNOW EVERYTHING ABOUT ALL THE USEFUL THINGS, SO...
...A RECORD OF THINGS WE DON'T KNOW ABOUT?
GIMME MORE!
WE DON'T KNOW THAT MUCH ABOUT ANYTHING. SORRY.
I NEED MORE!
WE WATCHERS ARE JUST ALWAYS LOOKING UP AT THE SKY...
BUT CINNABAR MIGHT KNOW SOME-THING.

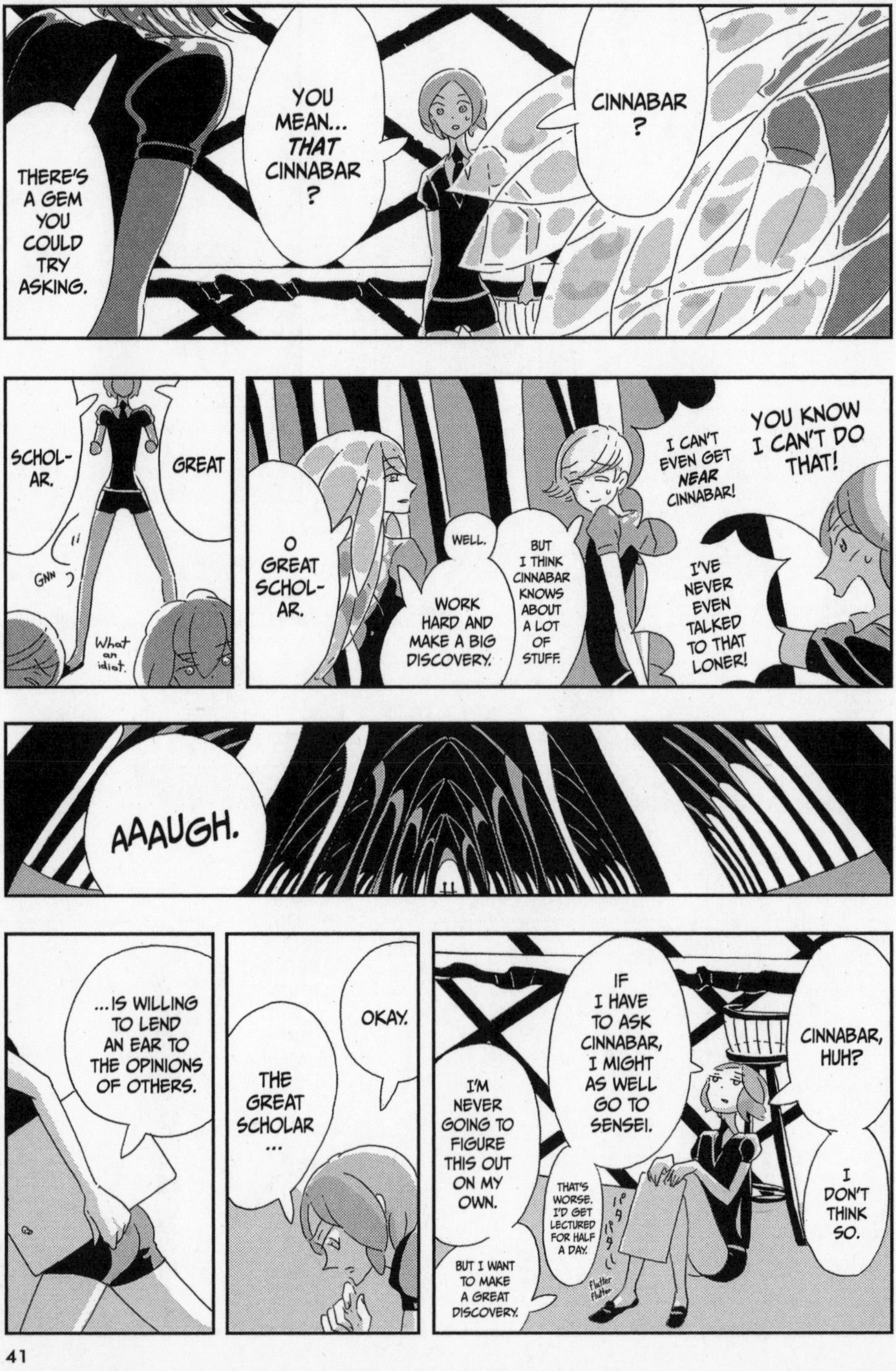
CINNABAR ?
YOU MEAN... THAT CINNABAR ?
THERE'S A GEM YOU COULD TRY ASKING.
YOU KNOW I CAN'T DO THAT!
I CAN'T EVEN GET NEAR CINNABAR!
I'VE NEVER EVEN TALKED TO THAT LONER!
BUT I THINK CINNABAR KNOWS ABOUT A LOT OF STUFF.
WELL.
WORK HARD AND MAKE A BIG DISCOVERY.
O GREAT SCHOL-AR.
GREAT
SCHOL-AR.
GNN
What an idiot.
AAAUGH.
CINNABAR, HUH?
I DON'T THINK SO.
IF I HAVE TO ASK CINNABAR, I MIGHT AS WELL GO TO SENSEI.
I'M NEVER GOING TO FIGURE THIS OUT ON MY OWN.
THAT'S WORSE. I'D GET LECTURED FOR HALF A DAY.
Flutter Flutter
BUT I WANT TO MAKE A GREAT DISCOVERY.
OKAY.
THE GREAT SCHOLAR ...
...IS WILLING TO LEND AN EAR TO THE OPINIONS OF OTHERS.

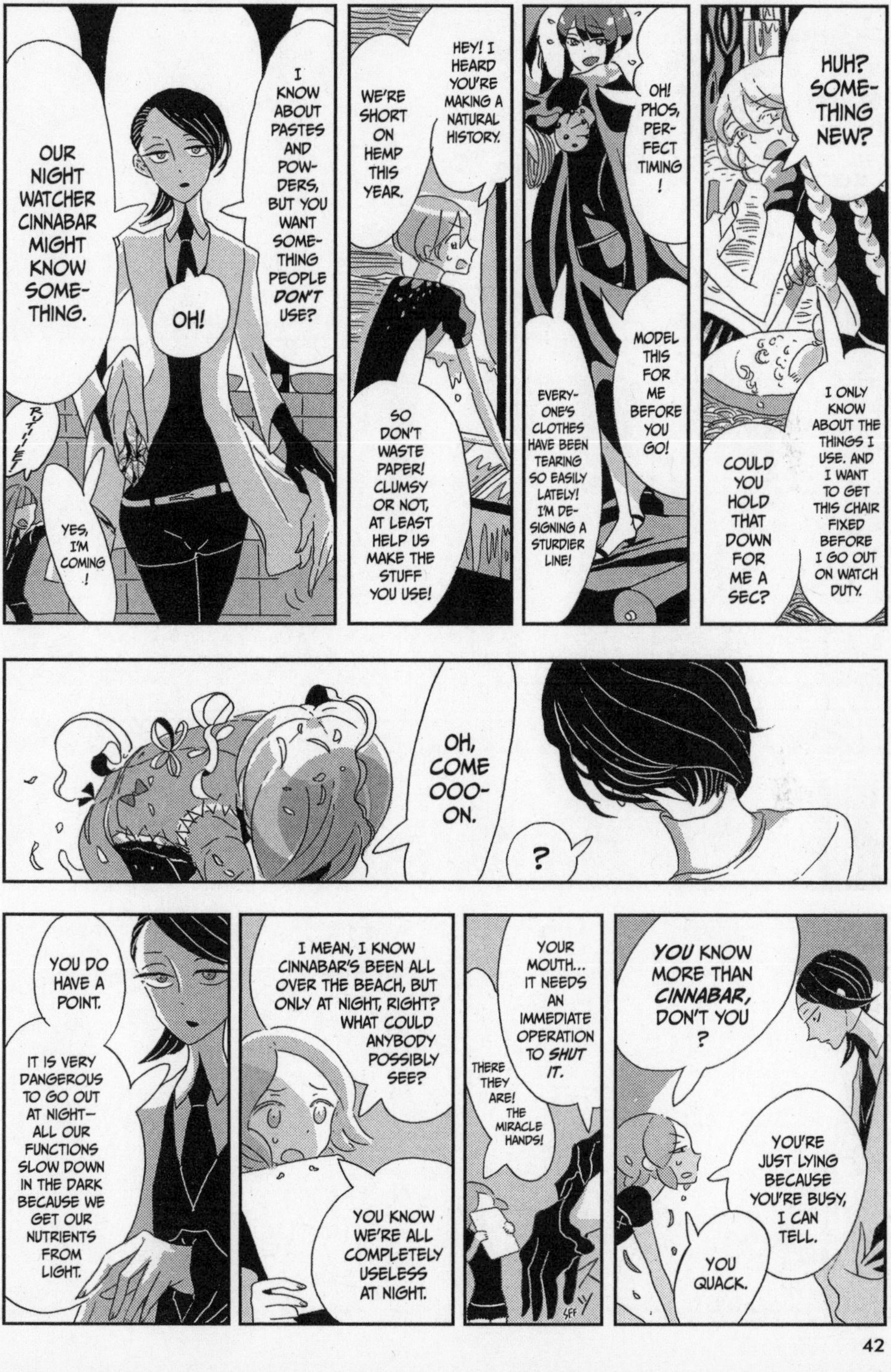
HUH? SOMETHING NEW?
I ONLY KNOW ABOUT THE THINGS I USE. AND I WANT TO GET THIS CHAIR FIXED BEFORE I GO OUT ON WATCH DUTY.
COULD YOU HOLD THAT DOWN FOR ME A SEC?
OH! PHOS, PERFECT TIMING!
MODEL THIS FOR ME BEFORE YOU GO!
EVERYONE'S CLOTHES HAVE BEEN TEARING SO EASILY LATELY! I'M DESIGNING A STURDIER LINE!
HEY! I HEARD YOU'RE MAKING A NATURAL HISTORY.
WE'RE SHORT ON HEMP THIS YEAR.
SO DON'T WASTE PAPER! CLUMSY OR NOT, AT LEAST HELP US MAKE THE STUFF YOU USE!
I KNOW ABOUT PASTES AND POWDERS, BUT YOU WANT SOMETHING PEOPLE DON'T USE?
OUR NIGHT WATCHER CINNABAR MIGHT KNOW SOMETHING.
OH!
RUTIIILE!
YES, I'M COMING!
OH, COME OOO-ON.
?
YOU KNOW MORE THAN CINNABAR, DON'T YOU?
YOU'RE JUST LYING BECAUSE YOU'RE BUSY, I CAN TELL.
YOU QUACK.
YOUR MOUTH... IT NEEDS AN IMMEDIATE OPERATION TO SHUT IT.
THERE THEY ARE! THE MIRACLE HANDS!
SFF
I MEAN, I KNOW CINNABAR'S BEEN ALL OVER THE BEACH, BUT ONLY AT NIGHT, RIGHT? WHAT COULD ANYBODY POSSIBLY SEE?
YOU KNOW WE'RE ALL COMPLETELY USELESS AT NIGHT.
YOU DO HAVE A POINT.
IT IS VERY DANGEROUS TO GO OUT AT NIGHT— ALL OUR FUNCTIONS SLOW DOWN IN THE DARK BECAUSE WE GET OUR NUTRIENTS FROM LIGHT.

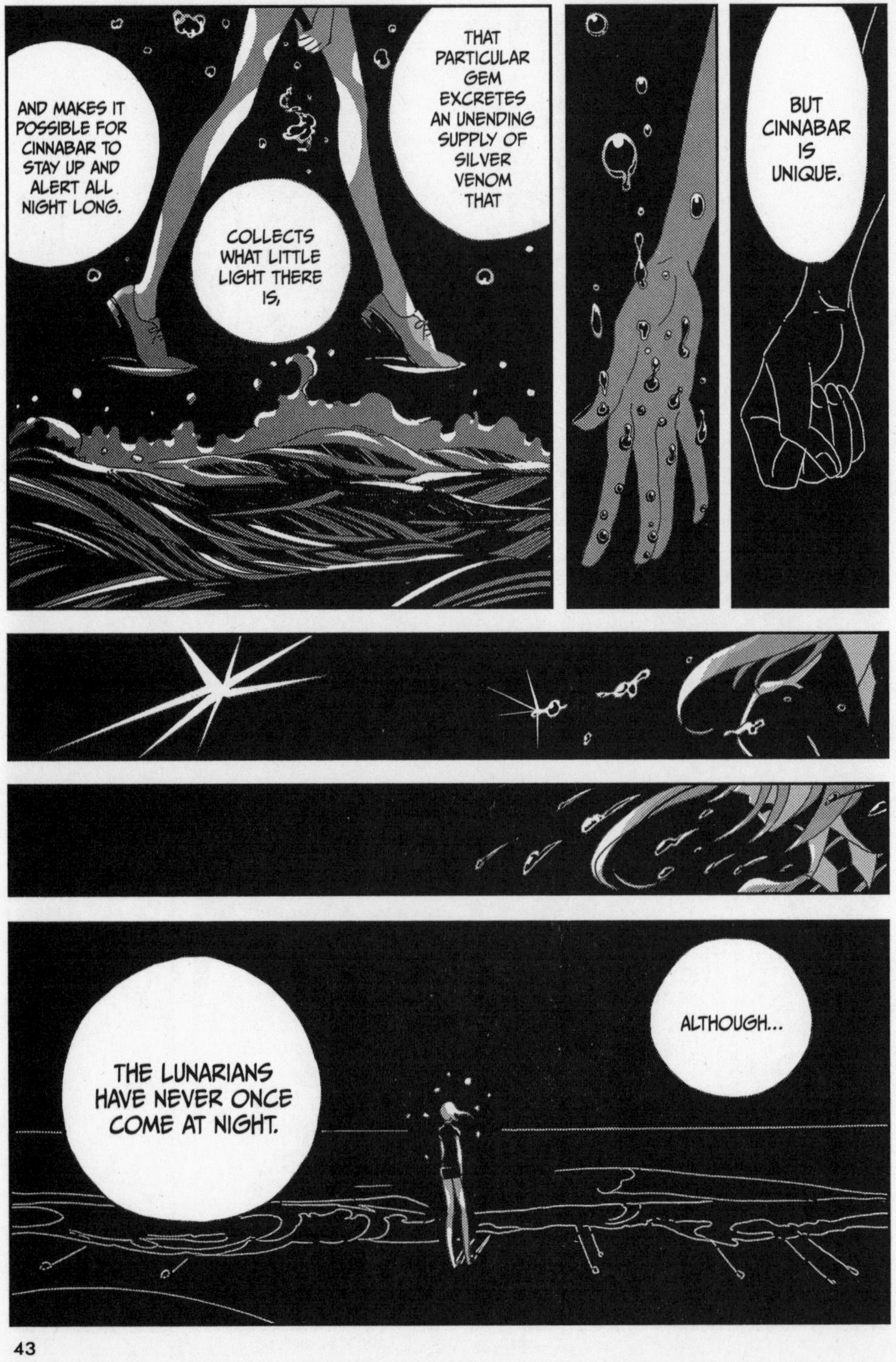

BUT CINNABAR IS UNIQUE.
THAT PARTICULAR GEM EXCRETES AN UNENDING SUPPLY OF SILVER VENOM THAT
COLLECTS WHAT LITTLE LIGHT THERE IS,
AND MAKES IT POSSIBLE FOR CINNABAR TO STAY UP AND ALERT ALL NIGHT LONG.
ALTHOUGH...
THE LUNARIANS HAVE NEVER ONCE COME AT NIGHT.

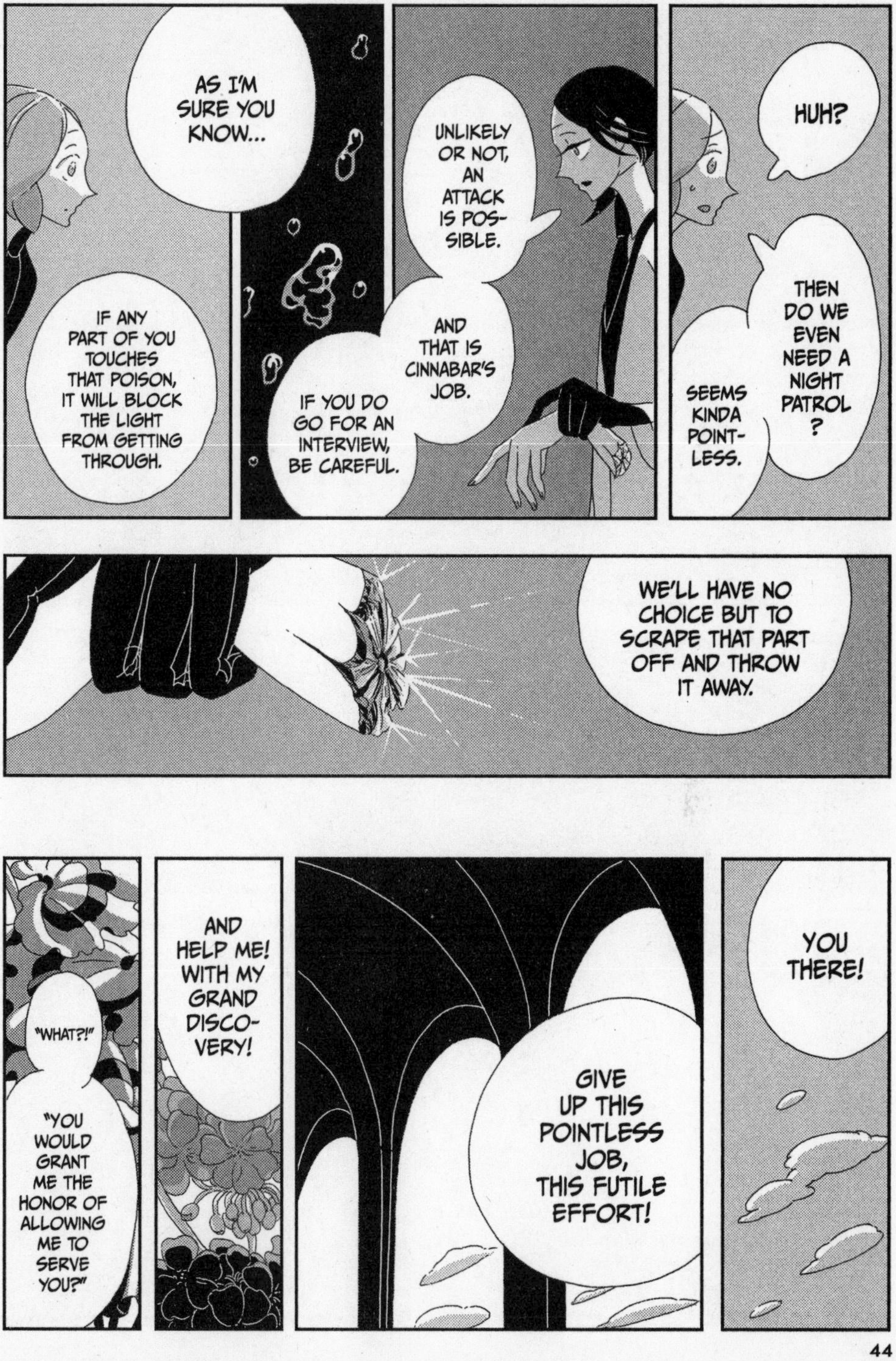
HUH?
THEN DO WE EVEN NEED A NIGHT PATROL?
SEEMS KINDA POINTLESS.
UNLIKELY OR NOT, AN ATTACK IS POSSIBLE.
AND THAT IS CINNABAR'S JOB.
IF YOU DO GO FOR AN INTERVIEW, BE CAREFUL.
AS I'M SURE YOU KNOW...
IF ANY PART OF YOU TOUCHES THAT POISON, IT WILL BLOCK THE LIGHT FROM GETTING THROUGH.
WE'LL HAVE NO CHOICE BUT TO SCRAPE THAT PART OFF AND THROW IT AWAY.
YOU THERE!
GIVE UP THIS POINTLESS JOB, THIS FUTILE EFFORT!
AND HELP ME! WITH MY GRAND DISCOVERY!
"WHAT?!"
"YOU WOULD GRANT ME THE HONOR OF ALLOWING ME TO SERVE YOU?"

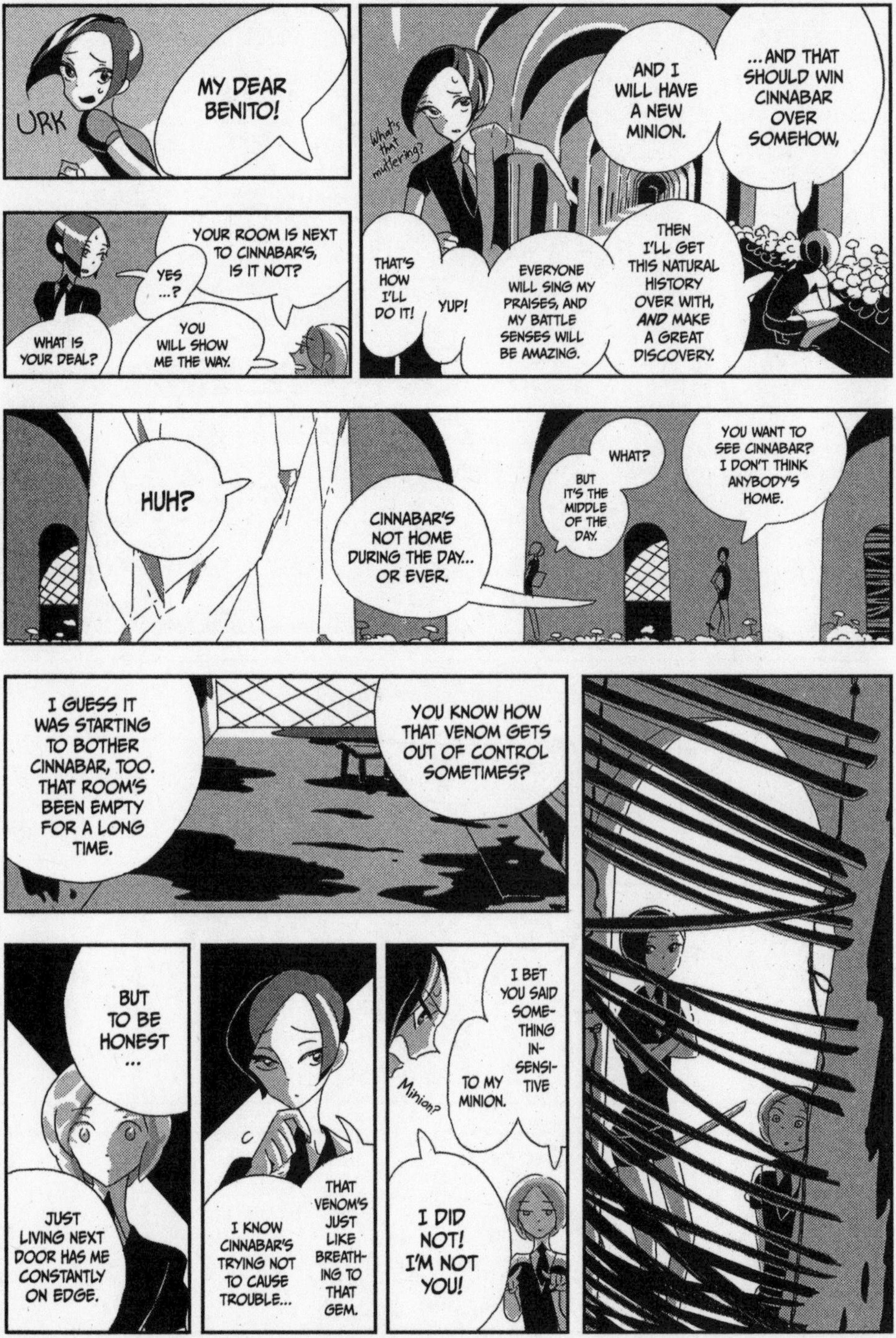
...AND THAT SHOULD WIN CINNABAR OVER SOMEHOW,
AND I WILL HAVE A NEW MINION.
What's that muttering?
THEN I'LL GET THIS NATURAL HISTORY OVER WITH, AND MAKE A GREAT DISCOVERY.
EVERYONE WILL SING MY PRAISES, AND MY BATTLE SENSES WILL BE AMAZING.
YUP!
THAT'S HOW I'LL DO IT!
MY DEAR BENITO!
URK
YOUR ROOM IS NEXT TO CINNABAR'S, IS IT NOT?
YES ...?
YOU WILL SHOW ME THE WAY.
WHAT IS YOUR DEAL?
YOU WANT TO SEE CINNABAR? I DON'T THINK ANYBODY'S HOME.
WHAT?
BUT IT'S THE MIDDLE OF THE DAY.
CINNABAR'S NOT HOME DURING THE DAY... OR EVER.
HUH?
YOU KNOW HOW THAT VENOM GETS OUT OF CONTROL SOMETIMES?
I GUESS IT WAS STARTING TO BOTHER CINNABAR, TOO. THAT ROOM'S BEEN EMPTY FOR A LONG TIME.
I BET YOU SAID SOME-THING IN-SENSI-TIVE
TO MY MINION.
Minion?
I DID NOT! I'M NOT YOU!
THAT VENOM'S JUST LIKE BREATH-ING TO THAT GEM.
I KNOW CINNABAR'S TRYING NOT TO CAUSE TROUBLE...
BUT TO BE HONEST ...
JUST LIVING NEXT DOOR HAS ME CONSTANTLY ON EDGE.

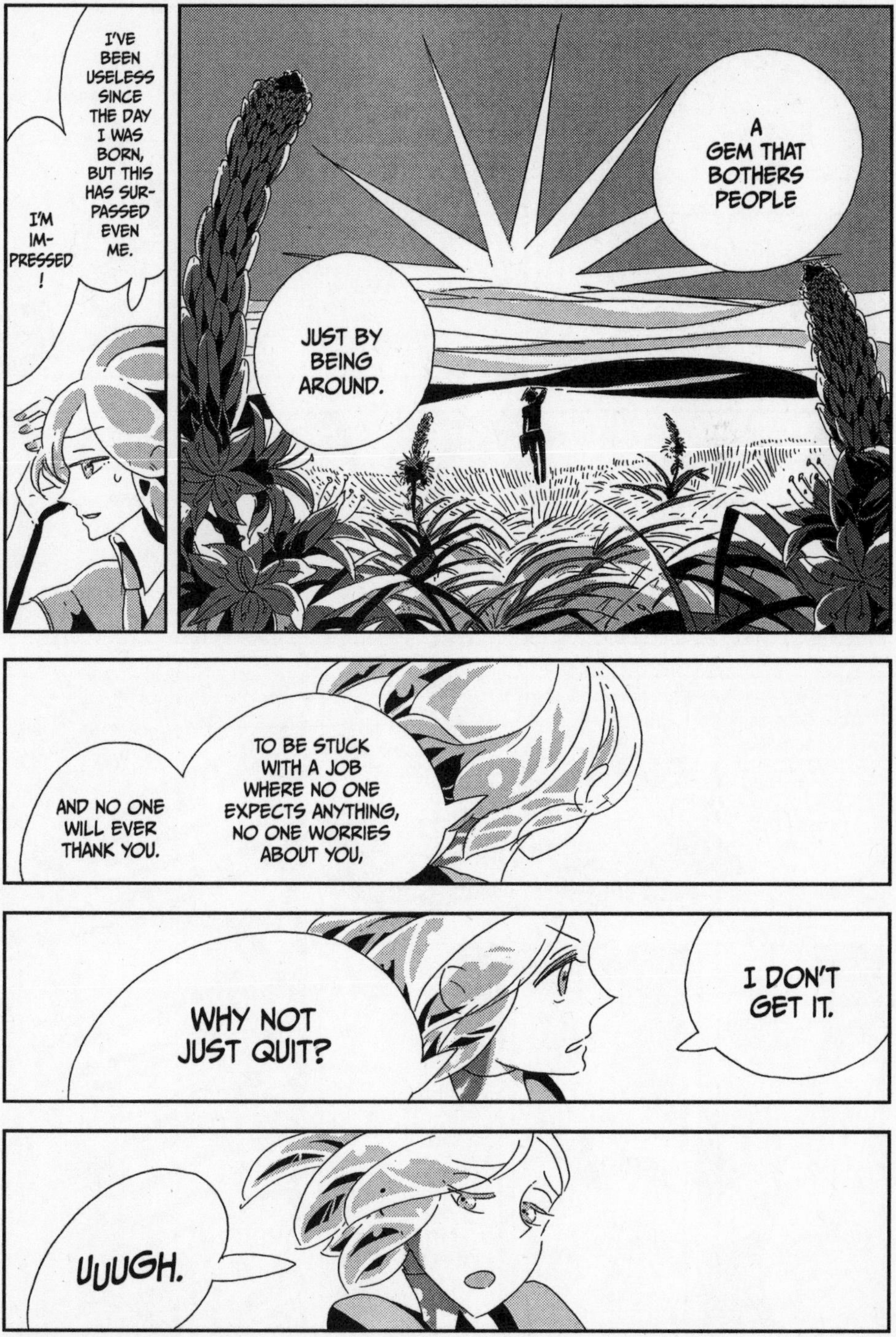
A GEM THAT BOTHERS PEOPLE
JUST BY BEING AROUND.
I'VE BEEN USELESS SINCE THE DAY I WAS BORN, BUT THIS HAS SURPASSED EVEN ME.
I'M IMPRESSED!
TO BE STUCK WITH A JOB WHERE NO ONE EXPECTS ANYTHING, NO ONE WORRIES ABOUT YOU,
AND NO ONE WILL EVER THANK YOU.
I DON'T GET IT.
WHY NOT JUST QUIT?
UUUGH.

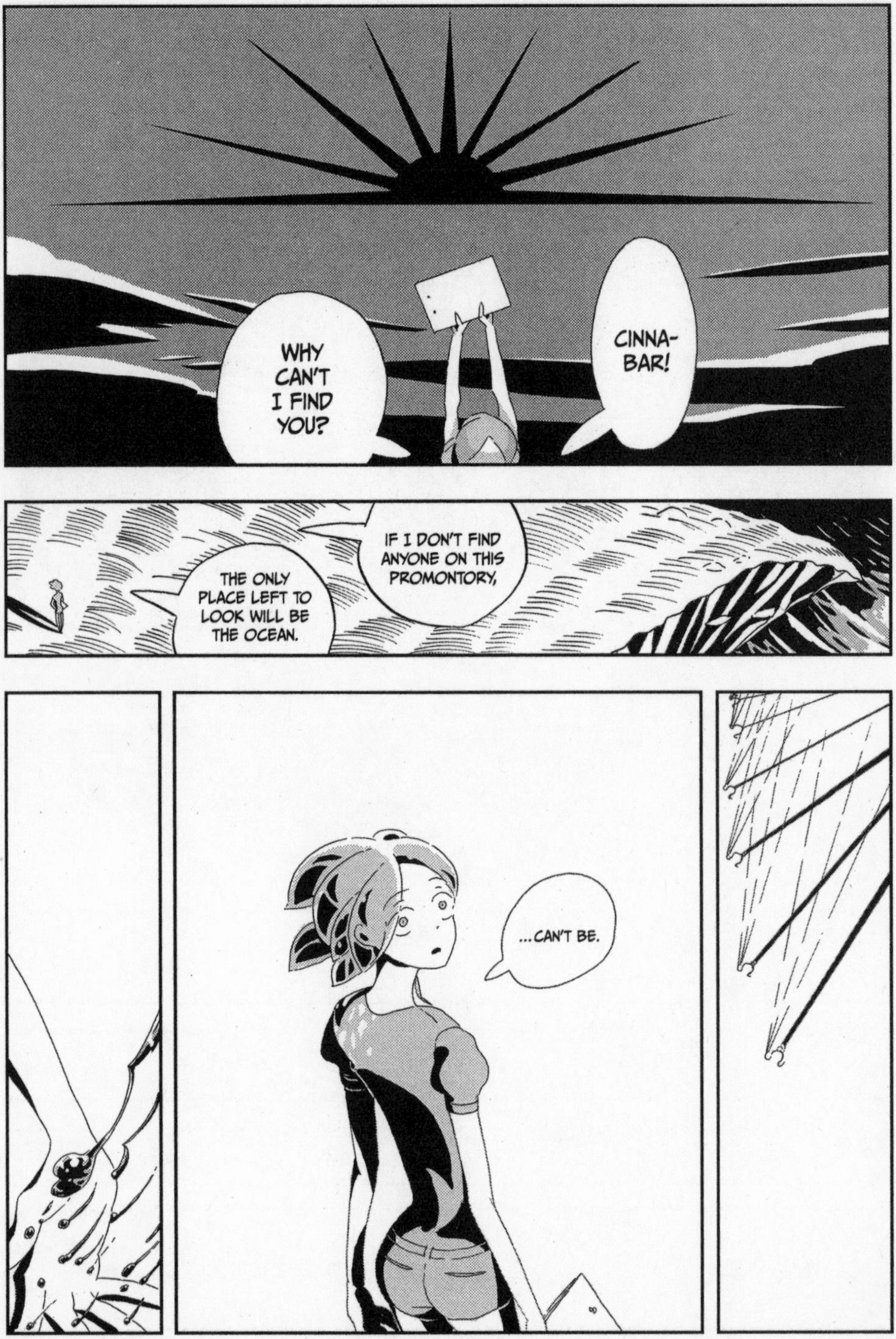
CINNA-BAR!
WHY CAN'T I FIND YOU?
IF I DON'T FIND ANYONE ON THIS PROMONTORY,
THE ONLY PLACE LEFT TO LOOK WILL BE THE OCEAN.
...CAN'T BE.

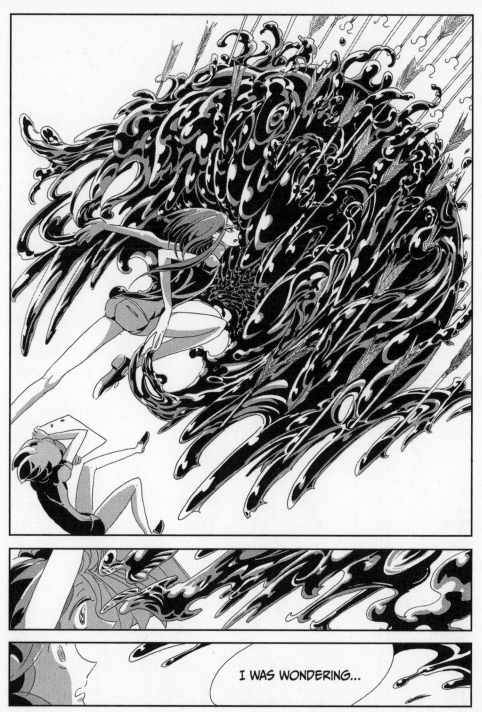

I WAS WONDERING...

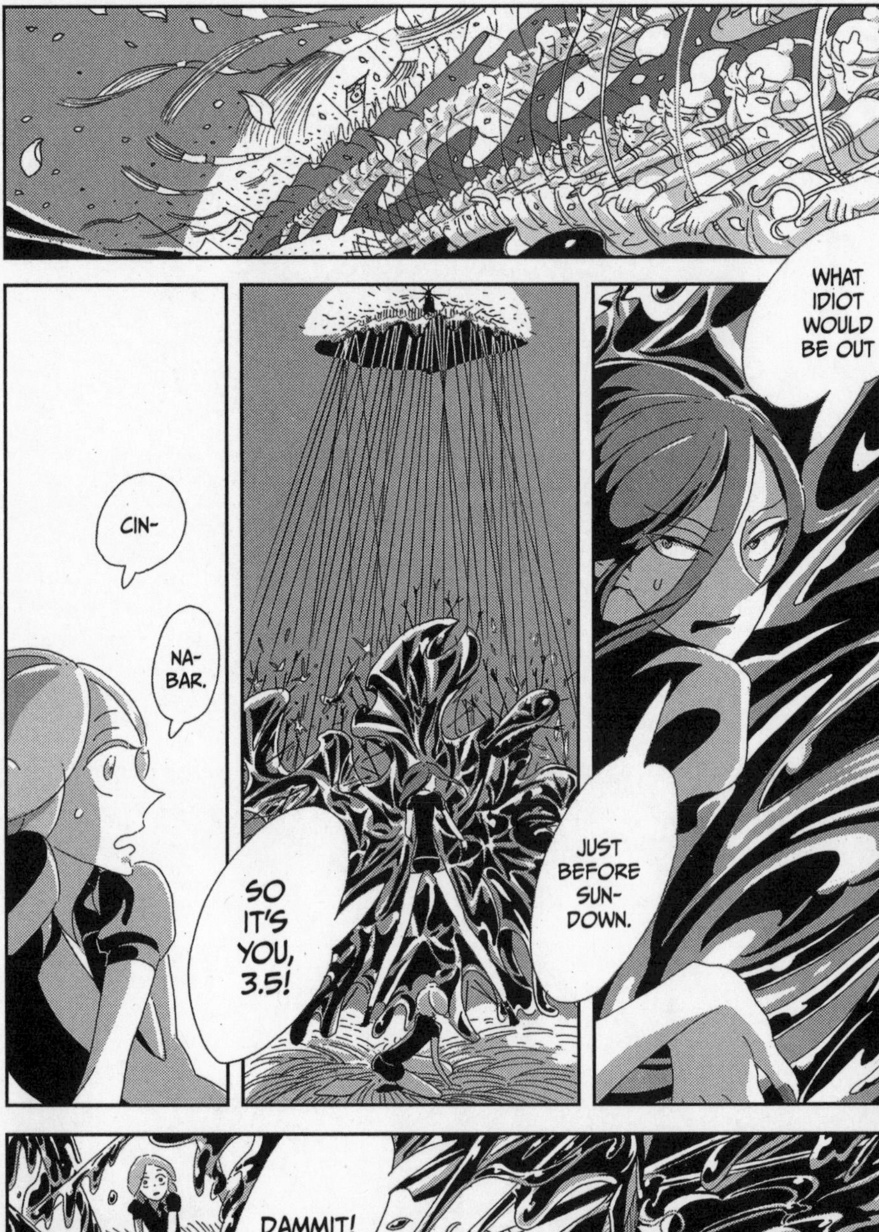
WHAT IDIOT WOULD BE OUT
JUST BEFORE SUN-DOWN.
SO IT'S YOU, 3.5!
CIN-
NA-BAR.
DAMMIT!

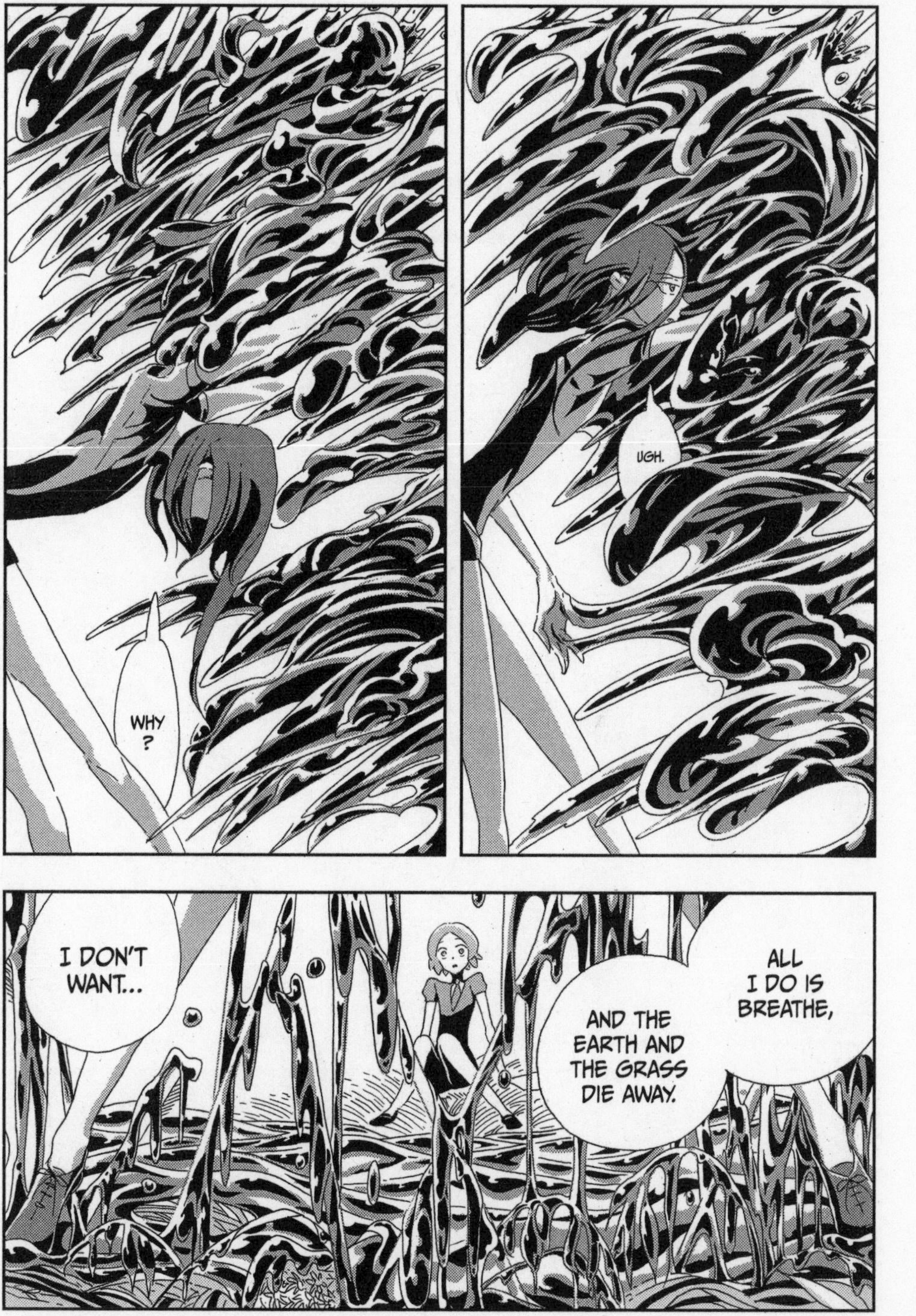
UGH.
WHY ?
ALL I DO IS BREATHE,
AND THE EARTH AND THE GRASS DIE AWAY.
I DON'T WANT...

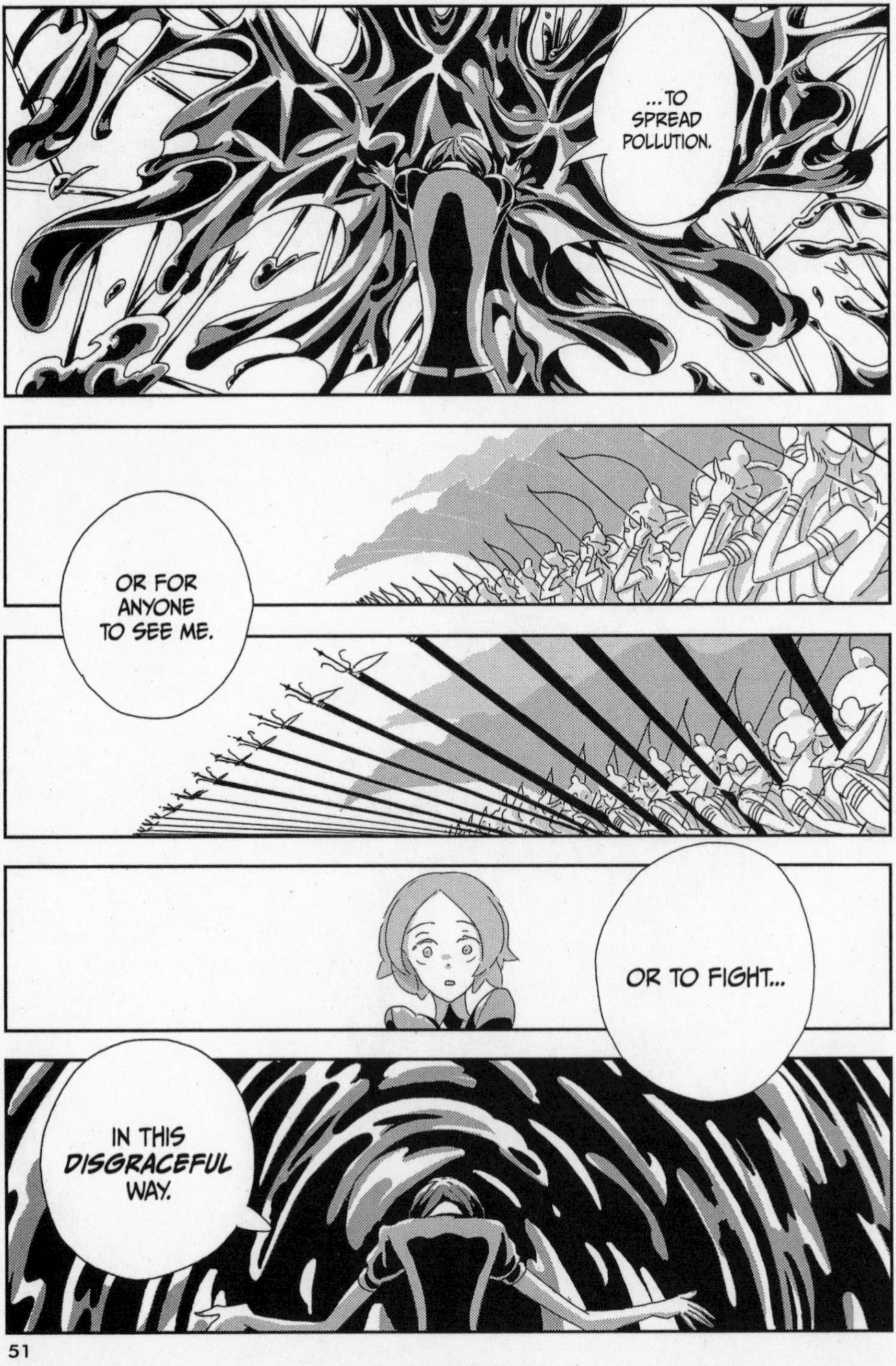
...TO SPREAD POLLUTION.
OR FOR ANYONE TO SEE ME.
OR TO FIGHT...
IN THIS DISGRACEFUL WAY.

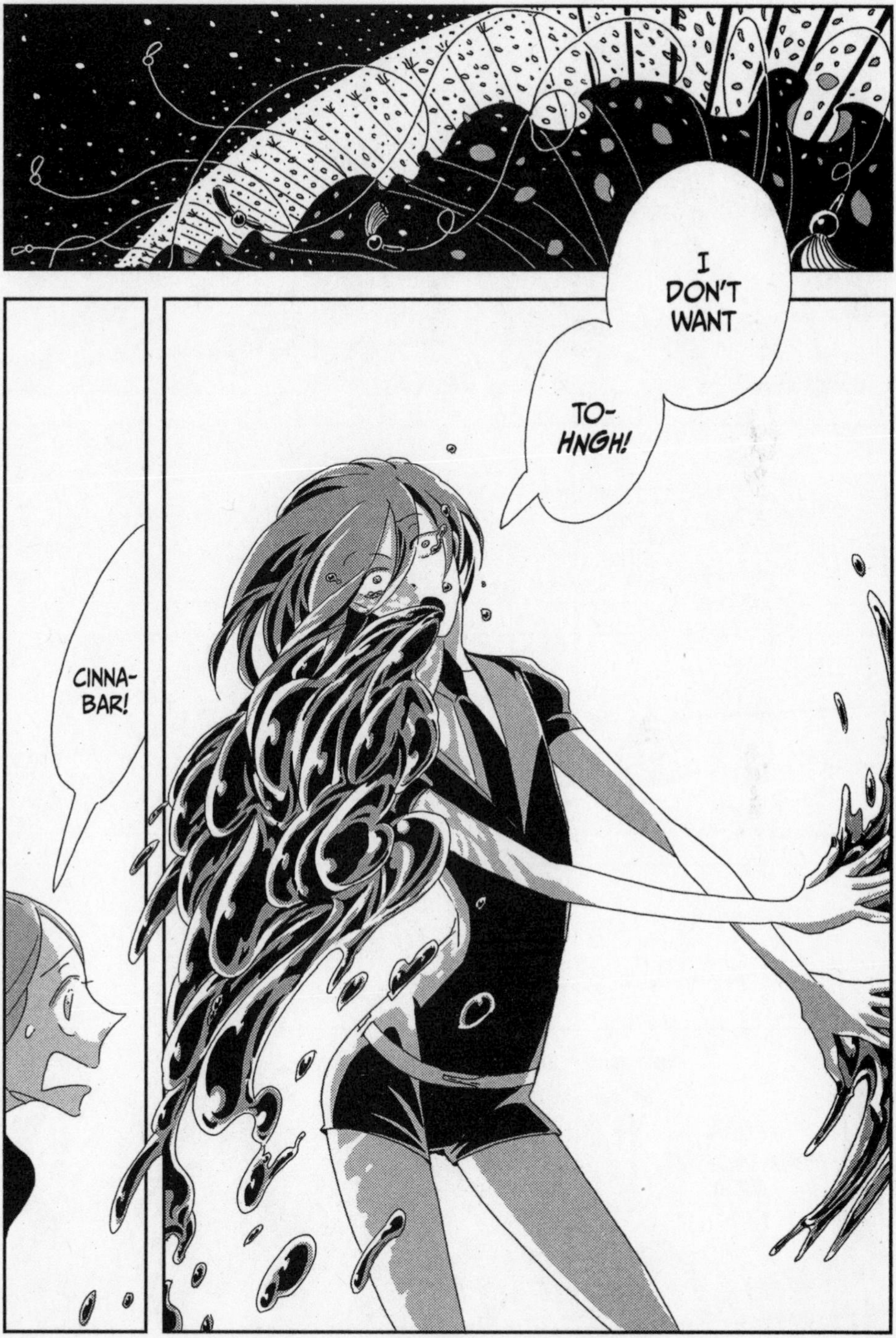
I DON'T WANT
TO- HNGH!
CINNA-BAR!

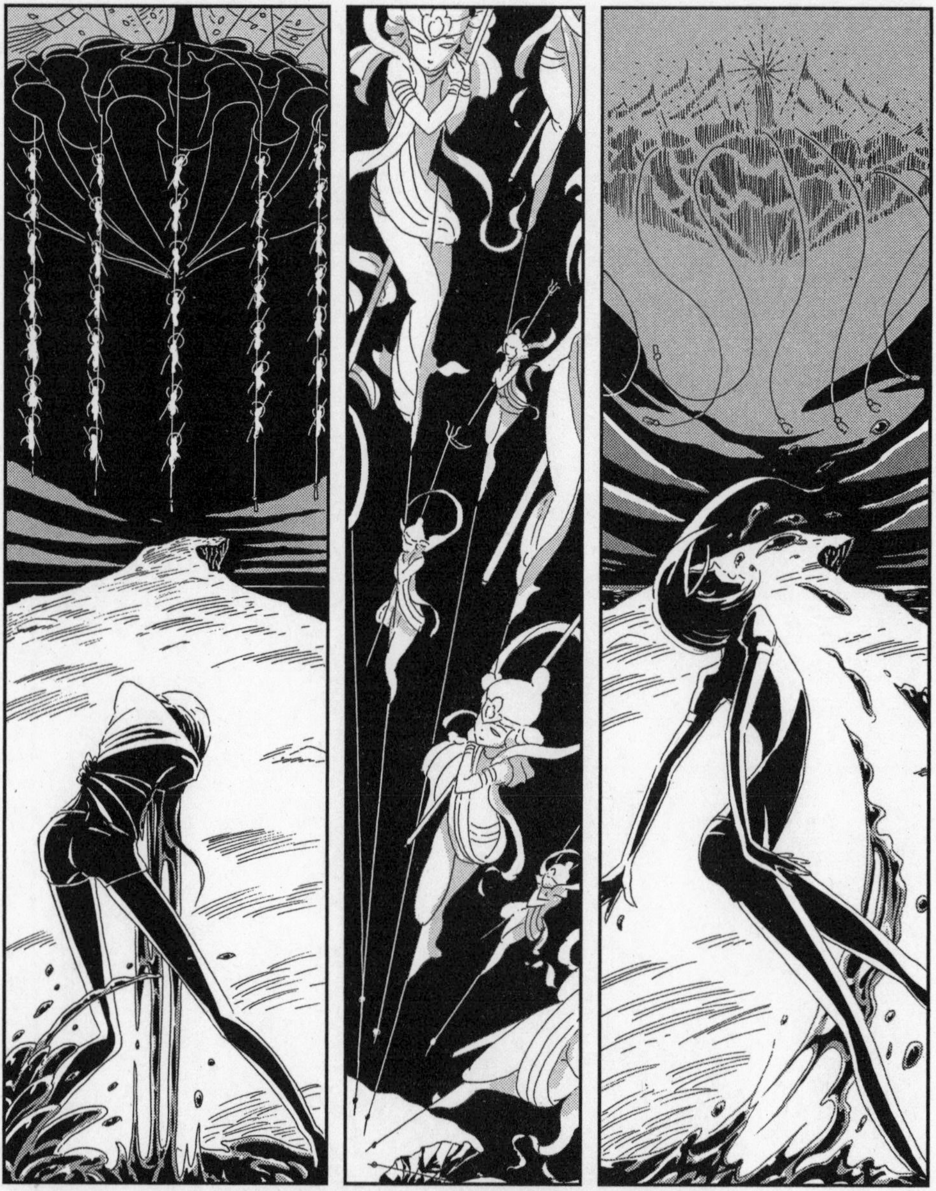
FIGHT.

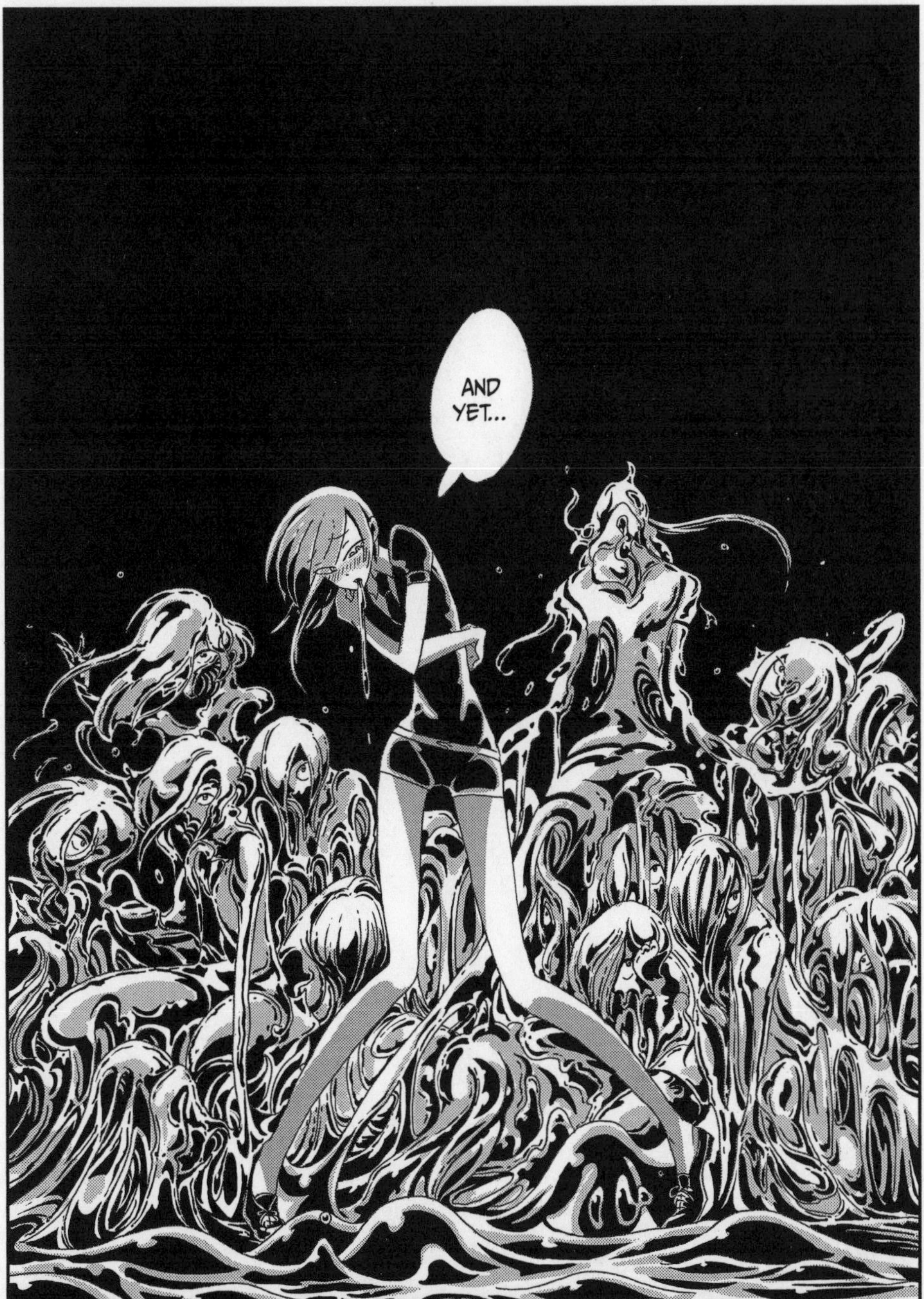
AND YET...

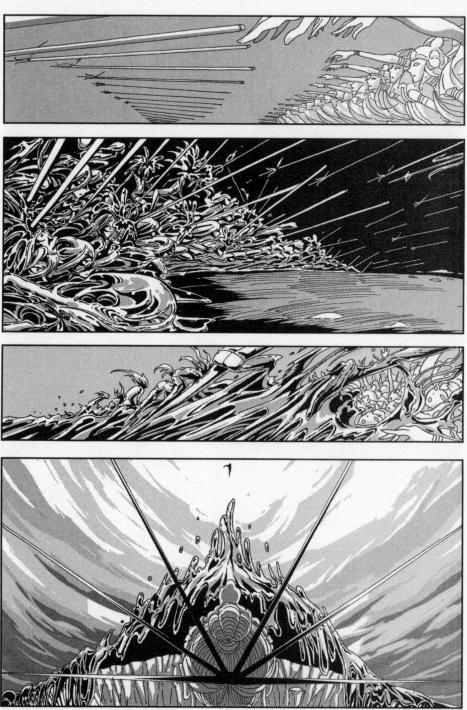

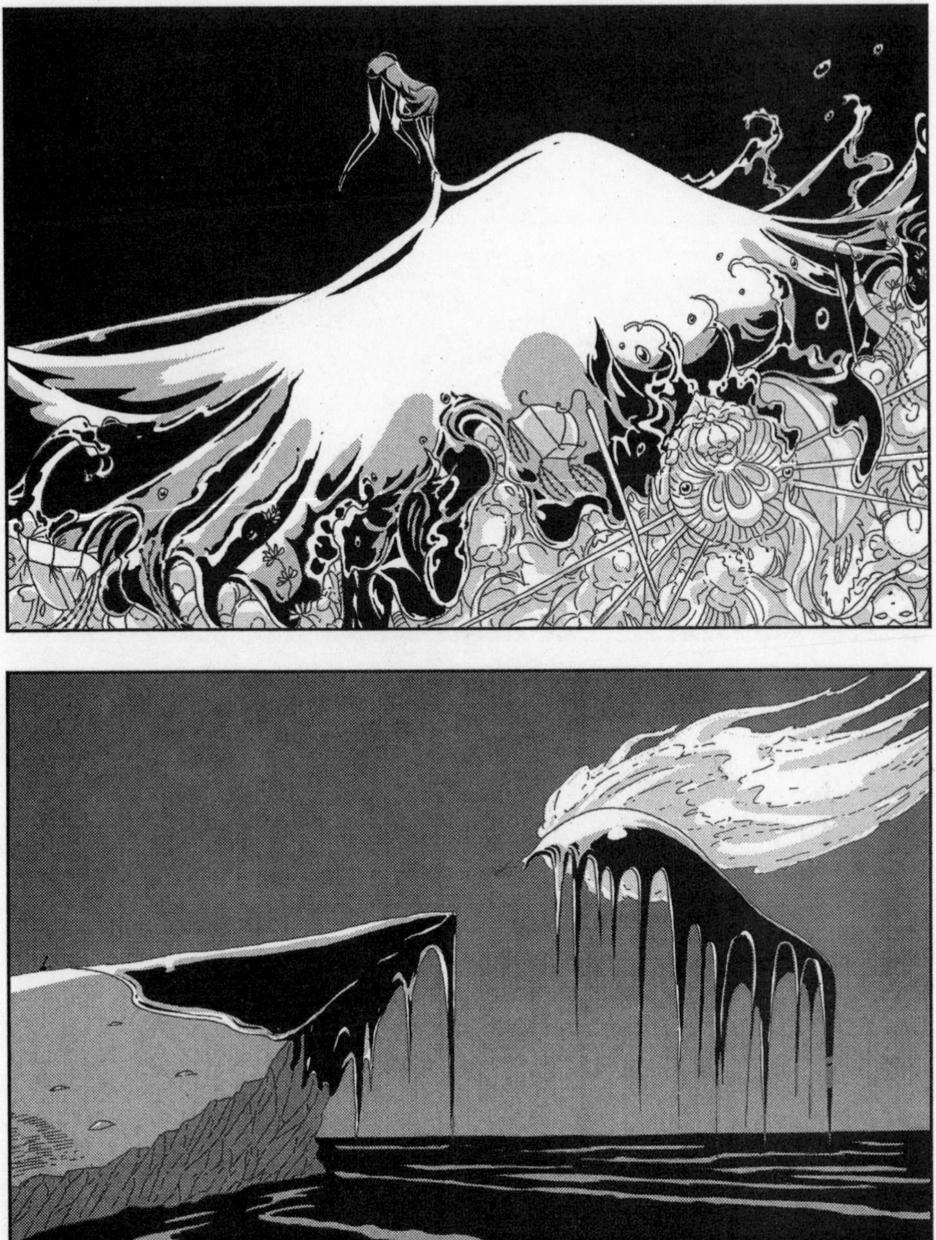

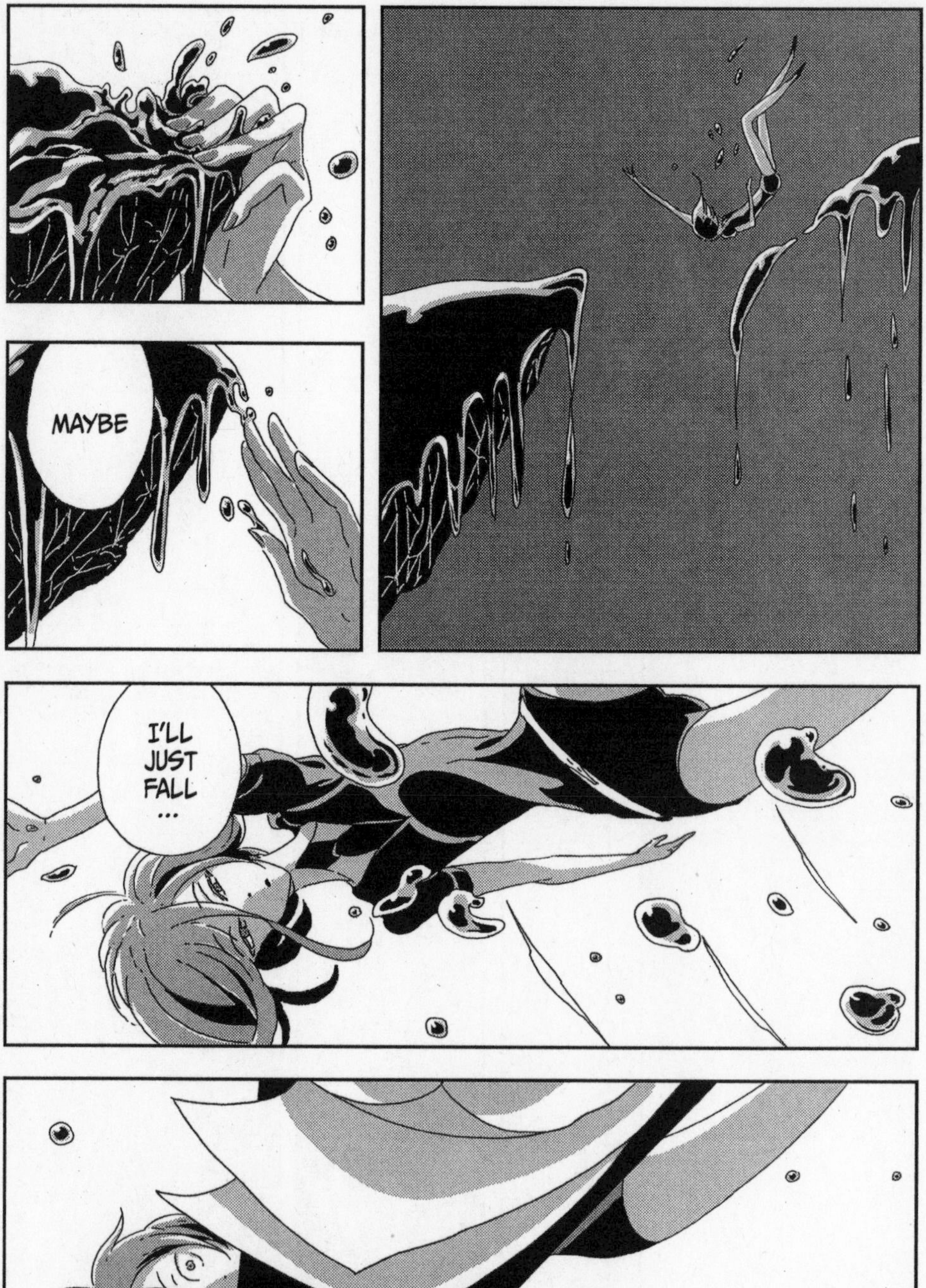
MAYBE
I'LL JUST FALL ...

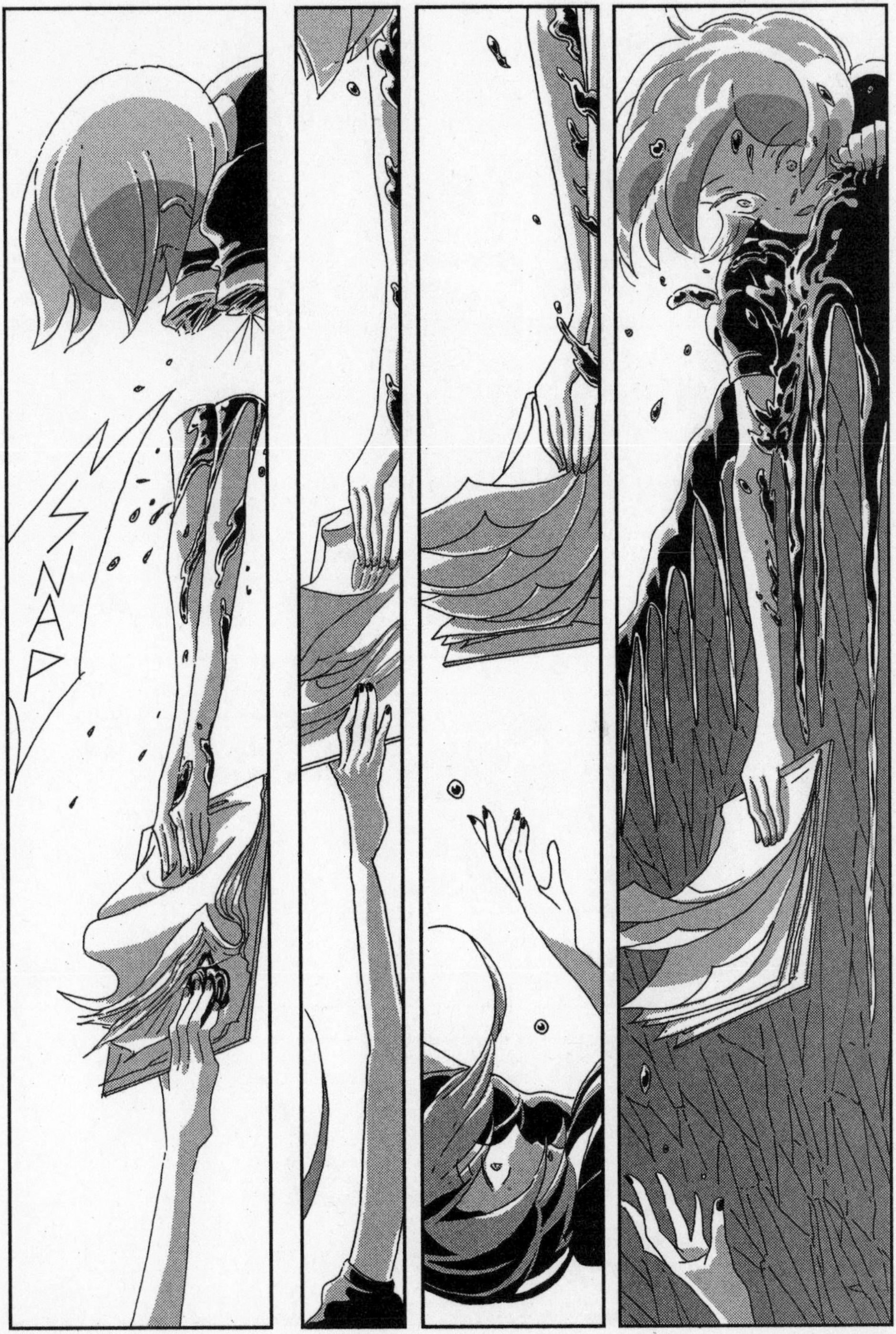
SNAP

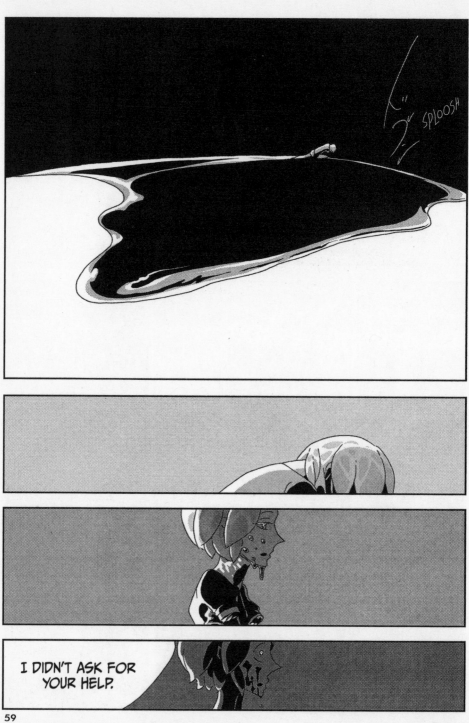

SPLOOSH

I DIDN'T ASK FOR
YOUR HELP.

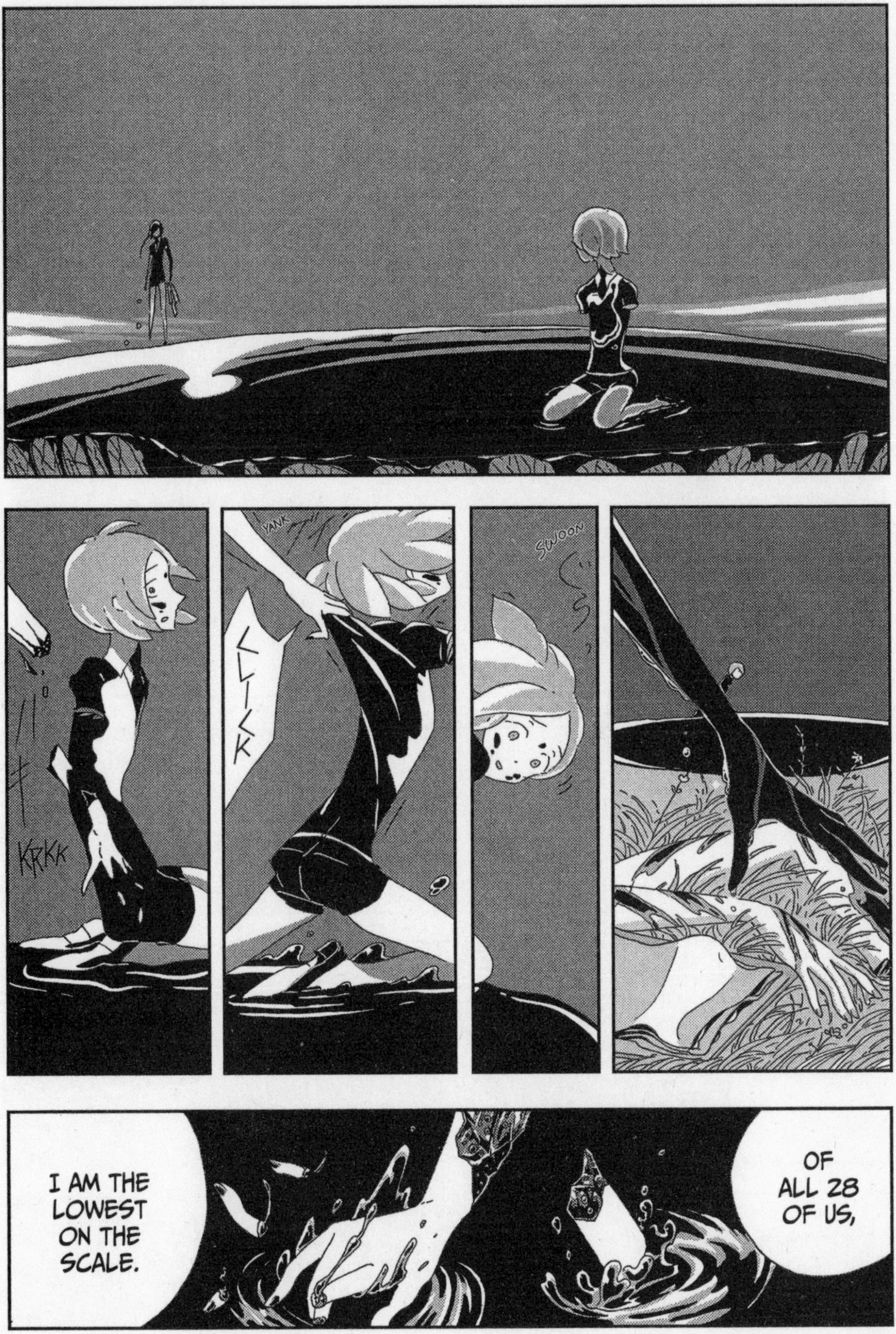
SWOON
YANK
CLICK
KRKK
OF ALL 28 OF US,
I AM THE LOWEST ON THE SCALE.

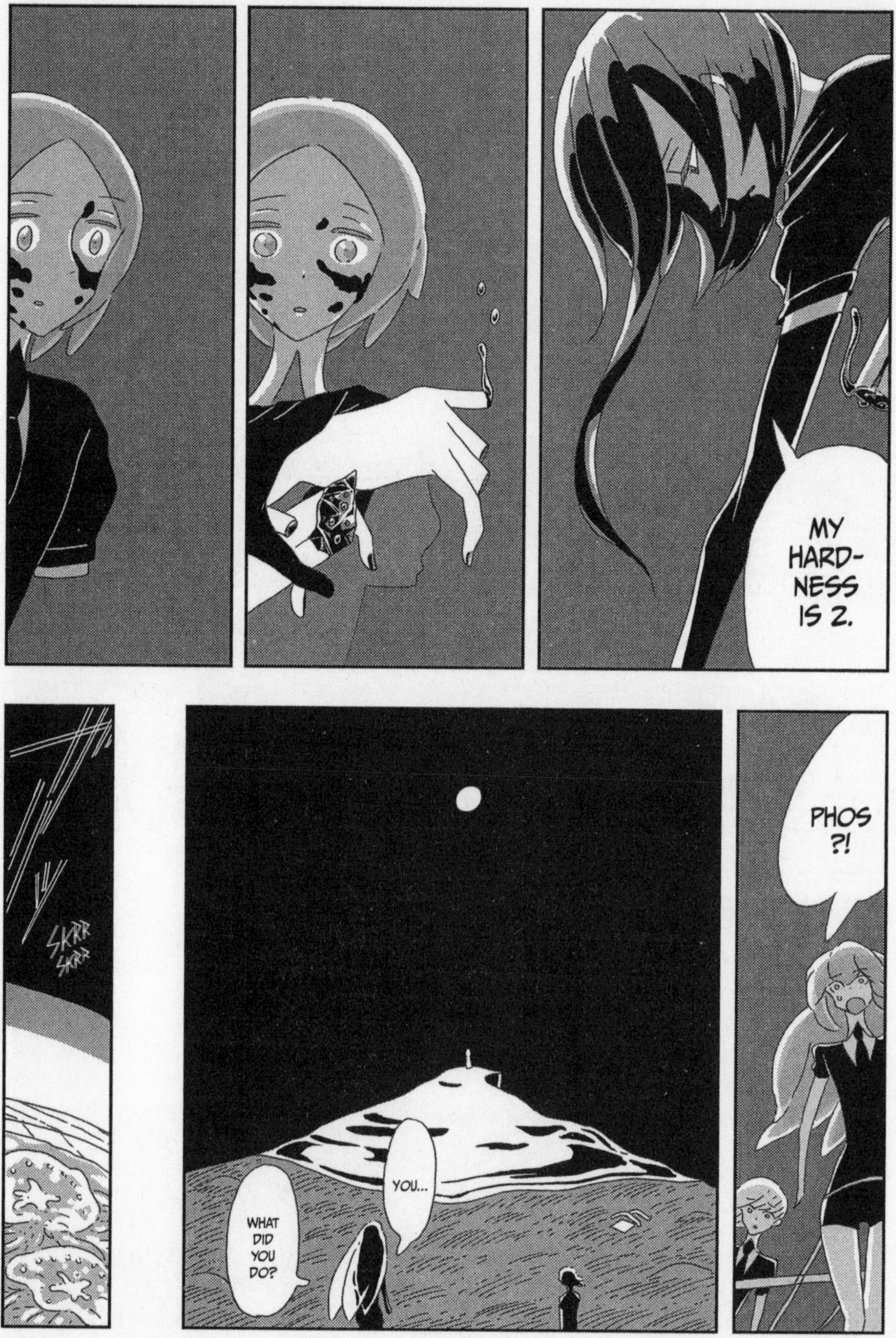
MY HARDNESS IS 2.
PHOS ?!
YOU...
WHAT DID YOU DO?
SKRR SKRR

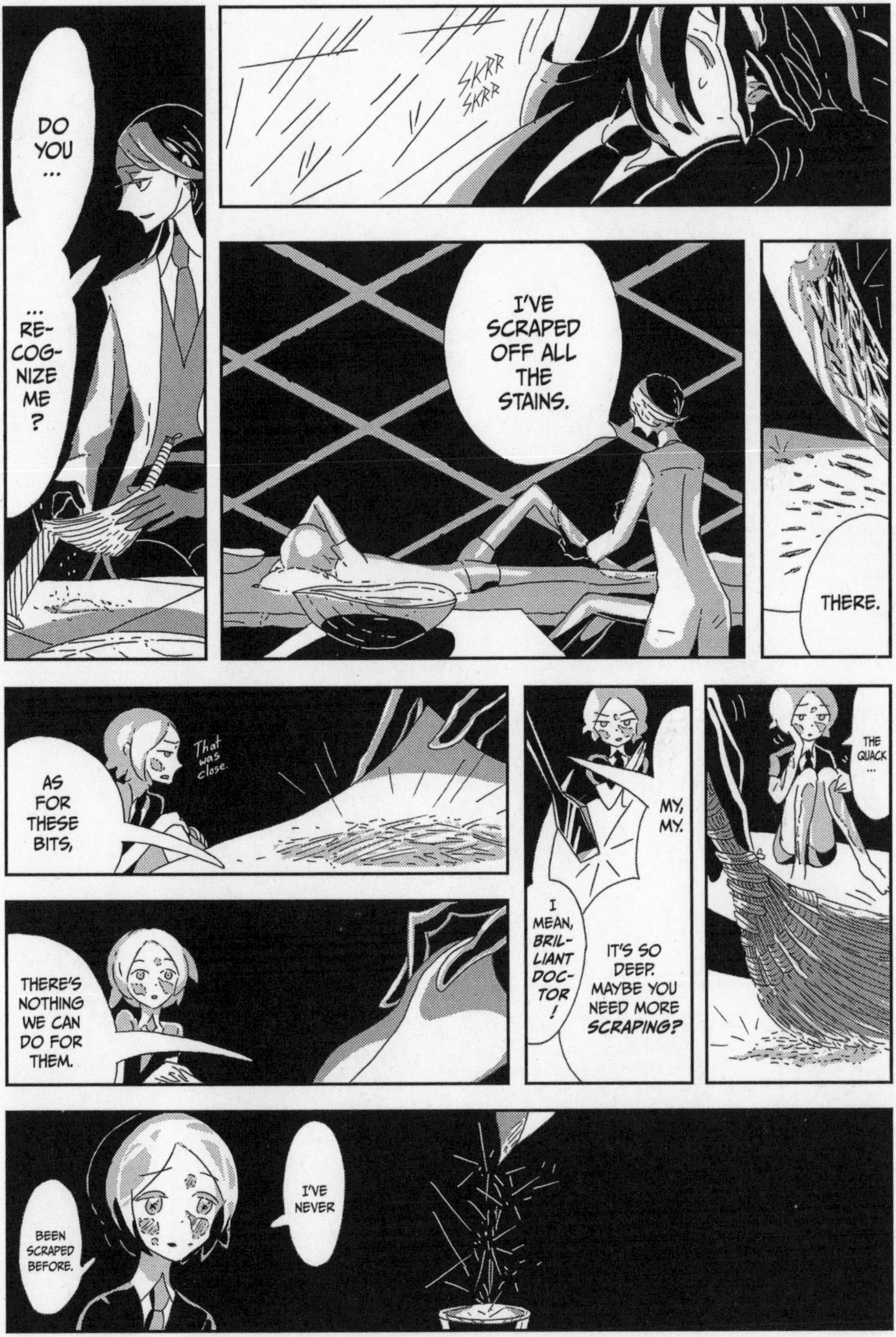
SKRR SKRR
THERE.
I'VE SCRAPED OFF ALL THE STAINS.
DO YOU ...
... RE-COGNIZE ME ?
THE QUACK ...
MY, MY.
IT'S SO DEEP. MAYBE YOU NEED MORE SCRAPING?
I MEAN, BRIL-LIANT DOC-TOR !
That was close.
AS FOR THESE BITS,
THERE'S NOTHING WE CAN DO FOR THEM.
I'VE NEVER
BEEN SCRAPED BEFORE.

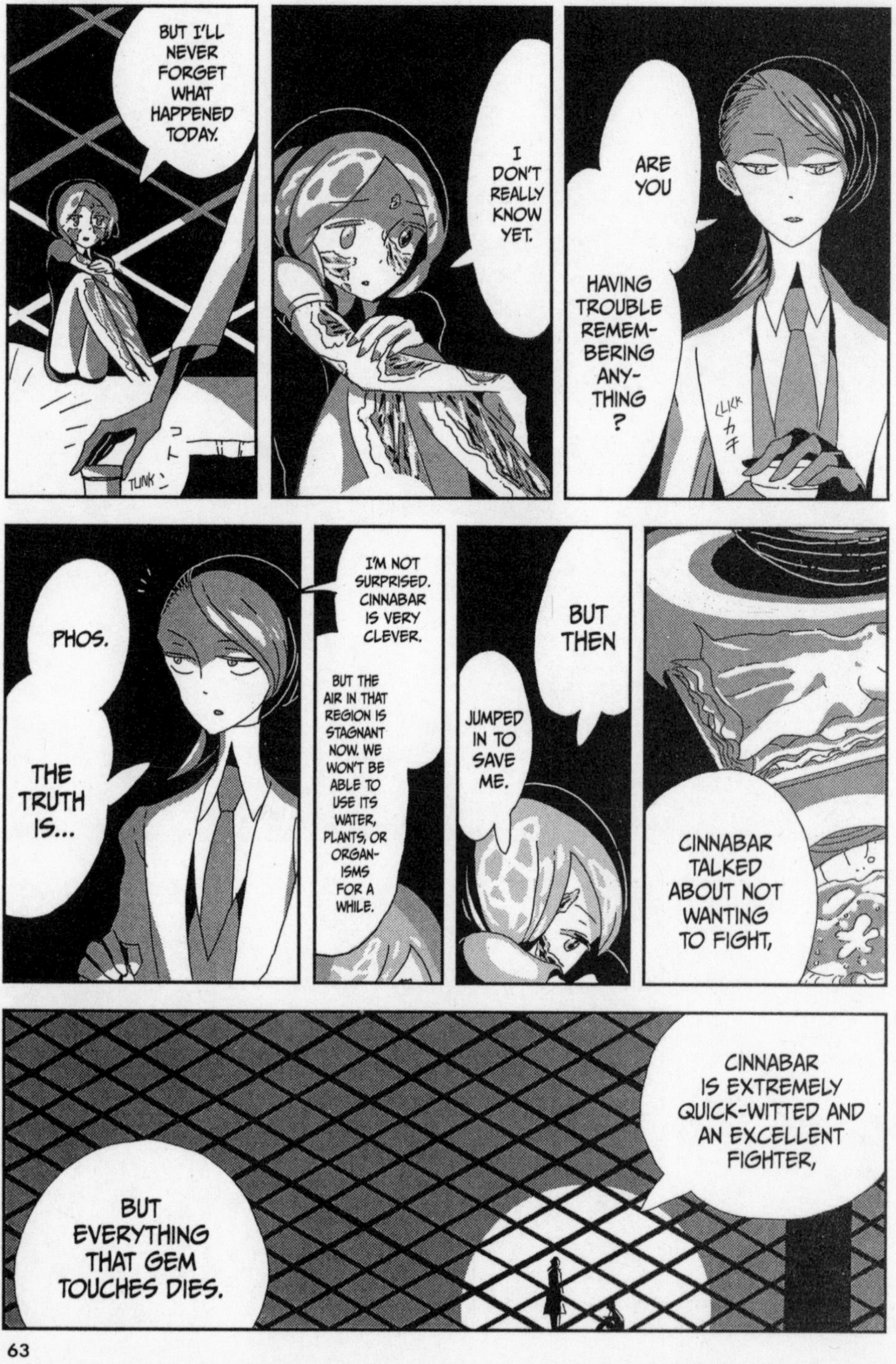
ARE YOU
HAVING TROUBLE REMEMBERING ANYTHING?
CLICK
カチ
I DON'T REALLY KNOW YET.
BUT I'LL NEVER FORGET WHAT HAPPENED TODAY.
コト
TUNK
CINNABAR TALKED ABOUT NOT WANTING TO FIGHT,
BUT THEN
JUMPED IN TO SAVE ME.
I'M NOT SURPRISED. CINNABAR IS VERY CLEVER.
BUT THE AIR IN THAT REGION IS STAGNANT NOW. WE WON'T BE ABLE TO USE ITS WATER, PLANTS, OR ORGANISMS FOR A WHILE.
PHOS.
THE TRUTH IS...
CINNABAR IS EXTREMELY QUICK-WITTED AND AN EXCELLENT FIGHTER,
BUT EVERYTHING THAT GEM TOUCHES DIES.

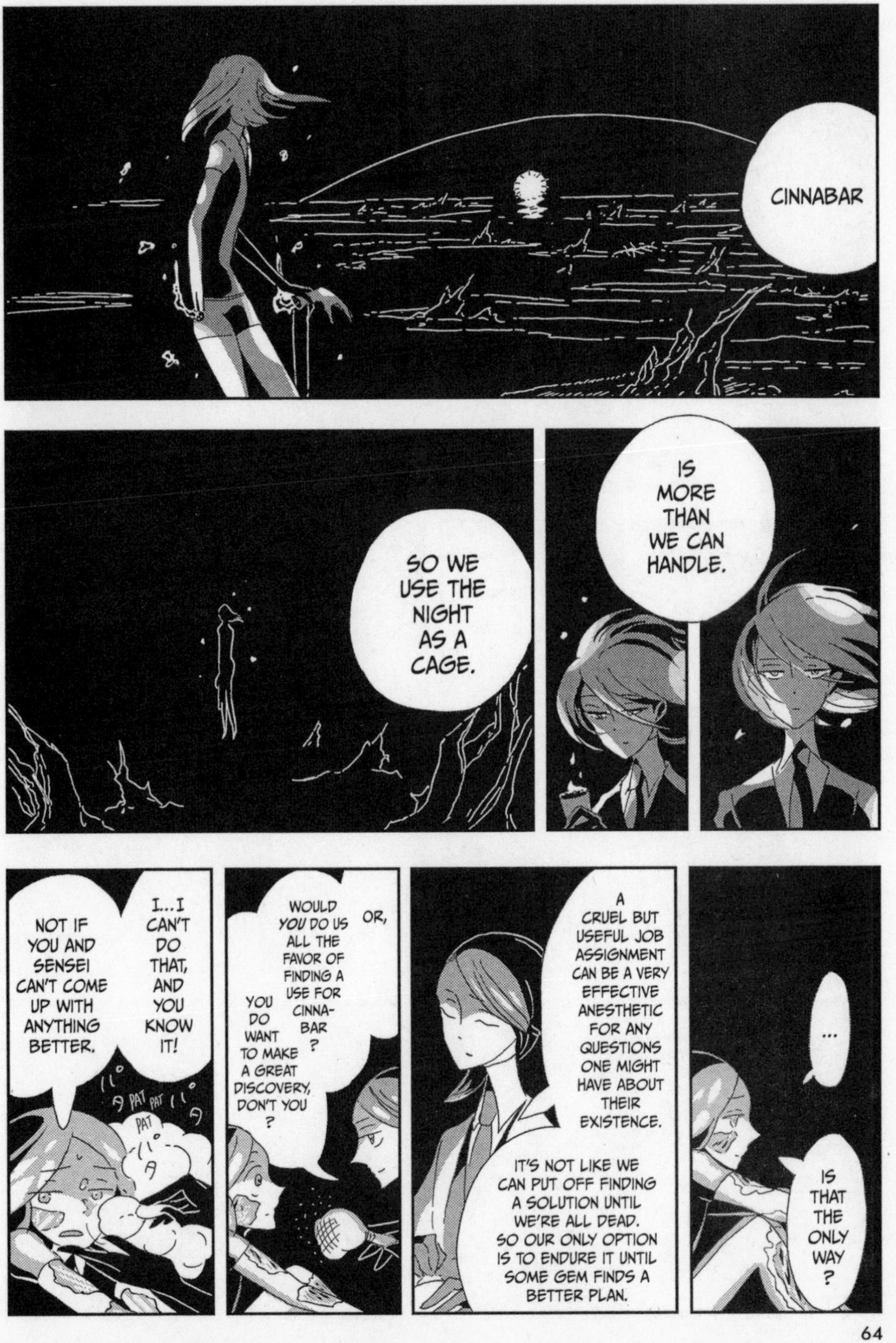
CINNABAR
IS MORE THAN WE CAN HANDLE.
SO WE USE THE NIGHT AS A CAGE.
...
IS THAT THE ONLY WAY?
A CRUEL BUT USEFUL JOB ASSIGNMENT CAN BE A VERY EFFECTIVE ANESTHETIC FOR ANY QUESTIONS ONE MIGHT HAVE ABOUT THEIR EXISTENCE.
IT'S NOT LIKE WE CAN PUT OFF FINDING A SOLUTION UNTIL WE'RE ALL DEAD. SO OUR ONLY OPTION IS TO ENDURE IT UNTIL SOME GEM FINDS A BETTER PLAN.
OR,
WOULD *YOU* DO US ALL THE FAVOR OF FINDING A USE FOR CINNA-BAR?
YOU DO WANT TO MAKE A GREAT DISCOVERY, DON'T YOU?
I...I CAN'T DO THAT, AND YOU KNOW IT!
NOT IF YOU AND SENSEI CAN'T COME UP WITH ANYTHING BETTER.
PAT PAT PAT

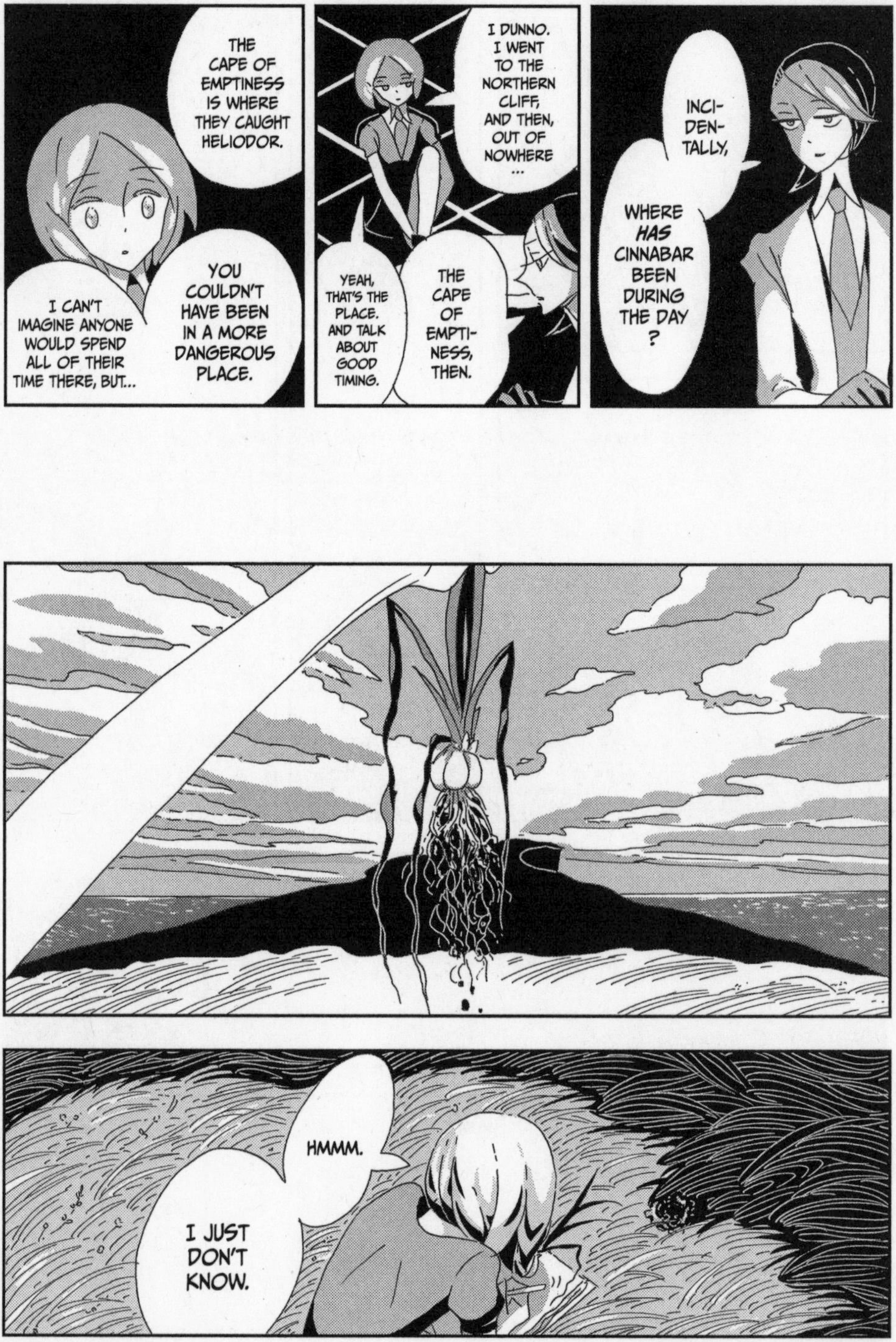
INCI-DENTALLY,
WHERE HAS CINNABAR BEEN DURING THE DAY?
I DUNNO. I WENT TO THE NORTHERN CLIFF, AND THEN, OUT OF NOWHERE...
THE CAPE OF EMPTI-NESS, THEN.
YEAH, THAT'S THE PLACE. AND TALK ABOUT GOOD TIMING.
THE CAPE OF EMPTINESS IS WHERE THEY CAUGHT HELIODOR.
YOU COULDN'T HAVE BEEN IN A MORE DANGEROUS PLACE.
I CAN'T IMAGINE ANYONE WOULD SPEND ALL OF THEIR TIME THERE, BUT...
HMMM.
I JUST DON'T KNOW.

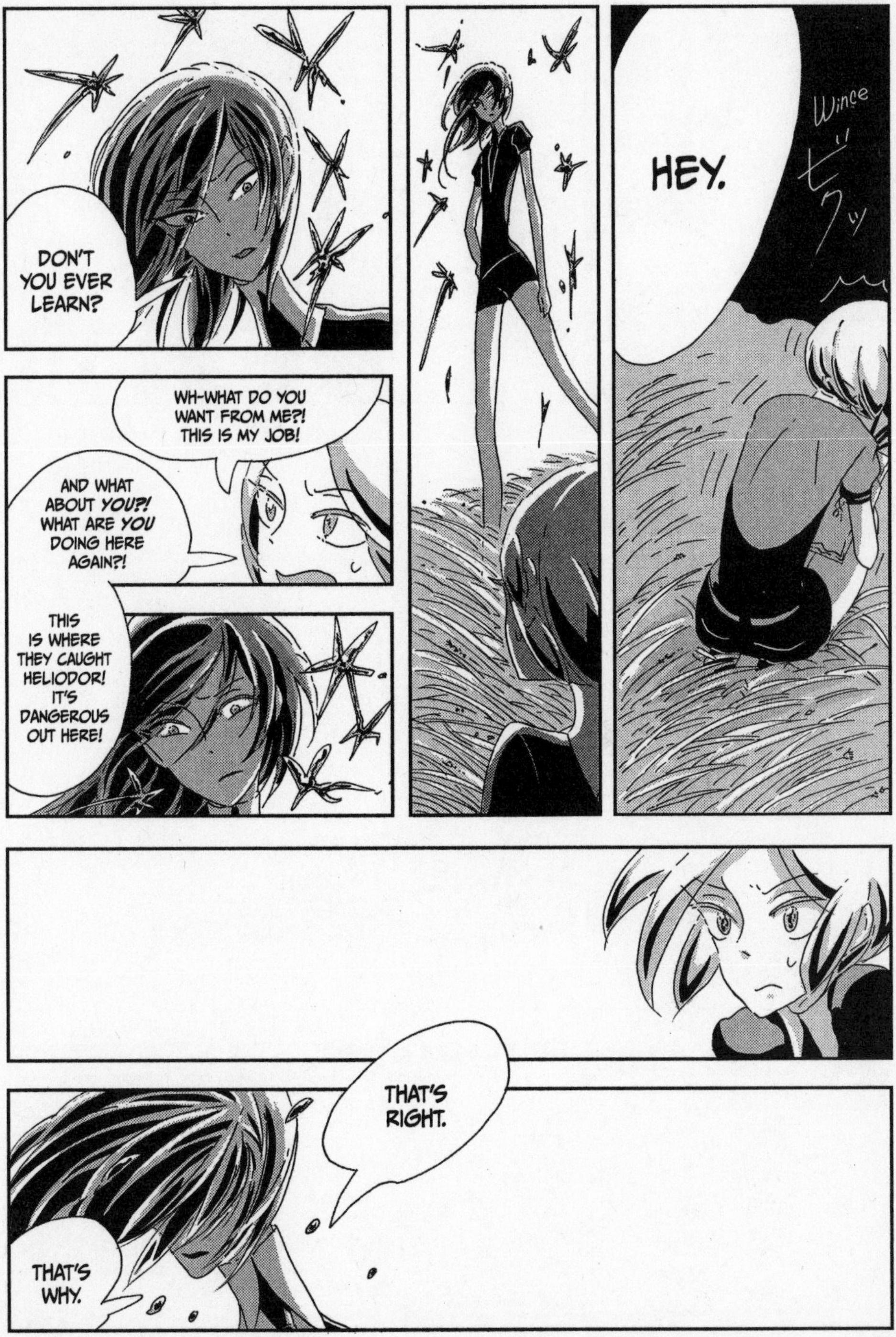
HEY.
Wince
ビクッ
DON'T YOU EVER LEARN?
WH-WHAT DO YOU WANT FROM ME?! THIS IS MY JOB!
AND WHAT ABOUT *YOU?!* WHAT ARE *YOU* DOING HERE AGAIN?!
THIS IS WHERE THEY CAUGHT HELIODOR! IT'S DANGEROUS OUT HERE!
THAT'S RIGHT.
THAT'S WHY.

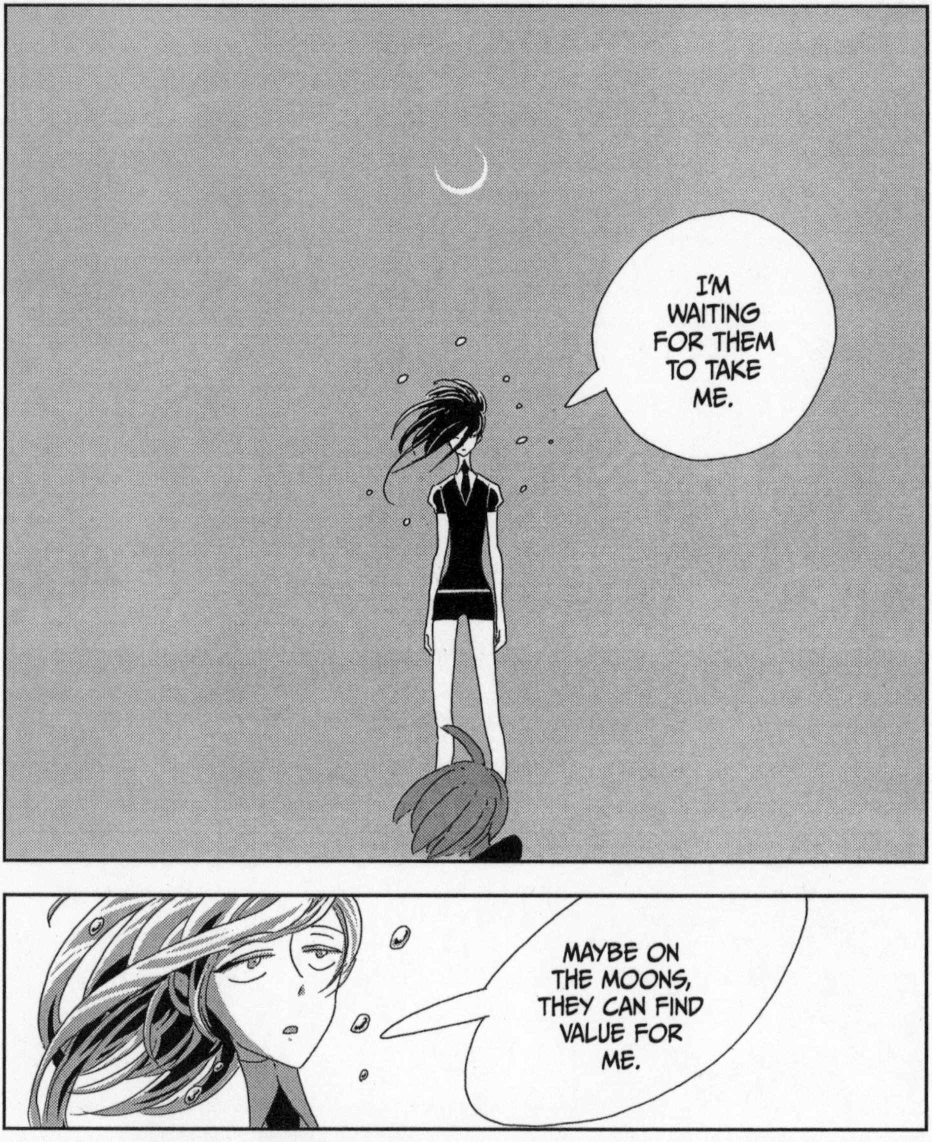
I'M WAITING FOR THEM TO TAKE ME.
MAYBE ON THE MOONS, THEY CAN FIND VALUE FOR ME.
I'VE WAITED ALL THIS TIME, BUT THEY NEVER COME.

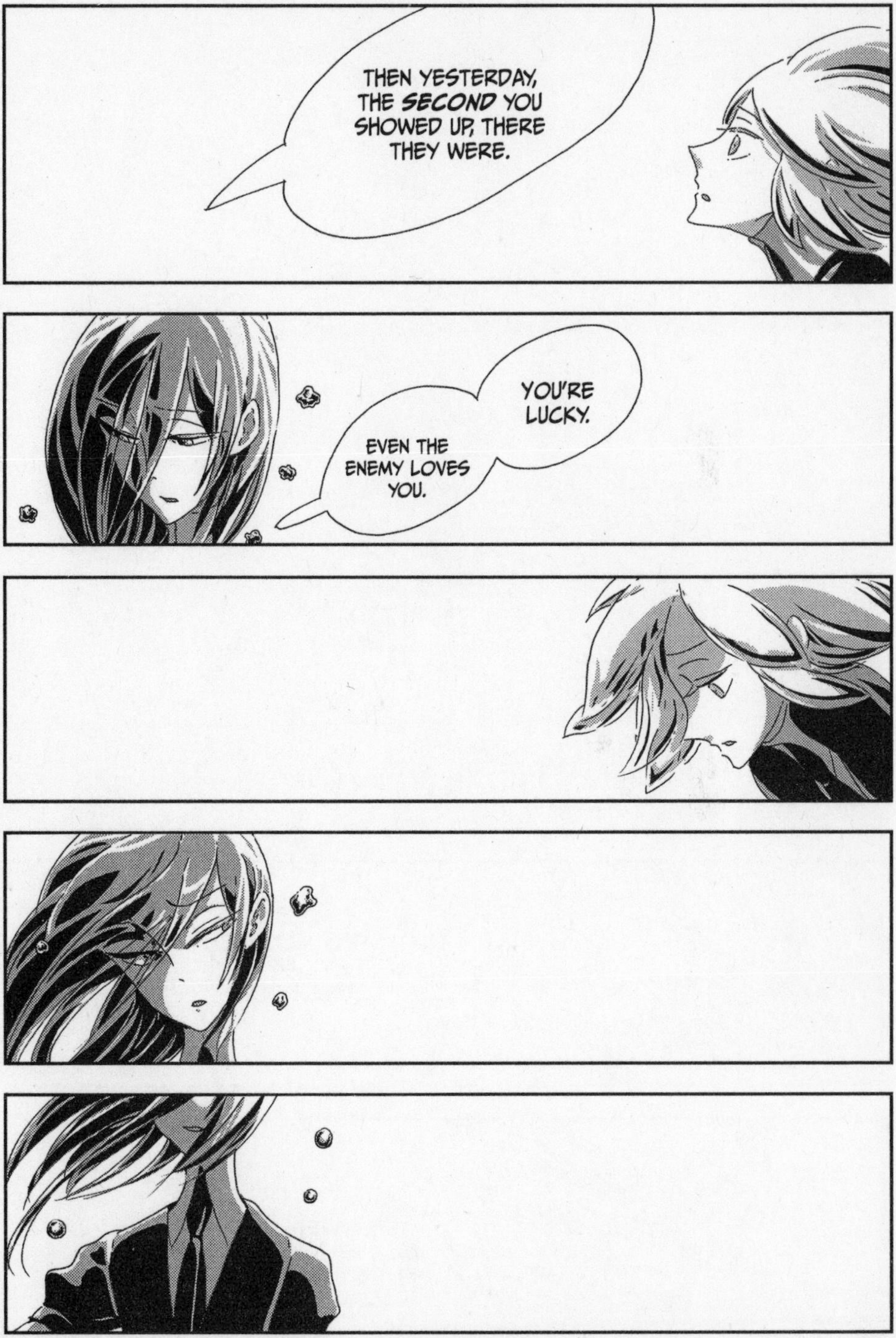
THEN YESTERDAY, THE *SECOND* YOU SHOWED UP, THERE THEY WERE.
YOU'RE LUCKY.
EVEN THE ENEMY LOVES YOU.

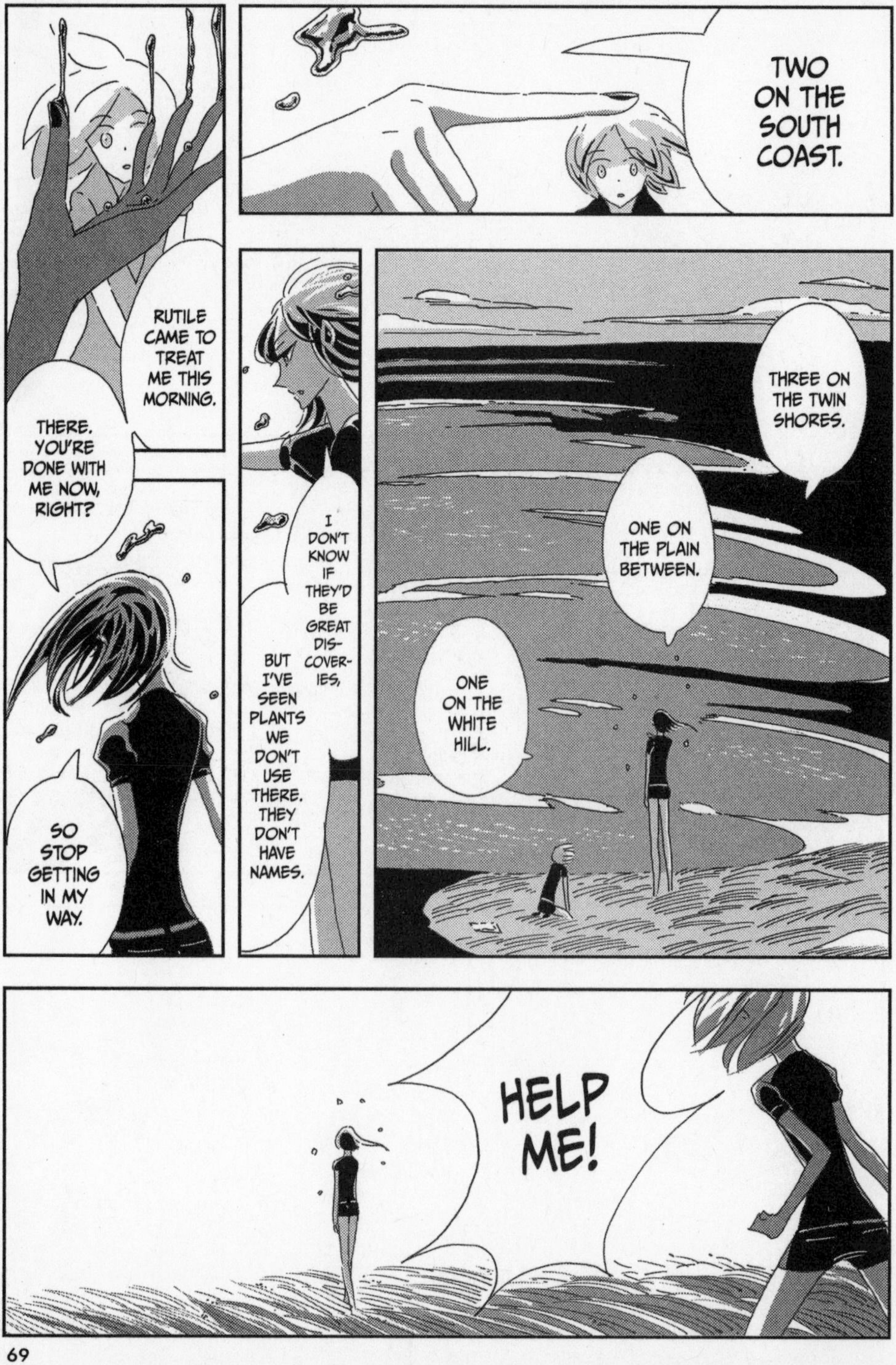
TWO ON THE SOUTH COAST.
THREE ON THE TWIN SHORES.
ONE ON THE PLAIN BETWEEN.
ONE ON THE WHITE HILL.
I DON'T KNOW IF THEY'D BE GREAT DIS-COVER-IES,
BUT I'VE SEEN PLANTS WE DON'T USE THERE. THEY DON'T HAVE NAMES.
RUTILE CAME TO TREAT ME THIS MORNING.
THERE. YOU'RE DONE WITH ME NOW, RIGHT?
SO STOP GETTING IN MY WAY.
HELP ME!

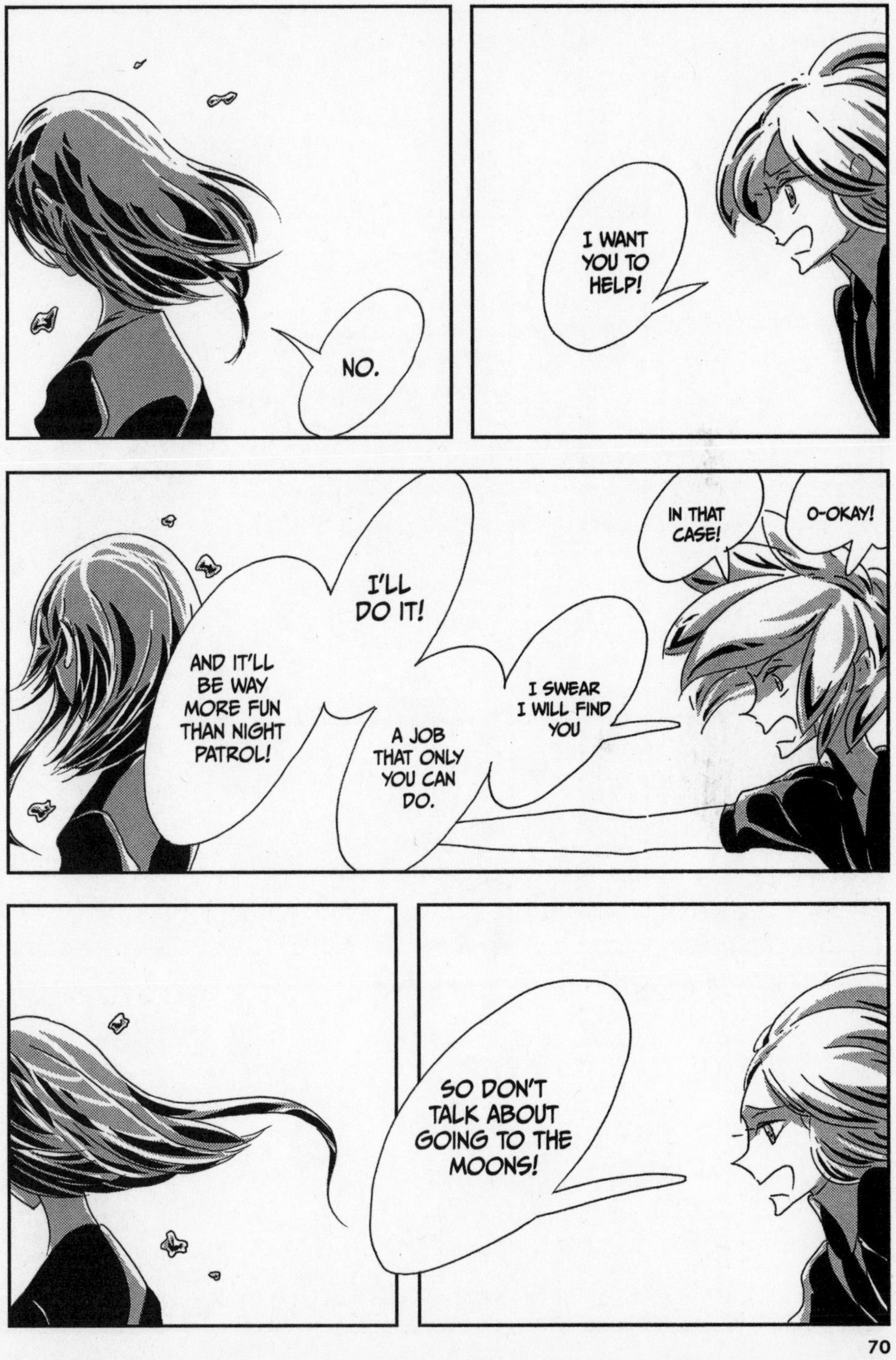
I WANT YOU TO HELP!
NO.
O-OKAY!
IN THAT CASE!
I SWEAR I WILL FIND YOU
A JOB THAT ONLY YOU CAN DO.
I'LL DO IT!
AND IT'LL BE WAY MORE FUN THAN NIGHT PATROL!
SO DON'T TALK ABOUT GOING TO THE MOONS!

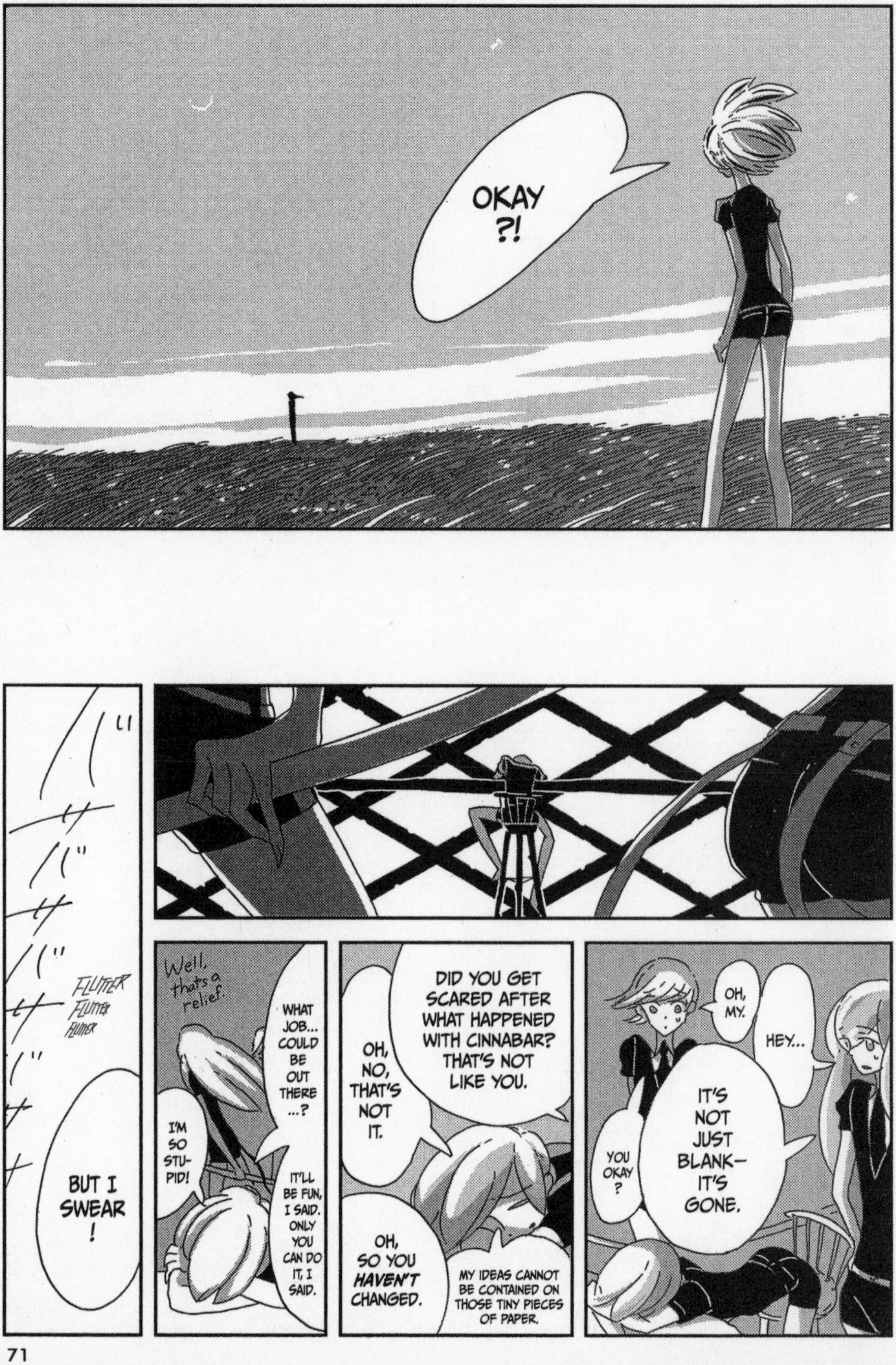
OKAY ?!
OH, MY.
HEY...
IT'S NOT JUST BLANK— IT'S GONE.
YOU OKAY ?
DID YOU GET SCARED AFTER WHAT HAPPENED WITH CINNABAR? THAT'S NOT LIKE YOU.
OH, NO, THAT'S NOT IT.
MY IDEAS CANNOT BE CONTAINED ON THOSE TINY PIECES OF PAPER.
OH, SO YOU ***HAVEN'T*** CHANGED.
WHAT JOB... COULD BE OUT THERE ...?
Well, that's a relief.
I'M SO STU- PID!
IT'LL BE FUN, I SAID. ONLY YOU CAN DO IT, I SAID.
バサバサバサバサ
FLUTTER FLUTTER FLUTTER
BUT I SWEAR !

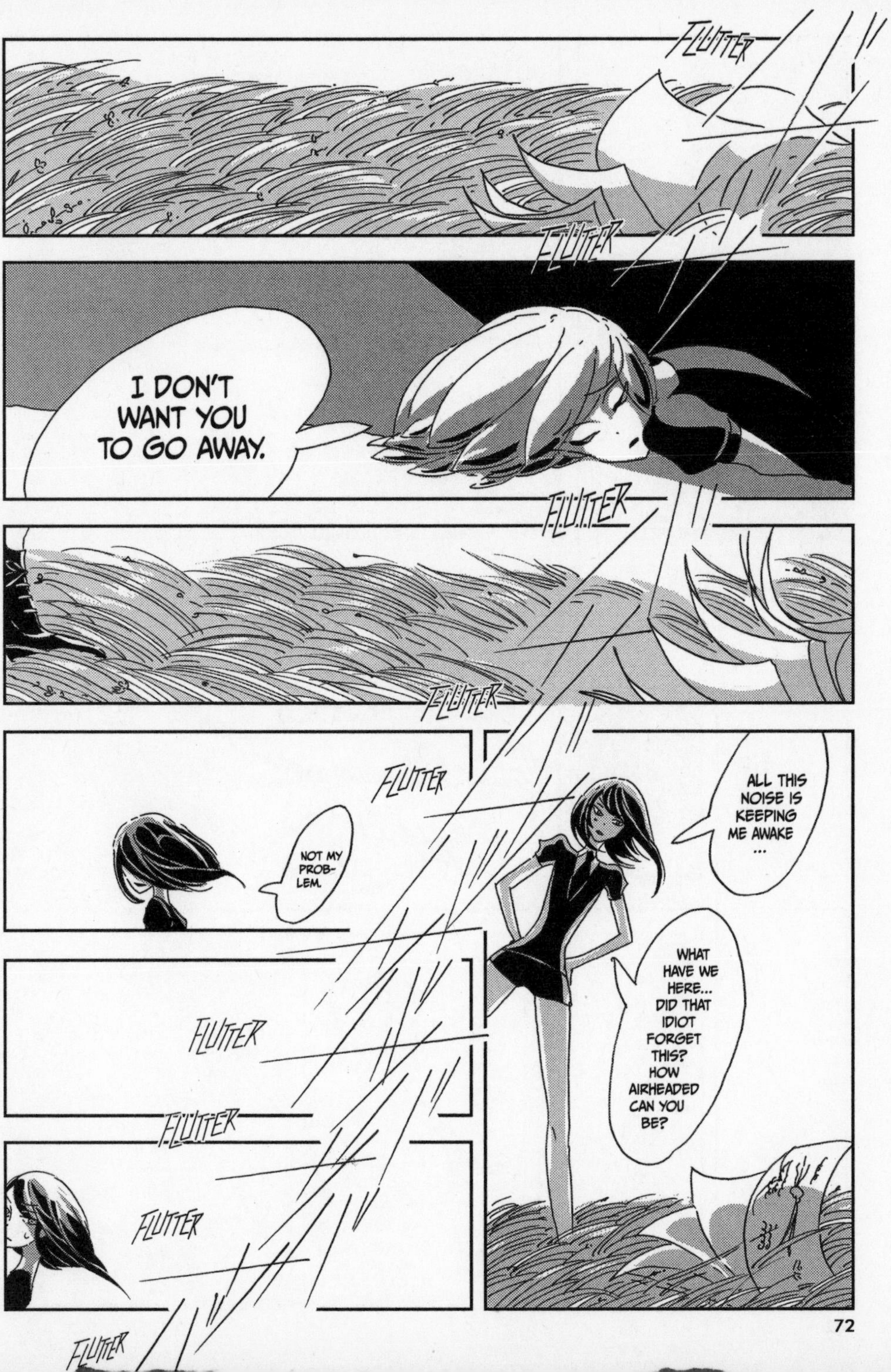
FLUTTER
FLUTTER
I DON'T WANT YOU TO GO AWAY.
FLUTTER
FLUTTER
ALL THIS NOISE IS KEEPING ME AWAKE ...
WHAT HAVE WE HERE... DID THAT IDIOT FORGET THIS? HOW AIRHEADED CAN YOU BE?
FLUTTER
NOT MY PROB-LEM.
FLUTTER
FLUTTER
FLUTTER
FLUTTER

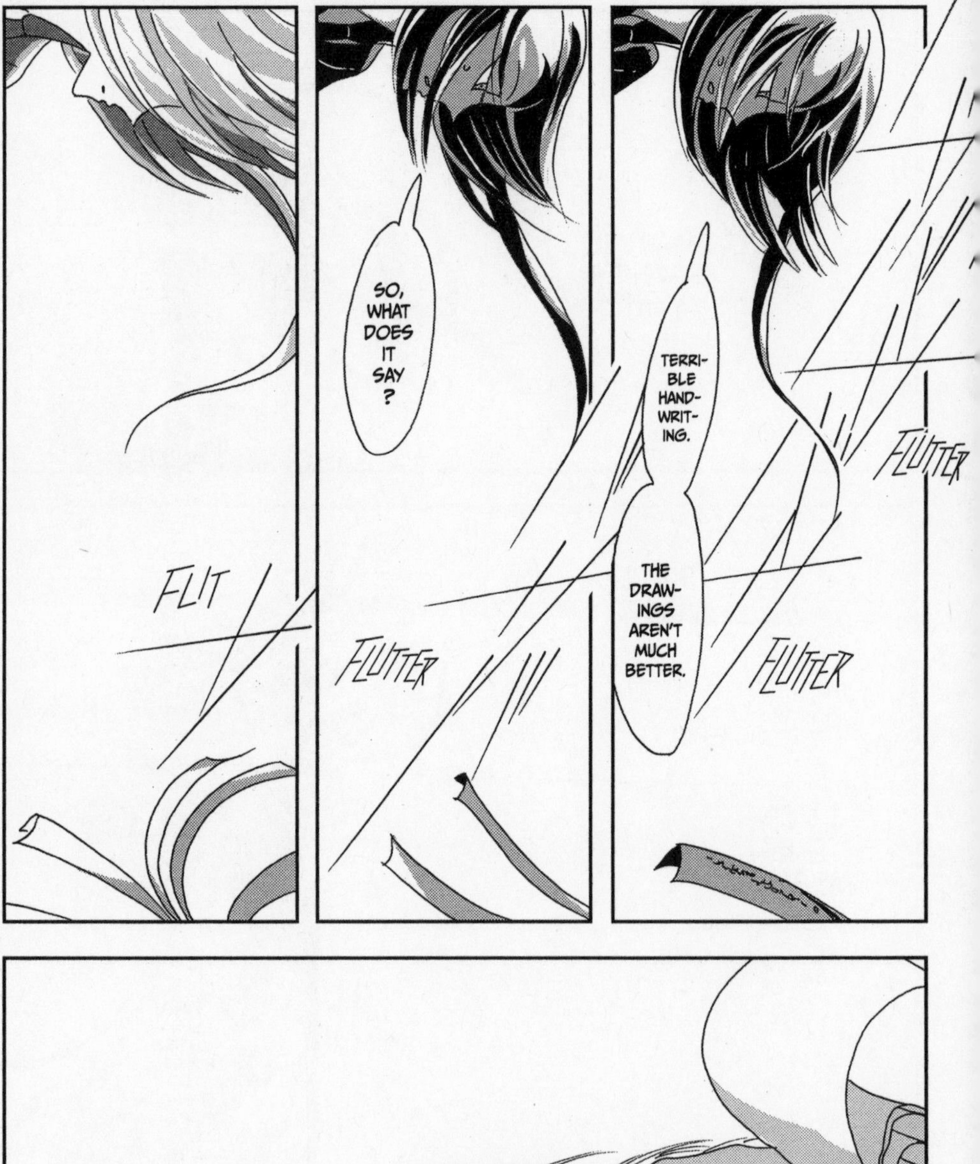
FLUTTER
TERRIBLE HANDWRITING.
THE DRAWINGS AREN'T MUCH BETTER.
FLUTTER
SO, WHAT DOES IT SAY?
FLUTTER
FLIT

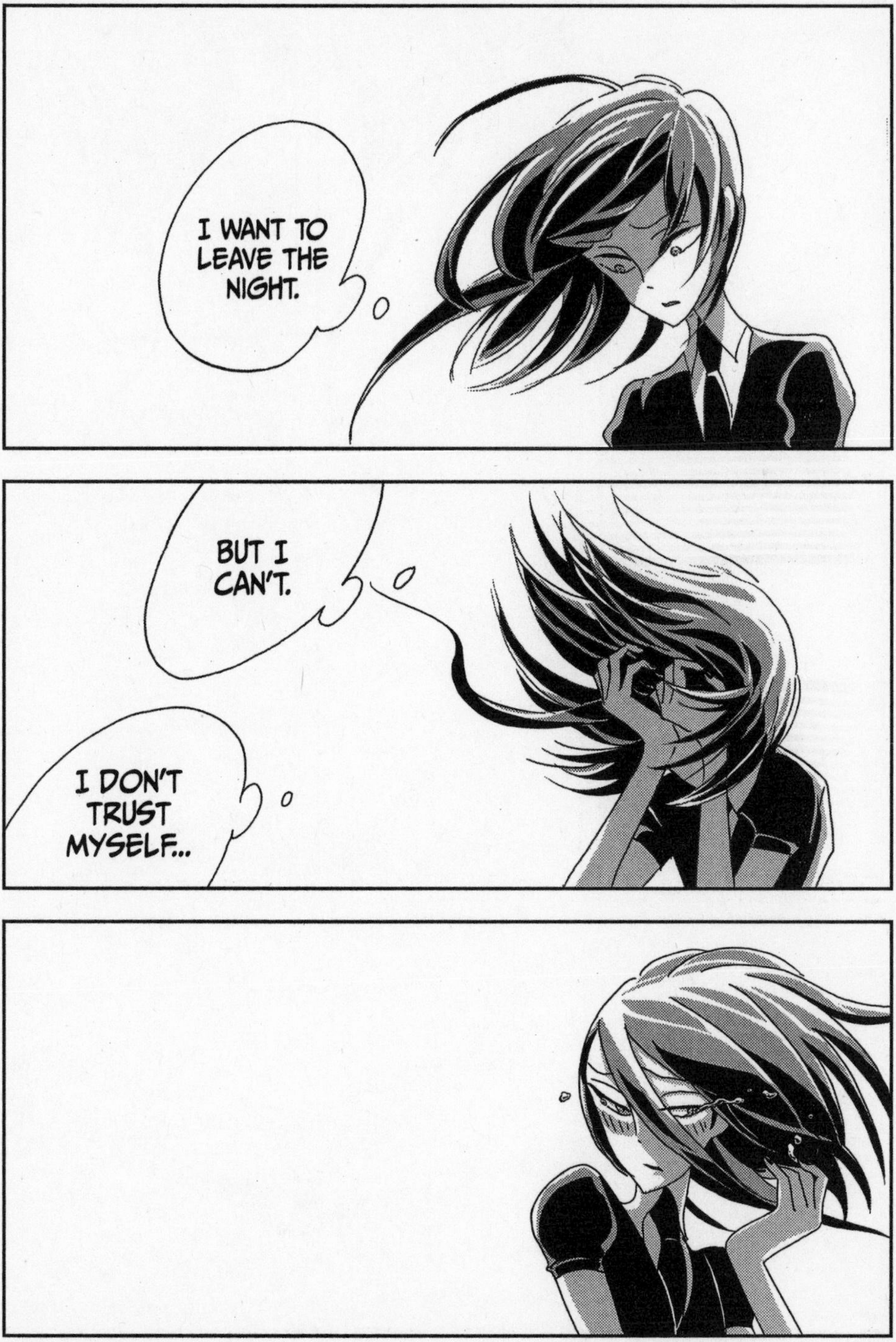
I WANT TO LEAVE THE NIGHT.
BUT I CAN'T.
I DON'T TRUST MYSELF...

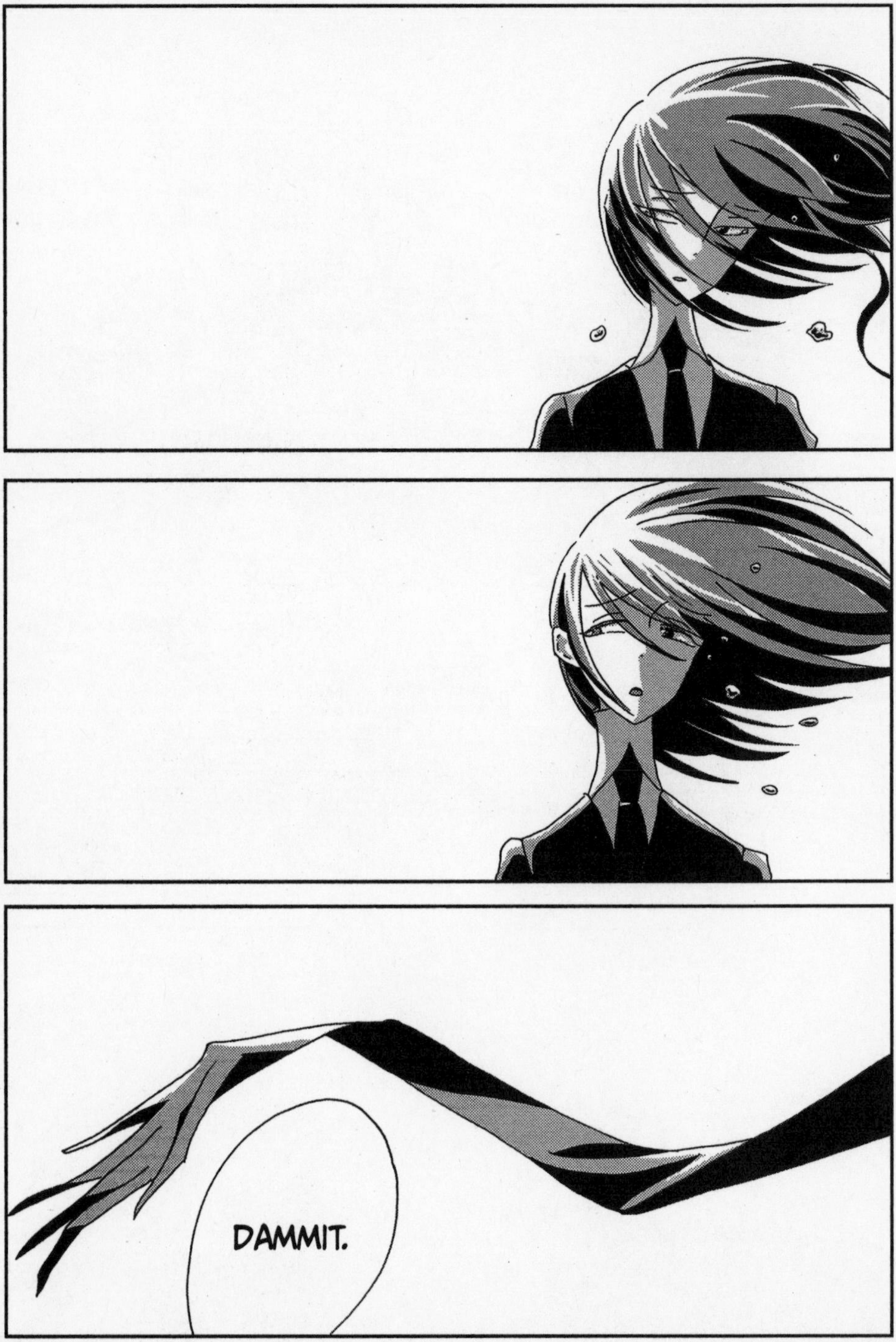
DAMMIT.

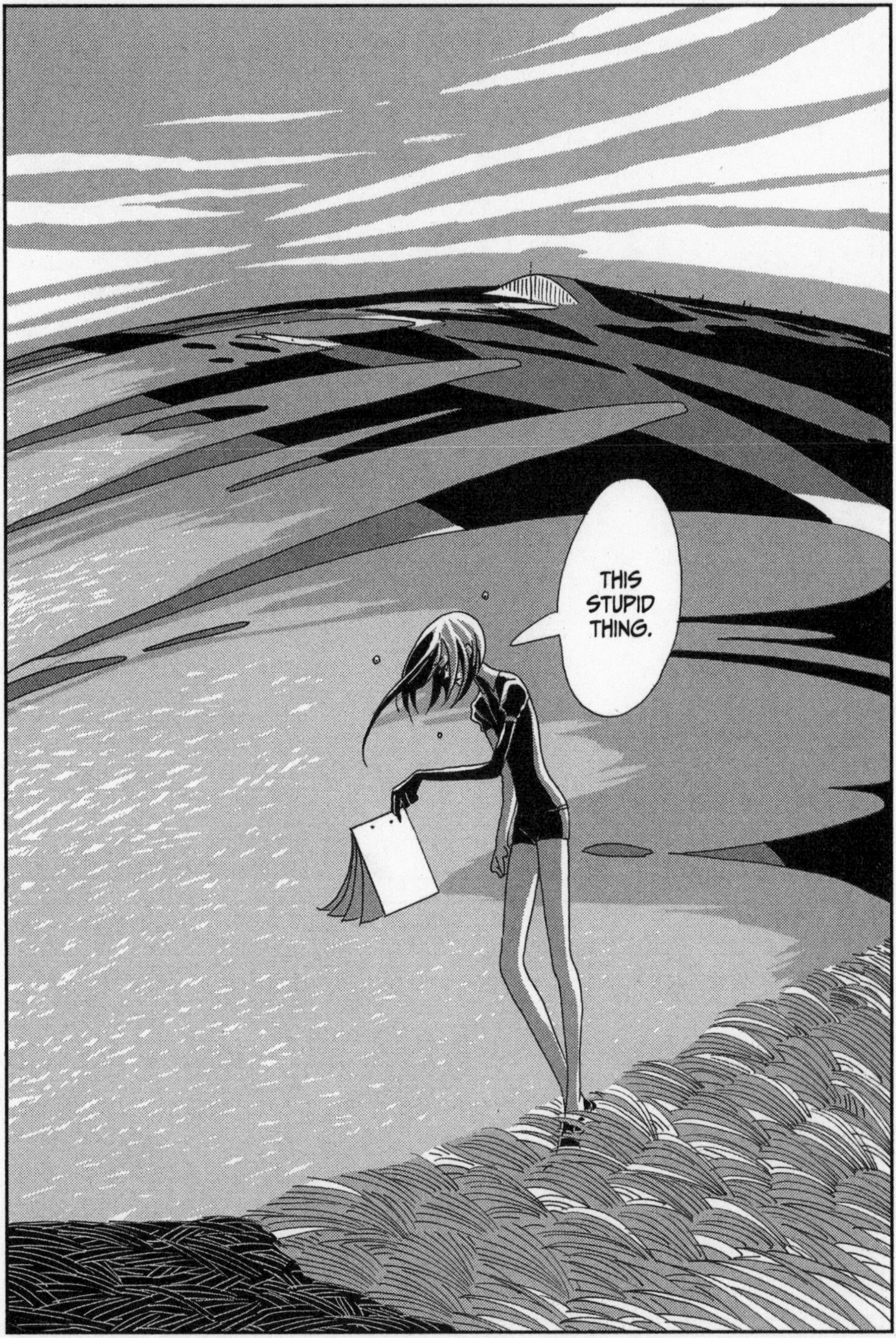
THIS STUPID THING.

CHAPTER 2: Cinnabar END

CHAPTER 3:

Diamond

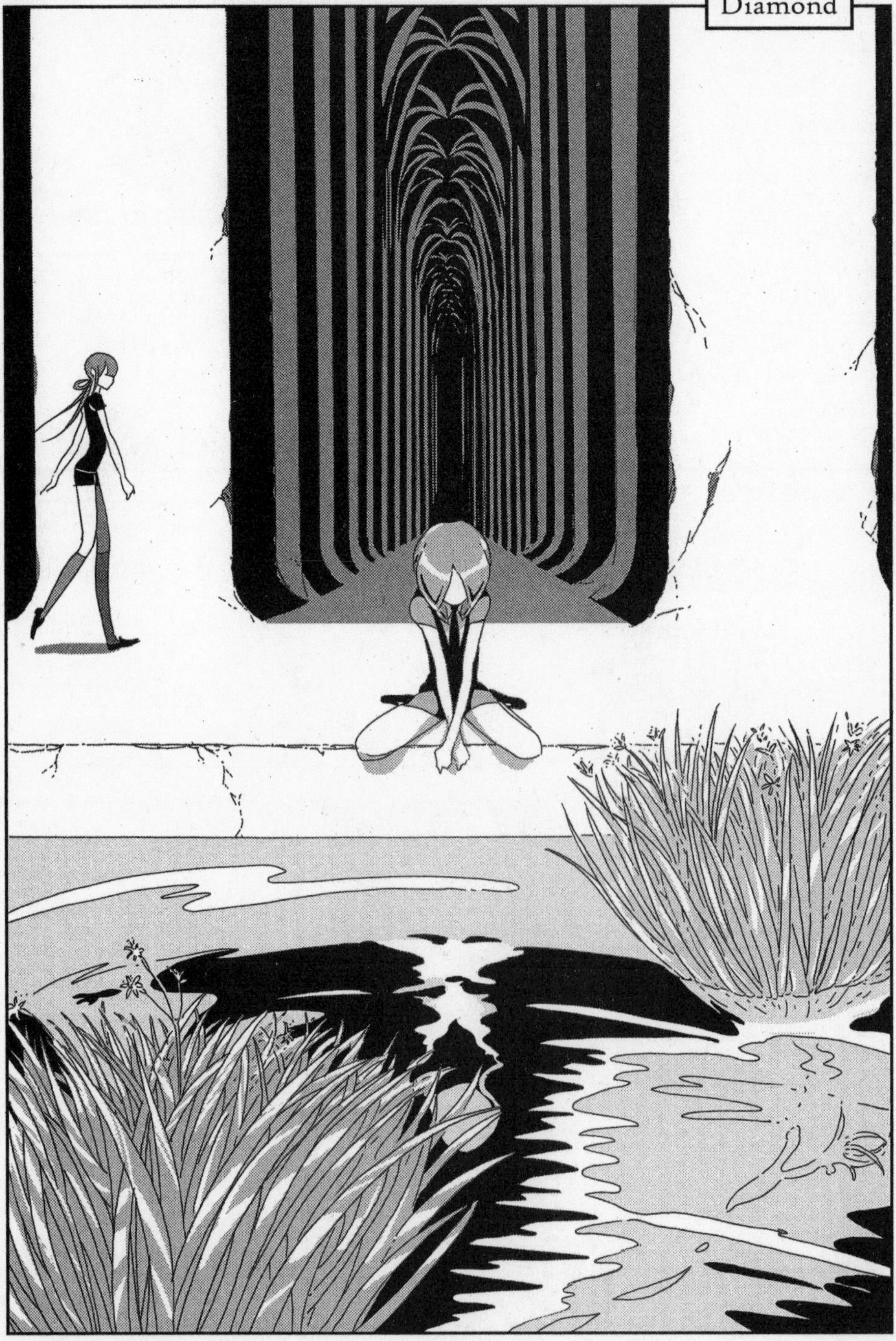

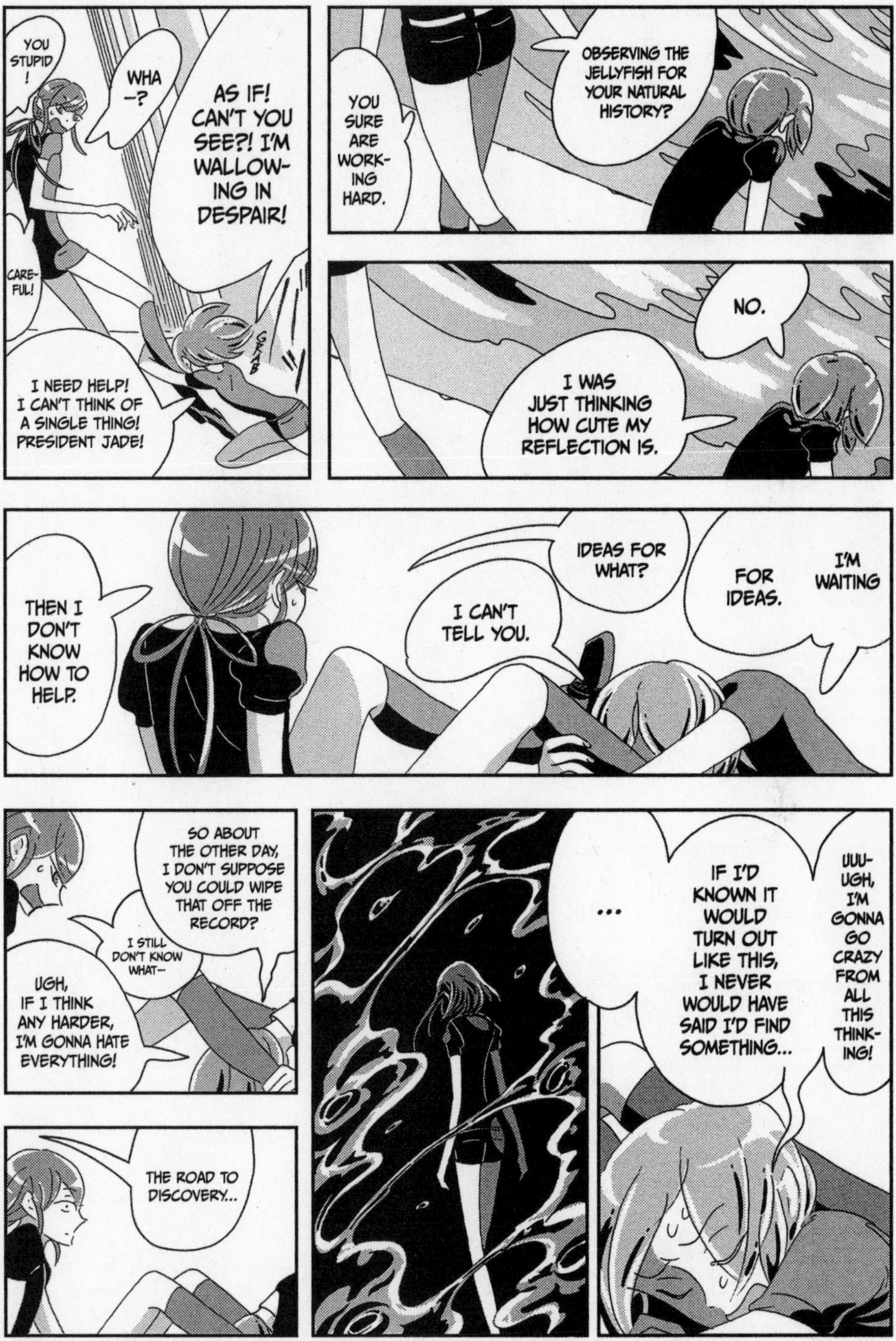

OBSERVING THE JELLYFISH FOR YOUR NATURAL HISTORY?
YOU SURE ARE WORKING HARD.
NO.
I WAS JUST THINKING HOW CUTE MY REFLECTION IS.
YOU STUPID!
WHA-?
AS IF! CAN'T YOU SEE?! I'M WALLOWING IN DESPAIR!
CAREFUL!
GRAB
I NEED HELP! I CAN'T THINK OF A SINGLE THING! PRESIDENT JADE!
I'M WAITING FOR IDEAS.
IDEAS FOR WHAT?
I CAN'T TELL YOU.
THEN I DON'T KNOW HOW TO HELP.
UUU-UGH, I'M GONNA GO CRAZY FROM ALL THIS THINKING!
IF I'D KNOWN IT WOULD TURN OUT LIKE THIS, I NEVER WOULD HAVE SAID I'D FIND SOMETHING...
...
SO ABOUT THE OTHER DAY, I DON'T SUPPOSE YOU COULD WIPE THAT OFF THE RECORD?
I STILL DON'T KNOW WHAT—
UGH, IF I THINK ANY HARDER, I'M GONNA HATE EVERYTHING!
THE ROAD TO DISCOVERY...

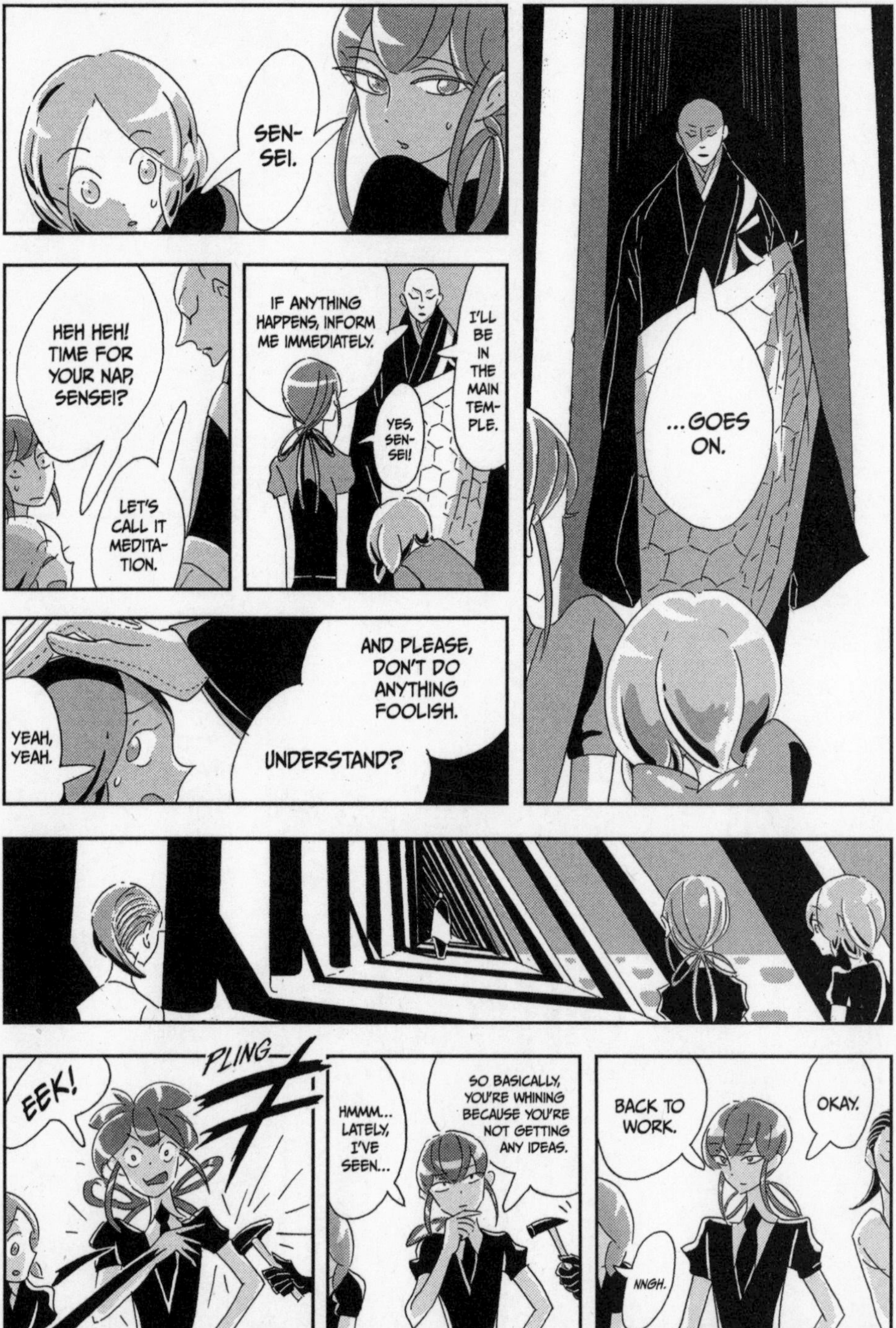
...GOES ON.
SEN-SEI.
IF ANYTHING HAPPENS, INFORM ME IMMEDIATELY.
I'LL BE IN THE MAIN TEMPLE.
YES, SEN-SEI!
HEH HEH! TIME FOR YOUR NAP, SENSEI?
LET'S CALL IT MEDITA-TION.
AND PLEASE, DON'T DO ANYTHING FOOLISH.
UNDERSTAND?
YEAH, YEAH.
OKAY.
BACK TO WORK.
NNGH.
SO BASICALLY, YOU'RE WHINING BECAUSE YOU'RE NOT GETTING ANY IDEAS.
HMMM... LATELY, I'VE SEEN...
PLING
EEK!

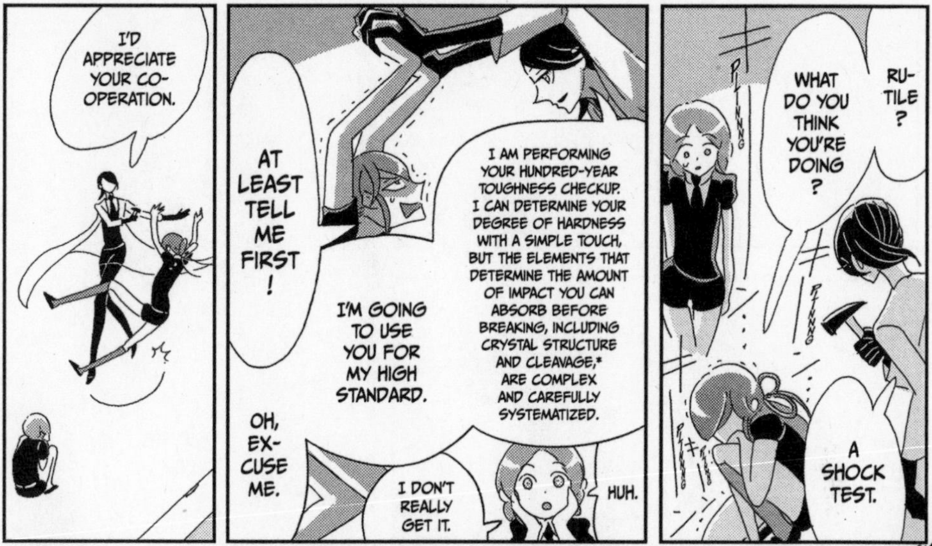
RU-TILE?
WHAT DO YOU THINK YOU'RE DOING?
A SHOCK TEST.
AT LEAST TELL ME FIRST!
I AM PERFORMING YOUR HUNDRED-YEAR TOUGHNESS CHECKUP. I CAN DETERMINE YOUR DEGREE OF HARDNESS WITH A SIMPLE TOUCH, BUT THE ELEMENTS THAT DETERMINE THE AMOUNT OF IMPACT YOU CAN ABSORB BEFORE BREAKING, INCLUDING CRYSTAL STRUCTURE AND CLEAVAGE,* ARE COMPLEX AND CAREFULLY SYSTEMATIZED.
I'M GOING TO USE YOU FOR MY HIGH STANDARD.
HUH.
I DON'T REALLY GET IT.
OH, EXCUSE ME.
I'D APPRECIATE YOUR CO-OPERATION.

*The tendency of hard materials to split along specific planes.

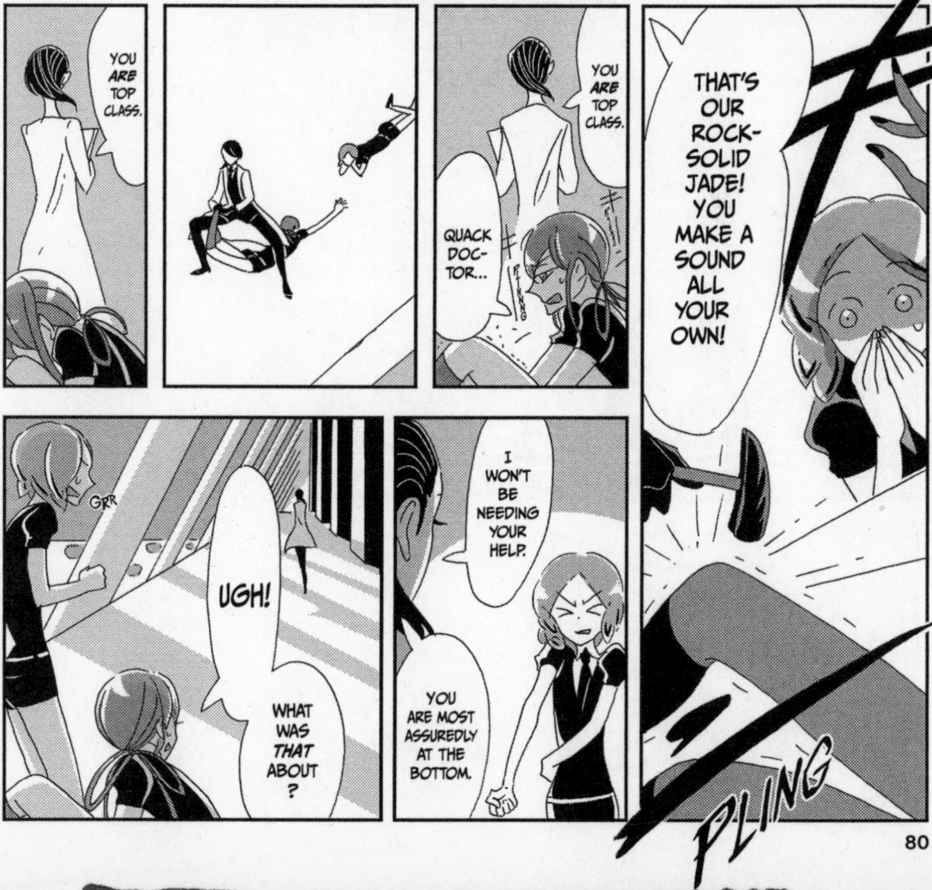
THAT'S OUR ROCK-SOLID JADE! YOU MAKE A SOUND ALL YOUR OWN!
PLING
YOU *ARE* TOP CLASS.
QUACK DOCTOR...
YOU *ARE* TOP CLASS.
I WON'T BE NEEDING YOUR HELP.
YOU ARE MOST ASSUREDLY AT THE BOTTOM.
UGH!
GRR
WHAT WAS *THAT* ABOUT?

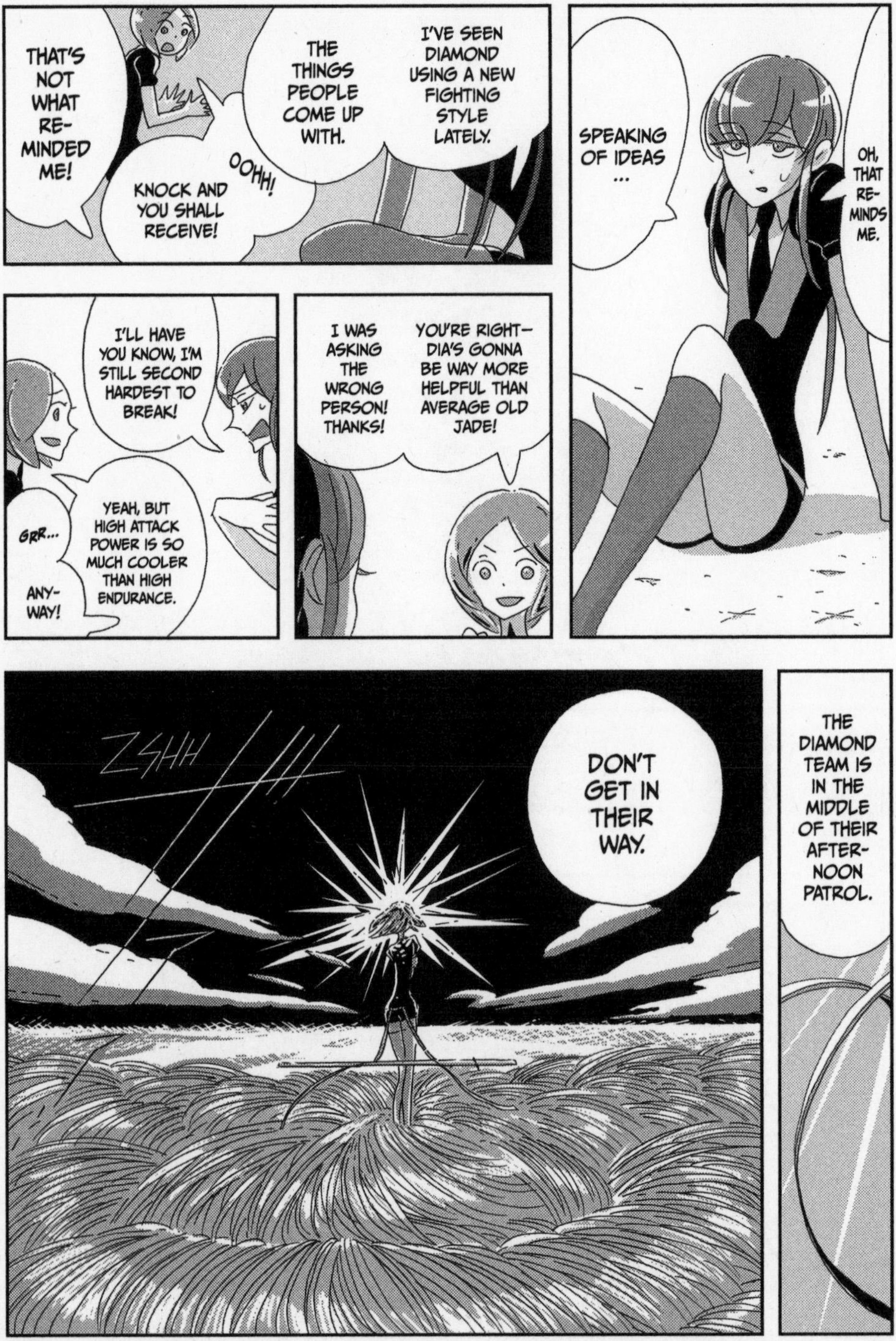
OH, THAT RE-MINDS ME.
SPEAKING OF IDEAS ...
I'VE SEEN DIAMOND USING A NEW FIGHTING STYLE LATELY.
THE THINGS PEOPLE COME UP WITH.
THAT'S NOT WHAT RE-MINDED ME!
OOHH!
KNOCK AND YOU SHALL RECEIVE!
YOU'RE RIGHT— DIA'S GONNA BE WAY MORE HELPFUL THAN AVERAGE OLD JADE!
I WAS ASKING THE WRONG PERSON! THANKS!
I'LL HAVE YOU KNOW, I'M STILL SECOND HARDEST TO BREAK!
YEAH, BUT HIGH ATTACK POWER IS SO MUCH COOLER THAN HIGH ENDURANCE.
GRR...
ANY-WAY!
THE DIAMOND TEAM IS IN THE MIDDLE OF THEIR AFTER-NOON PATROL.
DON'T GET IN THEIR WAY.
ZSHH

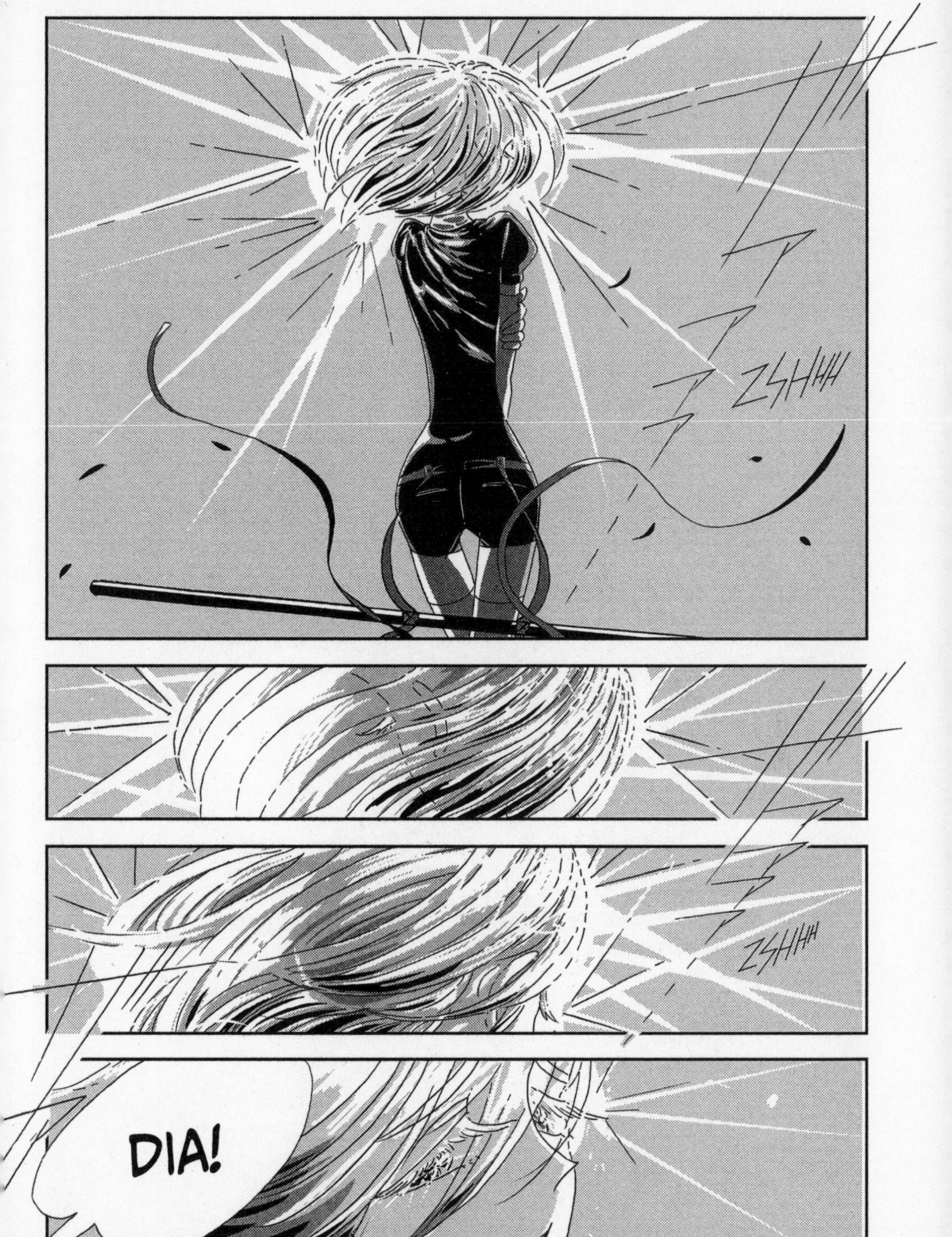
ZSHHH
ZSHHH
DIA!

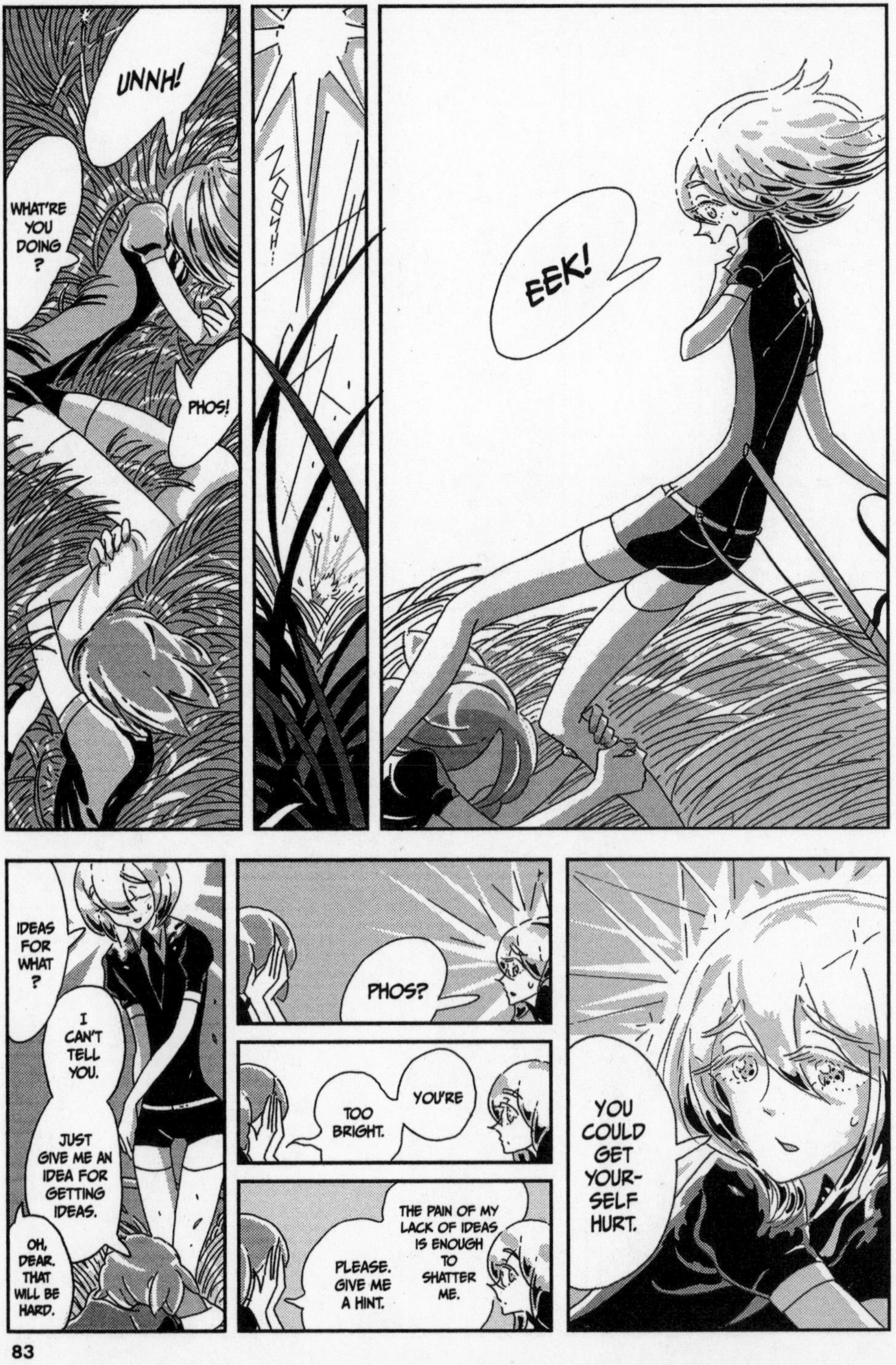
EEK!
ZOOSH!!
UNNH!
WHAT'RE YOU DOING?
PHOS!
YOU COULD GET YOURSELF HURT.
PHOS?
YOU'RE
TOO BRIGHT.
THE PAIN OF MY LACK OF IDEAS IS ENOUGH TO SHATTER ME.
PLEASE. GIVE ME A HINT.
IDEAS FOR WHAT?
I CAN'T TELL YOU.
JUST GIVE ME AN IDEA FOR GETTING IDEAS.
OH, DEAR. THAT WILL BE HARD.

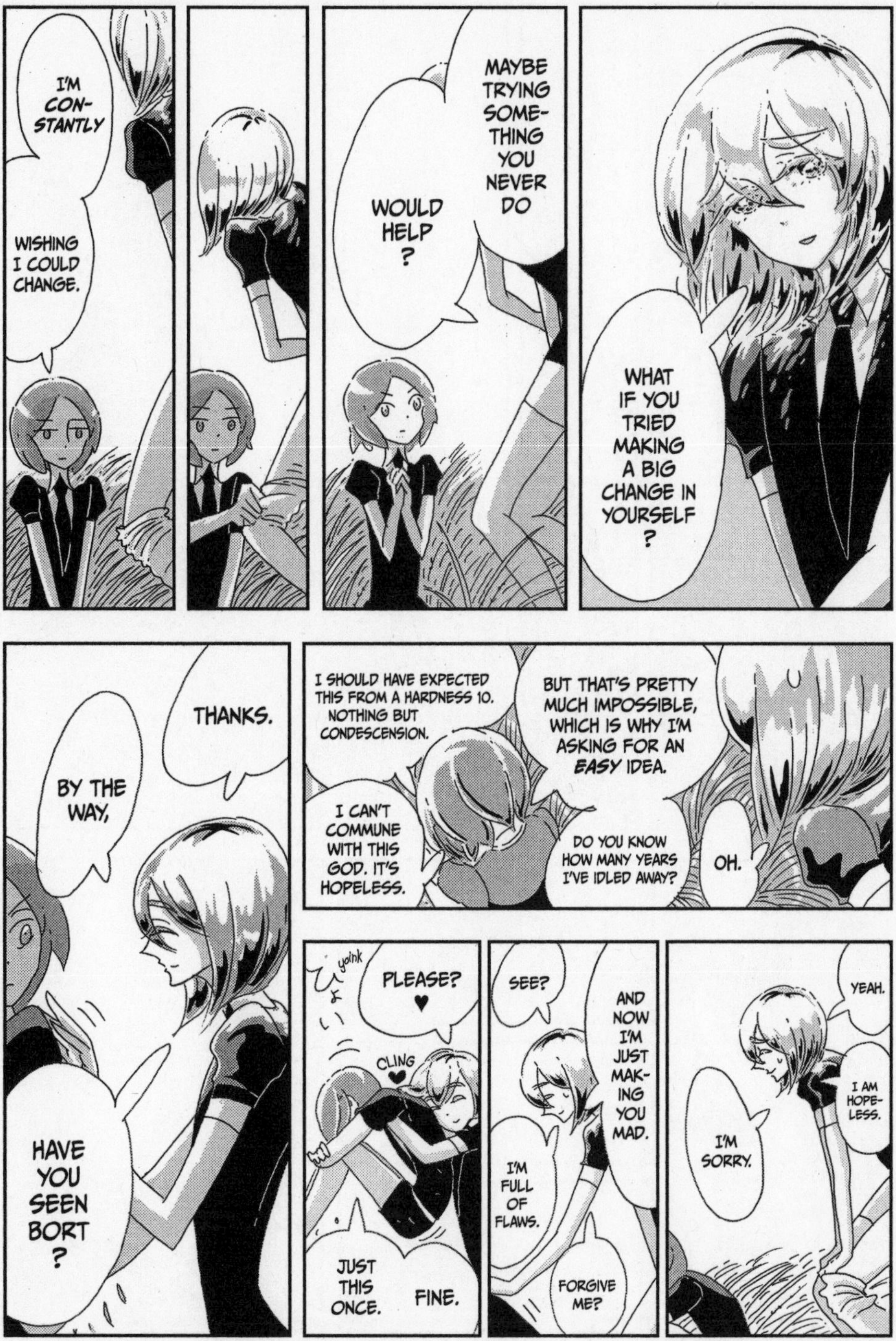
WHAT IF YOU TRIED MAKING A BIG CHANGE IN YOURSELF?
MAYBE TRYING SOMETHING YOU NEVER DO
WOULD HELP?
I'M CON-STANTLY
WISHING I COULD CHANGE.
OH.
BUT THAT'S PRETTY MUCH IMPOSSIBLE, WHICH IS WHY I'M ASKING FOR AN *EASY* IDEA.
DO YOU KNOW HOW MANY YEARS I'VE IDLED AWAY?
I SHOULD HAVE EXPECTED THIS FROM A HARDNESS 10. NOTHING BUT CONDESCENSION.
I CAN'T COMMUNE WITH THIS GOD. IT'S HOPELESS.
YEAH.
I AM HOPE-LESS.
I'M SORRY.
SEE?
AND NOW I'M JUST MAK-ING YOU MAD.
I'M FULL OF FLAWS.
FORGIVE ME?
PLEASE? ♥
yoink
CLING ♥
FINE.
JUST THIS ONCE.
THANKS.
BY THE WAY,
HAVE YOU SEEN BORT?

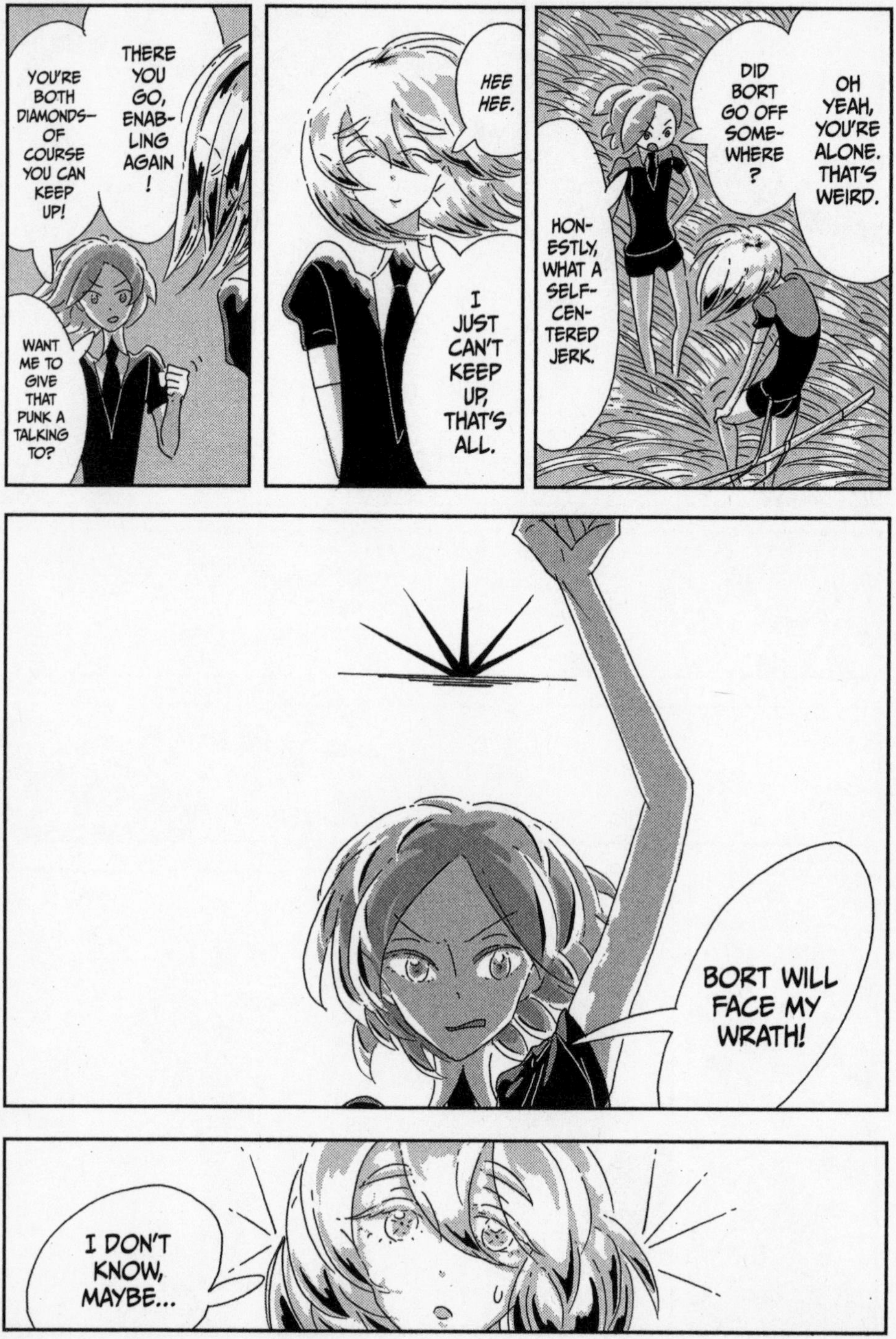
OH YEAH, YOU'RE ALONE. THAT'S WEIRD.
DID BORT GO OFF SOMEWHERE?
HONESTLY, WHAT A SELF-CENTERED JERK.
HEE HEE.
I JUST CAN'T KEEP UP, THAT'S ALL.
THERE YOU GO, ENABLING AGAIN!
YOU'RE BOTH DIAMONDS—OF COURSE YOU CAN KEEP UP!
WANT ME TO GIVE THAT PUNK A TALKING TO?
BORT WILL FACE MY WRATH!
I DON'T KNOW, MAYBE...

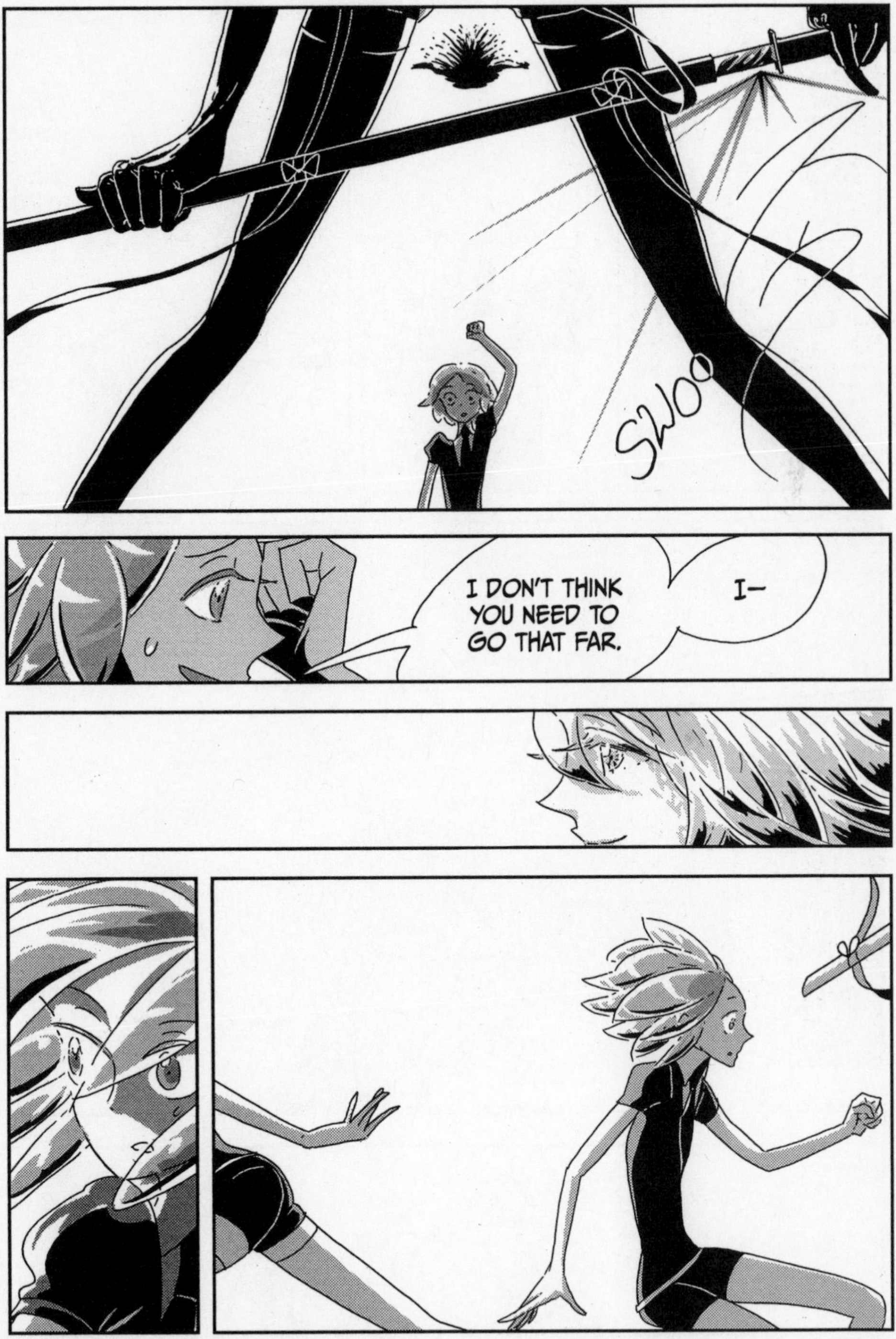
SWOO
I—
I DON'T THINK YOU NEED TO GO THAT FAR.

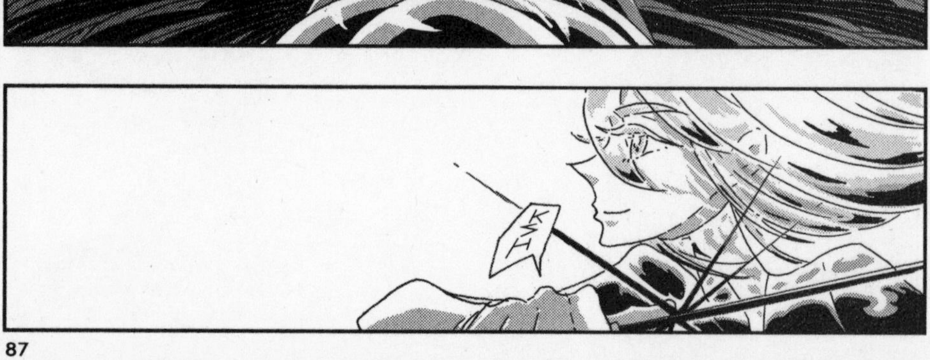
KSH
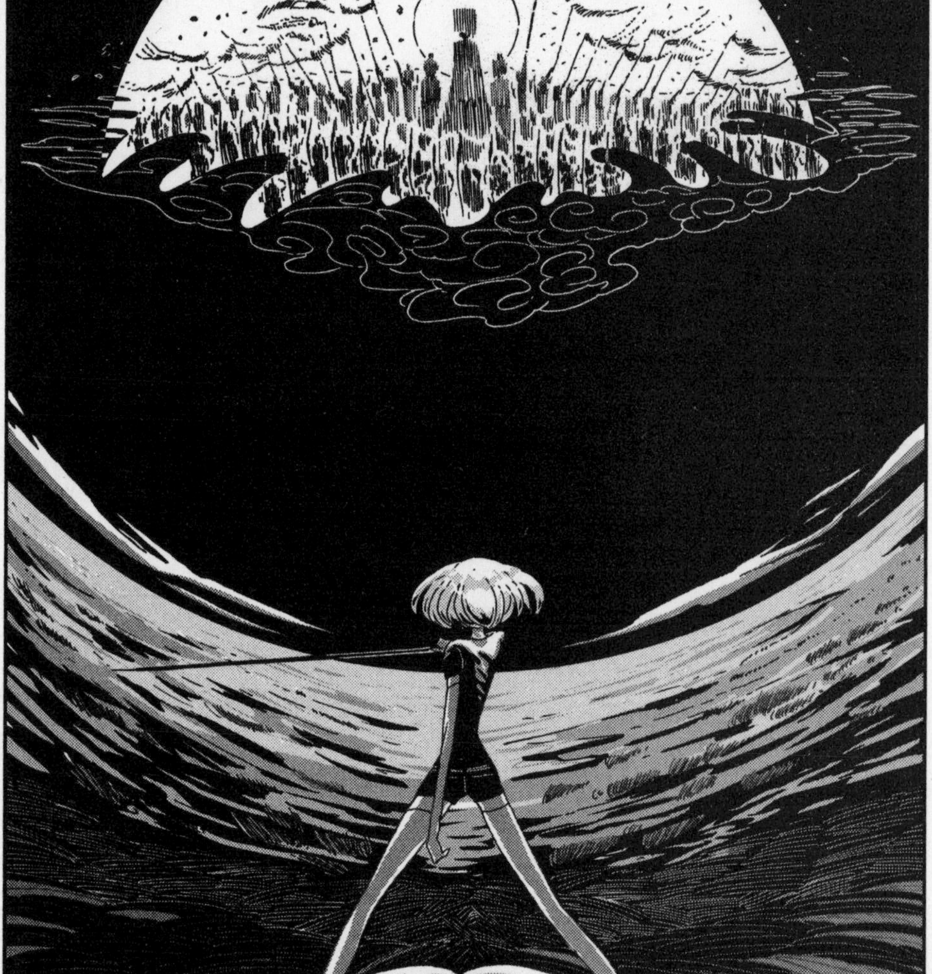

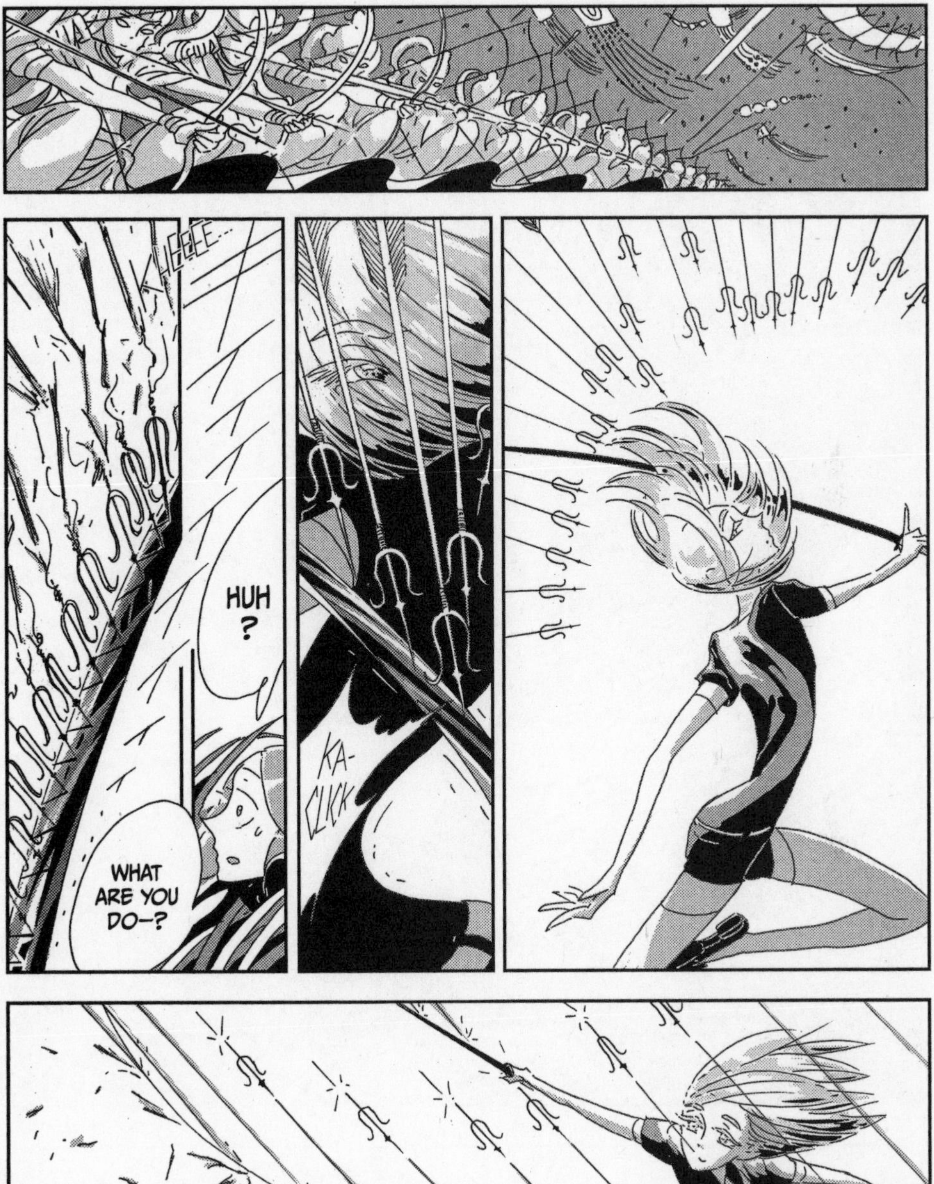
KA-CLICK
KHEEEE...
HUH?
WHAT ARE YOU DO-?

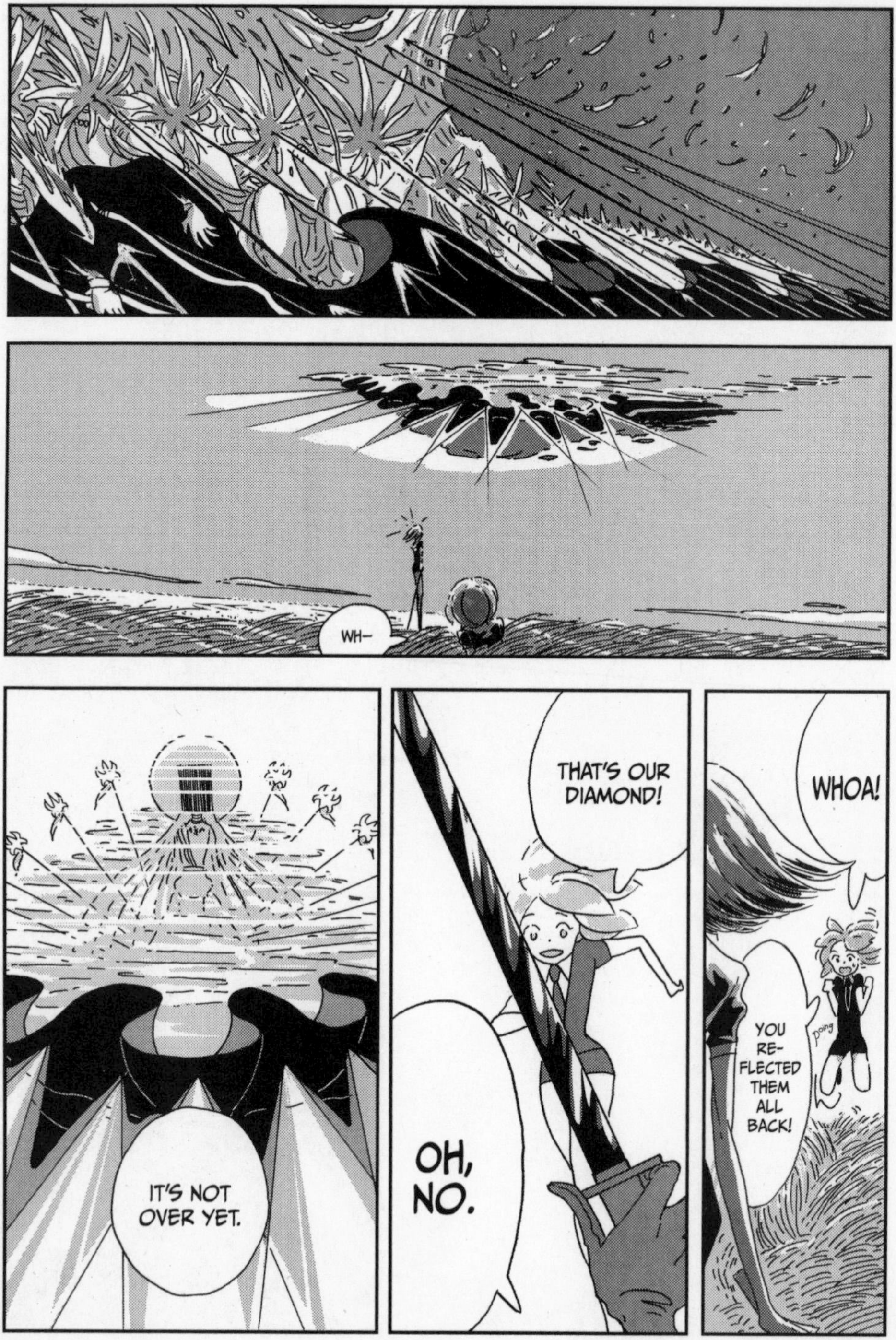
WH–
WHOA!
YOU RE-FLECTED THEM ALL BACK!
THAT'S OUR DIAMOND!
OH, NO.
IT'S NOT OVER YET.

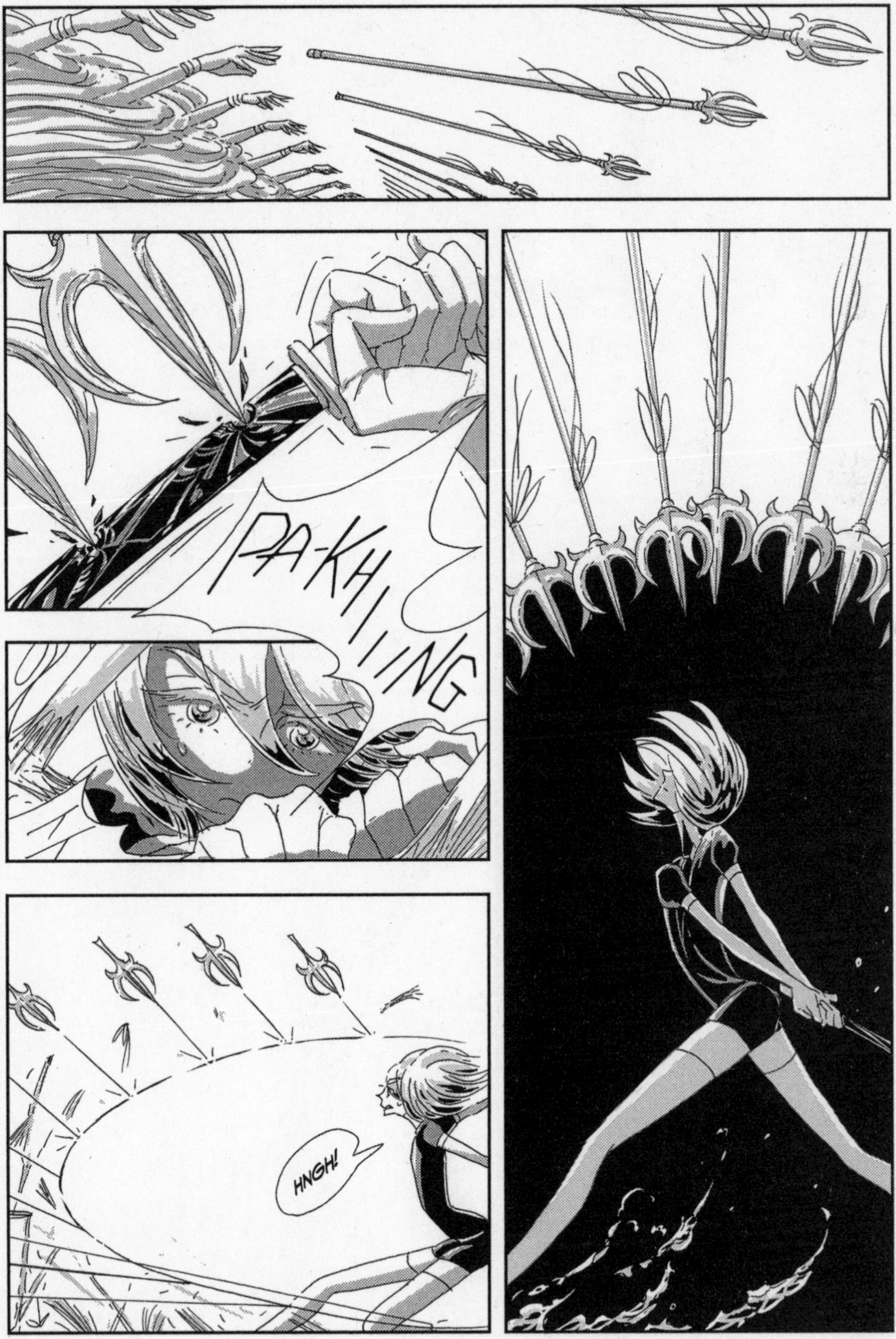
PA-KHIIIING
HNGH!

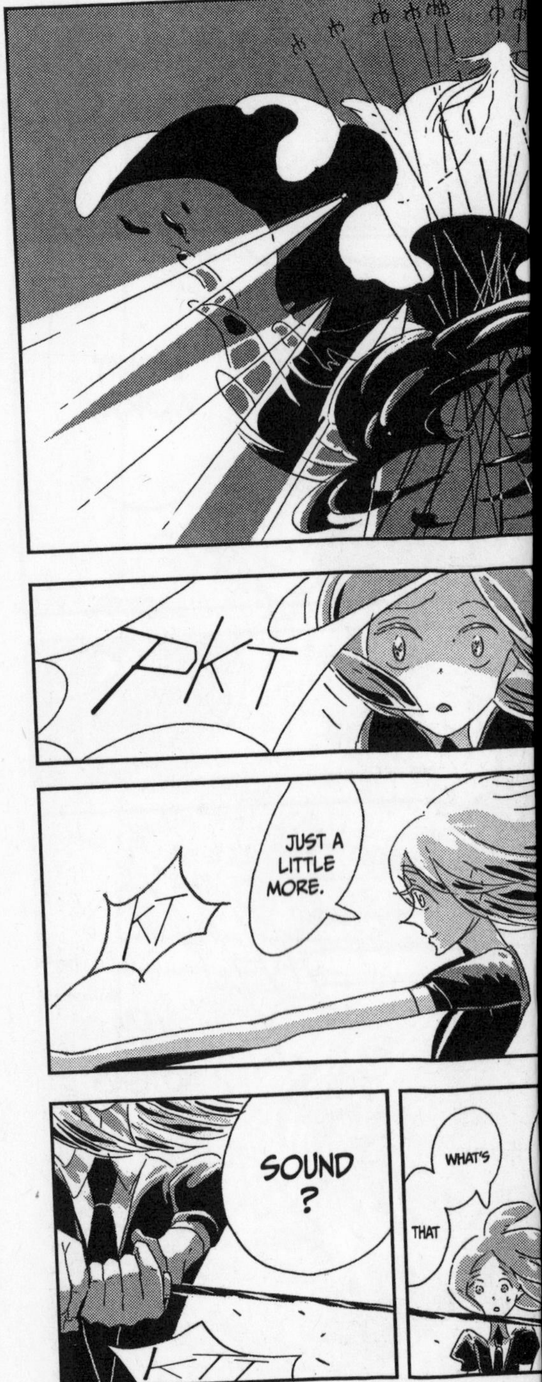
PKT
JUST A LITTLE MORE.
KT
WHAT'S
THAT
SOUND
?
KTT

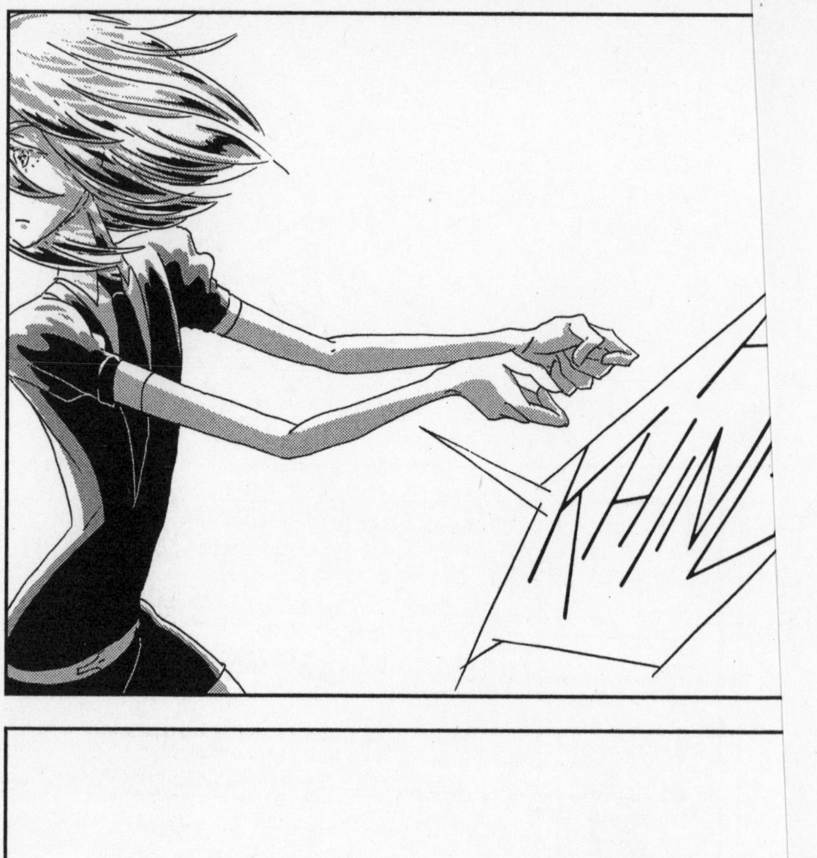

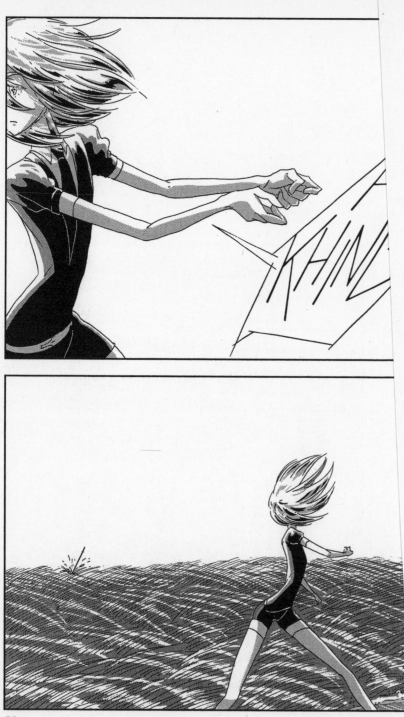

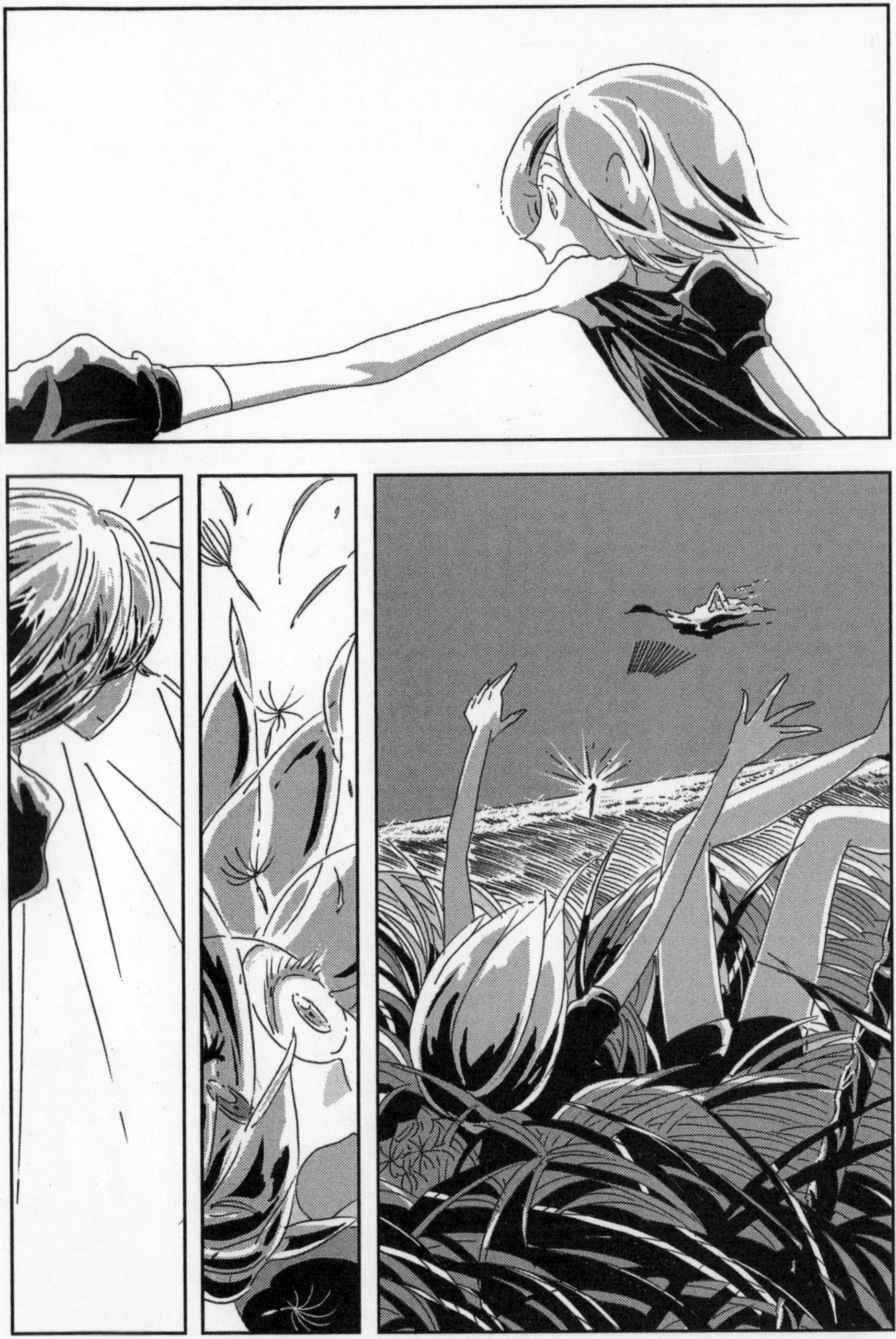

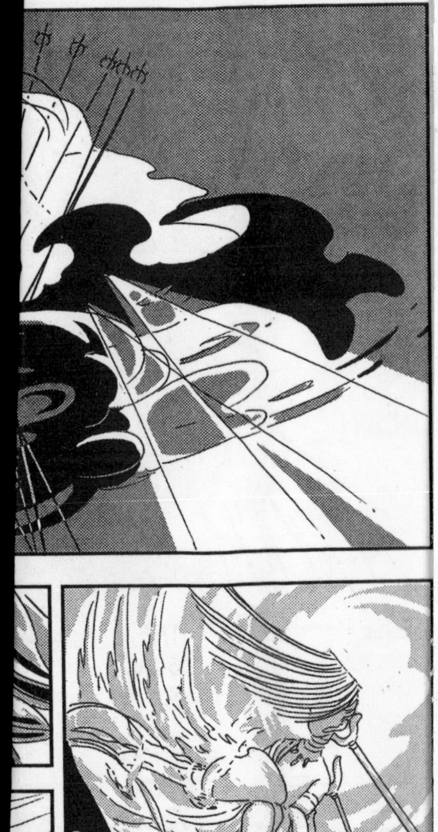
DIA
...?

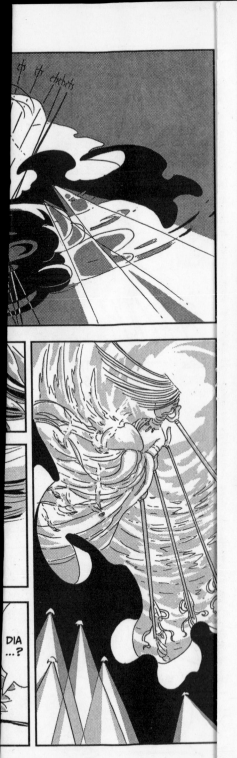

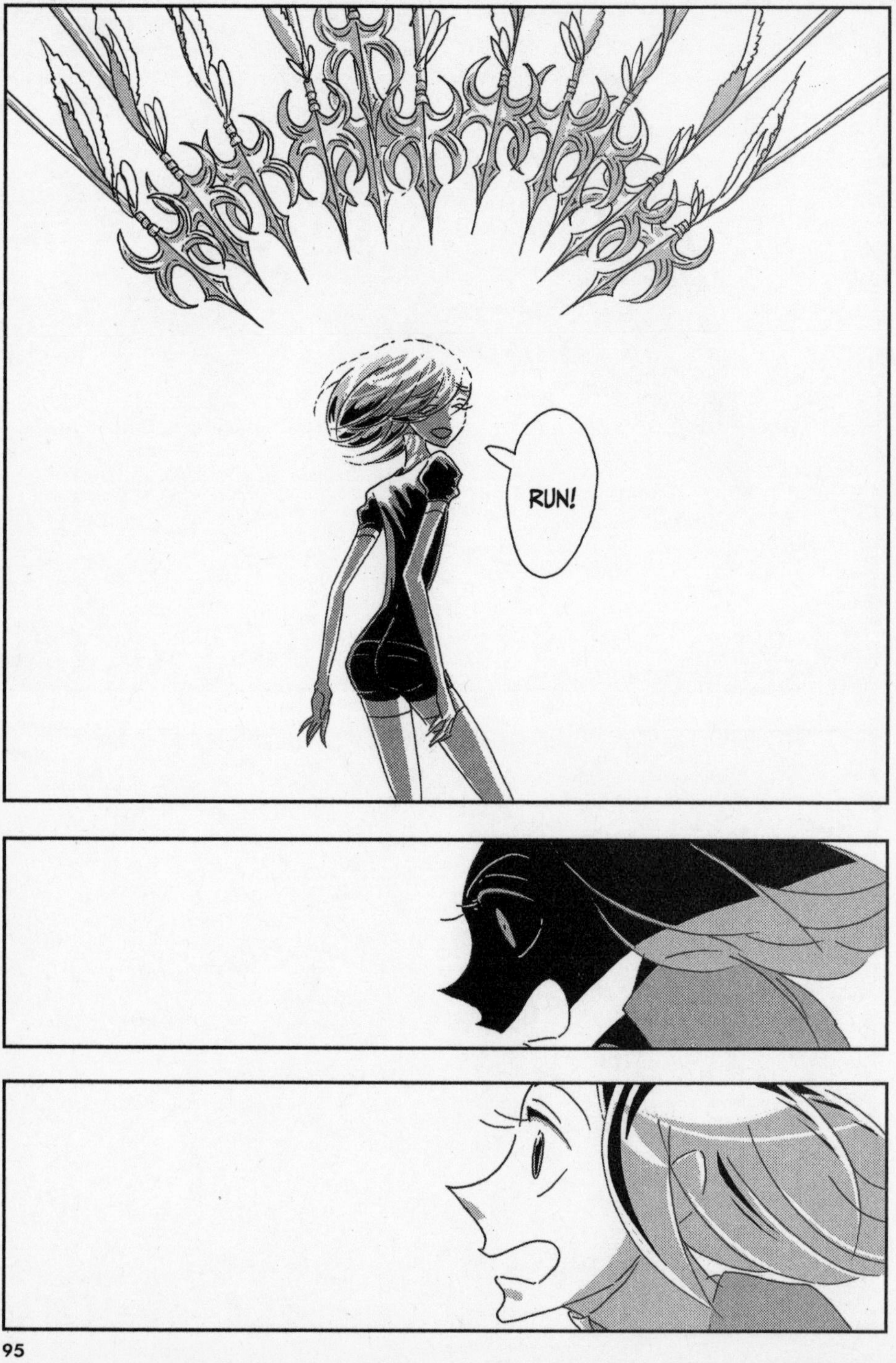
RUN!

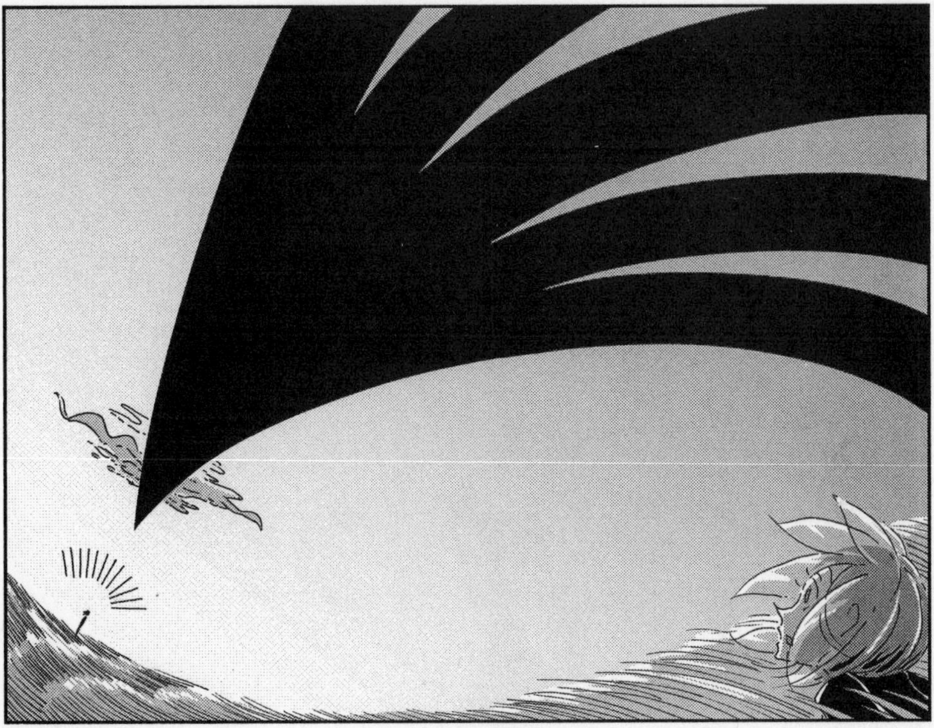

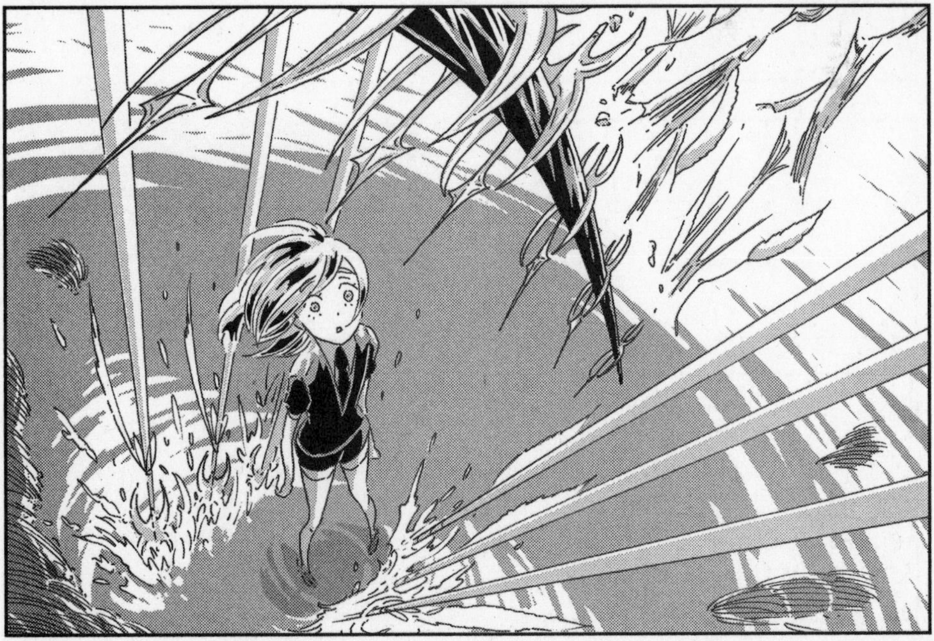

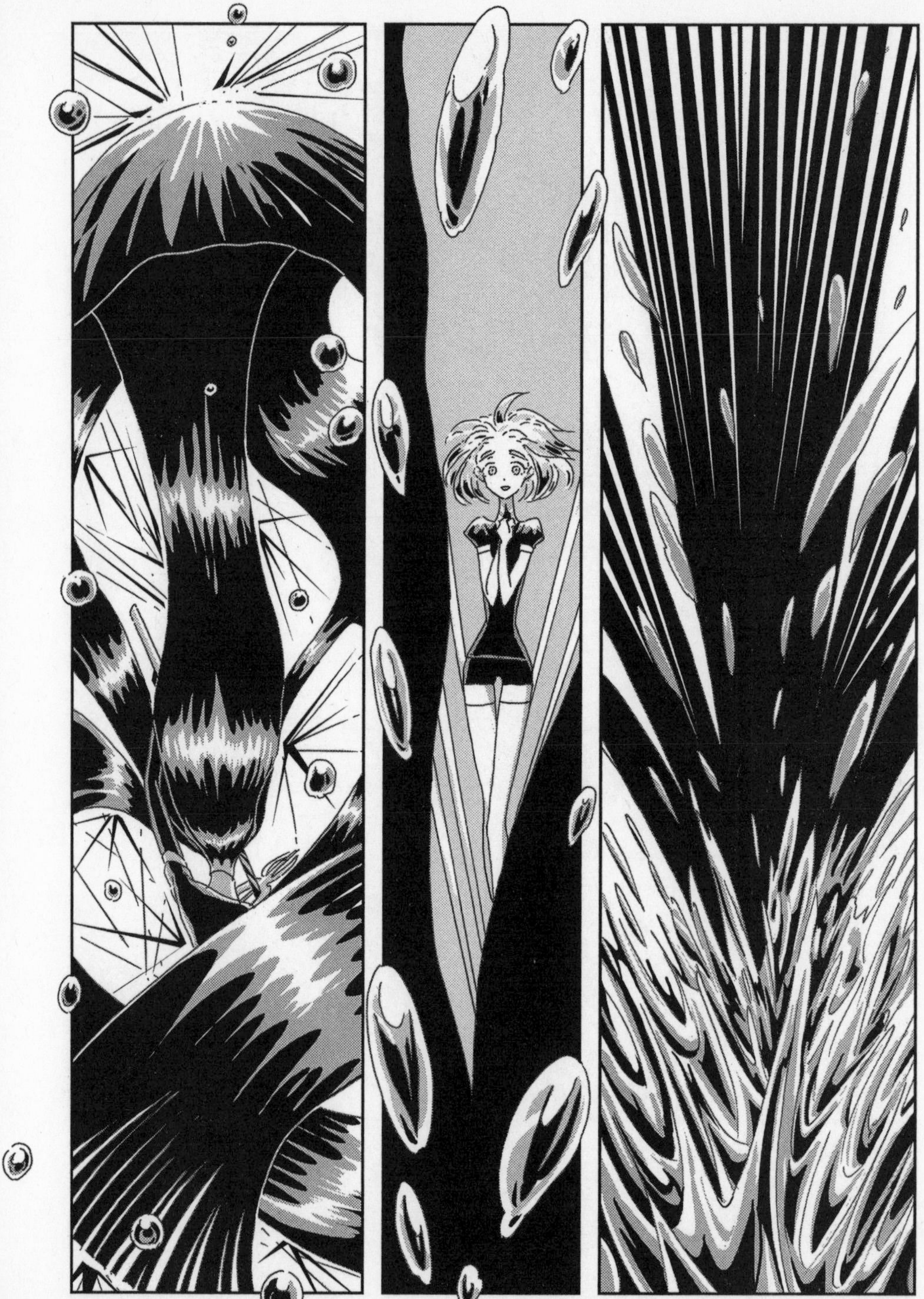

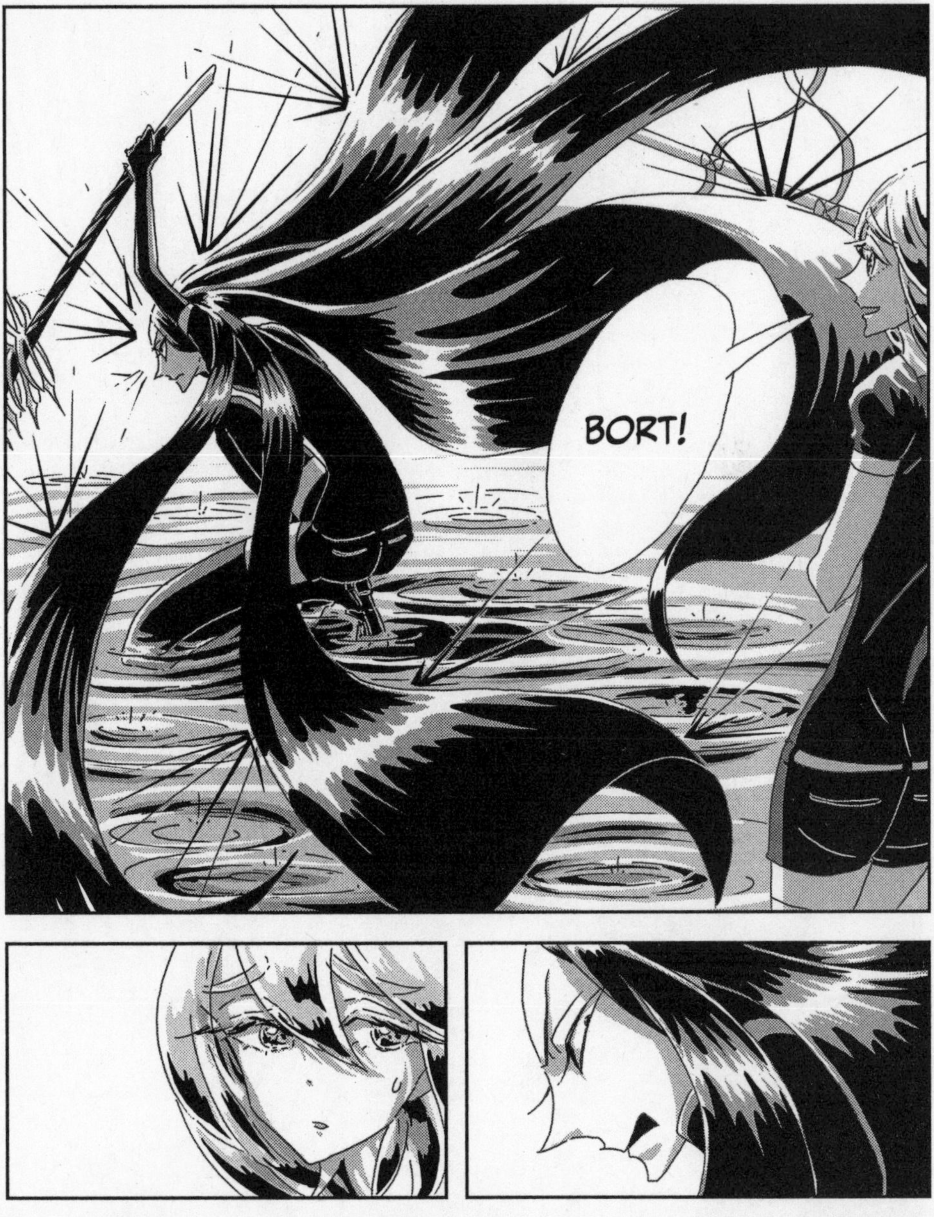
BORT!
TMP

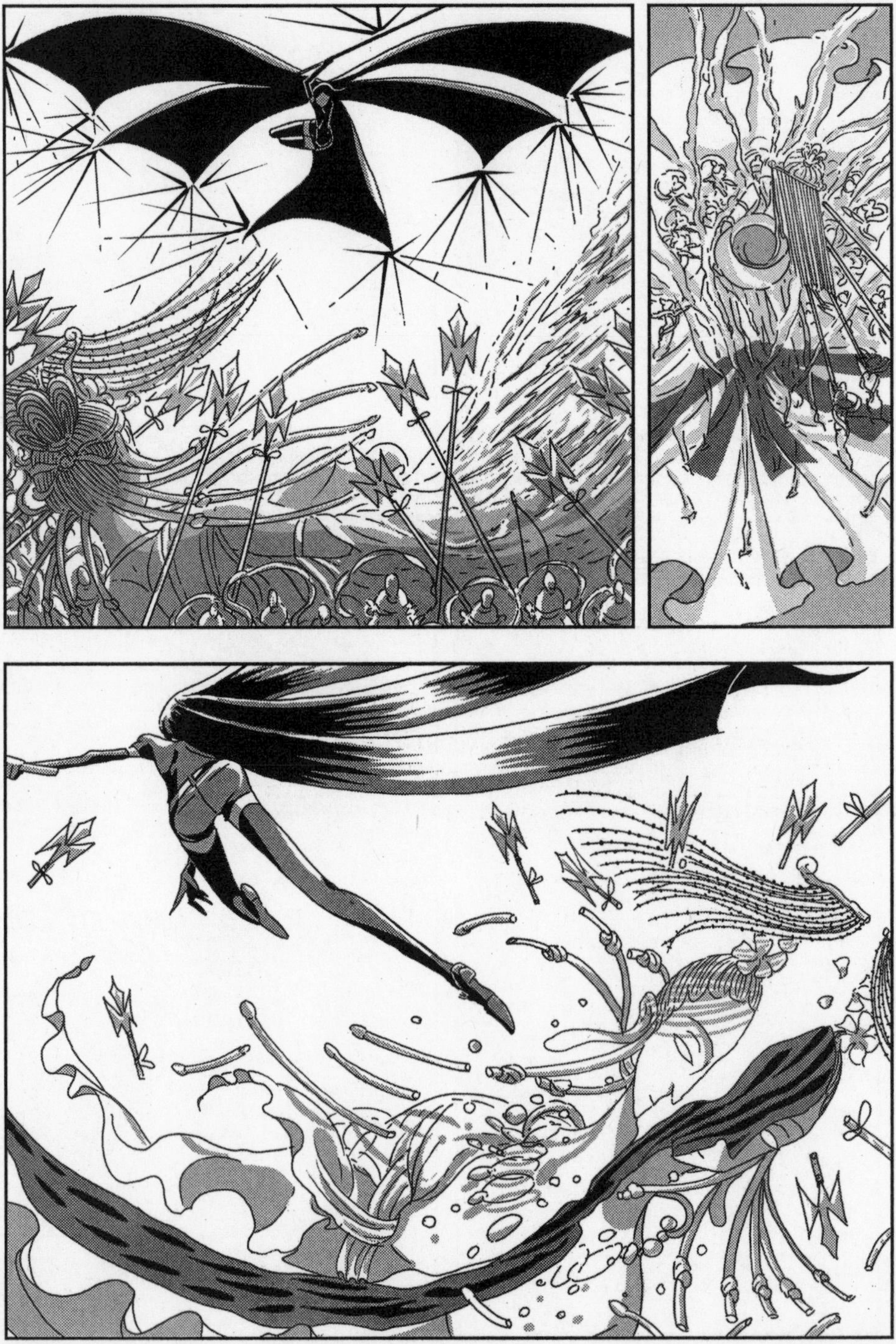

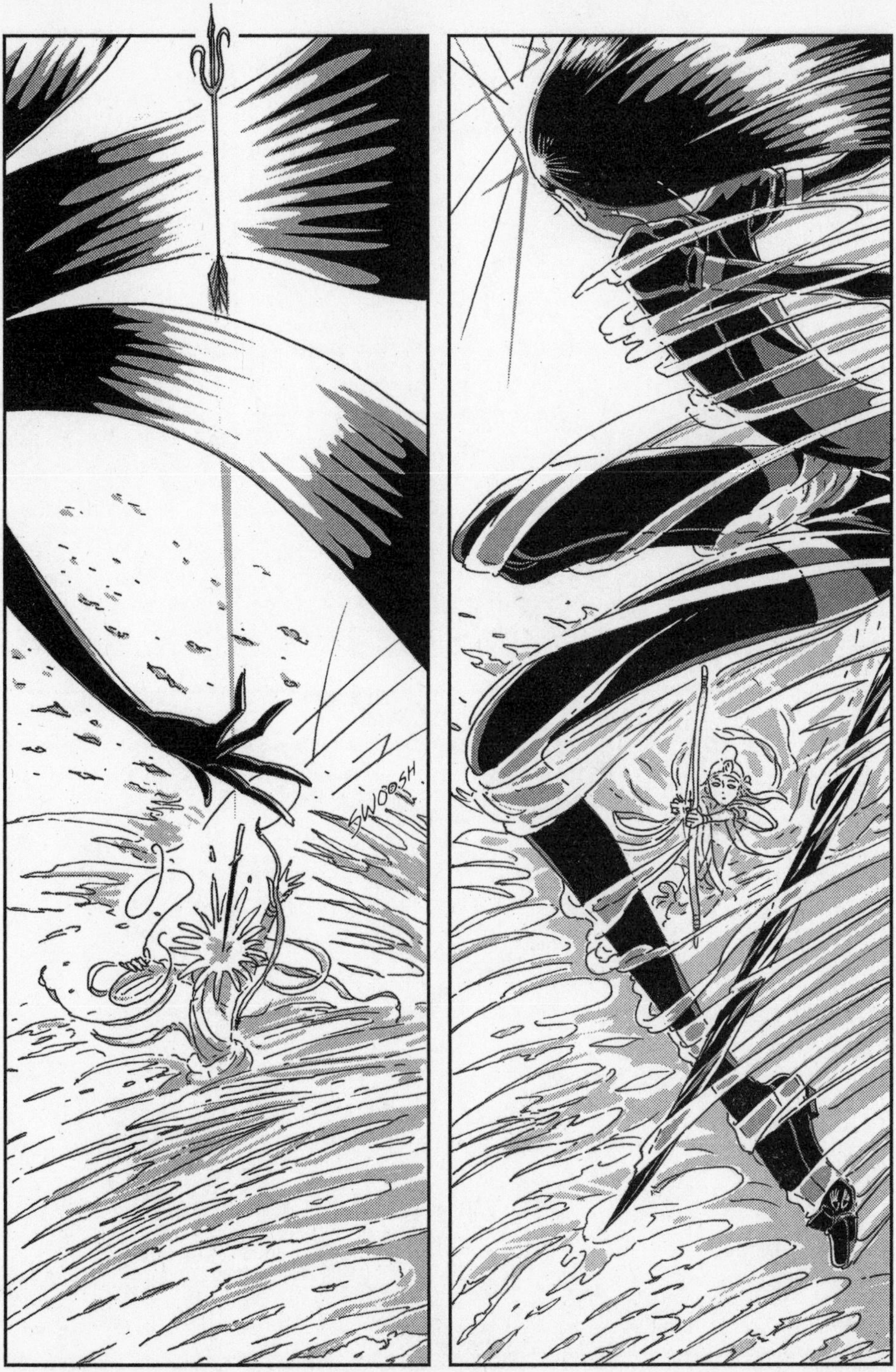
SWOOSH

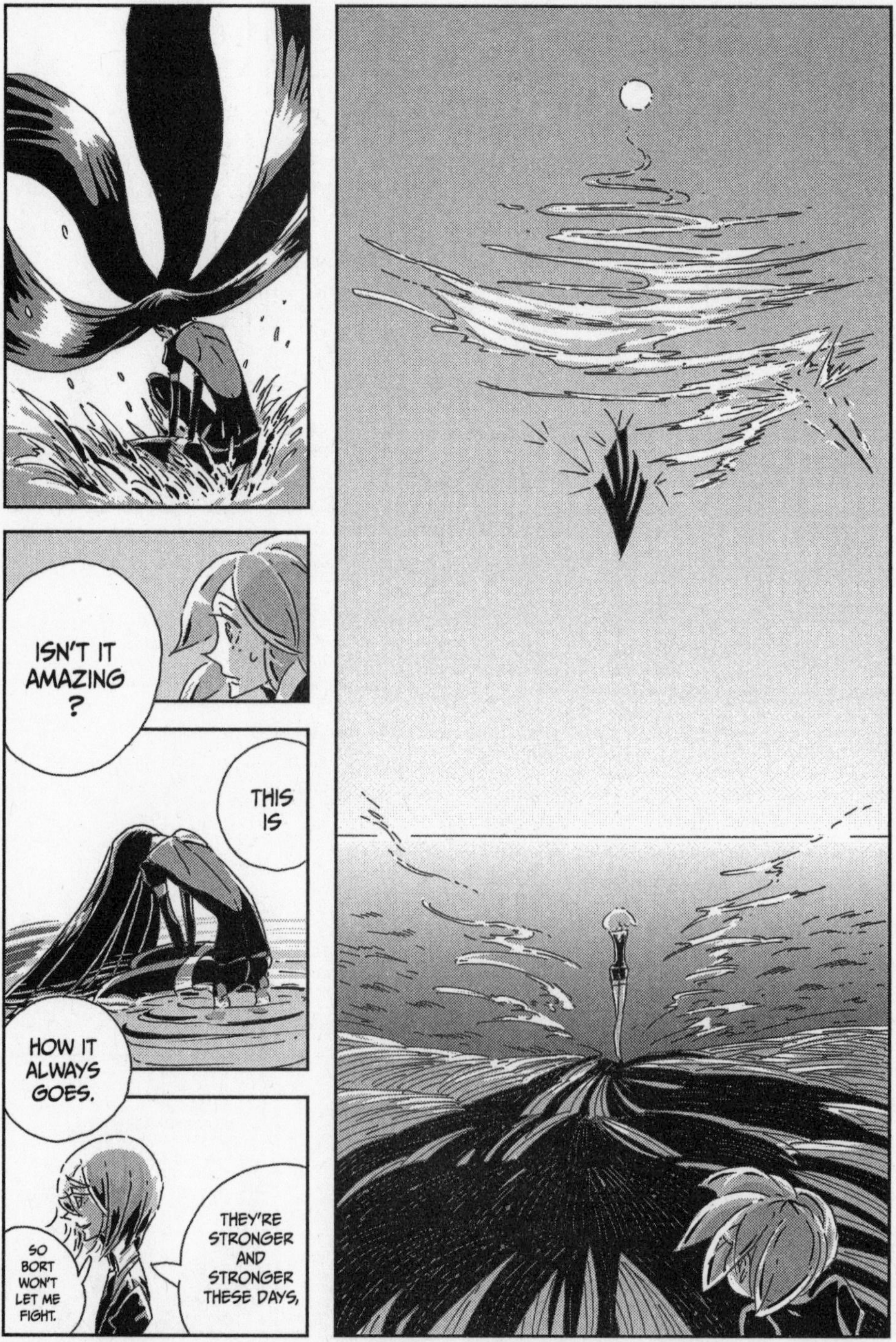
ISN'T IT AMAZING?
THIS IS
HOW IT ALWAYS GOES.
THEY'RE STRONGER AND STRONGER THESE DAYS,
SO BORT WON'T LET ME FIGHT.

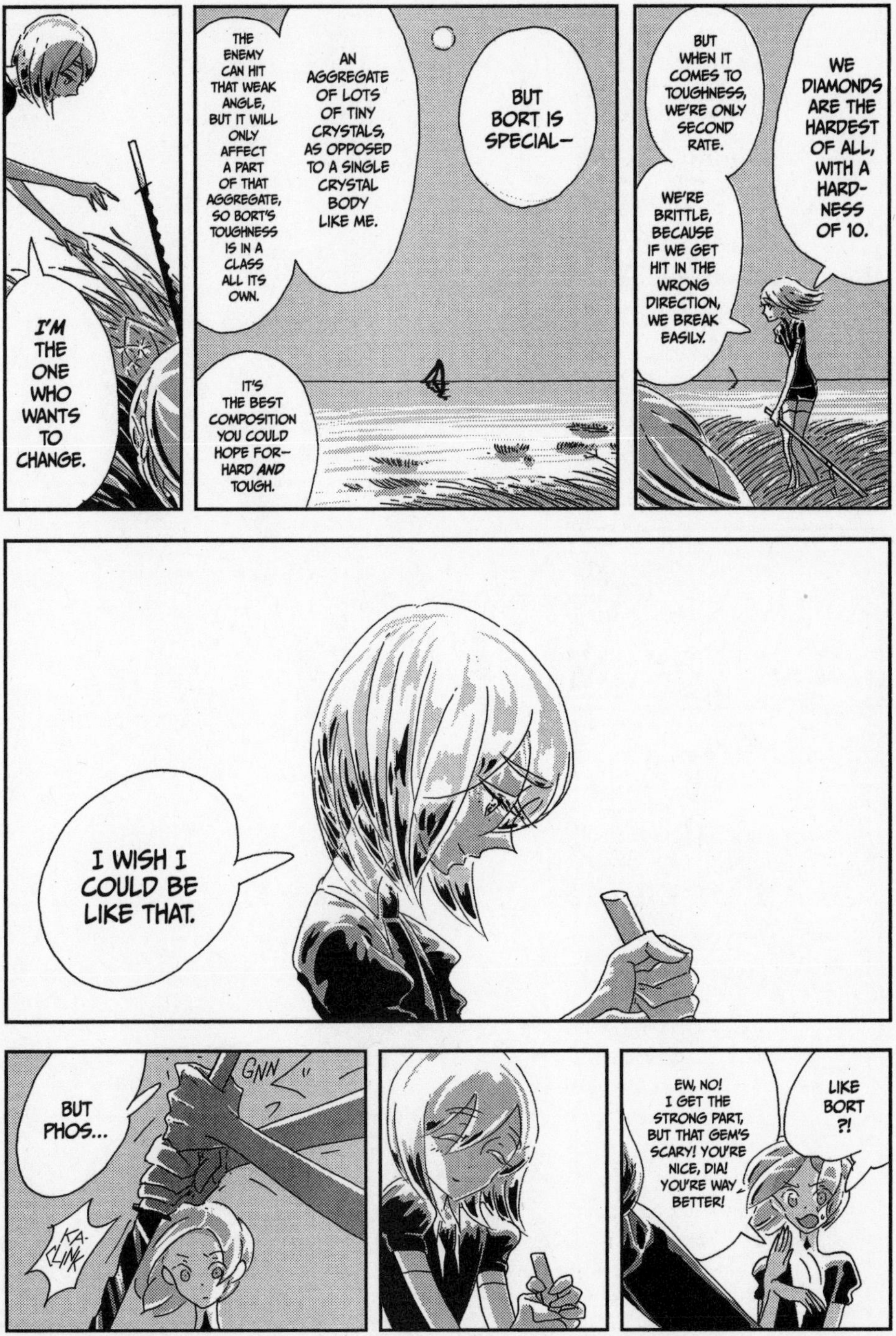
WE DIAMONDS ARE THE HARDEST OF ALL, WITH A HARDNESS OF 10.
BUT WHEN IT COMES TO TOUGHNESS, WE'RE ONLY SECOND RATE.
WE'RE BRITTLE, BECAUSE IF WE GET HIT IN THE WRONG DIRECTION, WE BREAK EASILY.
BUT BORT IS SPECIAL—
AN AGGREGATE OF LOTS OF TINY CRYSTALS, AS OPPOSED TO A SINGLE CRYSTAL BODY LIKE ME.
THE ENEMY CAN HIT THAT WEAK ANGLE, BUT IT WILL ONLY AFFECT A PART OF THAT AGGREGATE, SO BORT'S TOUGHNESS IS IN A CLASS ALL ITS OWN.
IT'S THE BEST COMPOSITION YOU COULD HOPE FOR—HARD *AND* TOUGH.
I'M THE ONE WHO WANTS TO CHANGE.
I WISH I COULD BE LIKE THAT.
LIKE BORT ?!
EW, NO! I GET THE STRONG PART, BUT THAT GEM'S SCARY! YOU'RE NICE, DIA! YOU'RE WAY BETTER!
GNN
BUT PHOS...
KA-CLINK

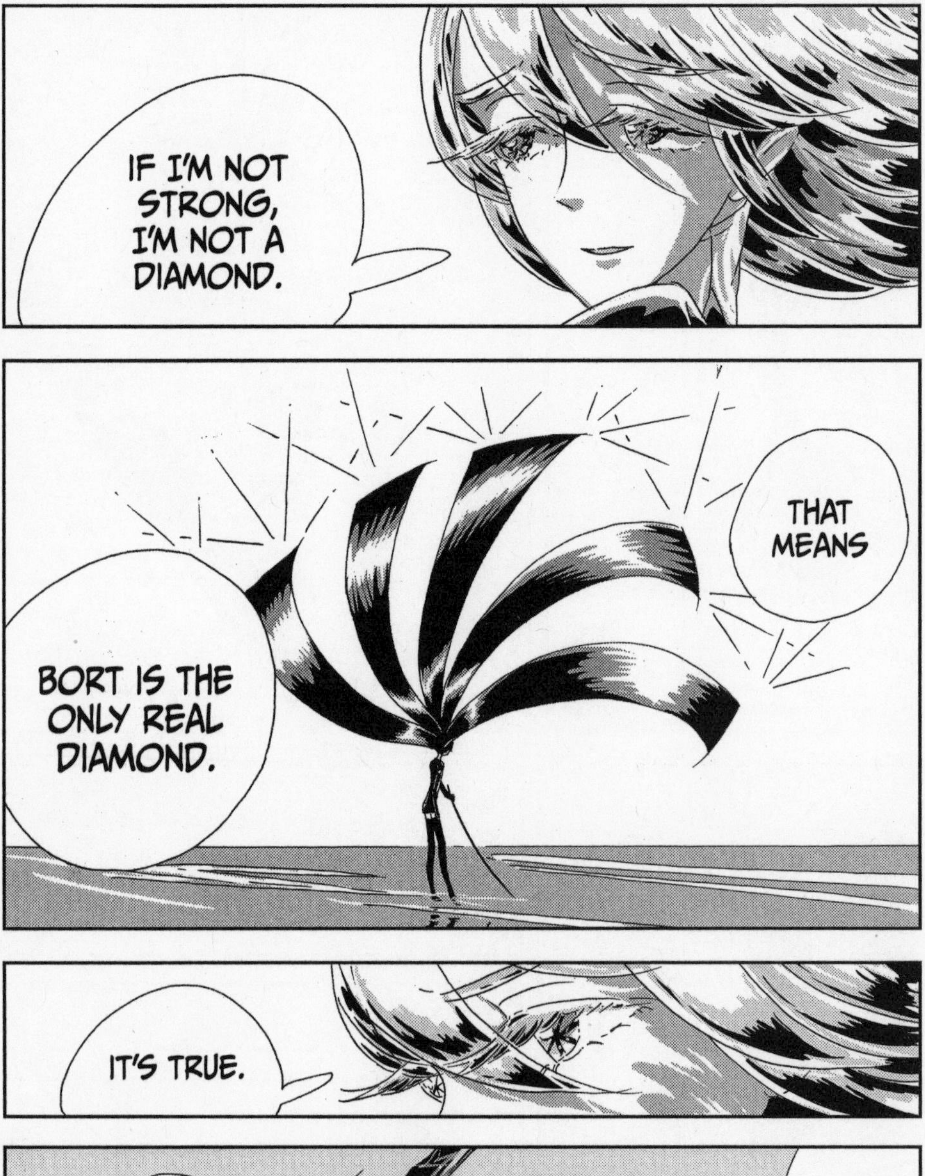
IF I'M NOT STRONG, I'M NOT A DIAMOND.
THAT MEANS
BORT IS THE ONLY REAL DIAMOND.
IT'S TRUE.
THAT'S WHY,
SOMETIMES,
JUST FOR A SECOND,
I'LL WISH...

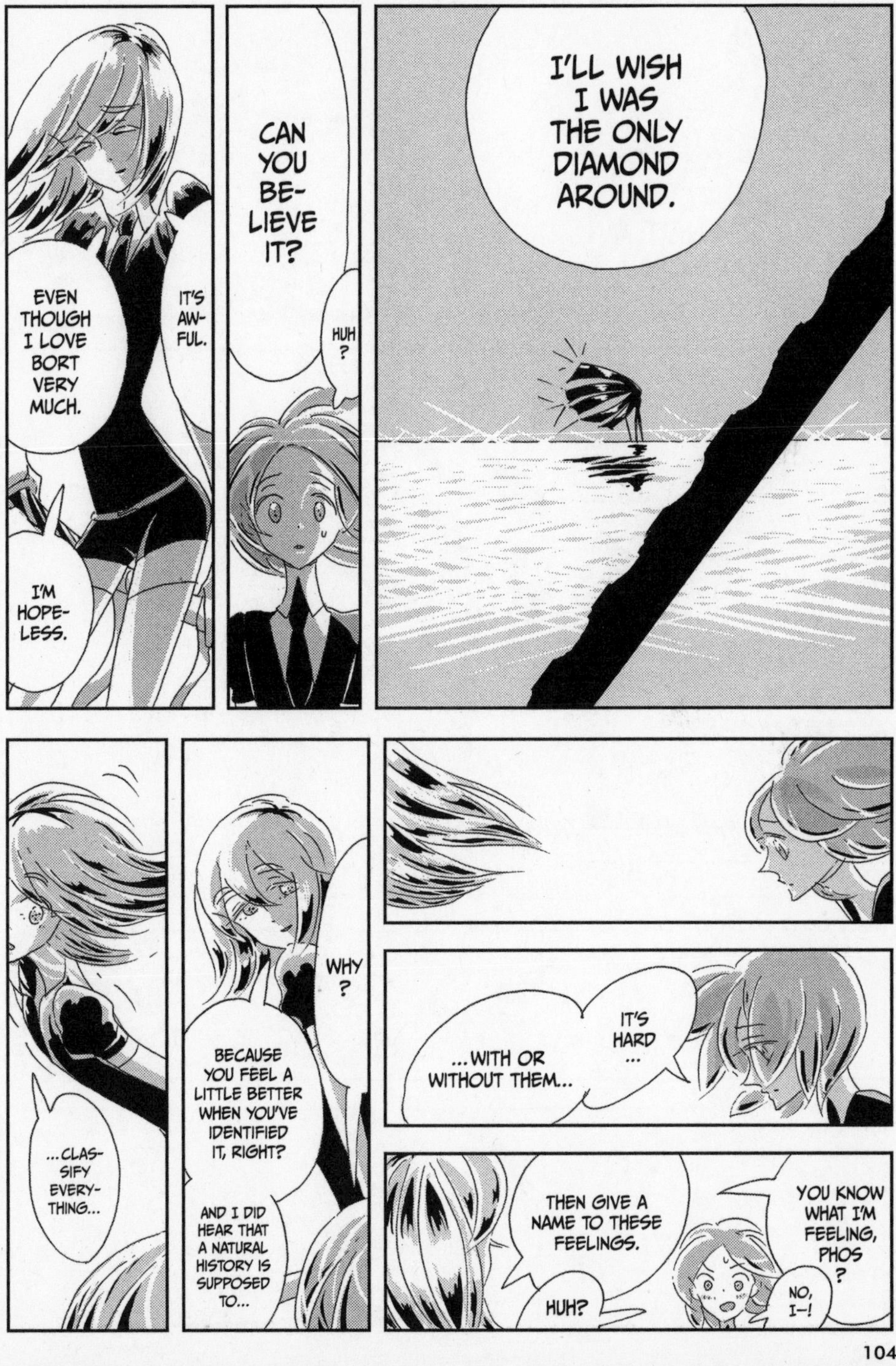
I'LL WISH I WAS THE ONLY DIAMOND AROUND.
CAN YOU BE-LIEVE IT?
HUH ?
IT'S AW-FUL.
EVEN THOUGH I LOVE BORT VERY MUCH.
I'M HOPE-LESS.
IT'S HARD ...
...WITH OR WITHOUT THEM...
YOU KNOW WHAT I'M FEELING, PHOS ?
THEN GIVE A NAME TO THESE FEELINGS.
NO, I–!
HUH?
WHY ?
BECAUSE YOU FEEL A LITTLE BETTER WHEN YOU'VE IDENTIFIED IT, RIGHT?
AND I DID HEAR THAT A NATURAL HISTORY IS SUPPOSED TO...
...CLAS-SIFY EVERY-THING...

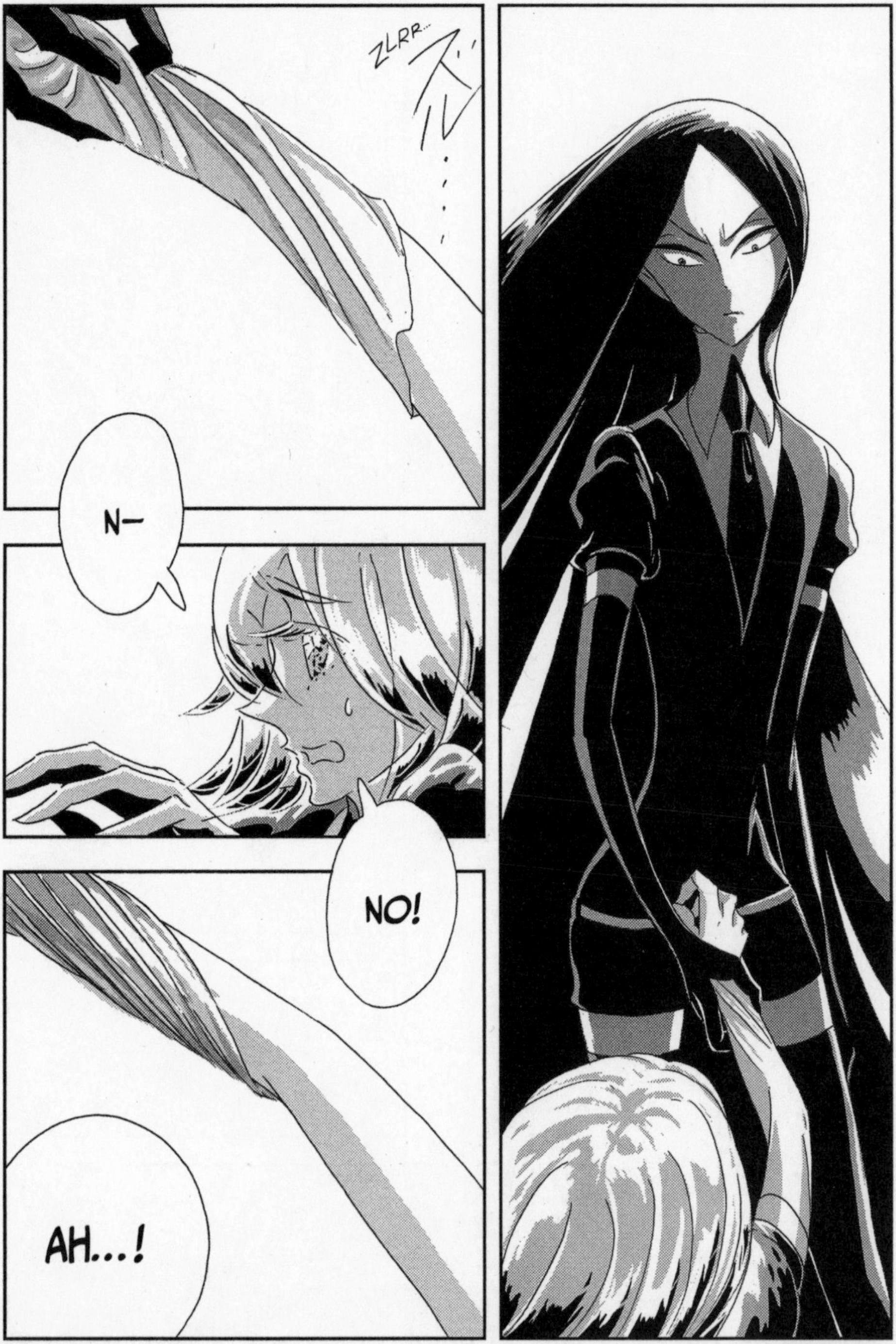
ZLRR...
ズル…
N—
NO!
AH...!

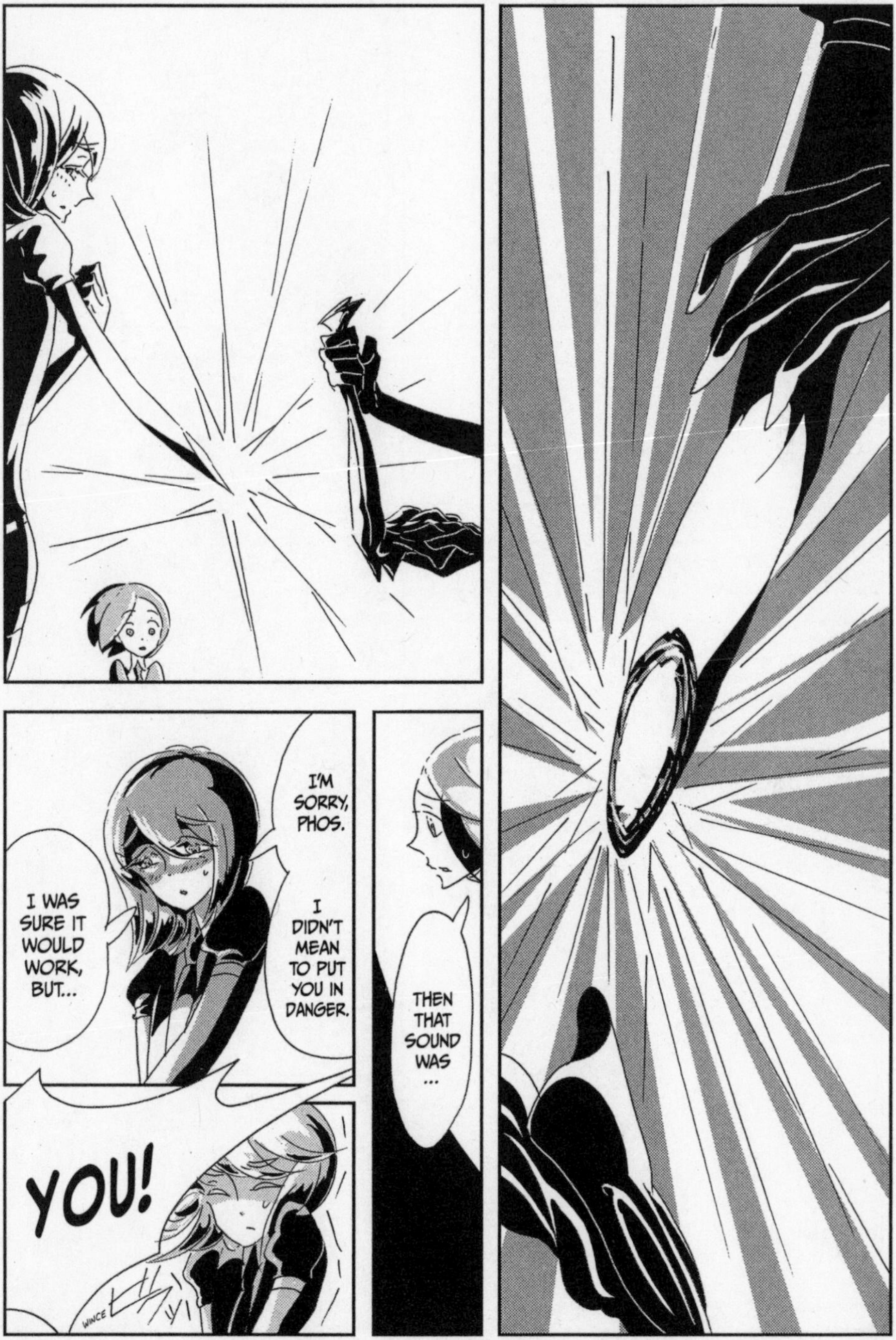
THEN THAT SOUND WAS...
I'M SORRY, PHOS.
I DIDN'T MEAN TO PUT YOU IN DANGER.
I WAS SURE IT WOULD WORK, BUT...
YOU!
WINCE

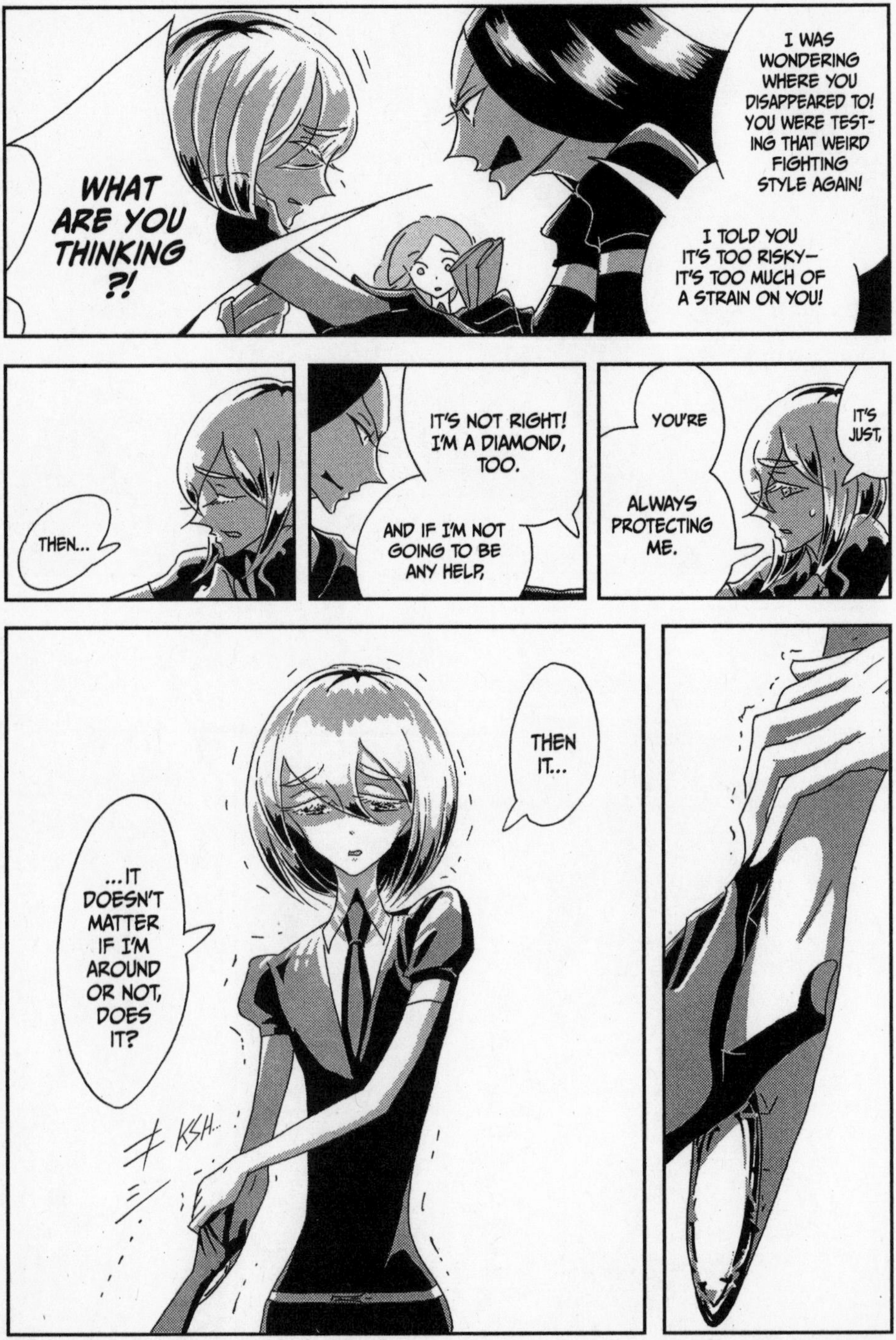
WHAT ARE YOU THINKING ?!
I WAS WONDERING WHERE YOU DISAPPEARED TO! YOU WERE TESTING THAT WEIRD FIGHTING STYLE AGAIN!
I TOLD YOU IT'S TOO RISKY— IT'S TOO MUCH OF A STRAIN ON YOU!
IT'S JUST,
YOU'RE
ALWAYS PROTECTING ME.
IT'S NOT RIGHT! I'M A DIAMOND, TOO.
AND IF I'M NOT GOING TO BE ANY HELP,
THEN...
THEN IT...
...IT DOESN'T MATTER IF I'M AROUND OR NOT, DOES IT?
KSH...

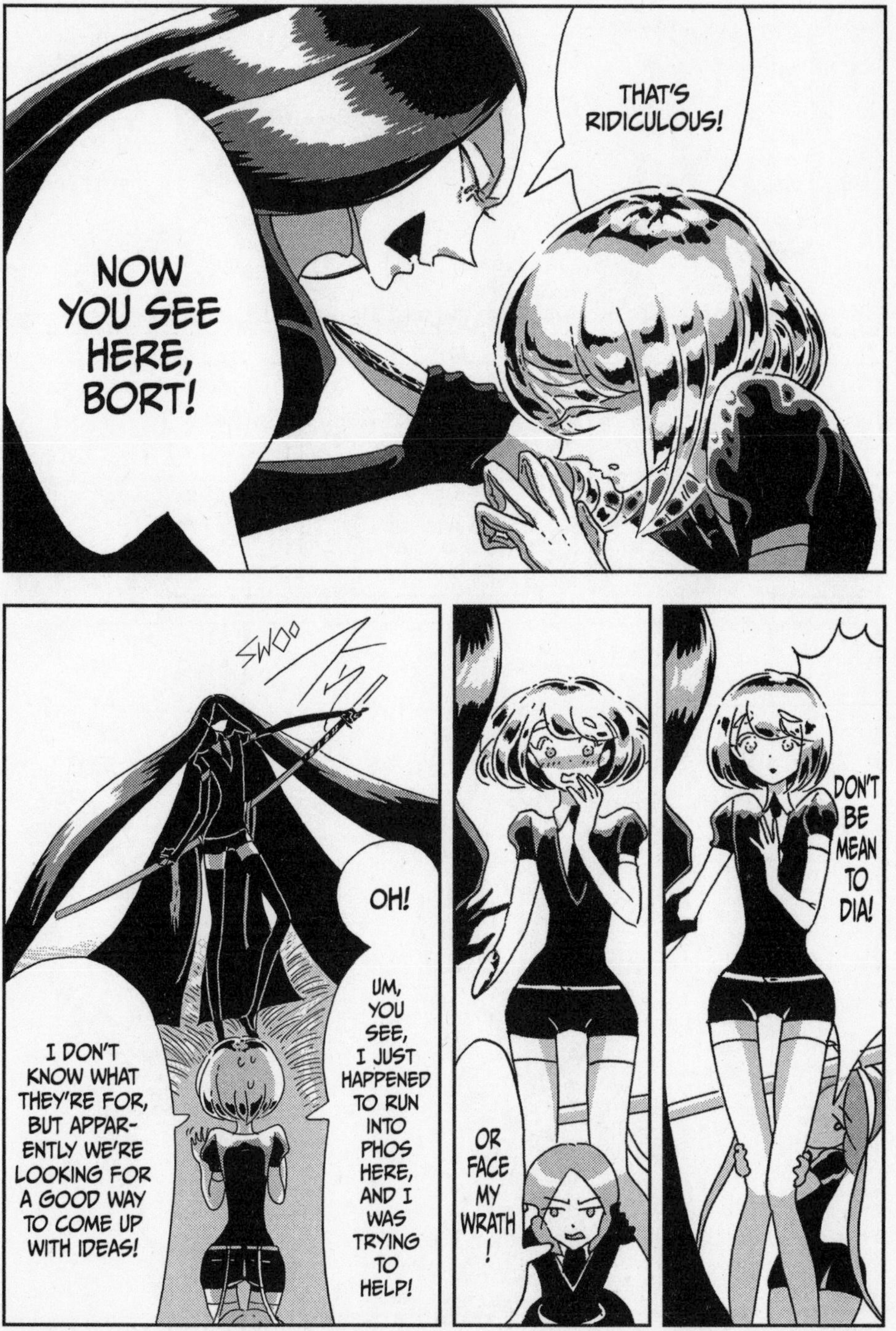
THAT'S RIDICULOUS!
NOW YOU SEE HERE, BORT!
DON'T BE MEAN TO DIA!
OR FACE MY WRATH!
SWOO
OH!
UM, YOU SEE, I JUST HAPPENED TO RUN INTO PHOS HERE, AND I WAS TRYING TO HELP!
I DON'T KNOW WHAT THEY'RE FOR, BUT APPARENTLY WE'RE LOOKING FOR A GOOD WAY TO COME UP WITH IDEAS!

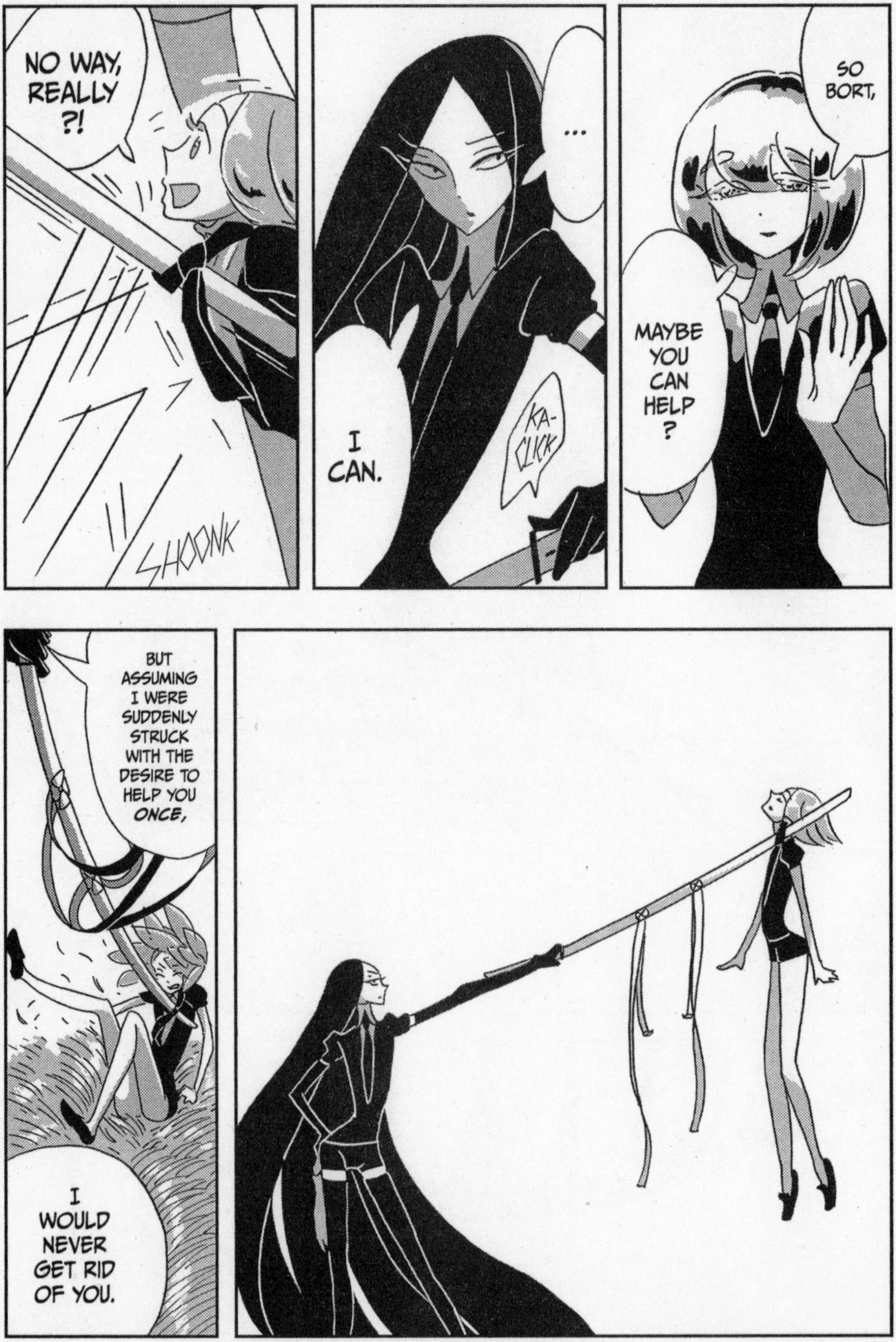
SO BORT,
MAYBE YOU CAN HELP?
...
KA-CLICK
I CAN.
NO WAY, REALLY?!
SHOONK
BUT ASSUMING I WERE SUDDENLY STRUCK WITH THE DESIRE TO HELP YOU *ONCE*,
I WOULD NEVER GET RID OF YOU.

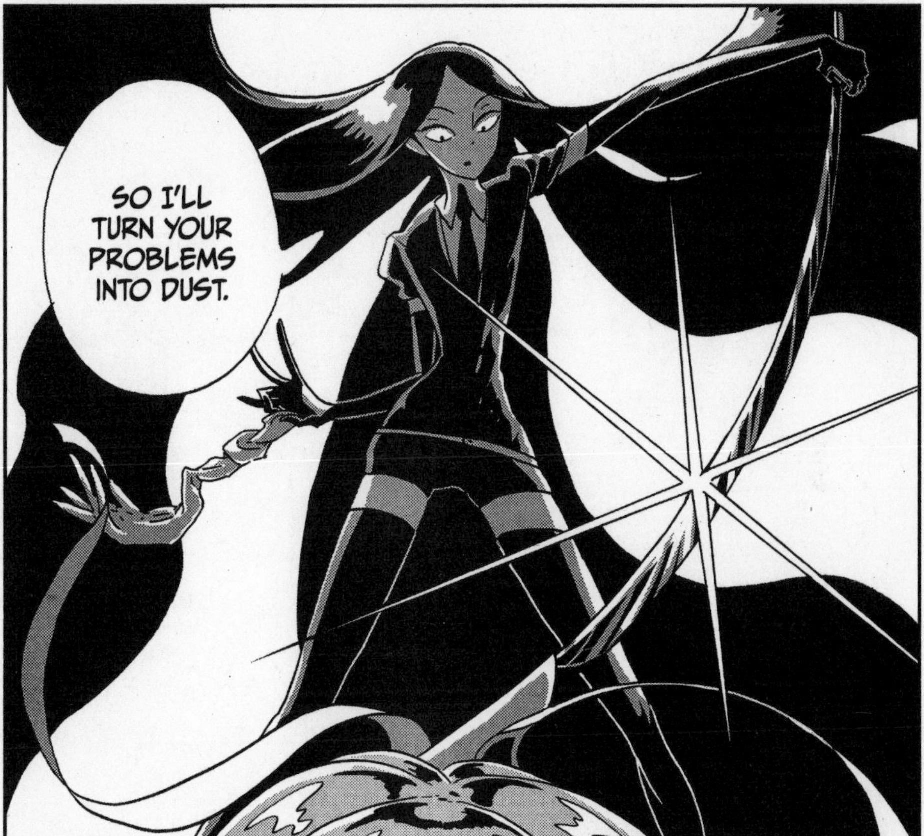
SO I'LL TURN YOUR PROBLEMS INTO DUST.

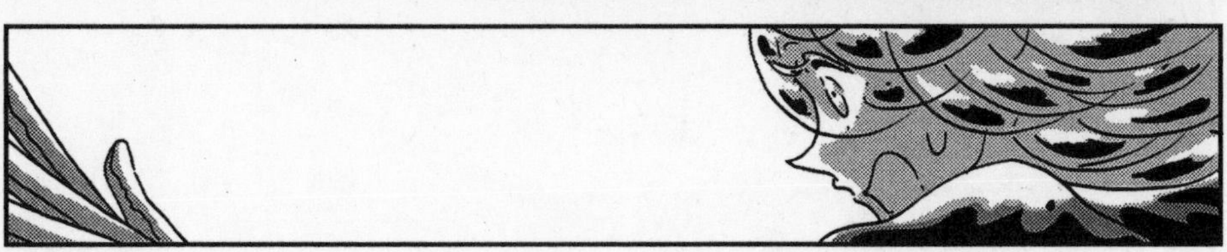

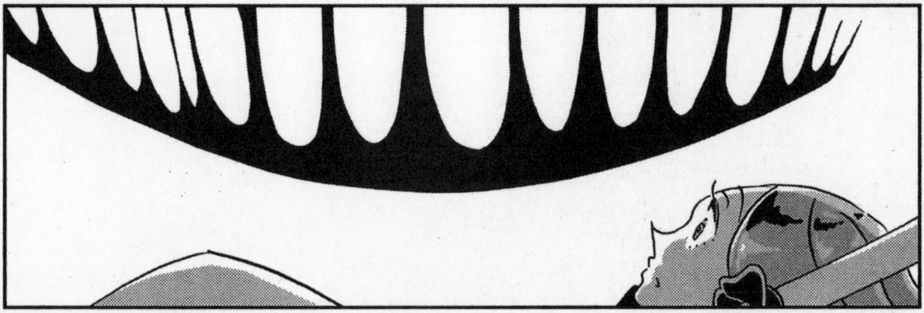

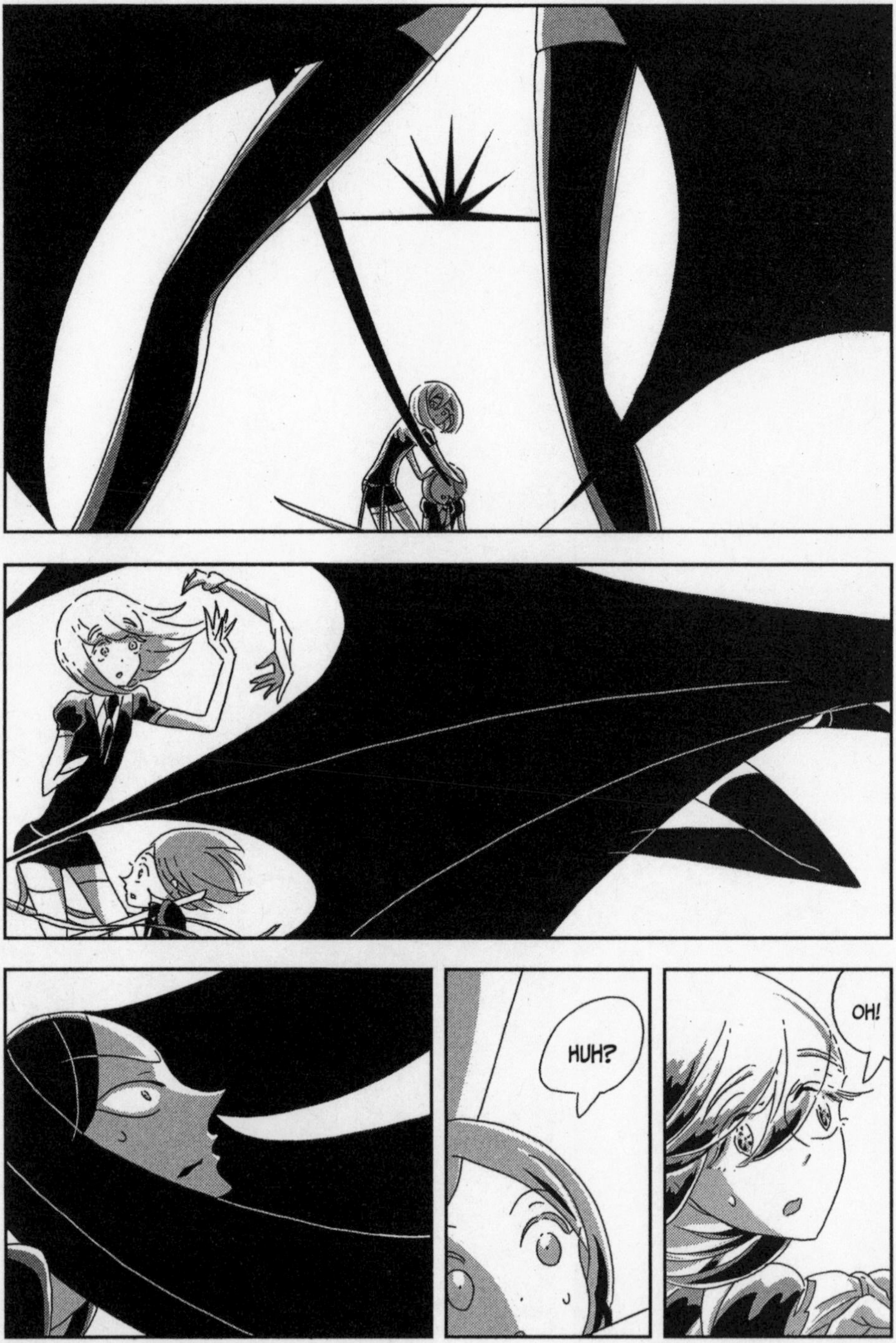
OH!
HUH?

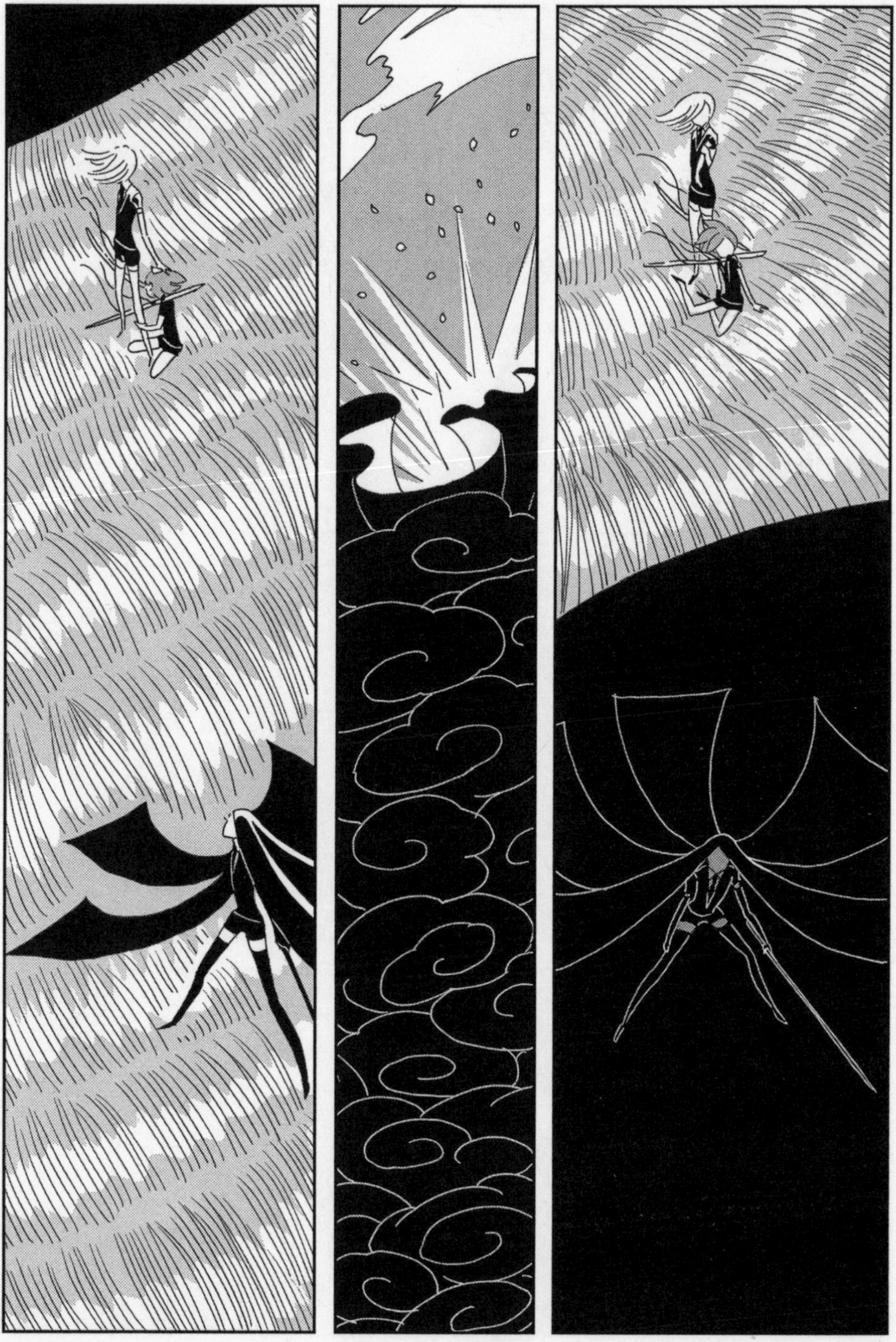

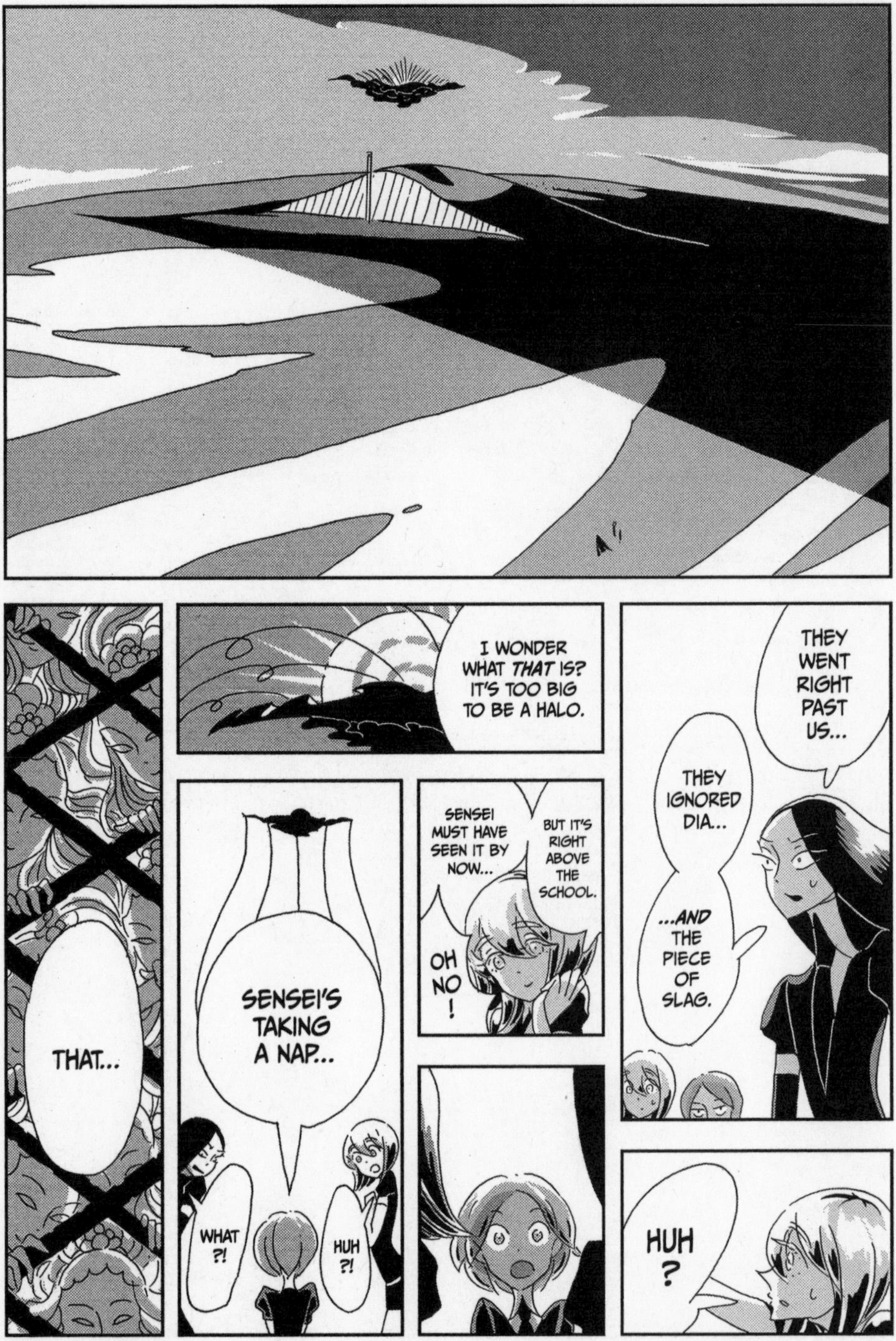
THEY WENT RIGHT PAST US...
THEY IGNORED DIA...
...AND THE PIECE OF SLAG.
I WONDER WHAT *THAT* IS? IT'S TOO BIG TO BE A HALO.
BUT IT'S RIGHT ABOVE THE SCHOOL.
SENSEI MUST HAVE SEEN IT BY NOW...
OH NO!
HUH?
SENSEI'S TAKING A NAP...
HUH?!
WHAT?!
THAT...

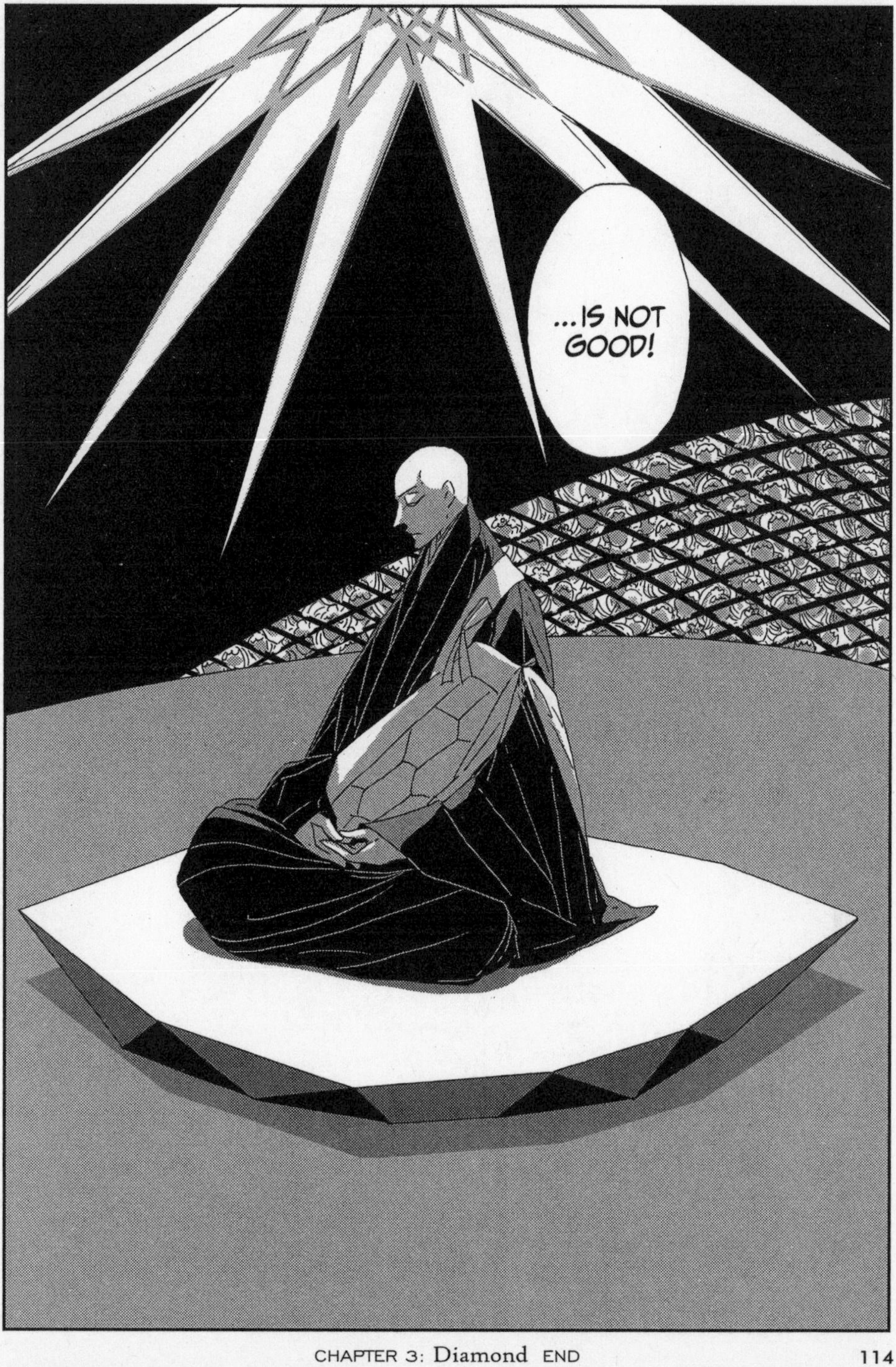
...IS NOT
GOOD!

CHAPTER 3: Diamond END

CHAPTER 4:

Cochlea

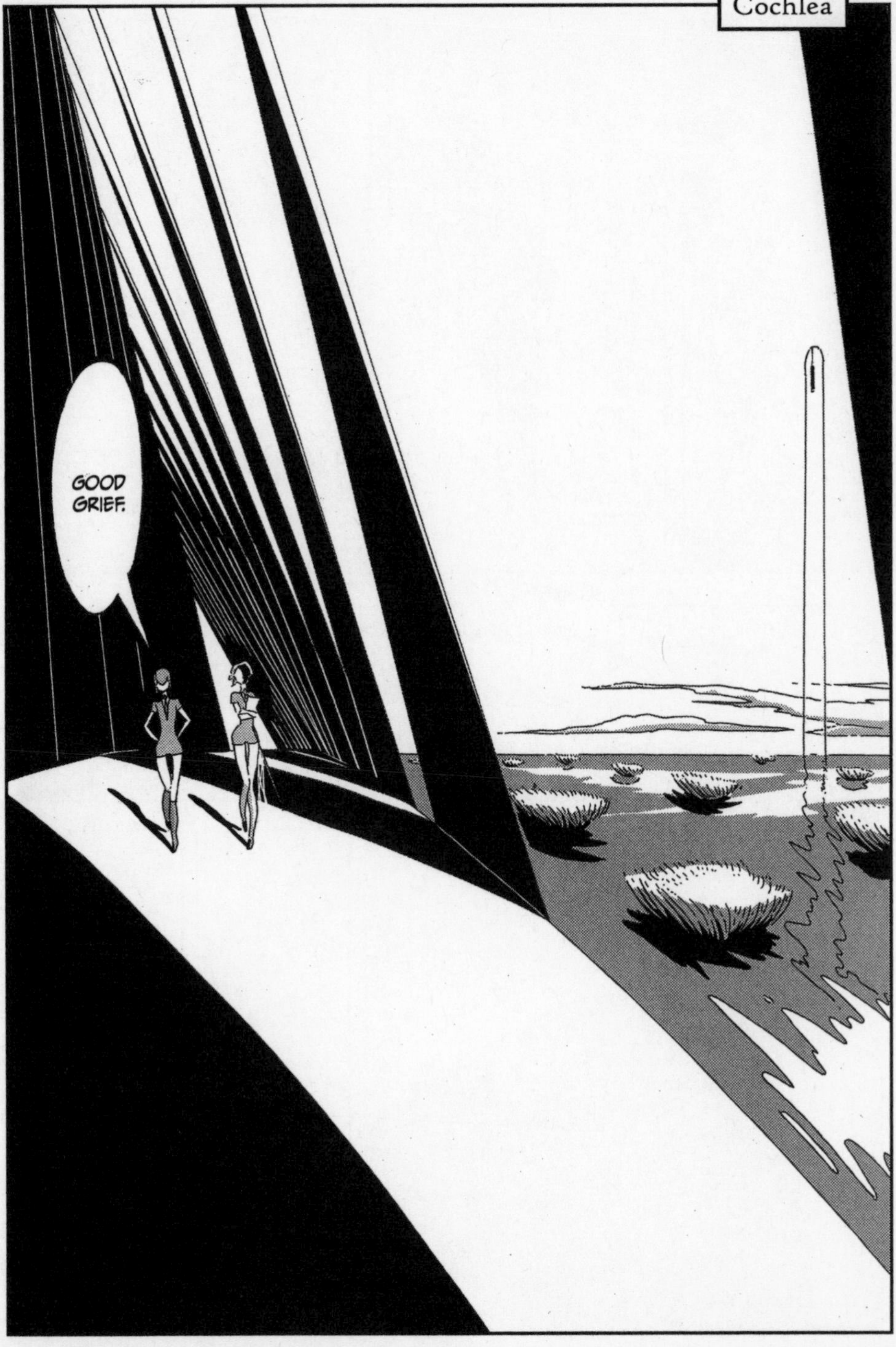
GOOD GRIEF.

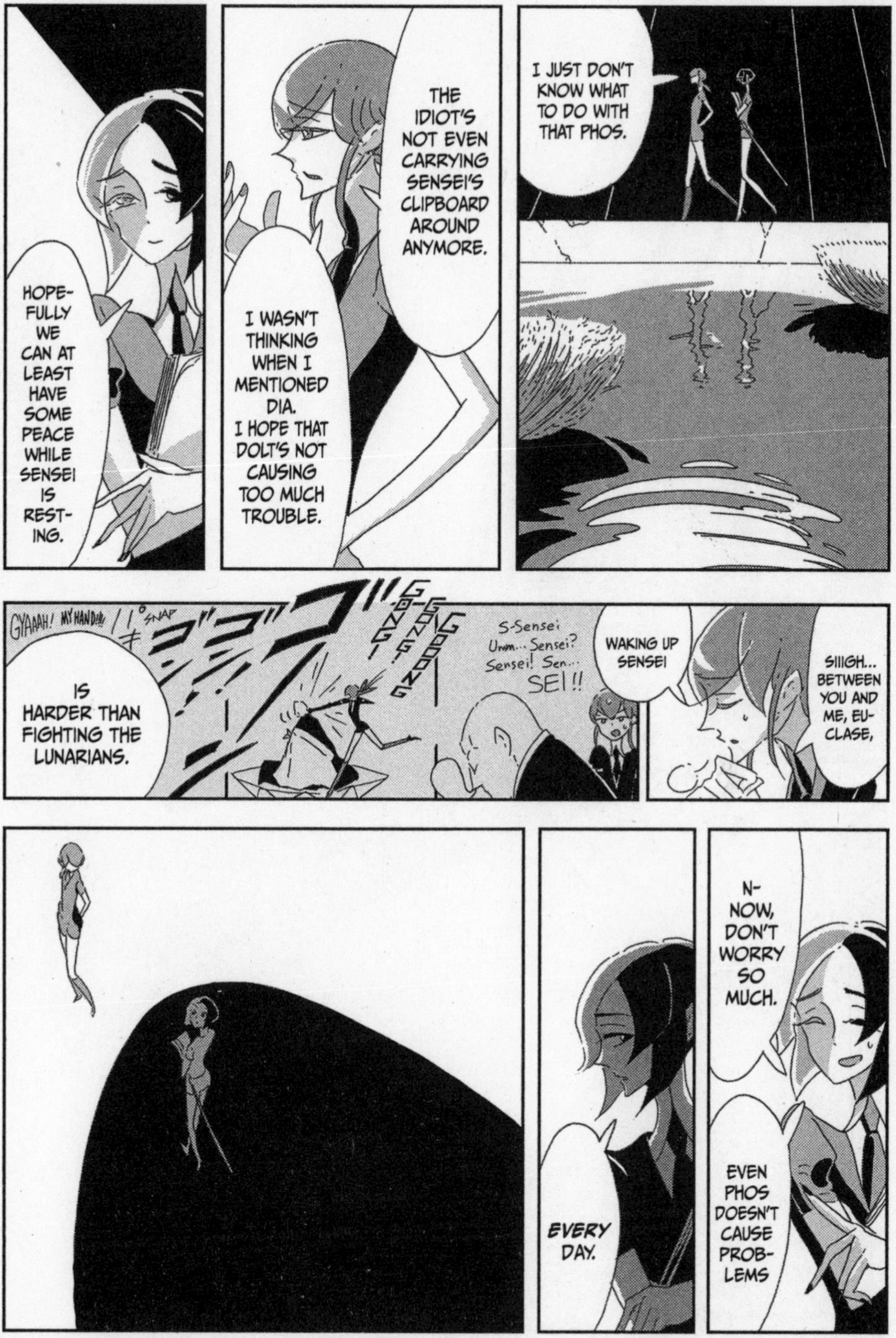
I JUST DON'T KNOW WHAT TO DO WITH THAT PHOS.
THE IDIOT'S NOT EVEN CARRYING SENSEI'S CLIPBOARD AROUND ANYMORE.
I WASN'T THINKING WHEN I MENTIONED DIA. I HOPE THAT DOLT'S NOT CAUSING TOO MUCH TROUBLE.
HOPE-FULLY WE CAN AT LEAST HAVE SOME PEACE WHILE SENSEI IS REST-ING.
SIIIGH... BETWEEN YOU AND ME, EU-CLASE,
WAKING UP SENSEI
S-Sensei Umm... Sensei? Sensei! Sen... SEI!!
GONG! GONG! GONG
SNAP
GYAAAH! MY HAND!!
IS HARDER THAN FIGHTING THE LUNARIANS.
N-NOW, DON'T WORRY SO MUCH.
EVEN PHOS DOESN'T CAUSE PROB-LEMS
EVERY DAY.

KER-SNAP
WHAM
WHOOOM
JADE! EUC!
LOOK UP!

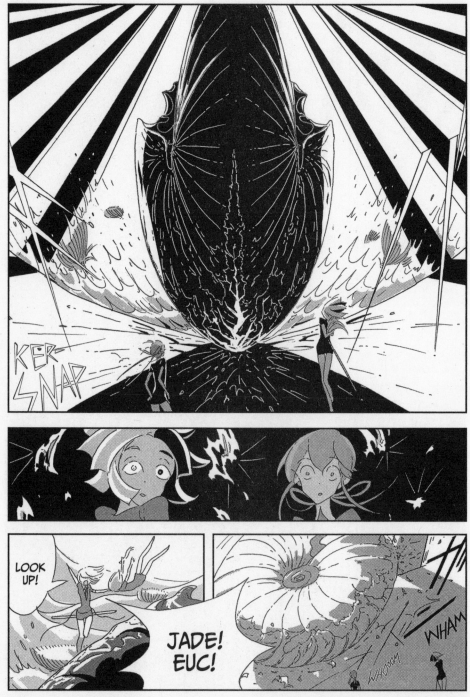

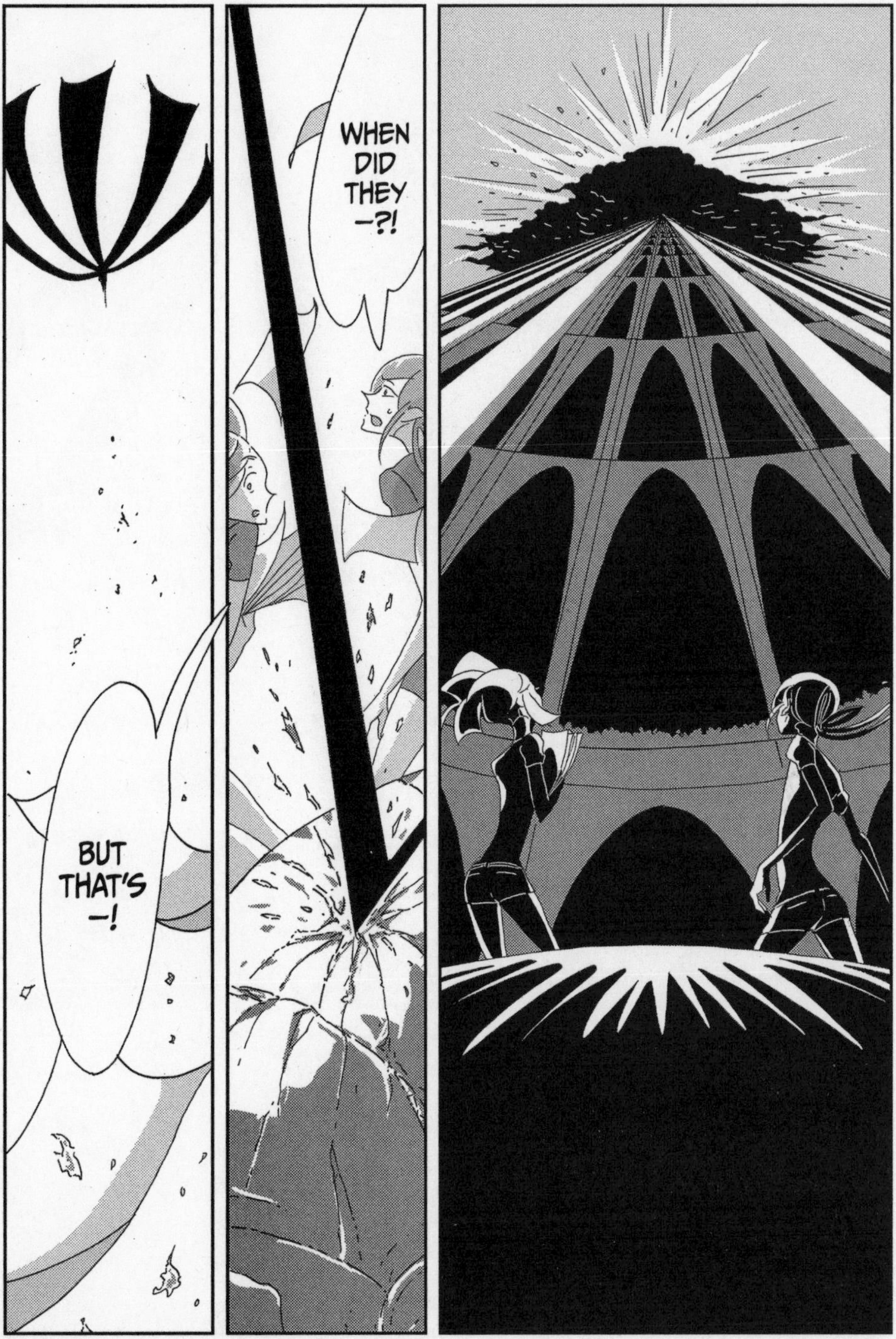
WHEN DID THEY —?!
BUT THAT'S —!

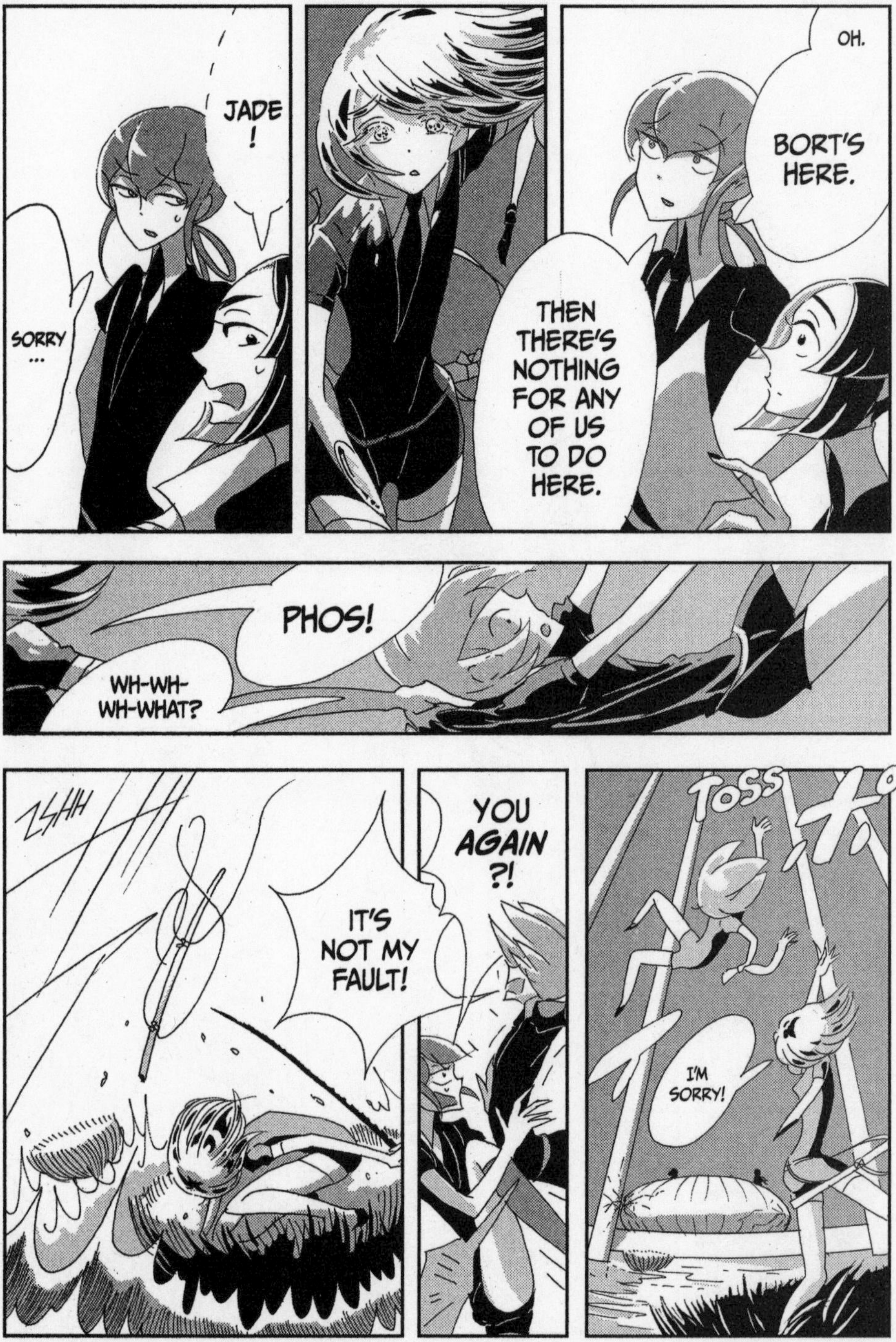
OH.
BORT'S HERE.
THEN THERE'S NOTHING FOR ANY OF US TO DO HERE.
JADE!
SORRY...
PHOS!
WH-WH-WH-WHAT?
TOSS
I'M SORRY!
YOU AGAIN?!
IT'S NOT MY FAULT!
ZSHH

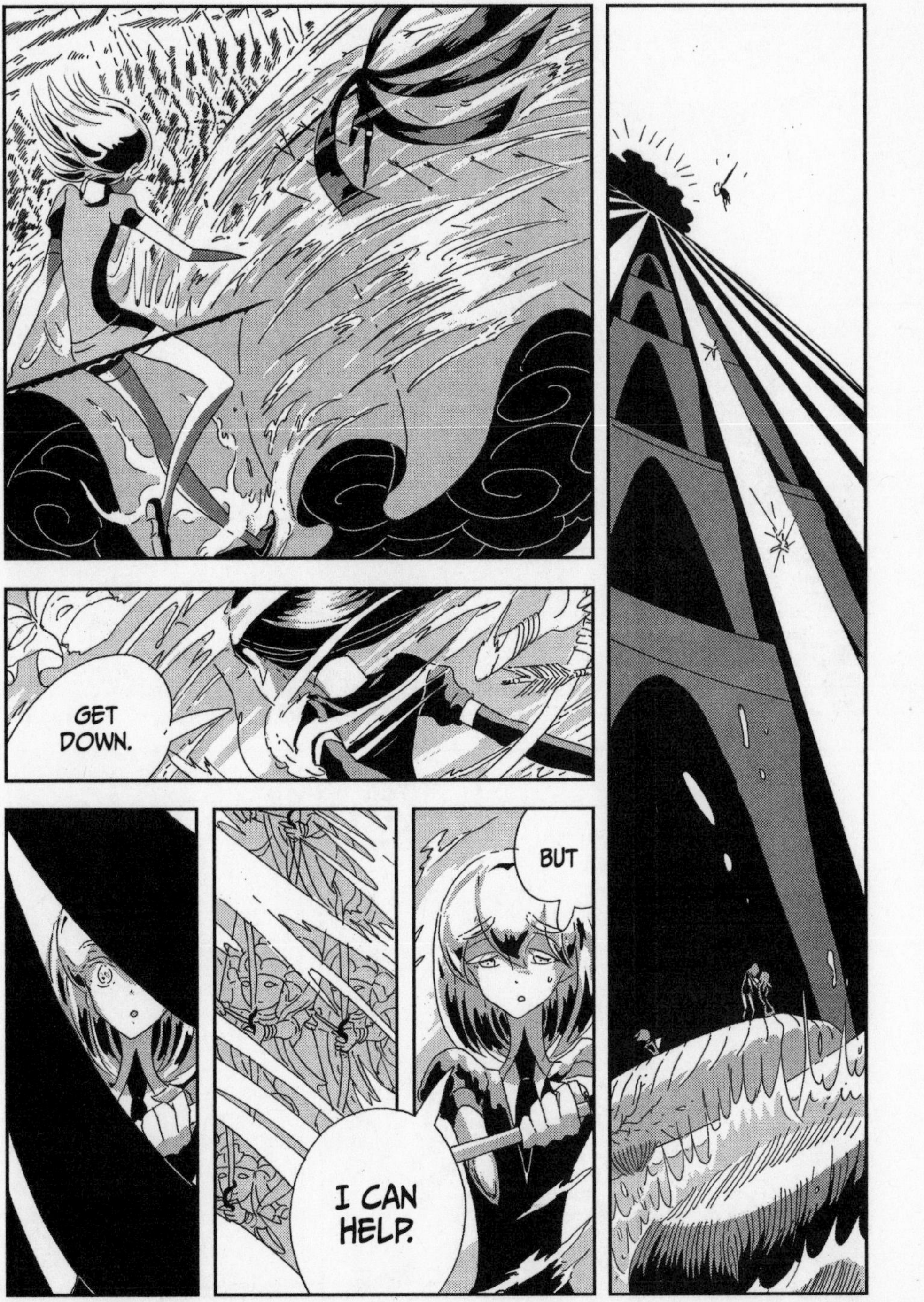
GET DOWN.
BUT
I CAN HELP.

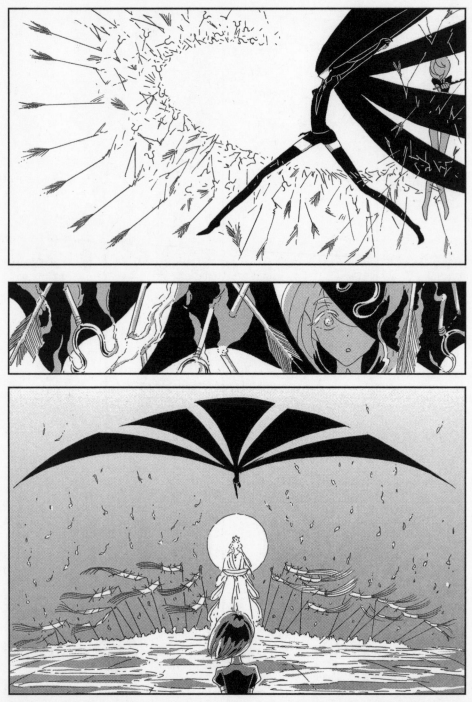

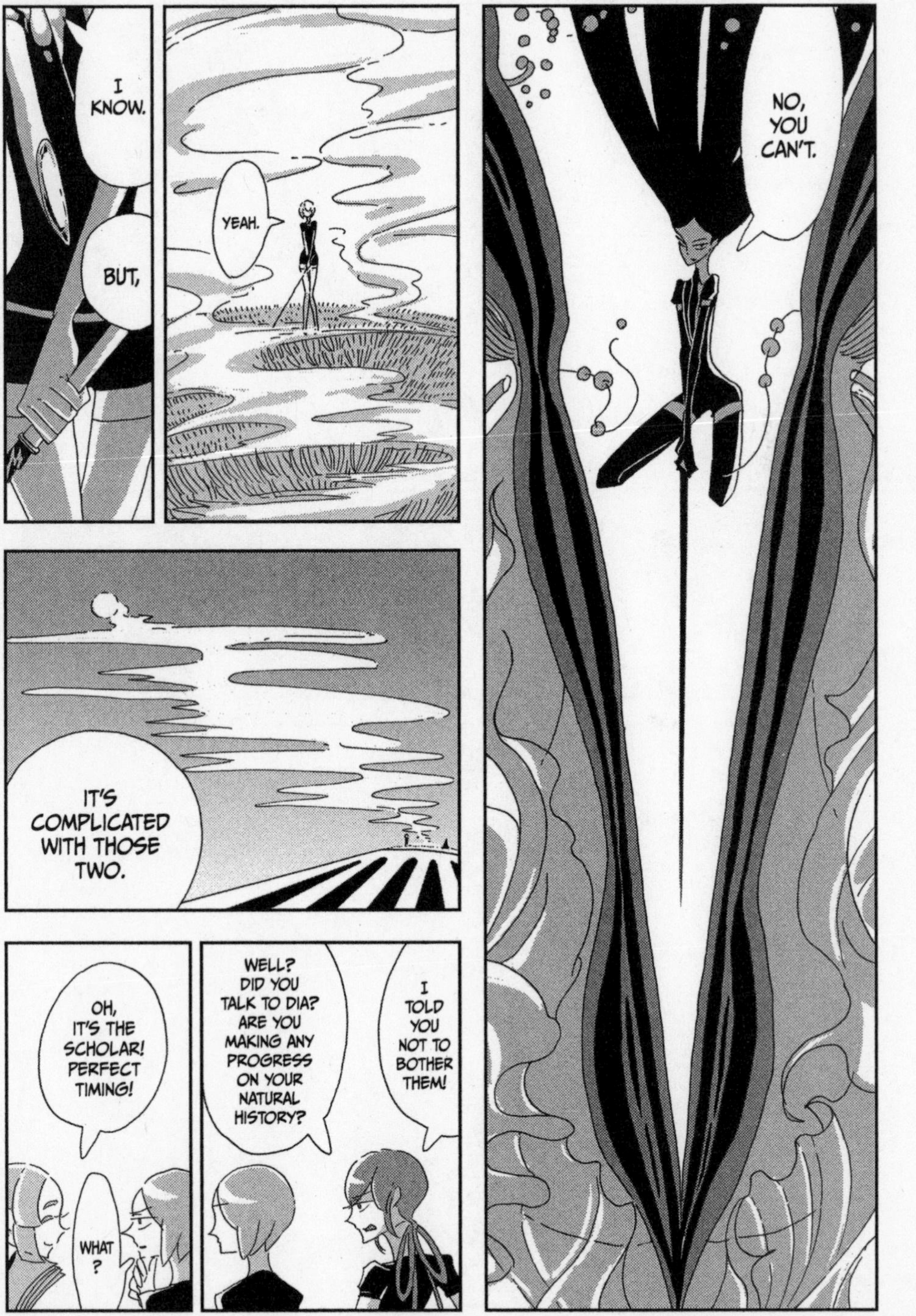
NO, YOU CAN'T.
YEAH.
I KNOW.
BUT,
IT'S COMPLICATED WITH THOSE TWO.
WELL? DID YOU TALK TO DIA? ARE YOU MAKING ANY PROGRESS ON YOUR NATURAL HISTORY?
I TOLD YOU NOT TO BOTHER THEM!
OH, IT'S THE SCHOLAR! PERFECT TIMING!
WHAT?

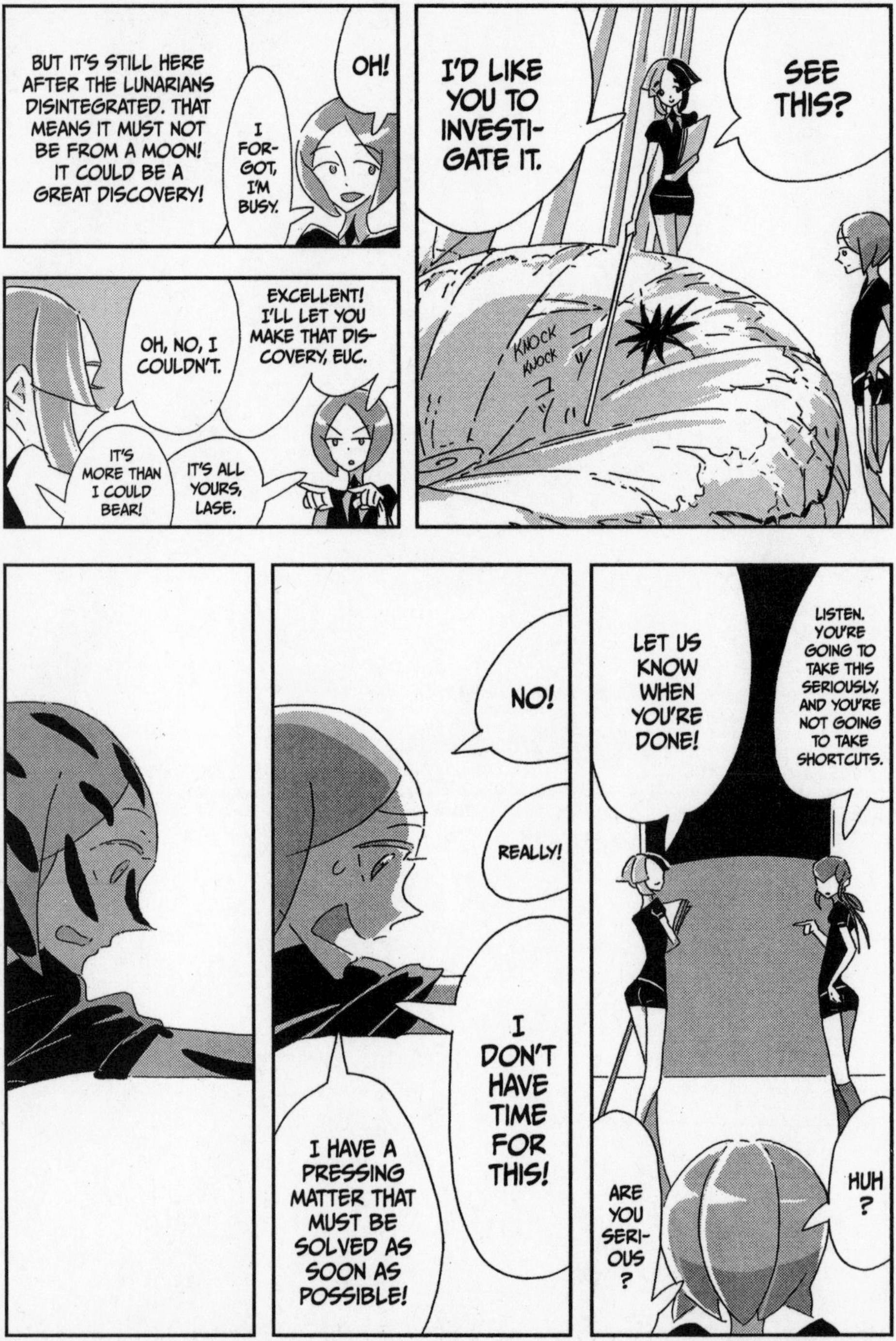
SEE THIS?
I'D LIKE YOU TO INVESTI-GATE IT.
KNOCK KNOCK
OH!
I FOR-GOT, I'M BUSY.
BUT IT'S STILL HERE AFTER THE LUNARIANS DISINTEGRATED. THAT MEANS IT MUST NOT BE FROM A MOON! IT COULD BE A GREAT DISCOVERY!
EXCELLENT! I'LL LET YOU MAKE THAT DIS-COVERY, EUC.
OH, NO, I COULDN'T.
IT'S ALL YOURS, LASE.
IT'S MORE THAN I COULD BEAR!
LISTEN. YOU'RE GOING TO TAKE THIS SERIOUSLY, AND YOU'RE NOT GOING TO TAKE SHORTCUTS.
LET US KNOW WHEN YOU'RE DONE!
HUH ?
ARE YOU SERI-OUS ?
NO!
REALLY!
I DON'T HAVE TIME FOR THIS!
I HAVE A PRESSING MATTER THAT MUST BE SOLVED AS SOON AS POSSIBLE!

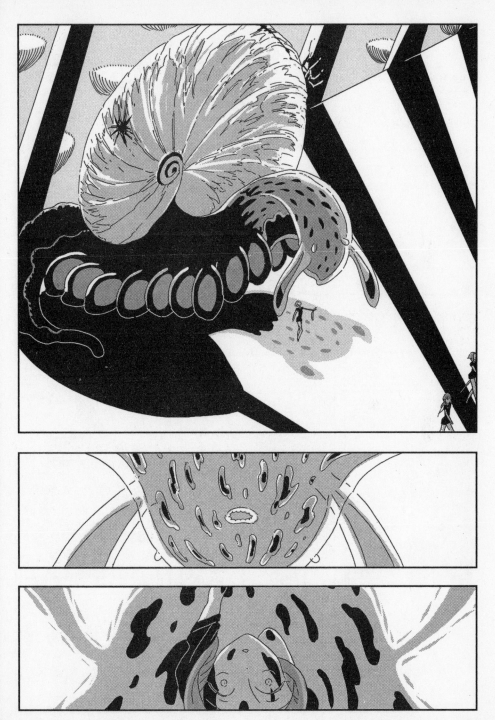

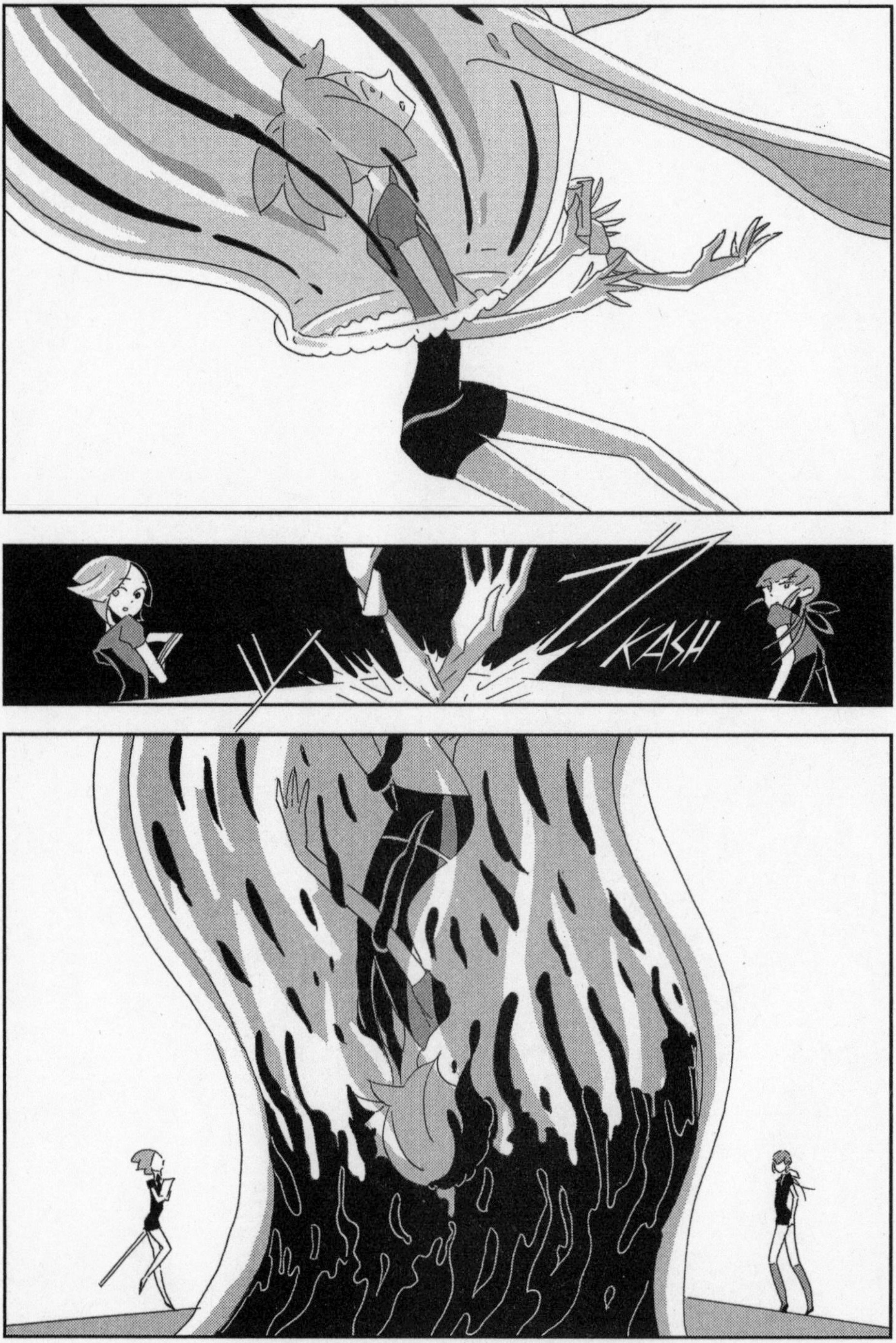
KASH

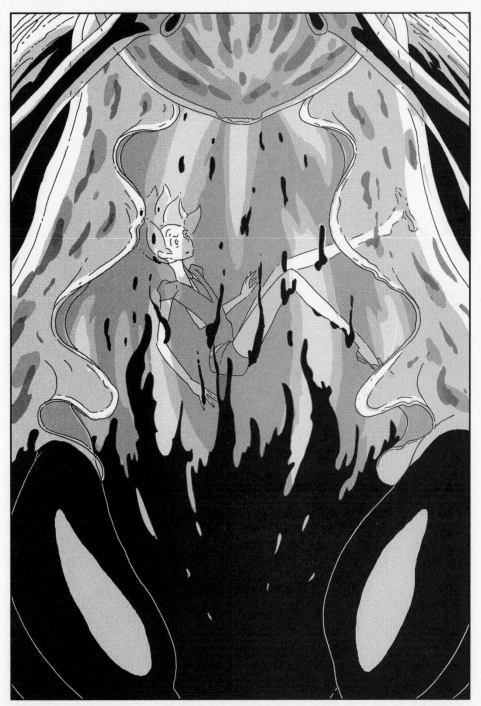

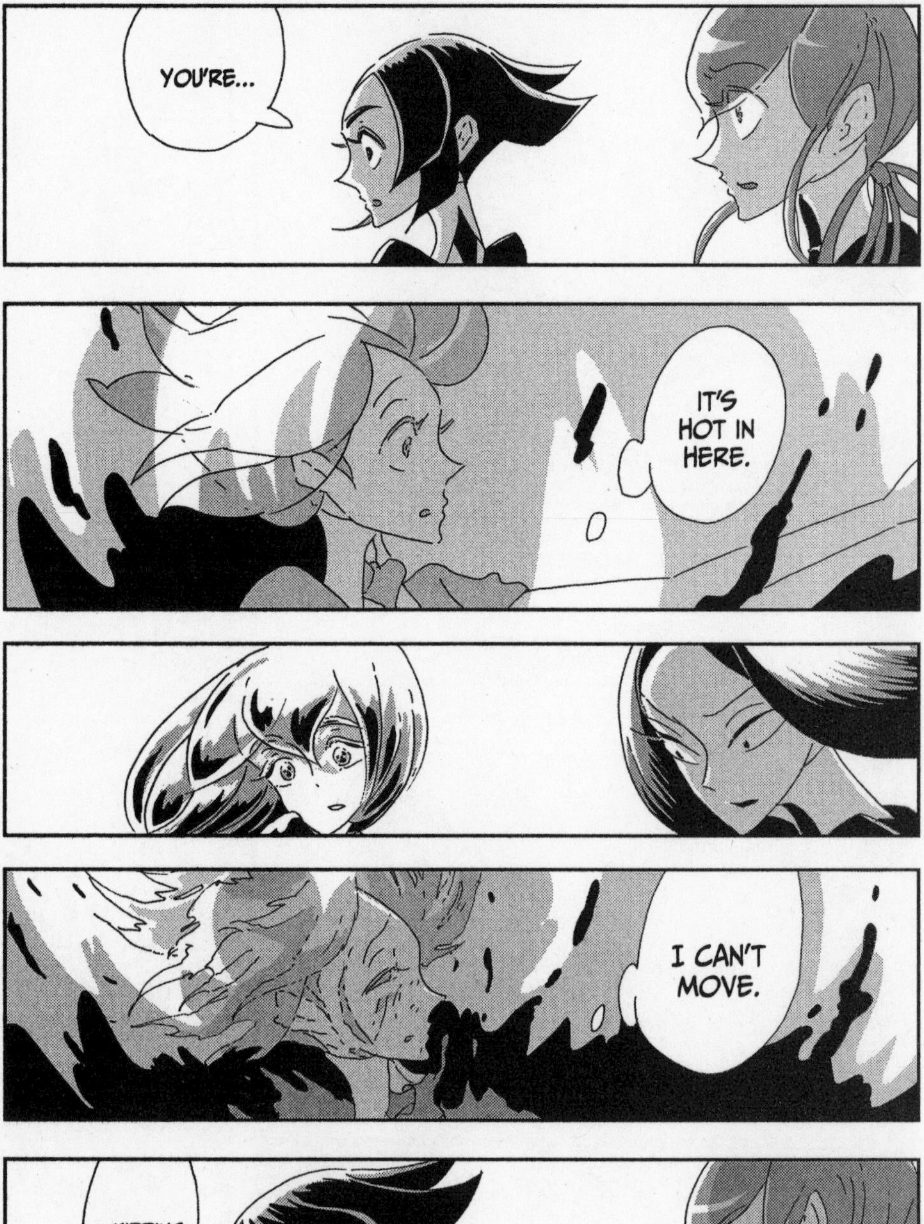
YOU'RE...
IT'S HOT IN HERE.
I CAN'T MOVE.
...KIDDING ME.

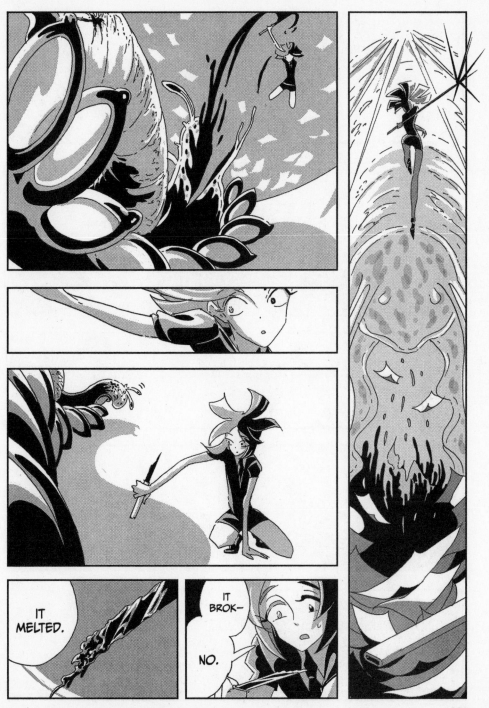

IT MELTED.

IT BROK—

NO.

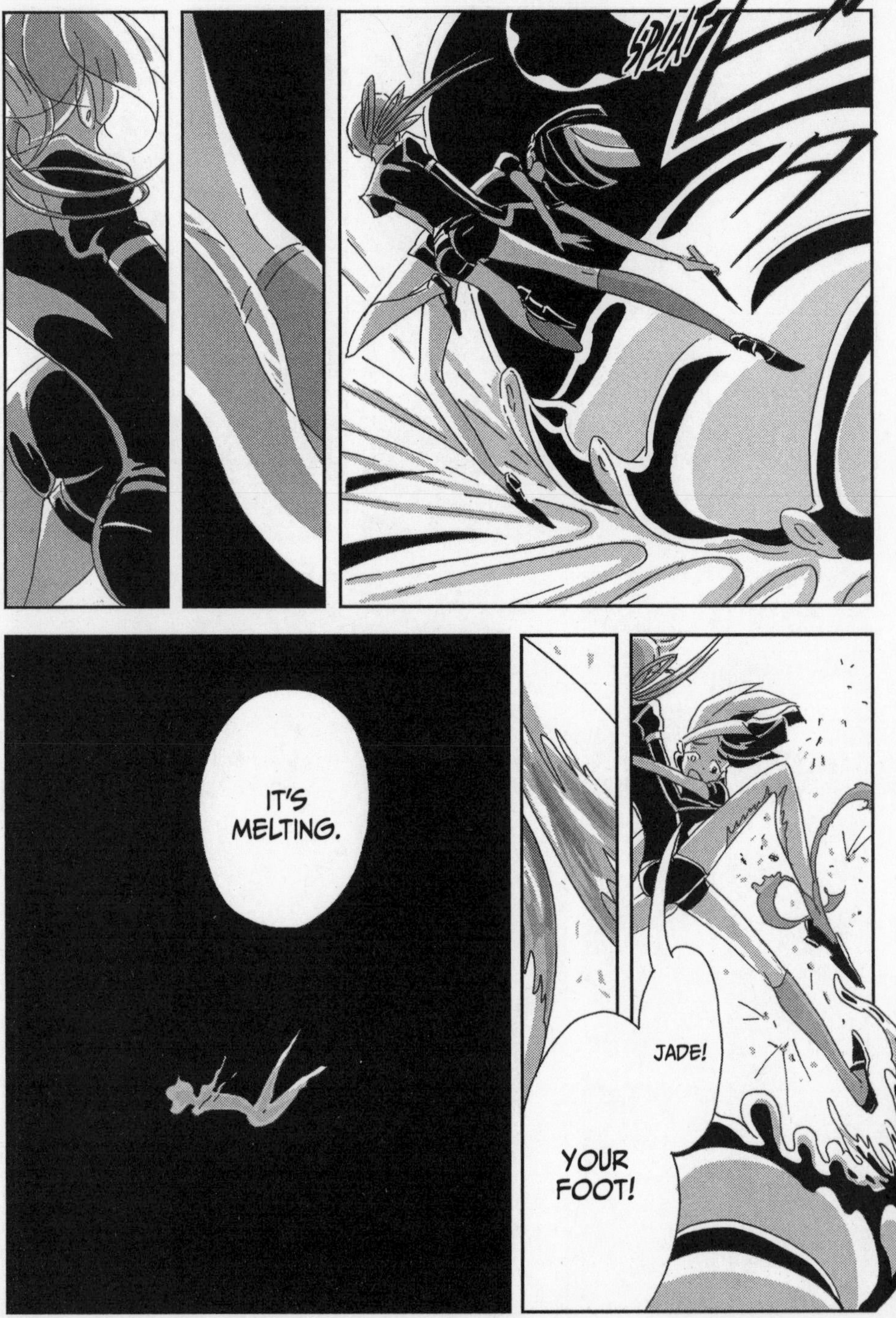
SPLAT
JADE!
YOUR FOOT!
IT'S MELTING.

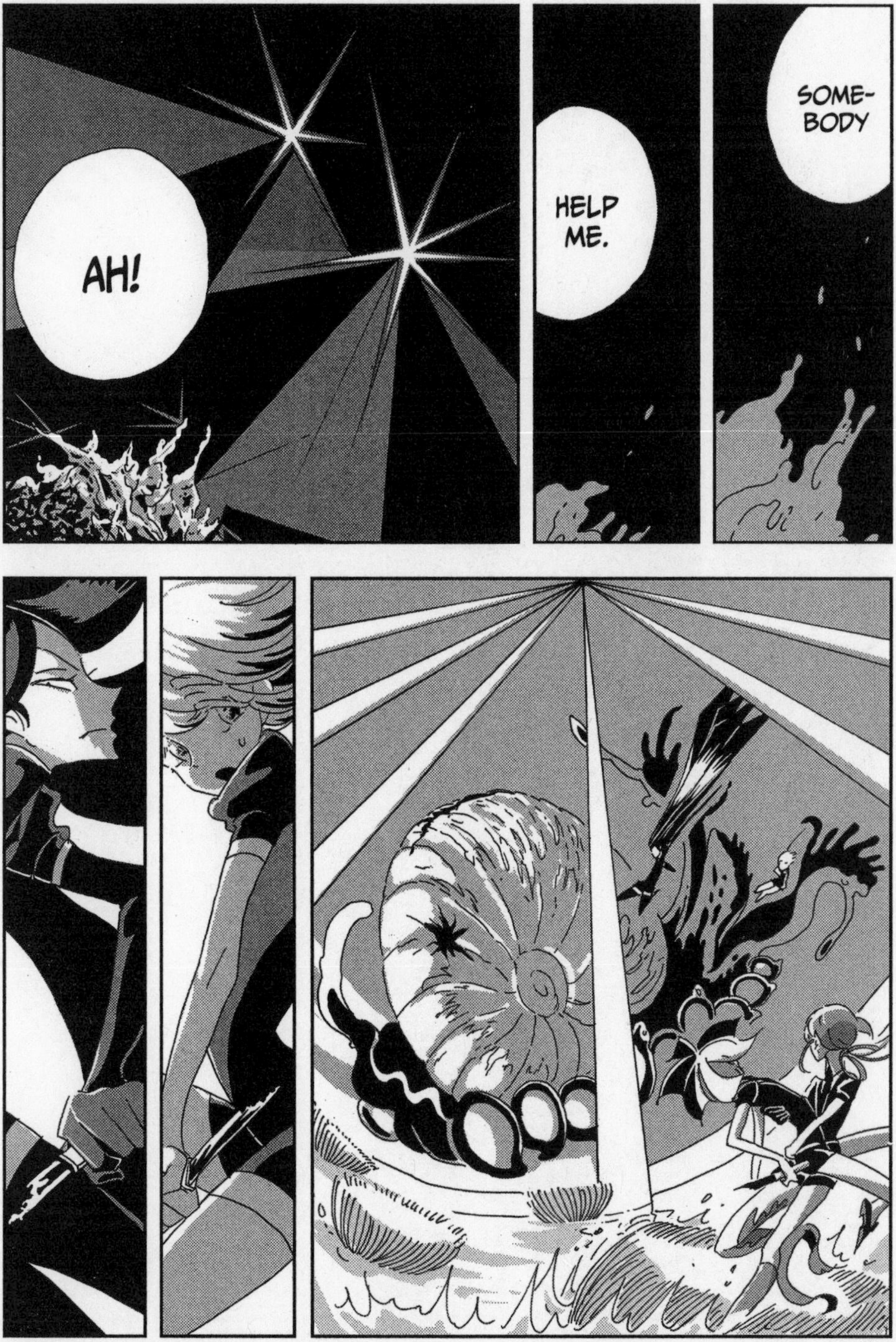
SOME-
BODY
HELP
ME.
AH!

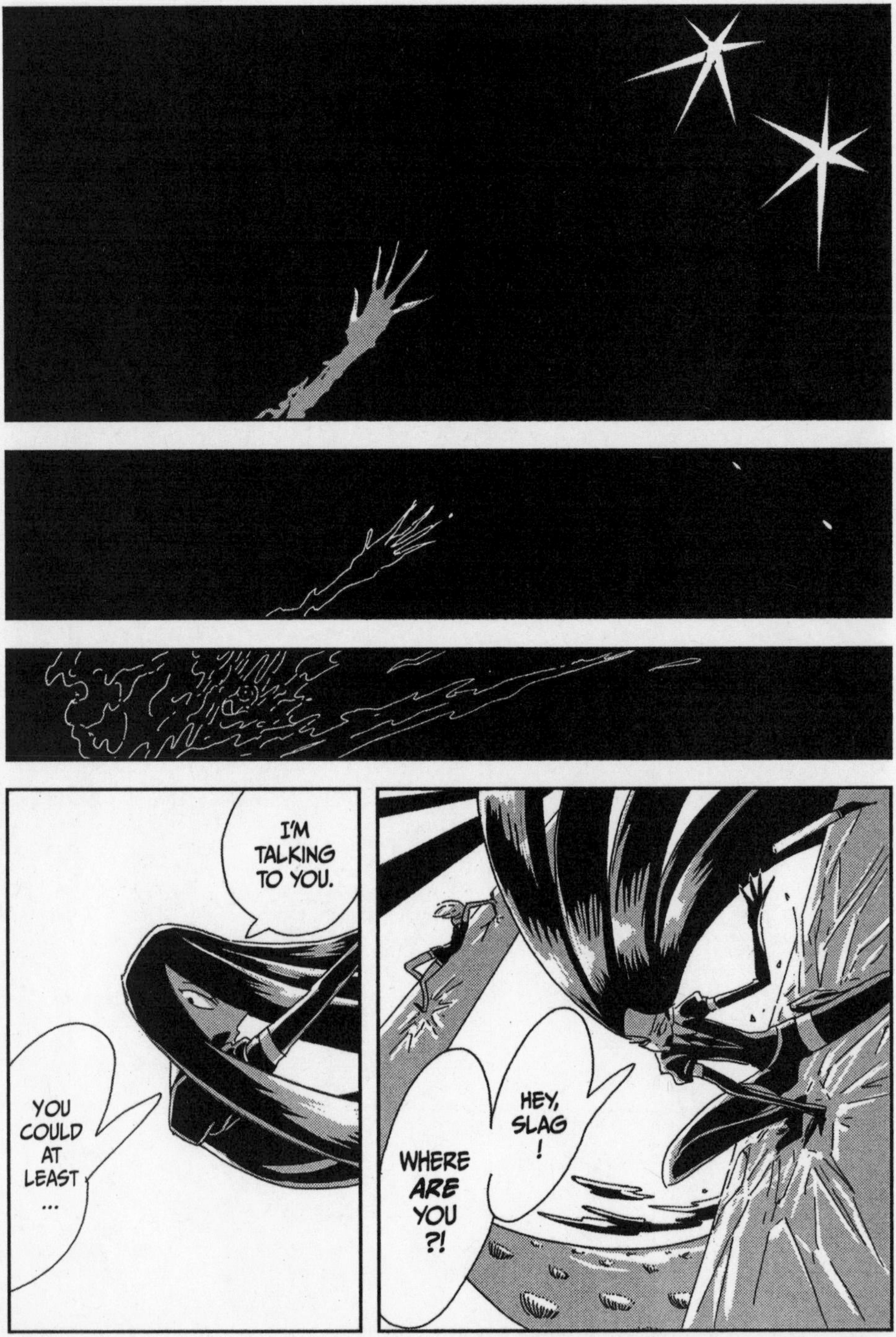
HEY, SLAG!
WHERE ARE YOU?!
I'M TALKING TO YOU.
YOU COULD AT LEAST...

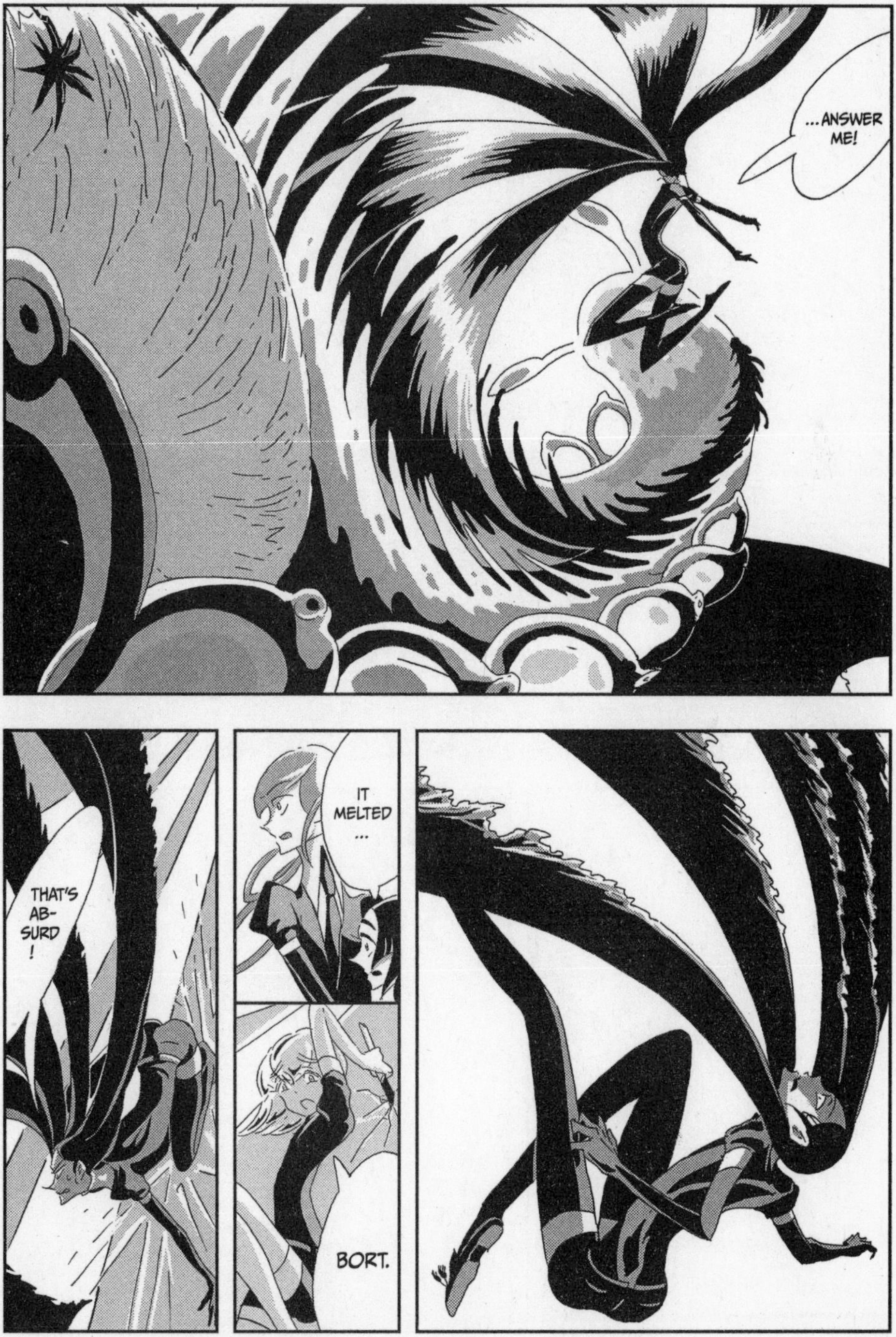
...ANSWER ME!
IT MELTED ...
BORT.
THAT'S ABSURD!

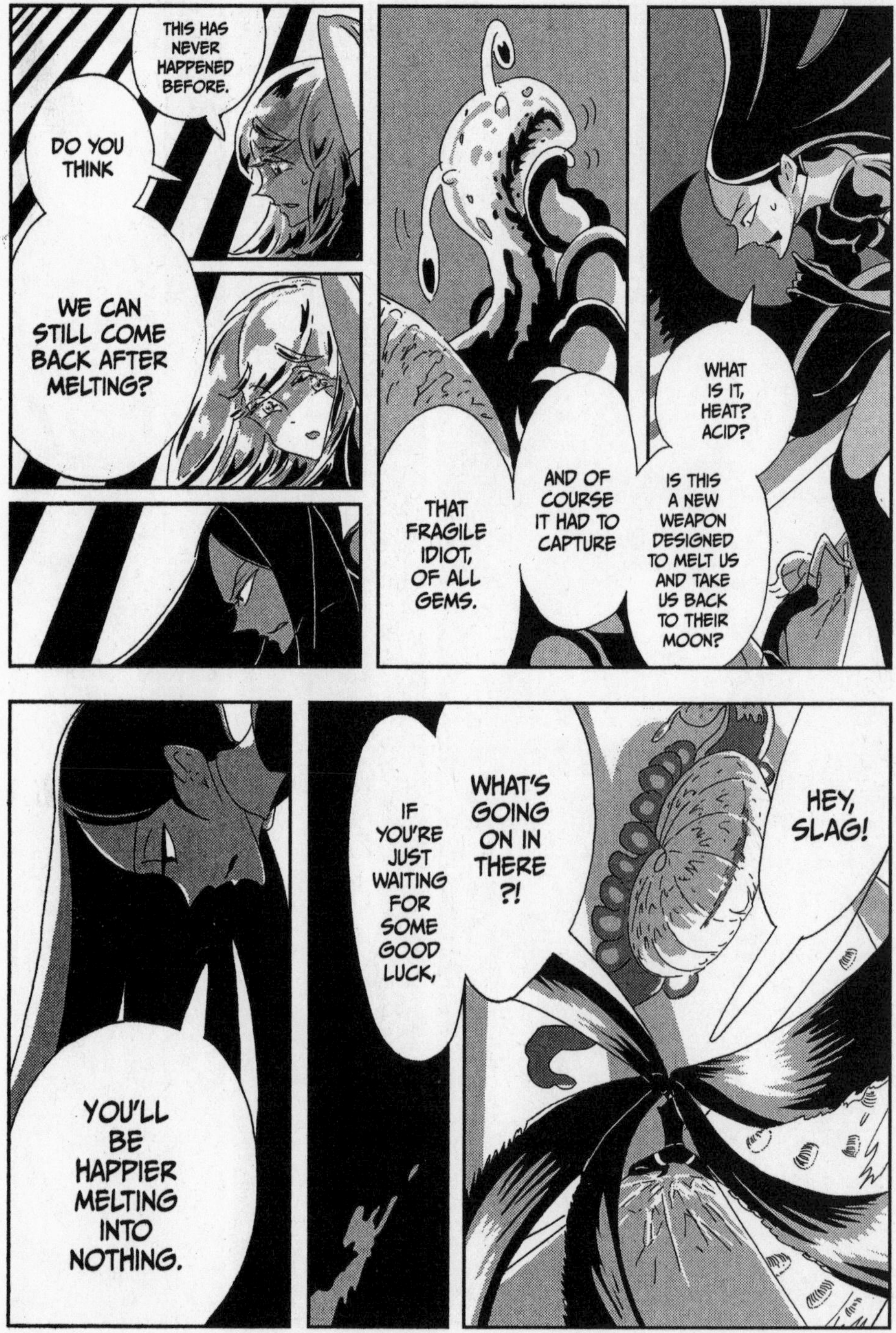
WHAT IS IT, HEAT? ACID?
IS THIS A NEW WEAPON DESIGNED TO MELT US AND TAKE US BACK TO THEIR MOON?
AND OF COURSE IT HAD TO CAPTURE
THAT FRAGILE IDIOT, OF ALL GEMS.
THIS HAS NEVER HAPPENED BEFORE.
DO YOU THINK
WE CAN STILL COME BACK AFTER MELTING?
HEY, SLAG!
WHAT'S GOING ON IN THERE?!
IF YOU'RE JUST WAITING FOR SOME GOOD LUCK,
YOU'LL BE HAPPIER MELTING INTO NOTHING.

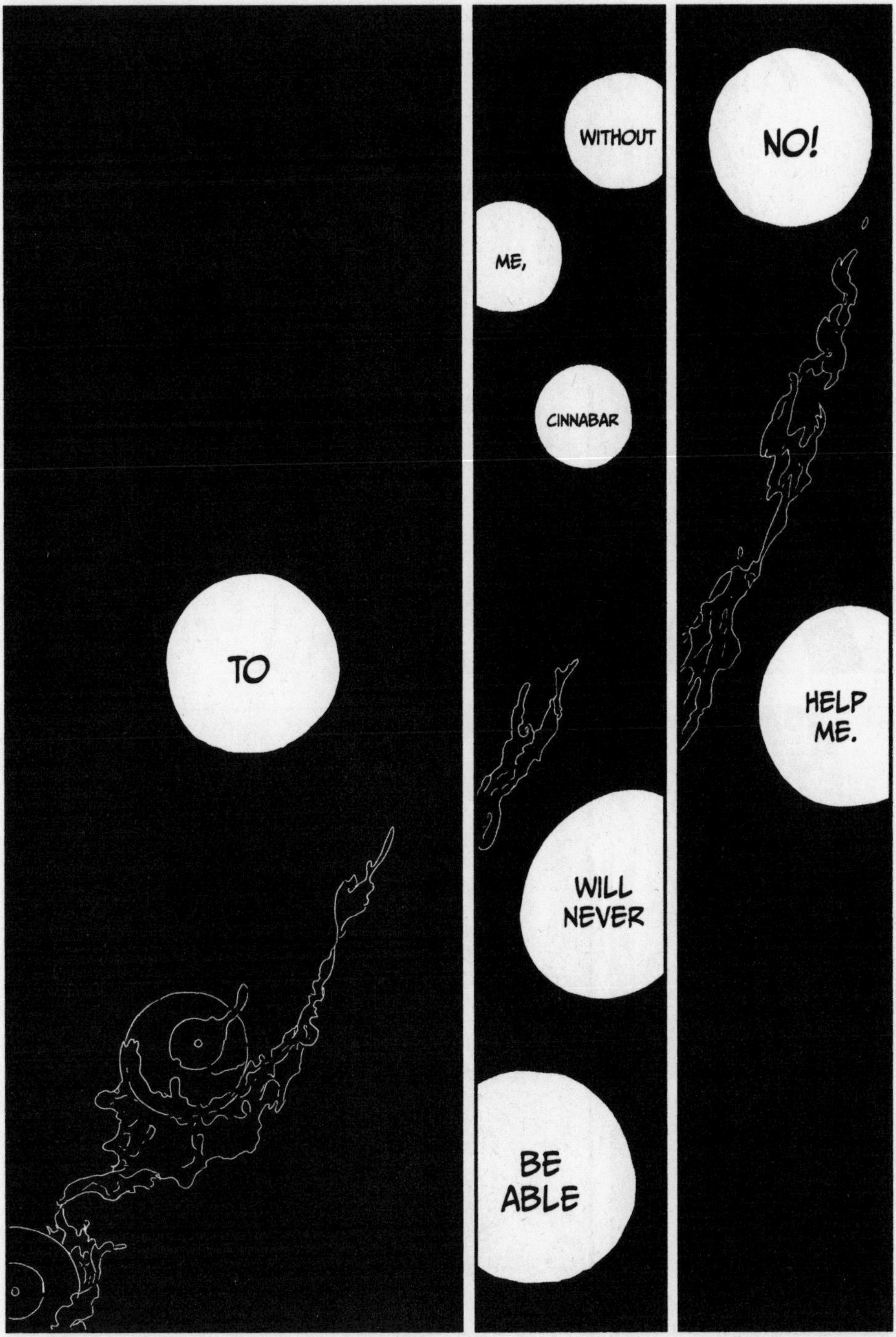
NO!
HELP ME.
WITHOUT
ME,
CINNABAR
WILL NEVER
BE ABLE
TO

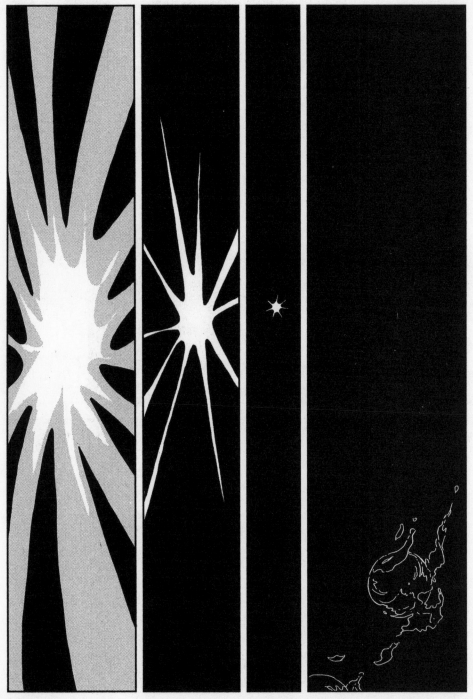

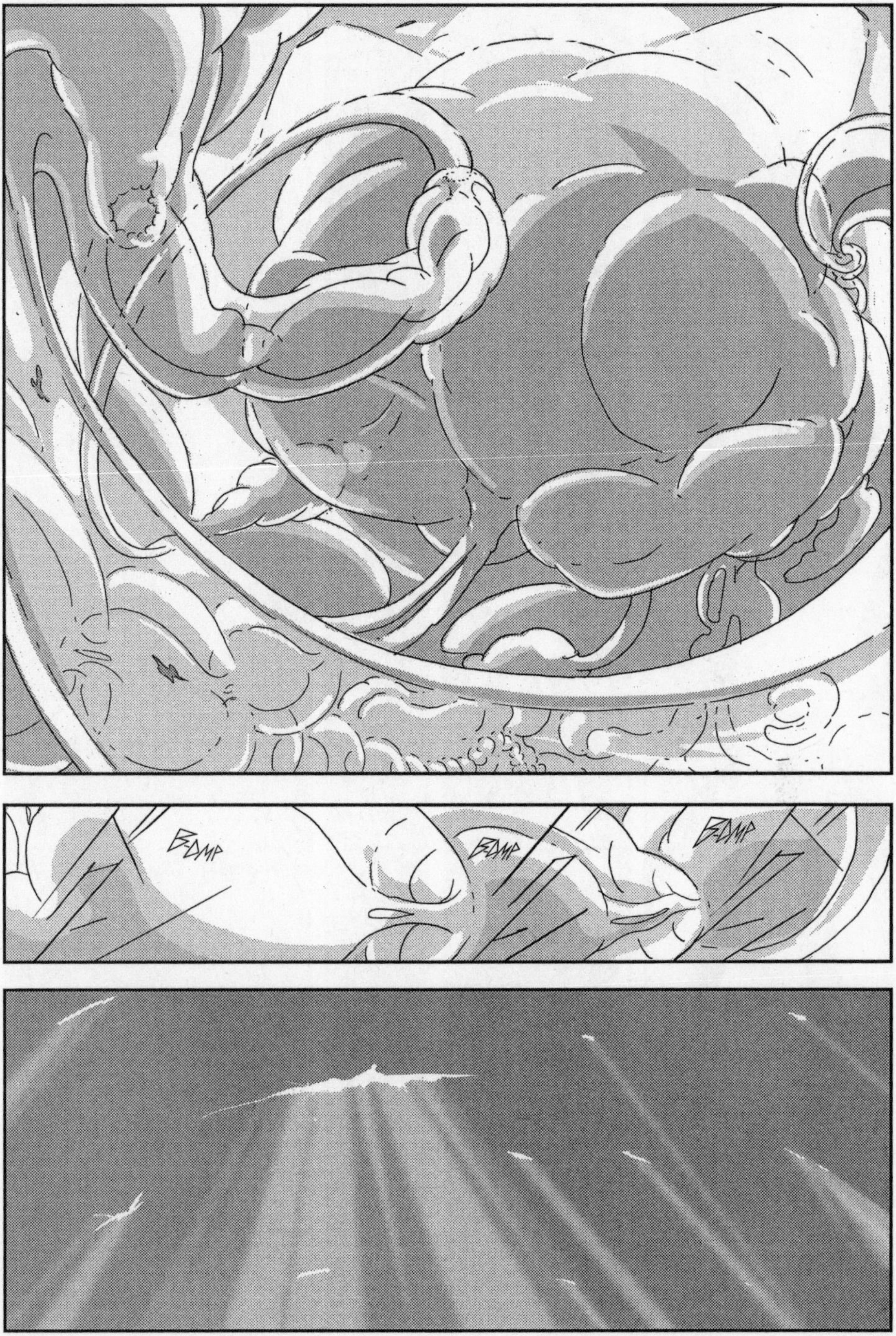
B-DMP
B-DMP
B-DMP

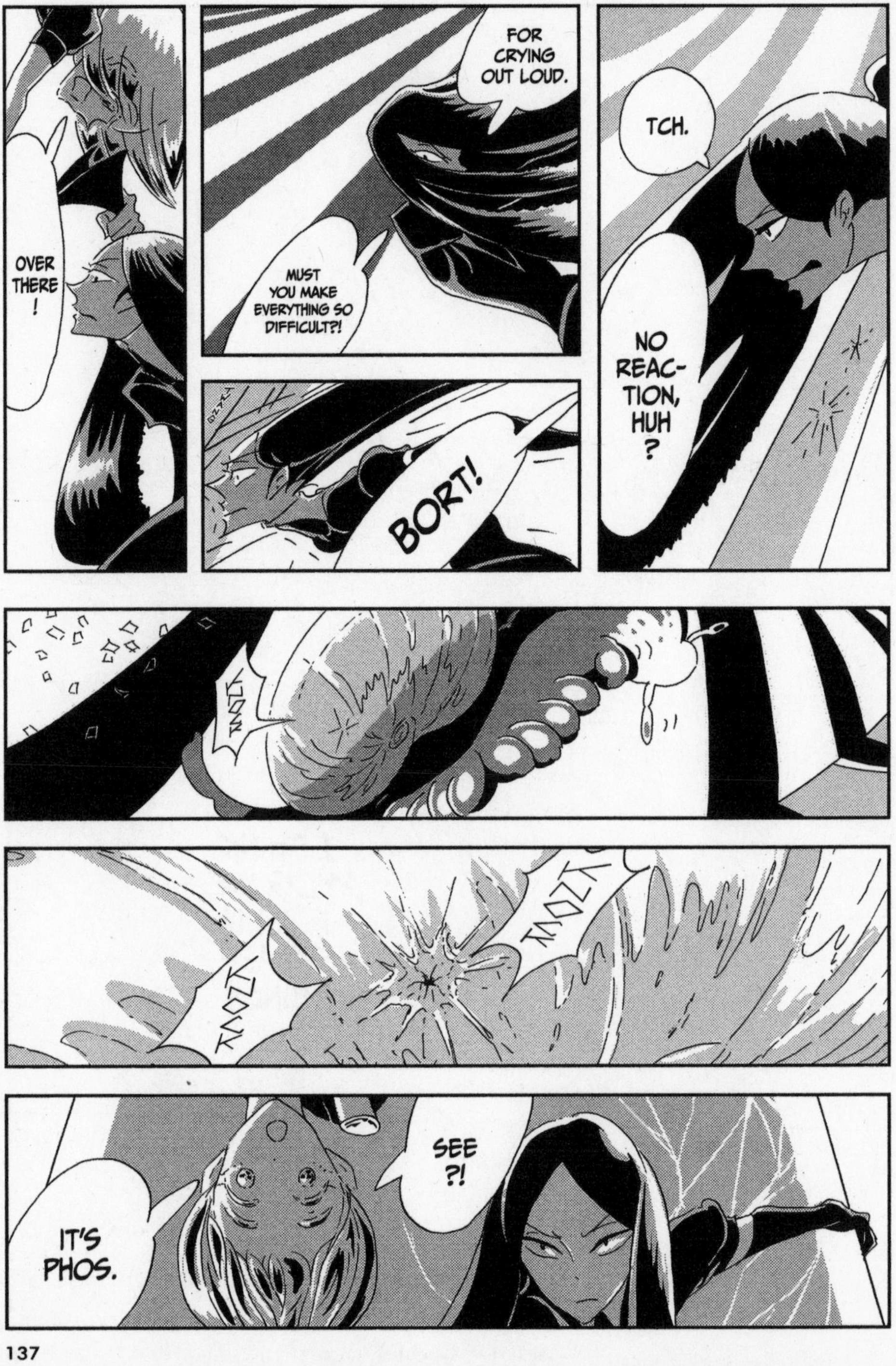
TCH.
NO REACTION, HUH?
FOR CRYING OUT LOUD.
MUST YOU MAKE EVERYTHING SO DIFFICULT?!
BORT!
OVER THERE!
KLOCK
KLOCK
KLOCK
SEE?!
IT'S PHOS.

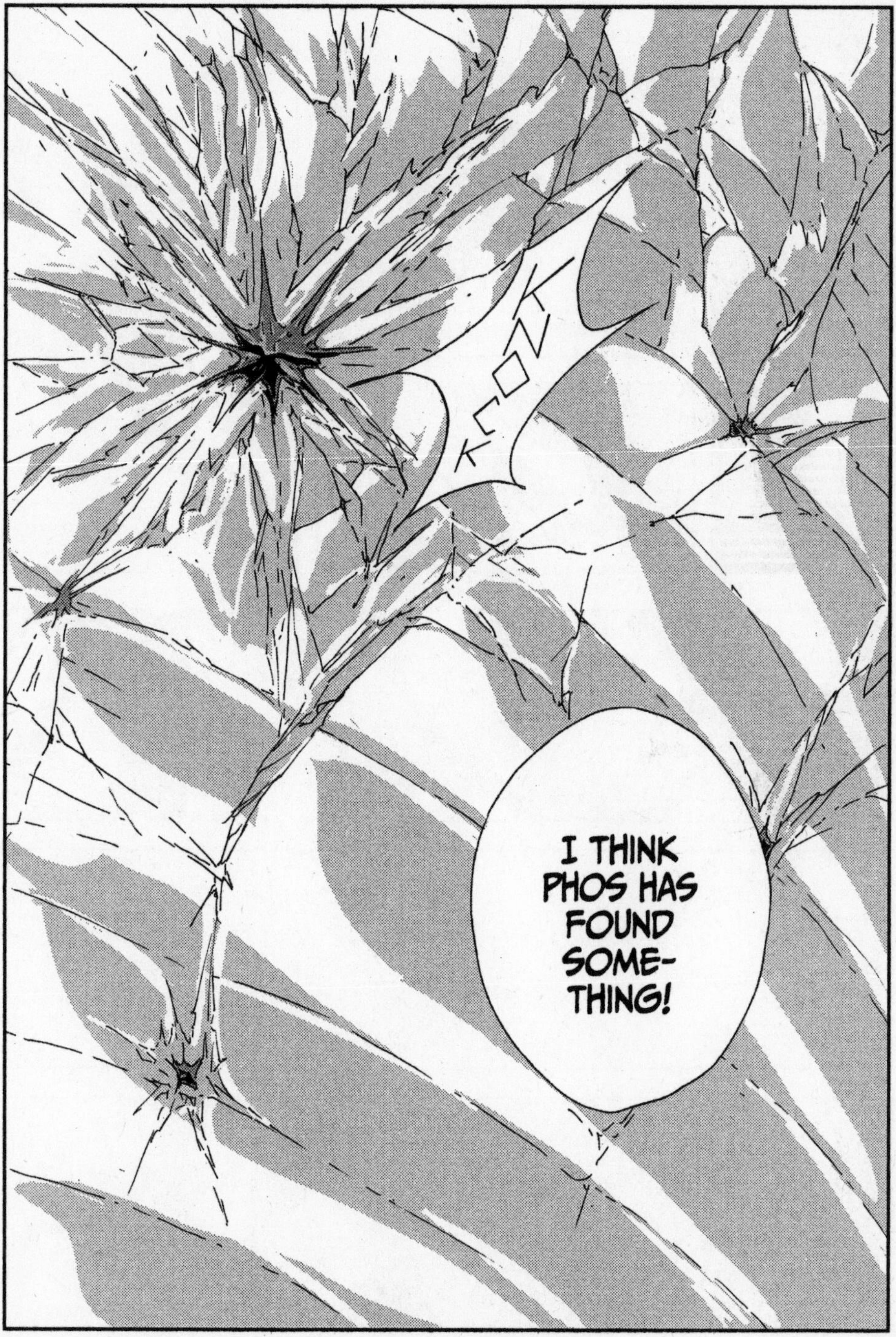
KCONK
I THINK PHOS HAS FOUND SOME-THING!

CHAPTER 4: Cochlea END

CHAPTER 5:

Metamorphosis

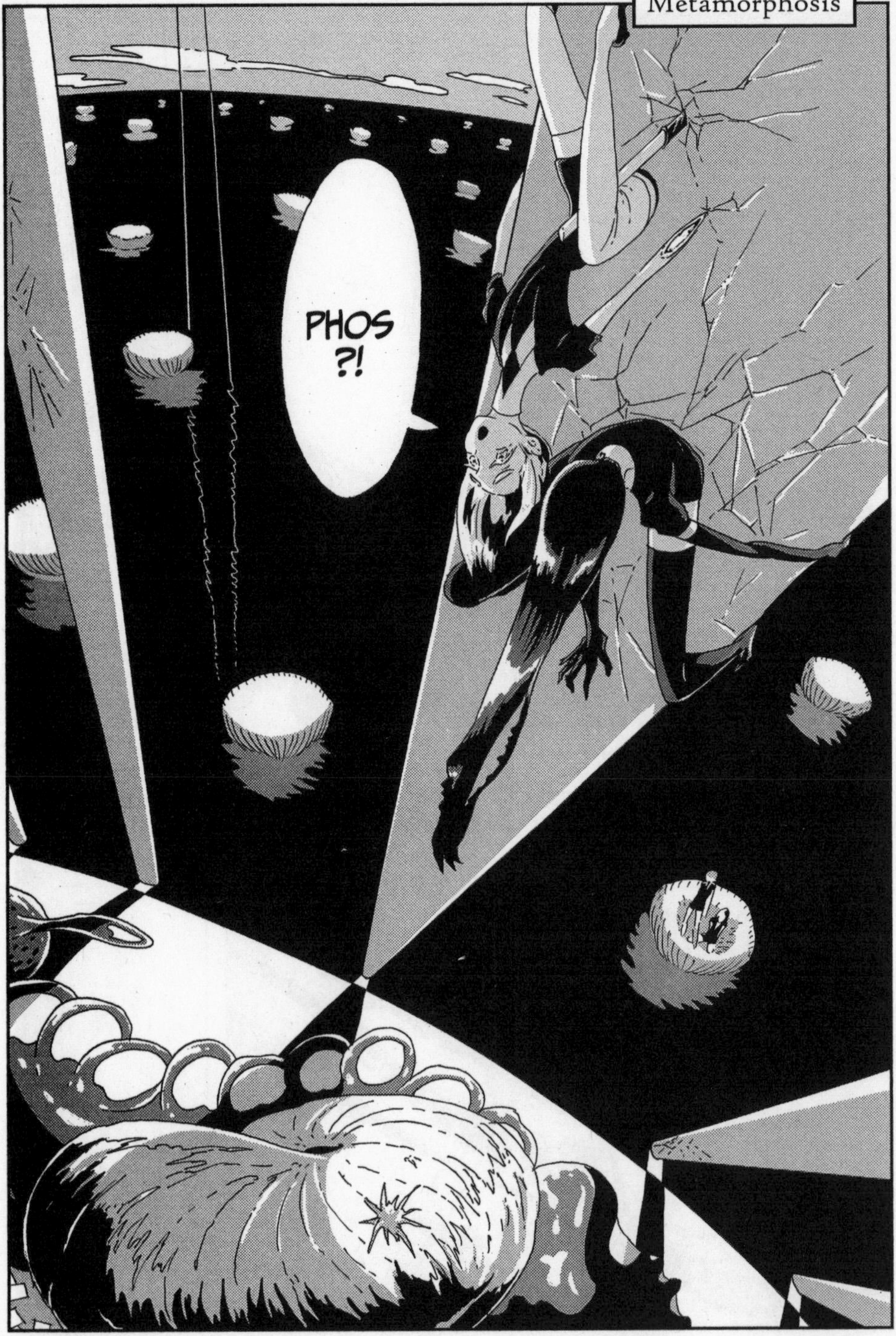
PHOS ?!

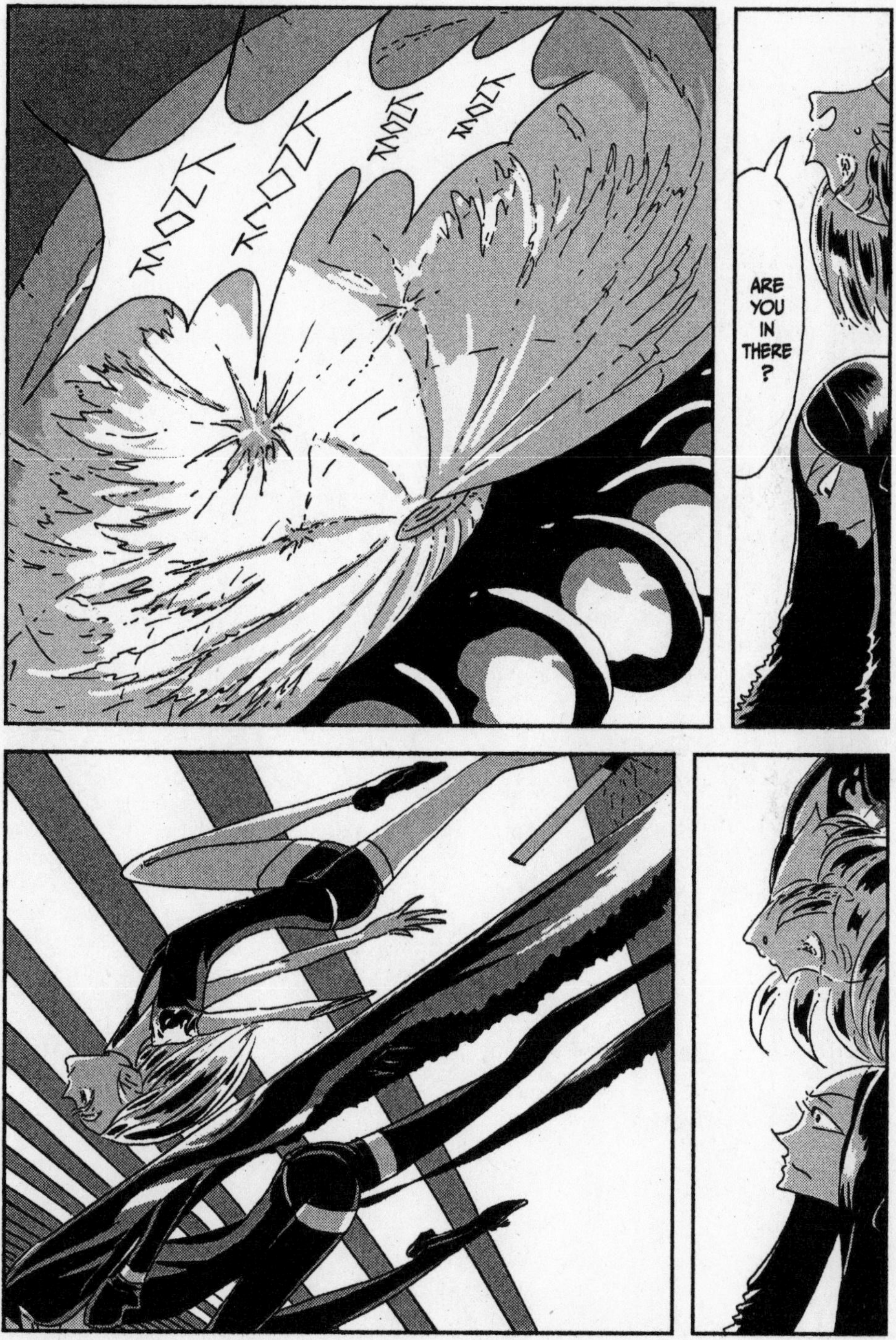
ARE YOU IN THERE ?
KNOCK
KNOCK
KNOCK
KNOCK

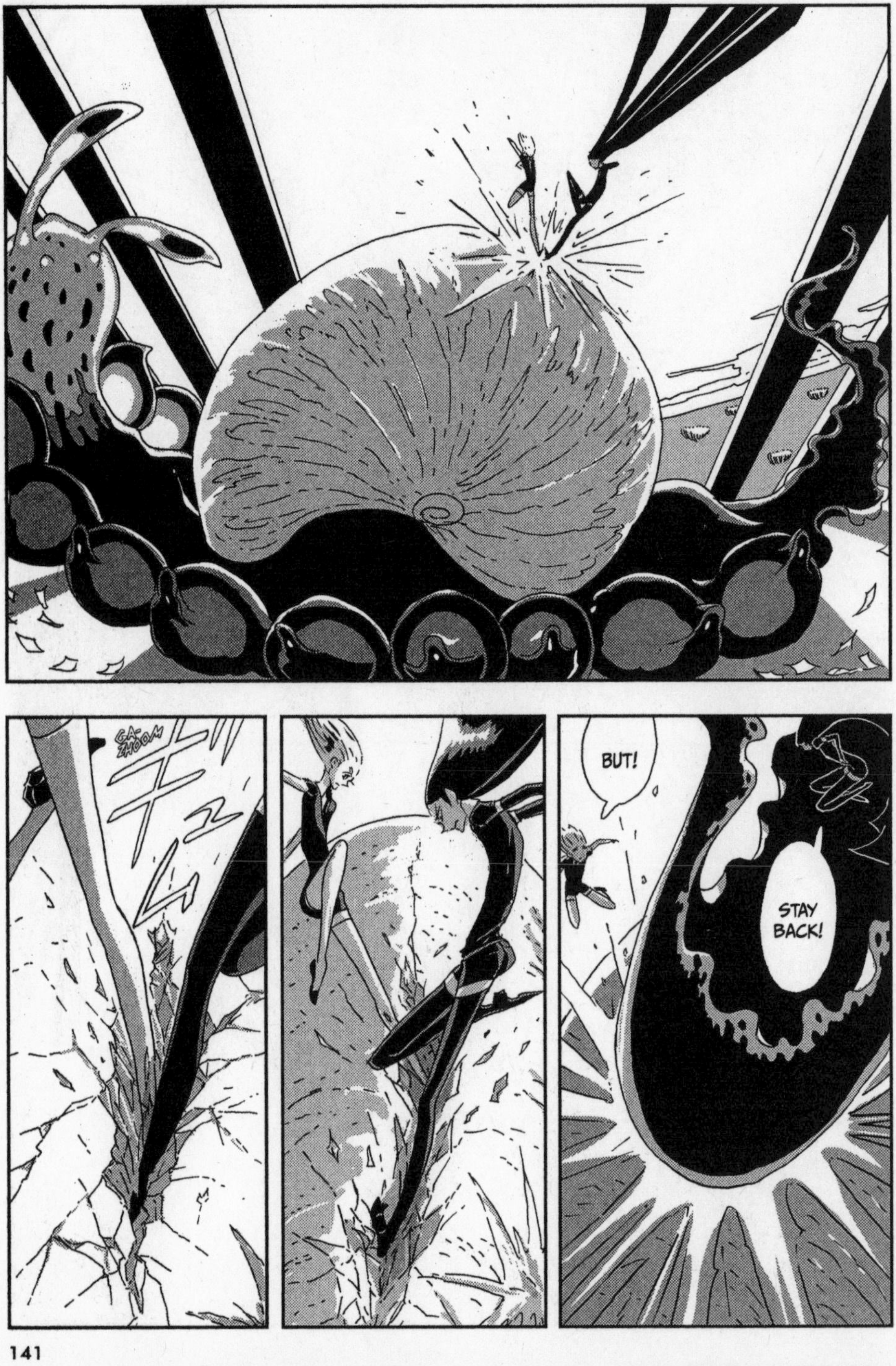
BUT!
STAY BACK!
GA-ZHOOM

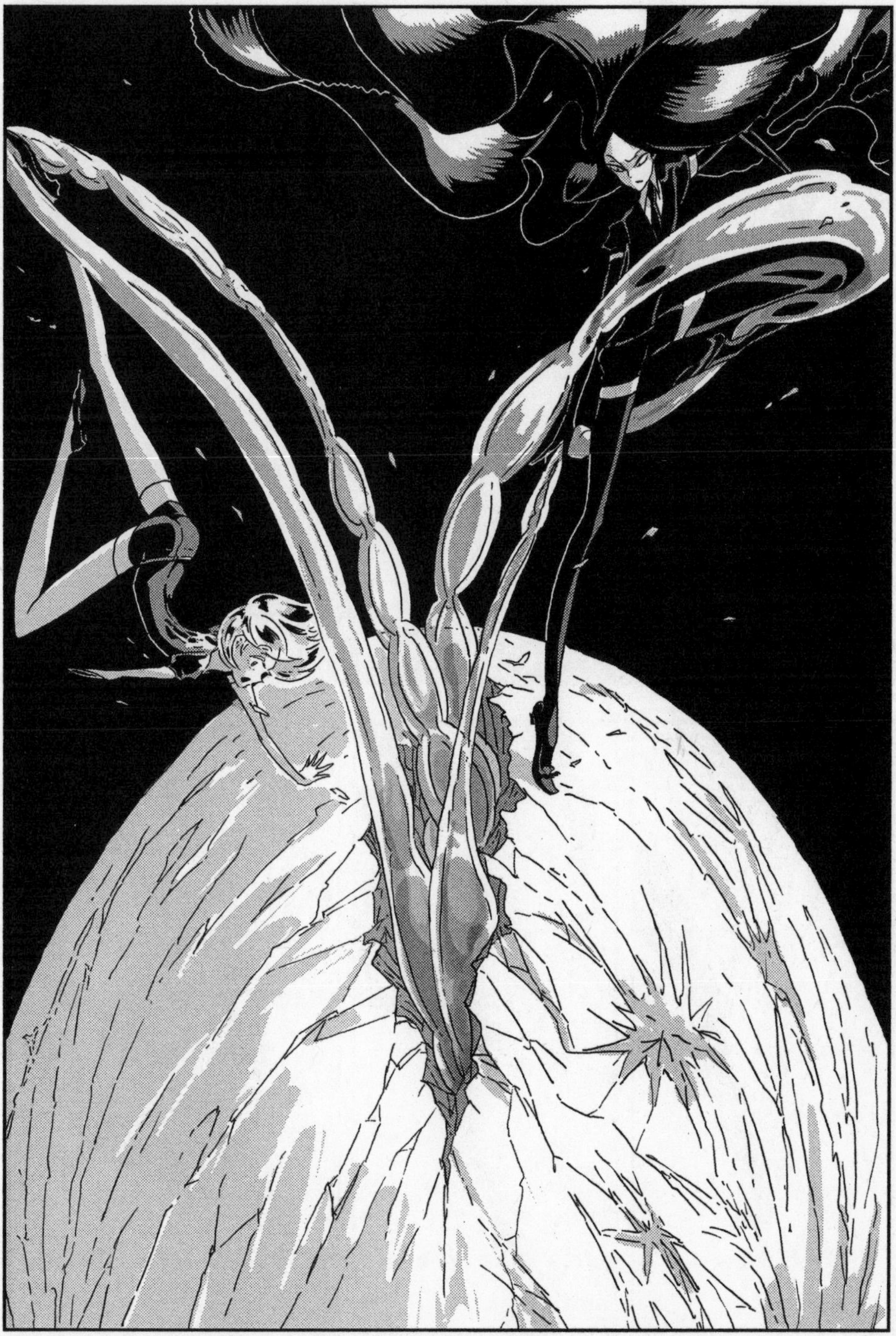

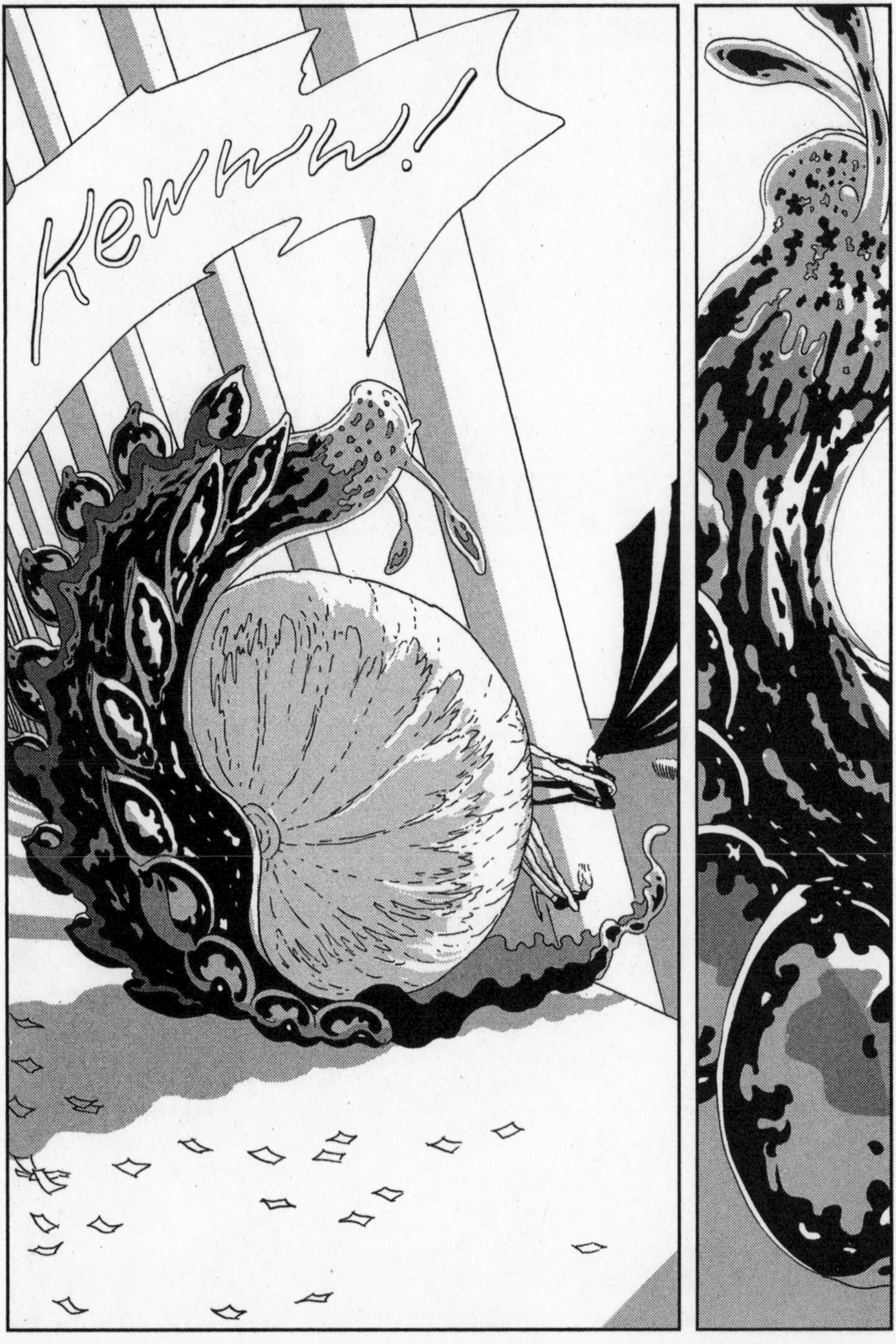
Kewww!

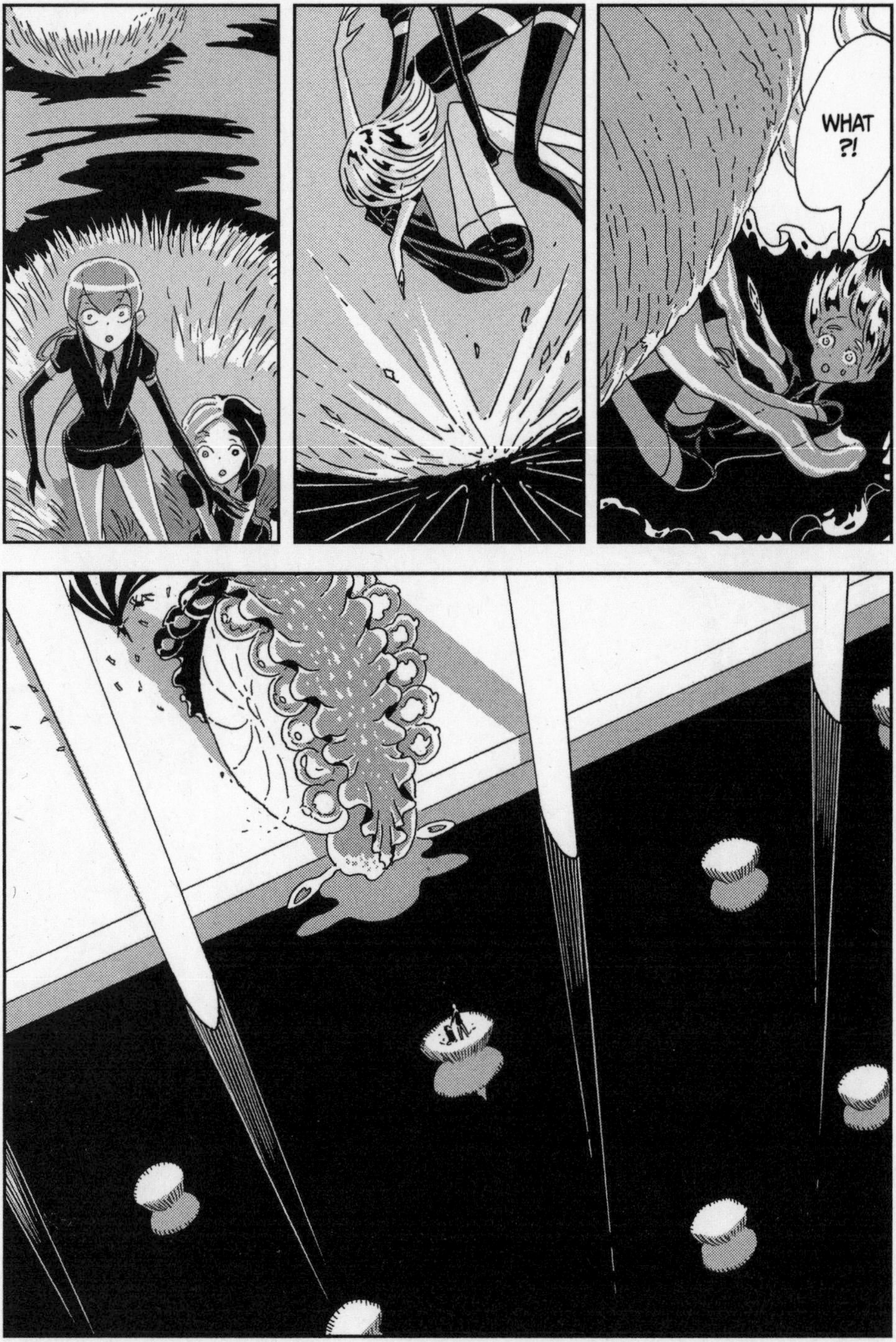
WHAT ?!

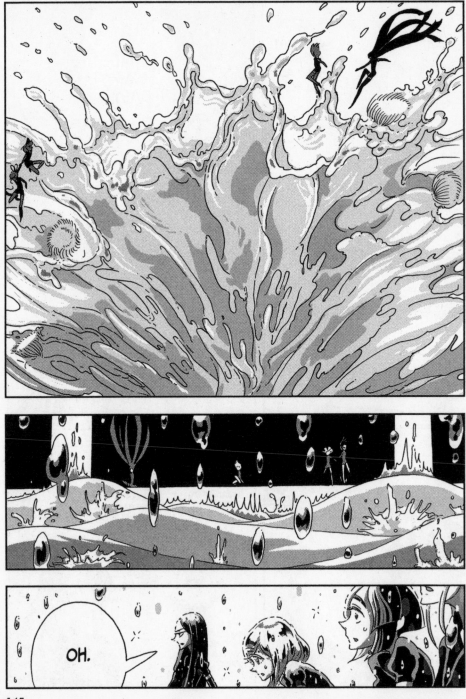

OH.

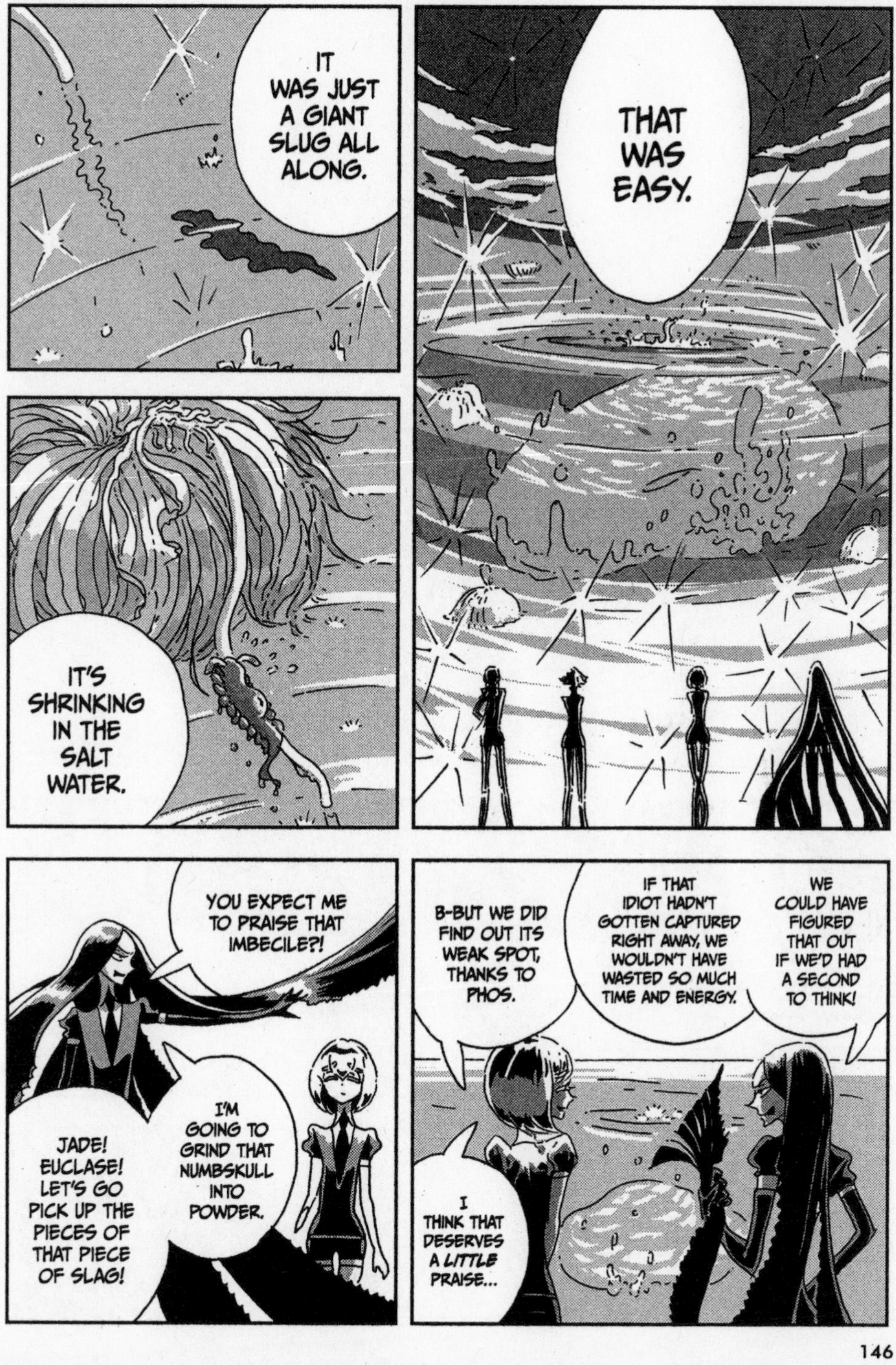
THAT WAS EASY.
IT WAS JUST A GIANT SLUG ALL ALONG.
IT'S SHRINKING IN THE SALT WATER.
WE COULD HAVE FIGURED THAT OUT IF WE'D HAD A SECOND TO THINK!
IF THAT IDIOT HADN'T GOTTEN CAPTURED RIGHT AWAY, WE WOULDN'T HAVE WASTED SO MUCH TIME AND ENERGY.
B-BUT WE DID FIND OUT ITS WEAK SPOT, THANKS TO PHOS.
I THINK THAT DESERVES A *LITTLE* PRAISE...
YOU EXPECT ME TO PRAISE THAT IMBECILE?!
I'M GOING TO GRIND THAT NUMBSKULL INTO POWDER.
JADE! EUCLASE! LET'S GO PICK UP THE PIECES OF THAT PIECE OF SLAG!

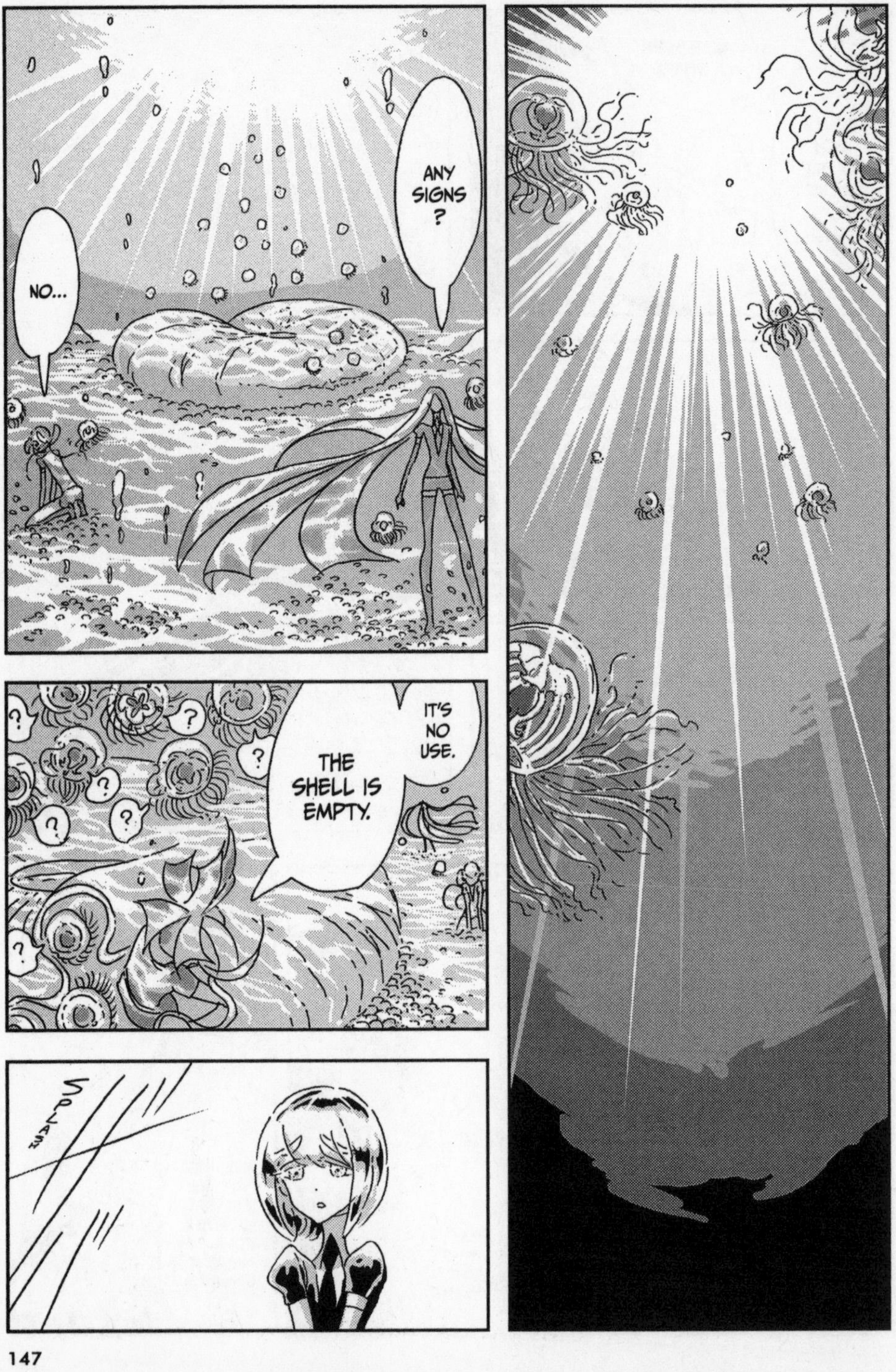
ANY SIGNS ?
NO...
IT'S NO USE.
THE SHELL IS EMPTY.
?
?
?
?
?
?
SPLASH

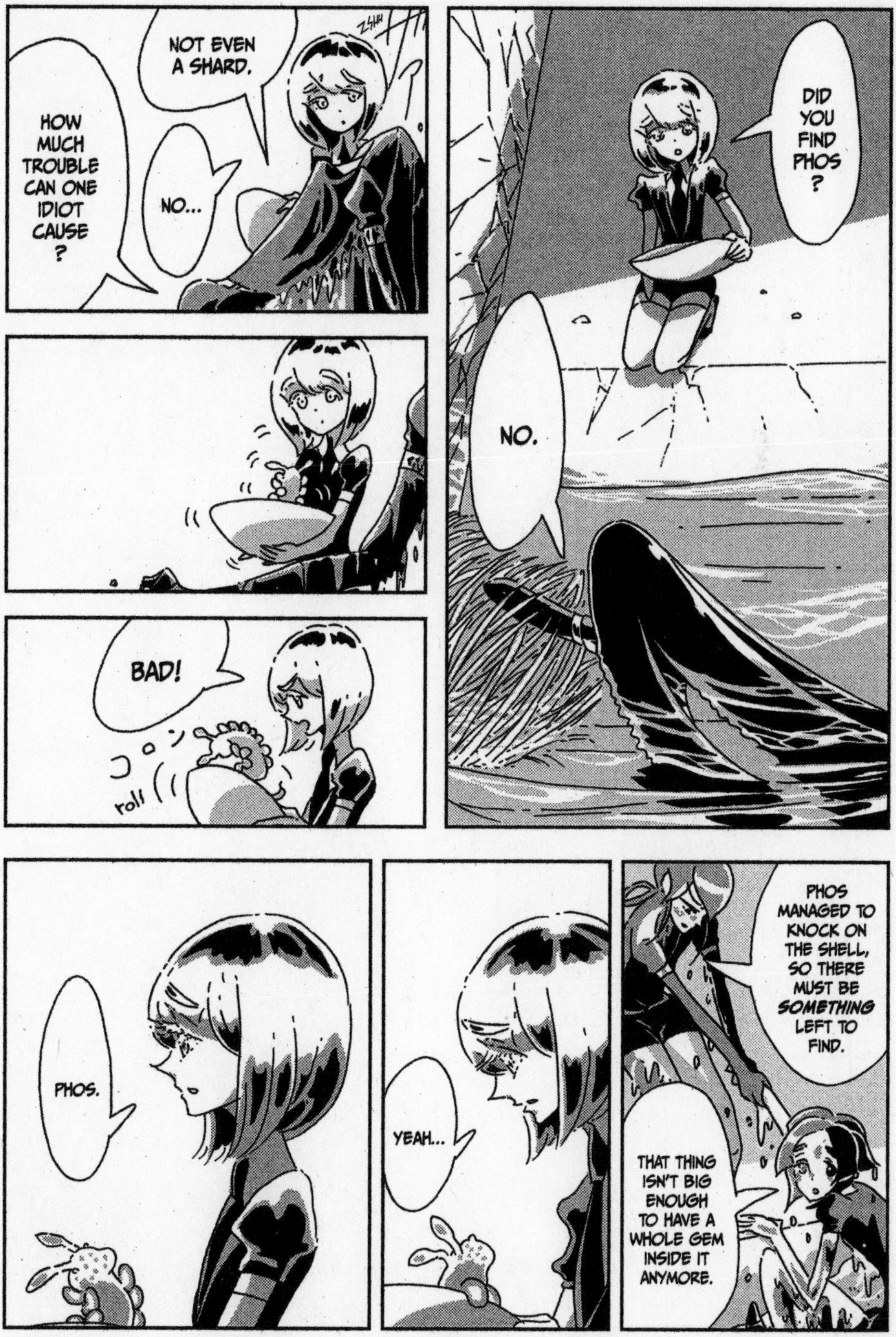
DID YOU FIND PHOS?
NO.
ZSHH
NOT EVEN A SHARD.
HOW MUCH TROUBLE CAN ONE IDIOT CAUSE?
NO...
BAD!
コロン
roll
PHOS MANAGED TO KNOCK ON THE SHELL, SO THERE MUST BE ***SOMETHING*** LEFT TO FIND.
THAT THING ISN'T BIG ENOUGH TO HAVE A WHOLE GEM INSIDE IT ANYMORE.
YEAH...
PHOS.

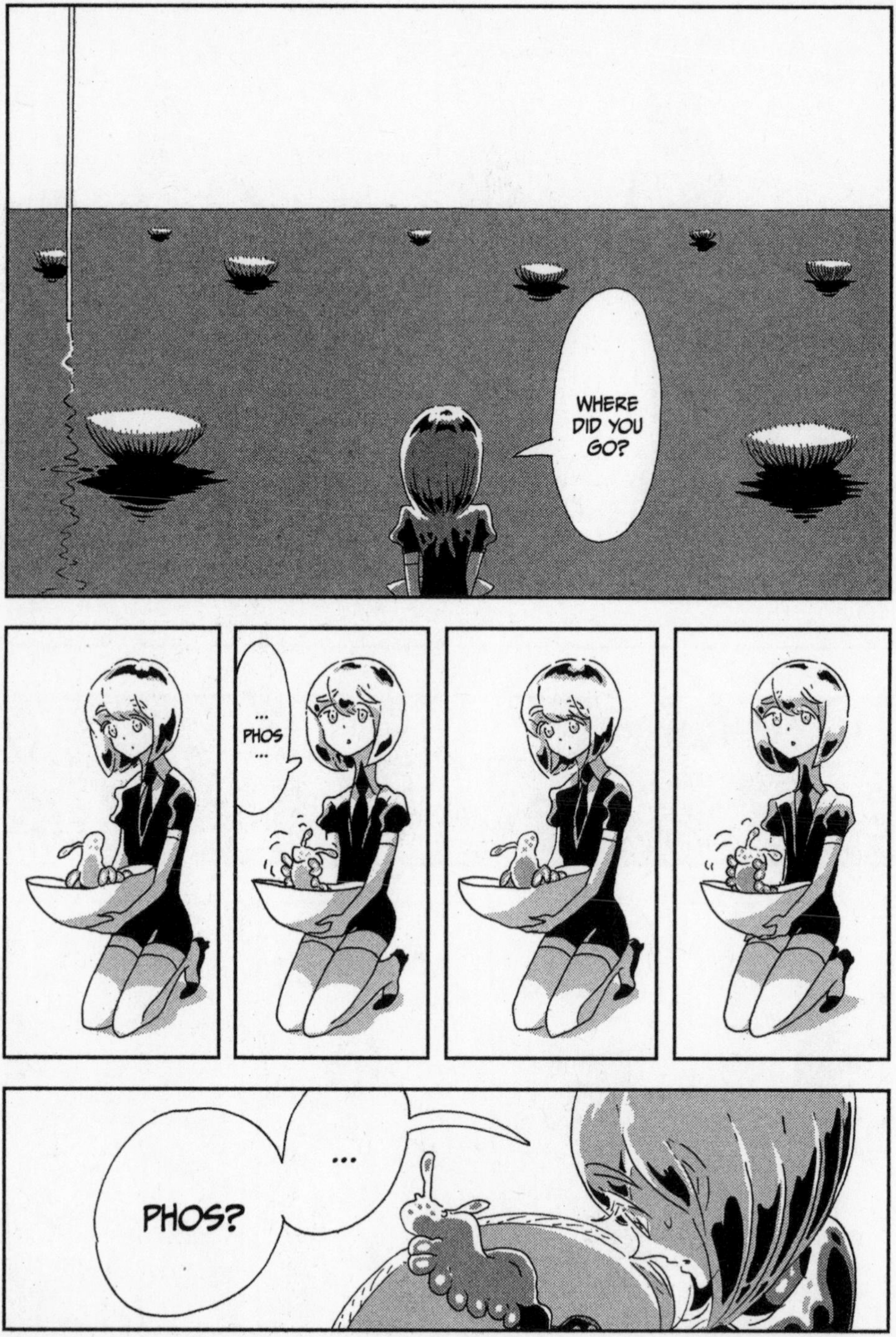
WHERE DID YOU GO?
... PHOS ...
...
PHOS?

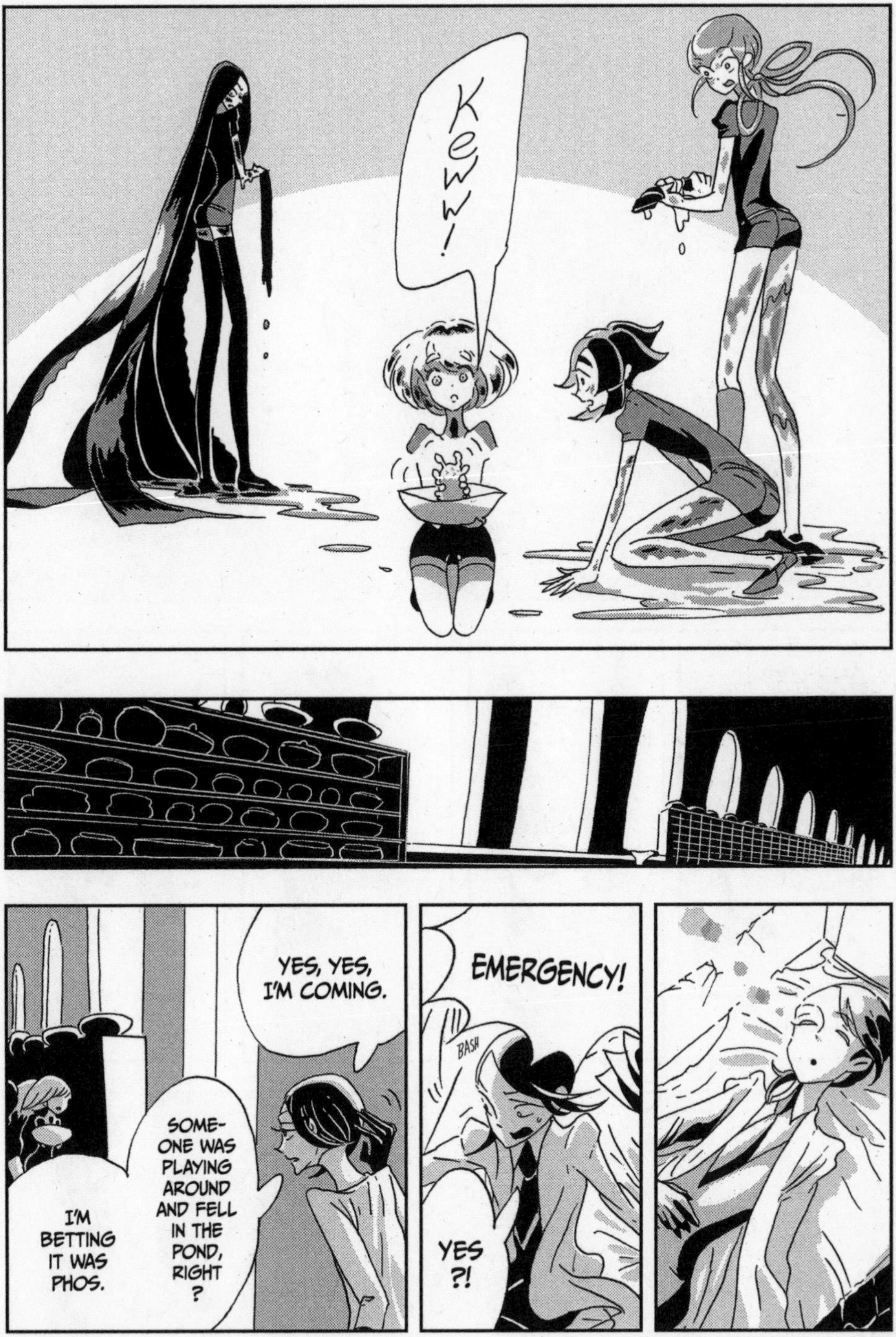
KEWW!
EMERGENCY!
BASH
YES ?!
YES, YES, I'M COMING.
SOME-ONE WAS PLAYING AROUND AND FELL IN THE POND, RIGHT ?
I'M BETTING IT WAS PHOS.

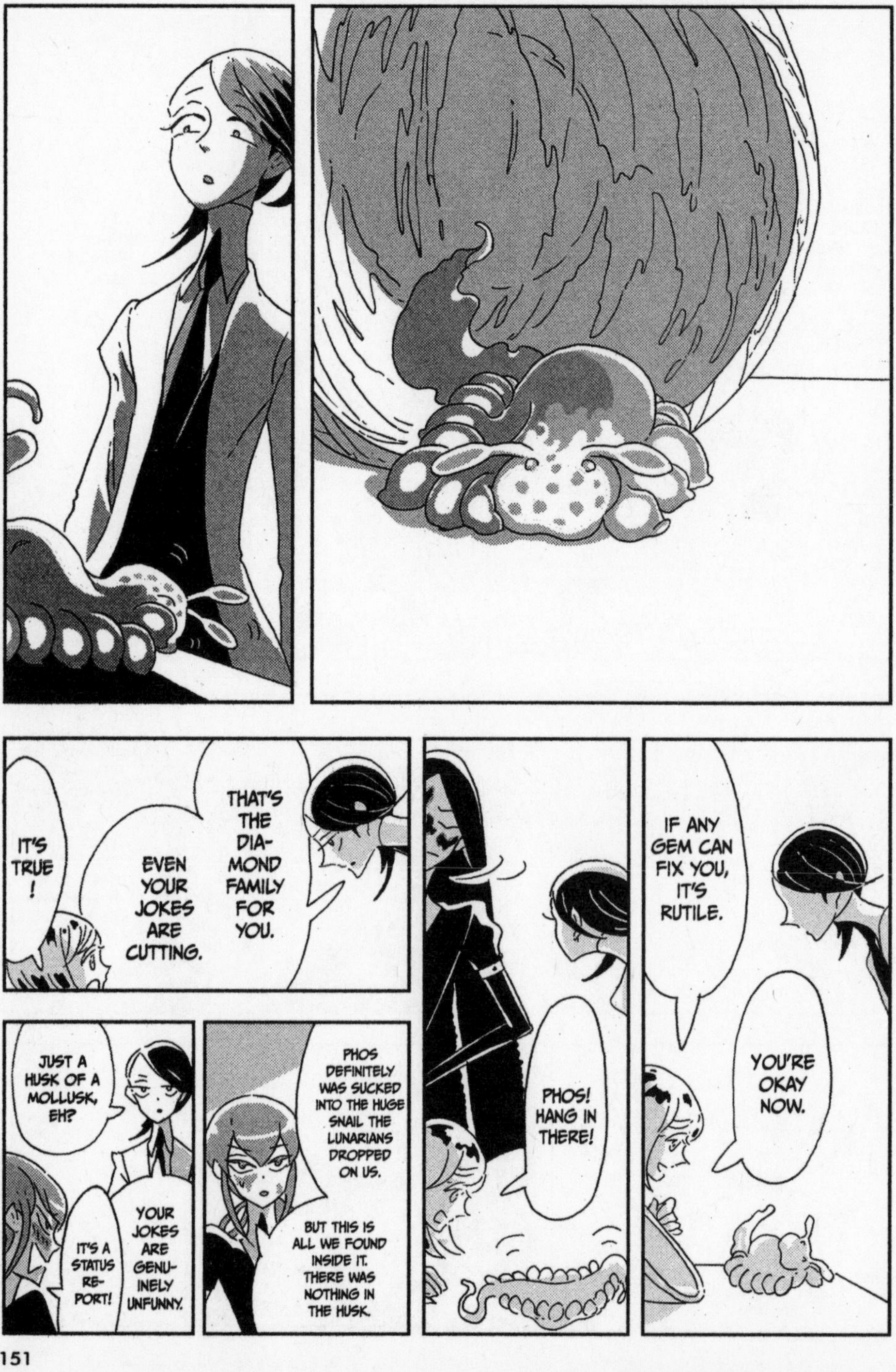
IF ANY GEM CAN FIX YOU, IT'S RUTILE.
YOU'RE OKAY NOW.
PHOS! HANG IN THERE!
THAT'S THE DIA-MOND FAMILY FOR YOU.
EVEN YOUR JOKES ARE CUTTING.
IT'S TRUE!
PHOS DEFINITELY WAS SUCKED INTO THE HUGE SNAIL THE LUNARIANS DROPPED ON US.
BUT THIS IS ALL WE FOUND INSIDE IT. THERE WAS NOTHING IN THE HUSK.
JUST A HUSK OF A MOLLUSK, EH?
YOUR JOKES ARE GENU-INELY UNFUNNY.
IT'S A STATUS RE-PORT!

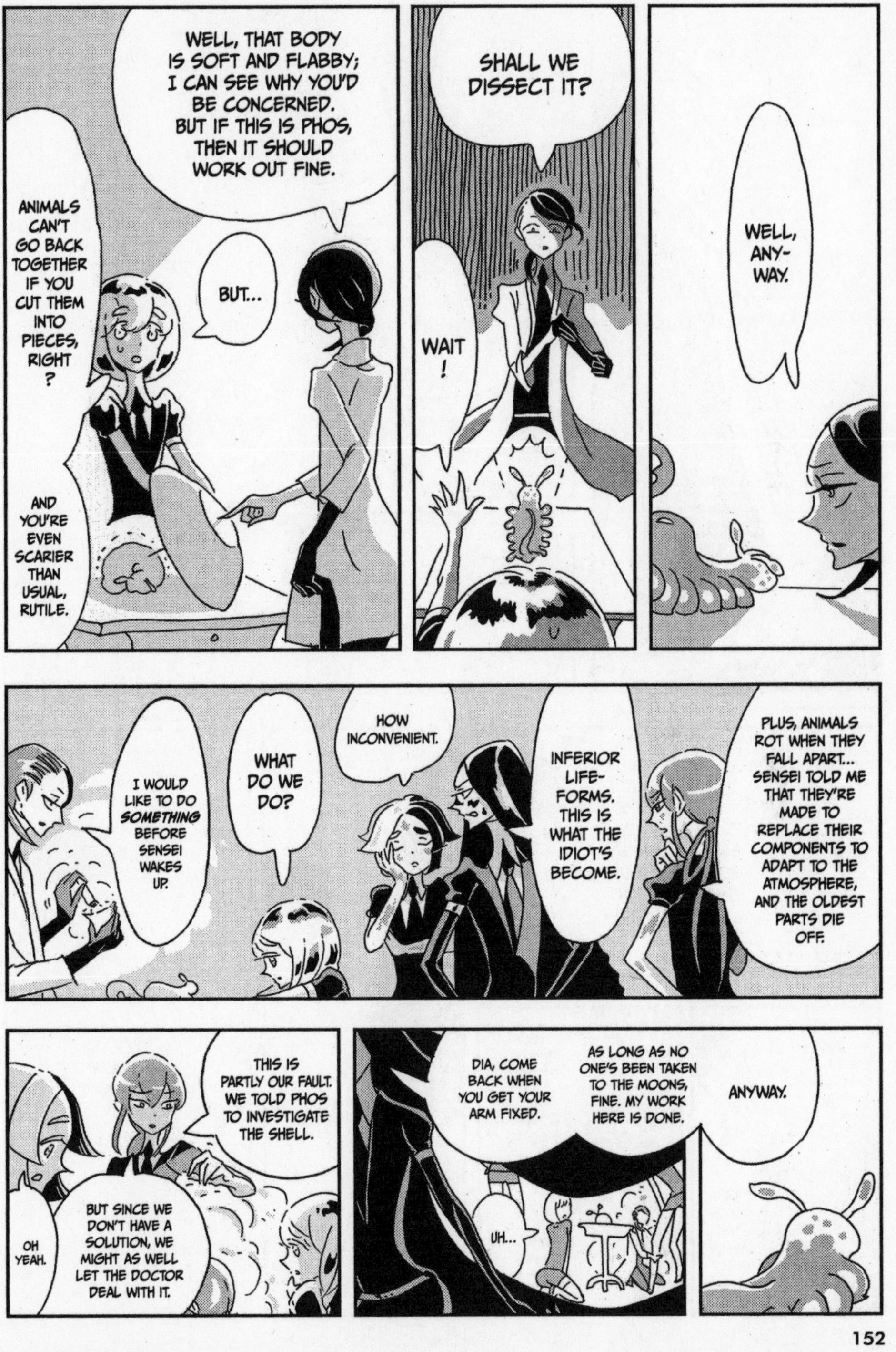
WELL, ANYWAY.
SHALL WE DISSECT IT?
WAIT!
WELL, THAT BODY IS SOFT AND FLABBY; I CAN SEE WHY YOU'D BE CONCERNED. BUT IF THIS IS PHOS, THEN IT SHOULD WORK OUT FINE.
BUT...
ANIMALS CAN'T GO BACK TOGETHER IF YOU CUT THEM INTO PIECES, RIGHT?
AND YOU'RE EVEN SCARIER THAN USUAL, RUTILE.
PLUS, ANIMALS ROT WHEN THEY FALL APART... SENSEI TOLD ME THAT THEY'RE MADE TO REPLACE THEIR COMPONENTS TO ADAPT TO THE ATMOSPHERE, AND THE OLDEST PARTS DIE OFF.
INFERIOR LIFE-FORMS. THIS IS WHAT THE IDIOT'S BECOME.
HOW INCONVENIENT.
WHAT DO WE DO?
I WOULD LIKE TO DO SOMETHING BEFORE SENSEI WAKES UP.
ANYWAY.
AS LONG AS NO ONE'S BEEN TAKEN TO THE MOONS, FINE. MY WORK HERE IS DONE.
DIA, COME BACK WHEN YOU GET YOUR ARM FIXED.
UH...
THIS IS PARTLY OUR FAULT. WE TOLD PHOS TO INVESTIGATE THE SHELL.
BUT SINCE WE DON'T HAVE A SOLUTION, WE MIGHT AS WELL LET THE DOCTOR DEAL WITH IT.
OH YEAH.

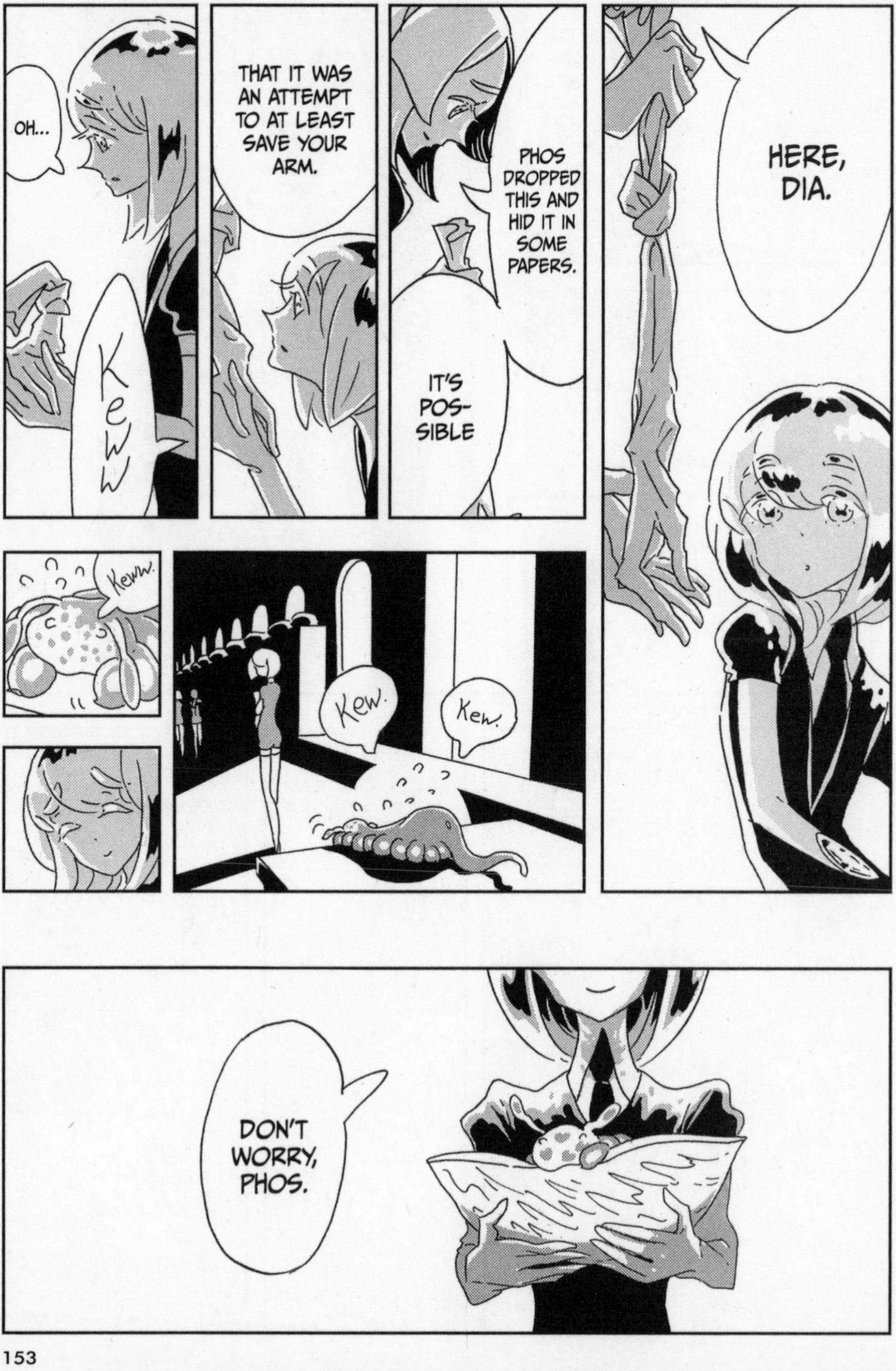
HERE, DIA.
PHOS DROPPED THIS AND HID IT IN SOME PAPERS.
IT'S POS-SIBLE
THAT IT WAS AN ATTEMPT TO AT LEAST SAVE YOUR ARM.
OH...
Keww
Kew.
Kew.
Keww.
DON'T WORRY, PHOS.

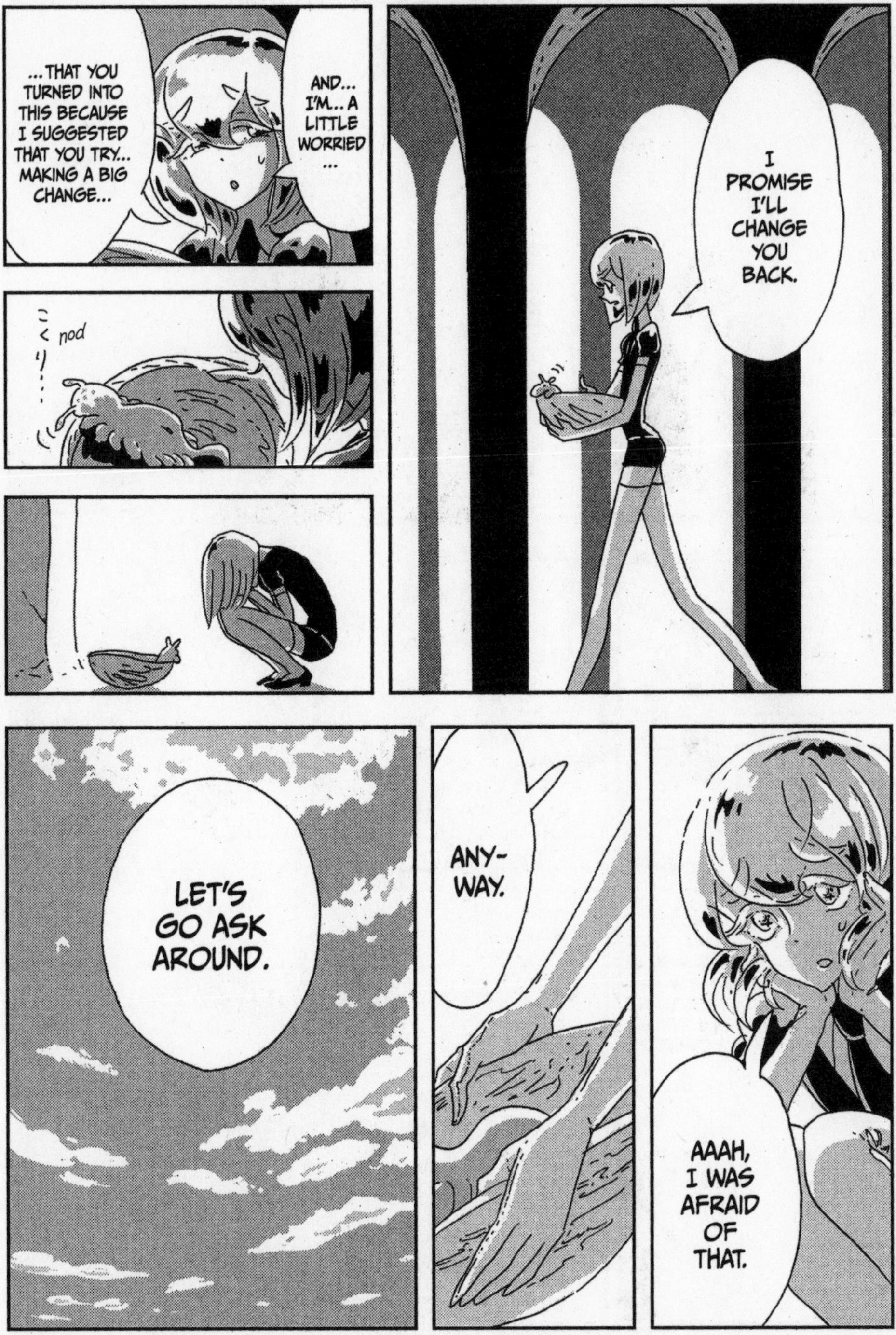
I PROMISE I'LL CHANGE YOU BACK.
AND... I'M... A LITTLE WORRIED ...
...THAT YOU TURNED INTO THIS BECAUSE I SUGGESTED THAT YOU TRY... MAKING A BIG CHANGE...
こくり…
nod
AAAH, I WAS AFRAID OF THAT.
ANY-WAY.
LET'S GO ASK AROUND.

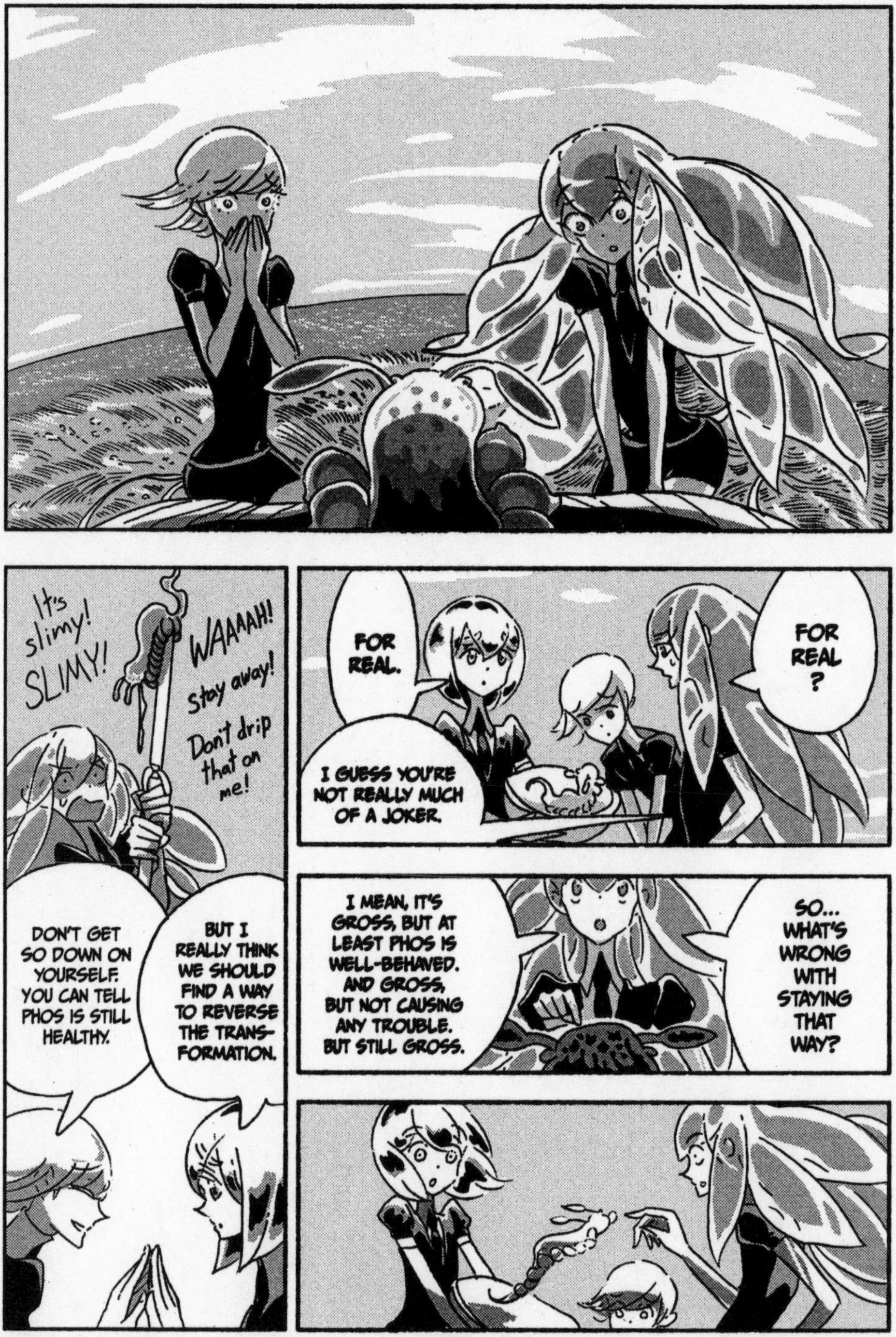
FOR REAL?
FOR REAL.
I GUESS YOU'RE NOT REALLY MUCH OF A JOKER.
SO... WHAT'S WRONG WITH STAYING THAT WAY?
I MEAN, IT'S GROSS, BUT AT LEAST PHOS IS WELL-BEHAVED. AND GROSS, BUT NOT CAUSING ANY TROUBLE. BUT STILL GROSS.
WAAAAH!
Stay away!
Don't drip that on me!
It's slimy! SLIMY!
BUT I REALLY THINK WE SHOULD FIND A WAY TO REVERSE THE TRANS-FORMATION.
DON'T GET SO DOWN ON YOURSELF. YOU CAN TELL PHOS IS STILL HEALTHY.

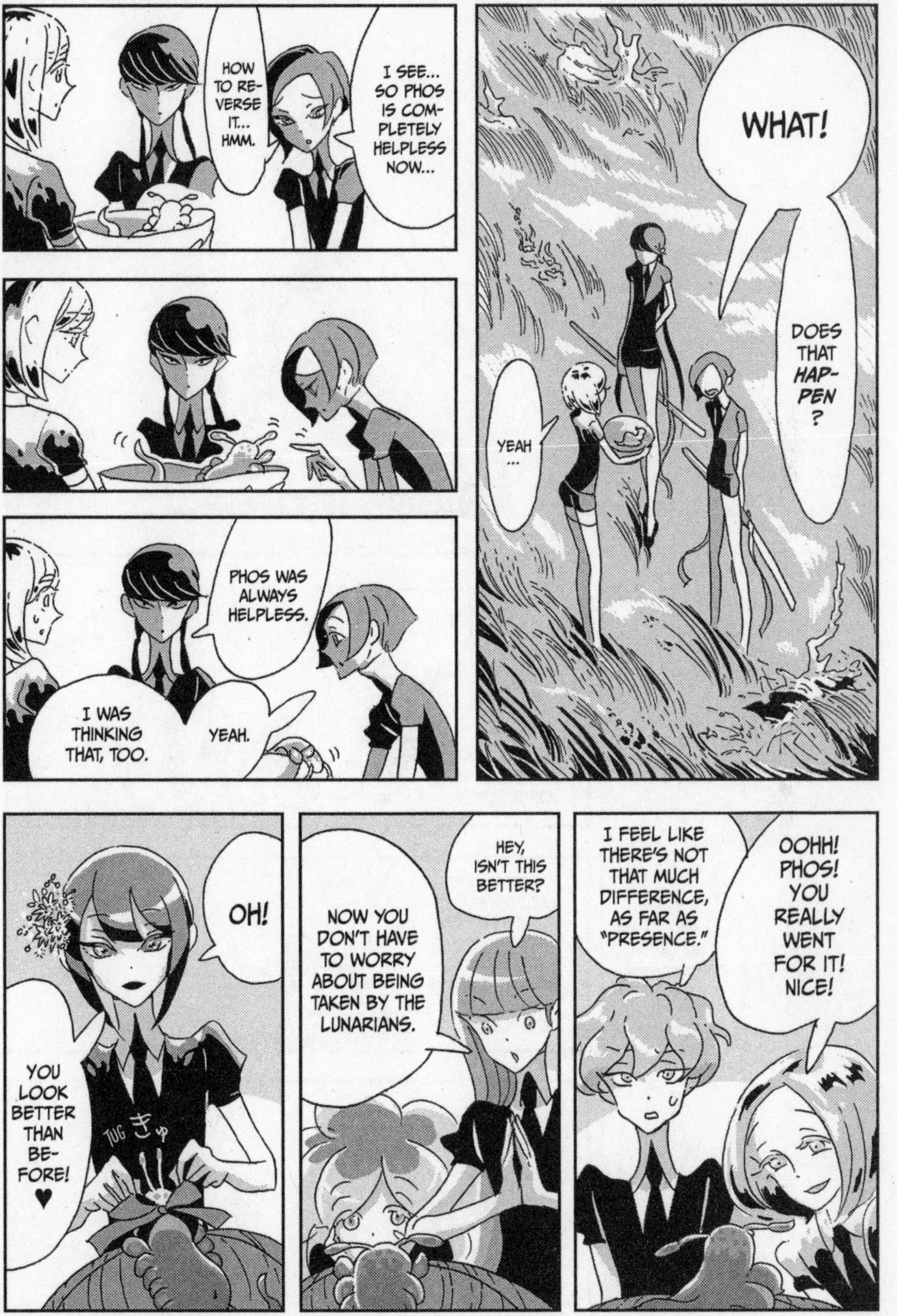
WHAT!
DOES THAT HAPPEN?
YEAH...
I SEE... SO PHOS IS COMPLETELY HELPLESS NOW...
HOW TO REVERSE IT... HMM.
PHOS WAS ALWAYS HELPLESS.
YEAH.
I WAS THINKING THAT, TOO.
OOHH! PHOS! YOU REALLY WENT FOR IT! NICE!
I FEEL LIKE THERE'S NOT THAT MUCH DIFFERENCE, AS FAR AS "PRESENCE."
HEY, ISN'T THIS BETTER?
NOW YOU DON'T HAVE TO WORRY ABOUT BEING TAKEN BY THE LUNARIANS.
OH!
TUG きゅ
YOU LOOK BETTER THAN BEFORE! ♥

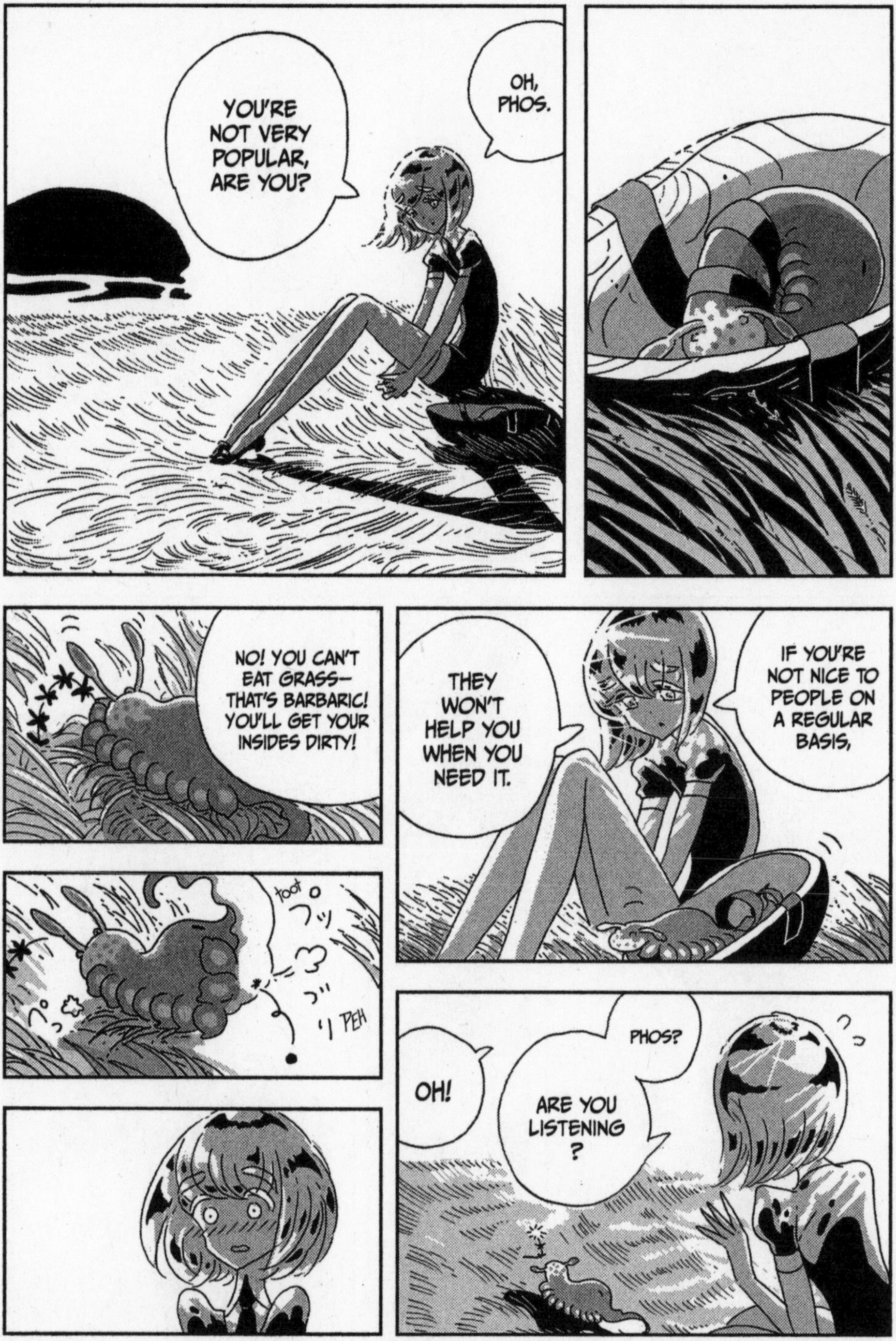
OH, PHOS.
YOU'RE NOT VERY POPULAR, ARE YOU?
IF YOU'RE NOT NICE TO PEOPLE ON A REGULAR BASIS,
THEY WON'T HELP YOU WHEN YOU NEED IT.
NO! YOU CAN'T EAT GRASS— THAT'S BARBARIC! YOU'LL GET YOUR INSIDES DIRTY!
toot
PEH
PHOS?
ARE YOU LISTENING ?
OH!

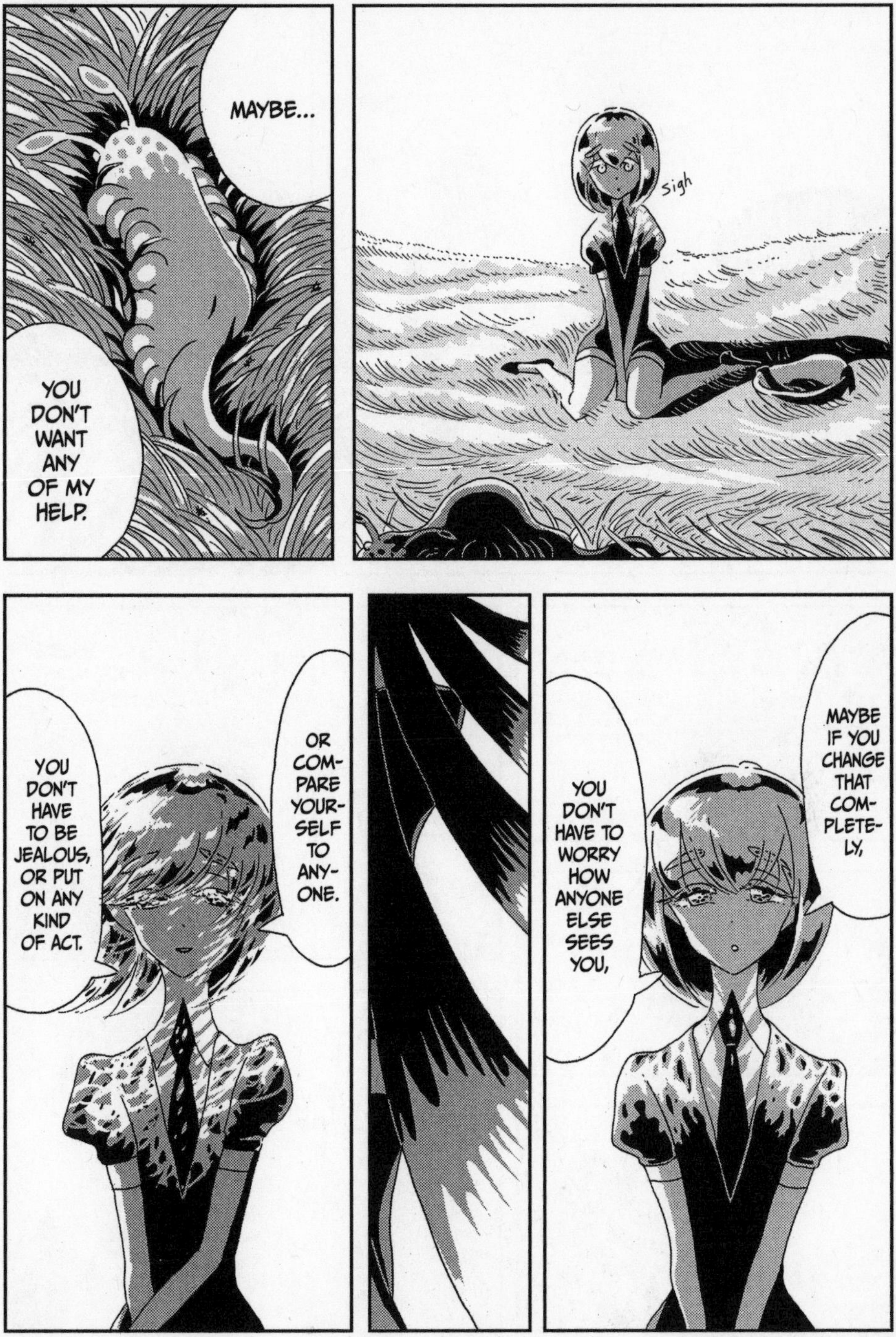
Sigh
MAYBE...
YOU DON'T WANT ANY OF MY HELP.
MAYBE IF YOU CHANGE THAT COMPLETELY,
YOU DON'T HAVE TO WORRY HOW ANYONE ELSE SEES YOU,
OR COMPARE YOURSELF TO ANYONE.
YOU DON'T HAVE TO BE JEALOUS, OR PUT ON ANY KIND OF ACT.

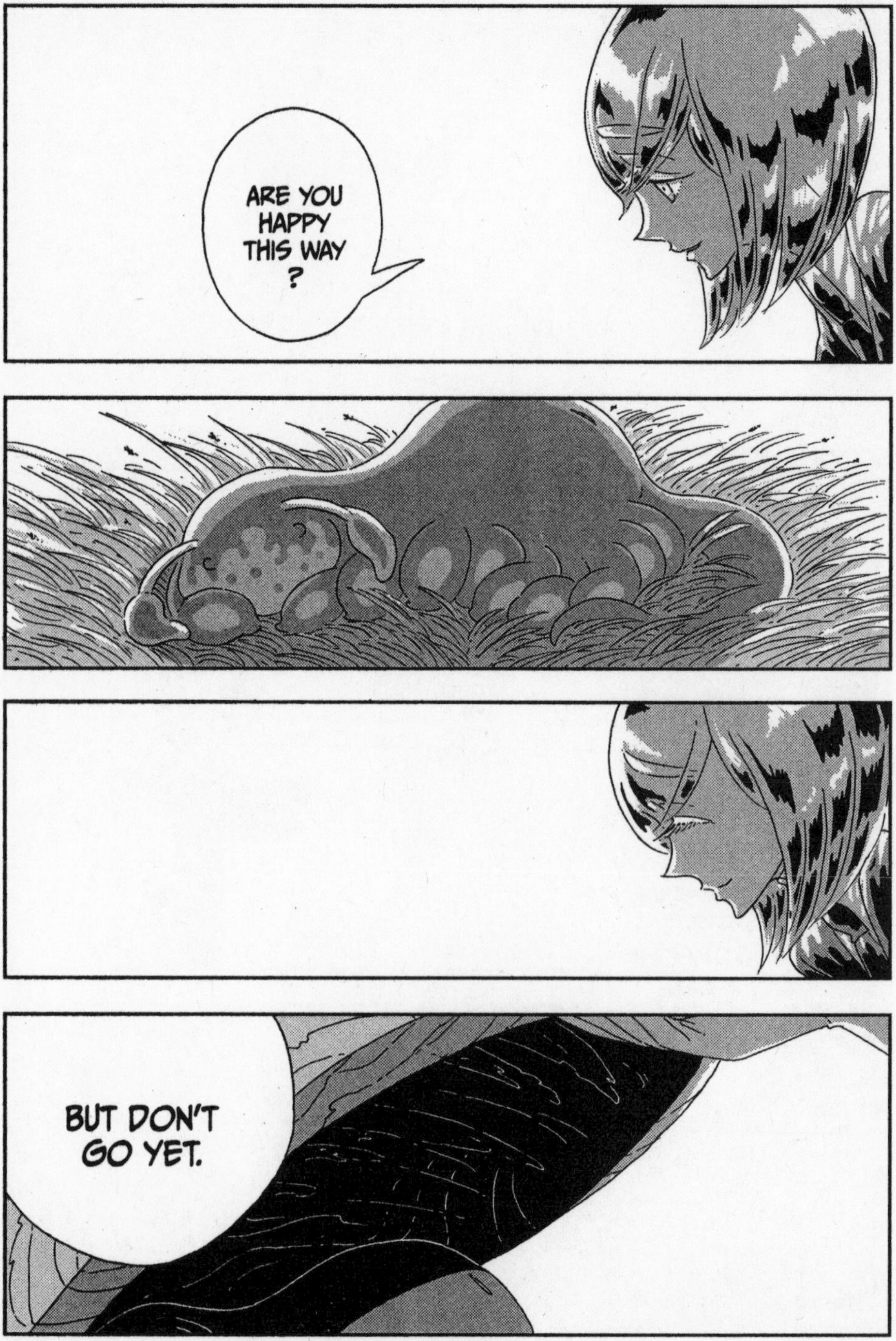
ARE YOU HAPPY THIS WAY ?
BUT DON'T GO YET.

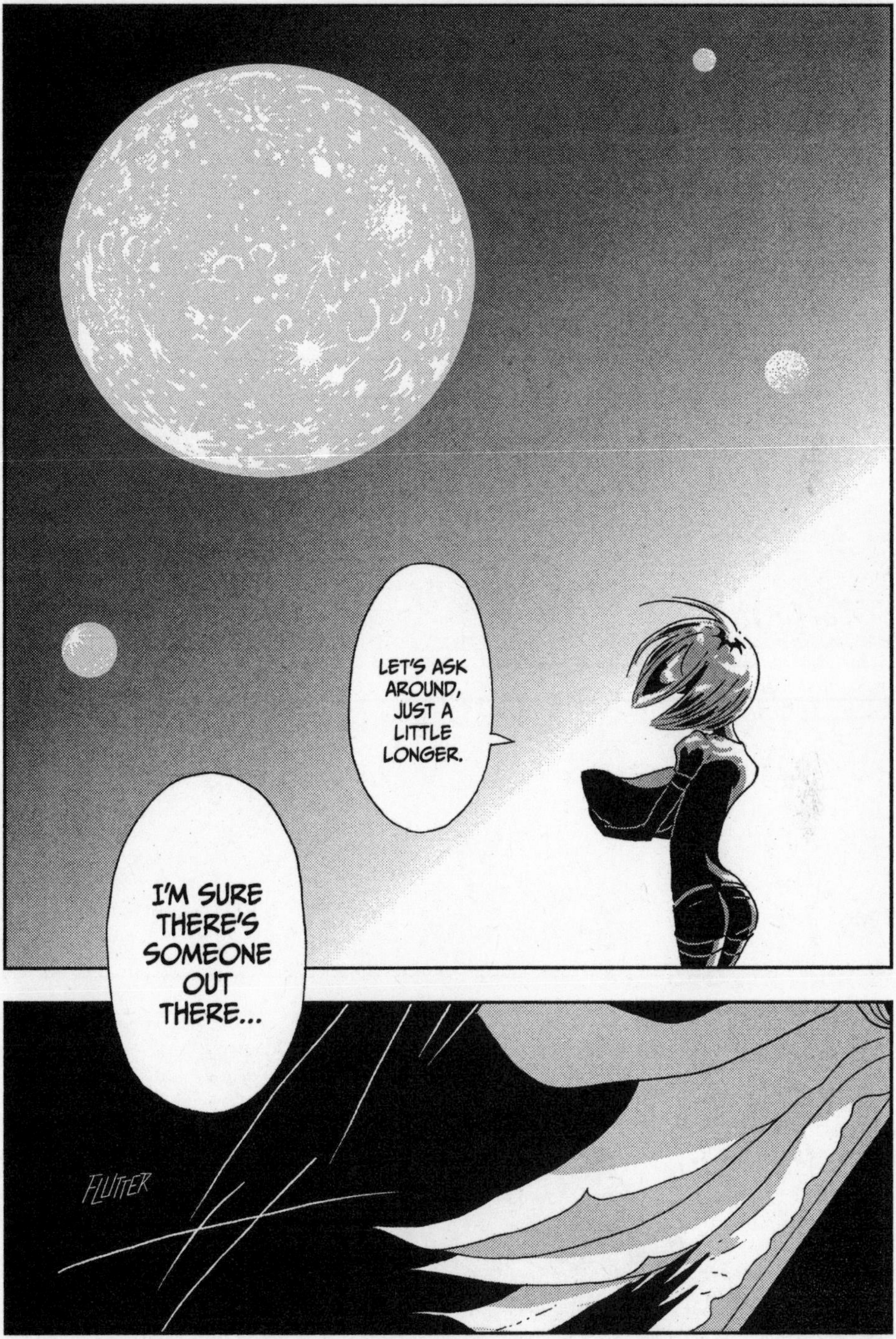
LET'S ASK AROUND, JUST A LITTLE LONGER.
I'M SURE THERE'S SOMEONE OUT THERE...
FLUTTER

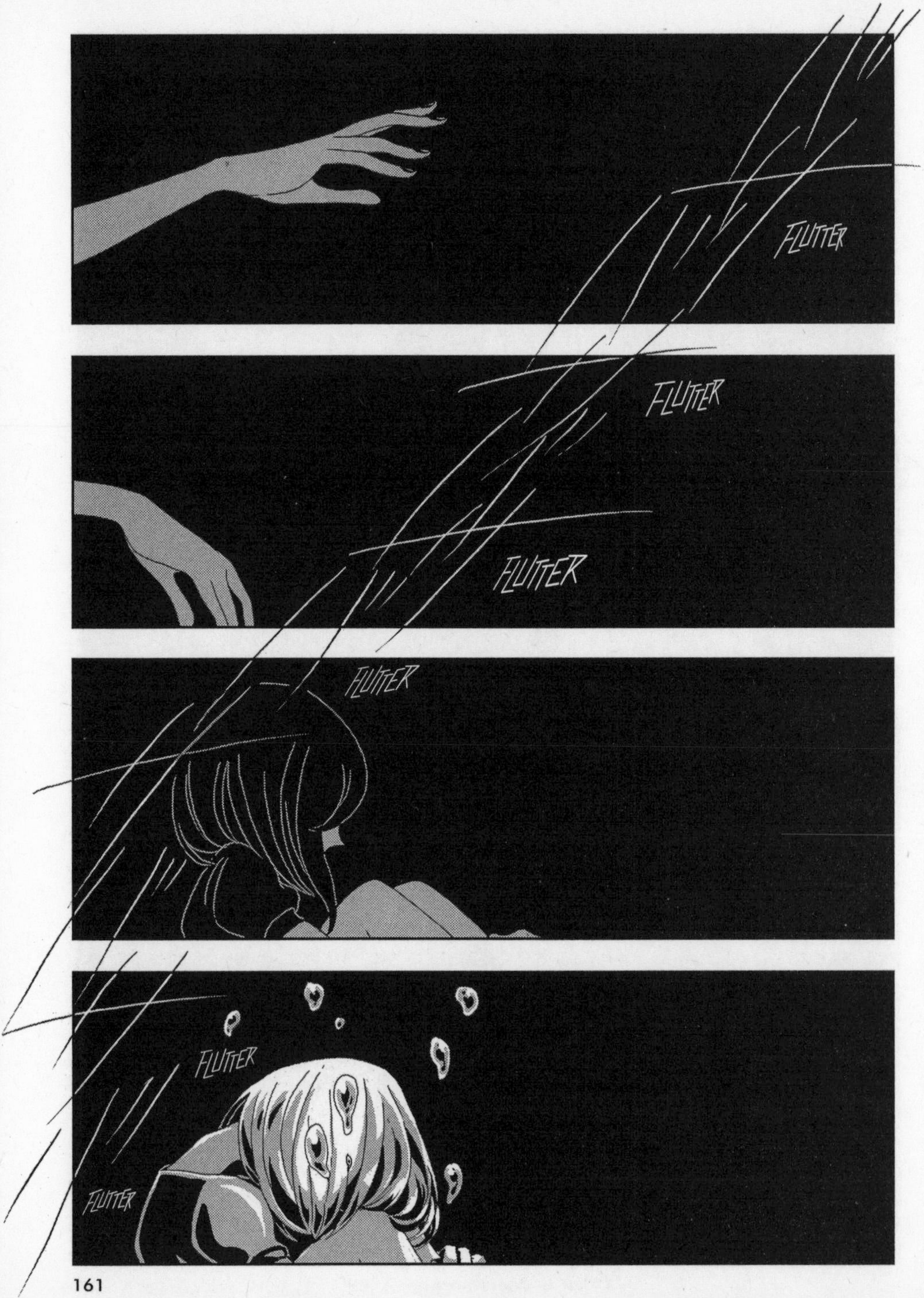
FLUTTER
FLUTTER
FLUTTER
FLUTTER
FLUTTER
FLUTTER

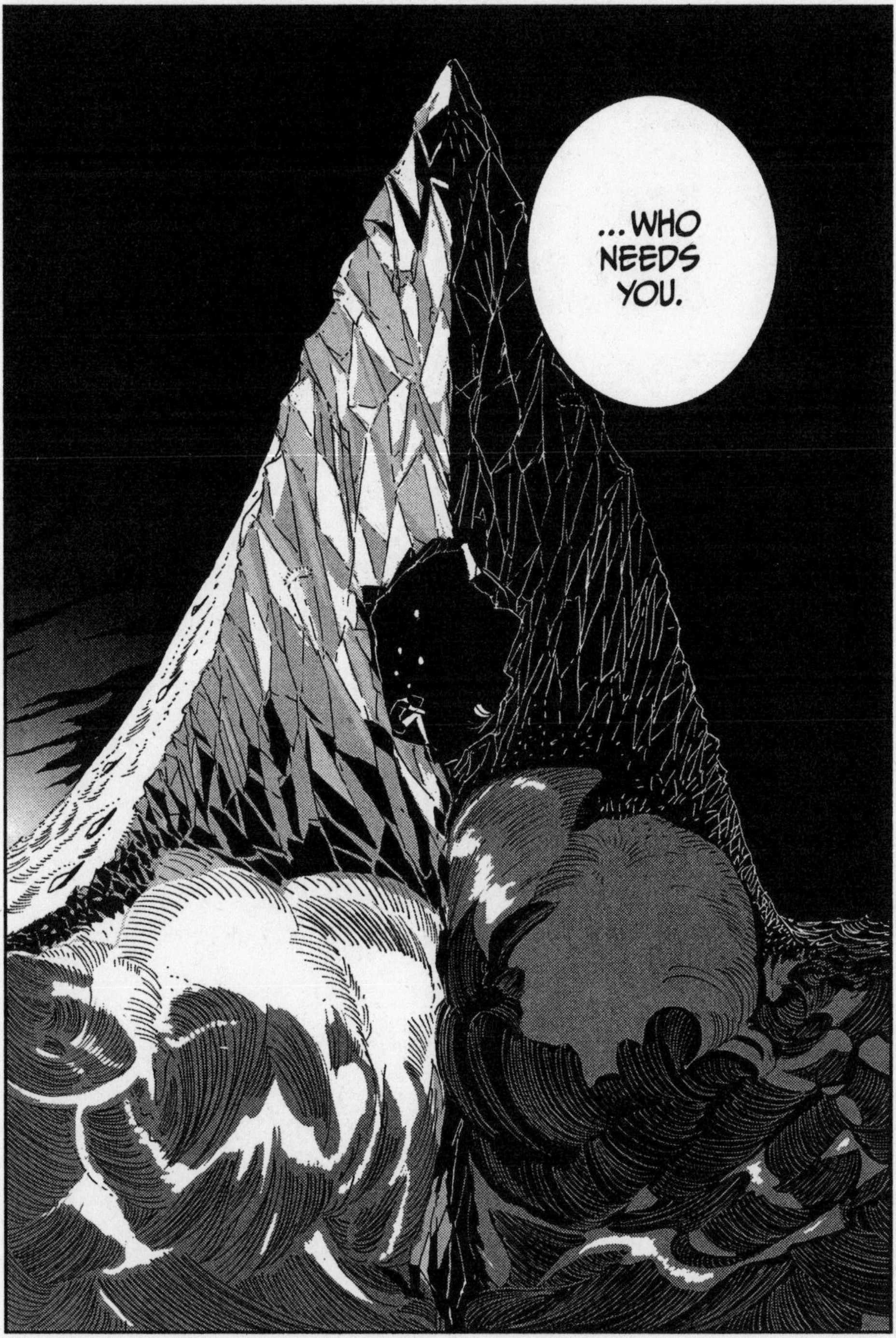
...WHO
NEEDS
YOU.

CHAPTER 5: Metamorphosis END

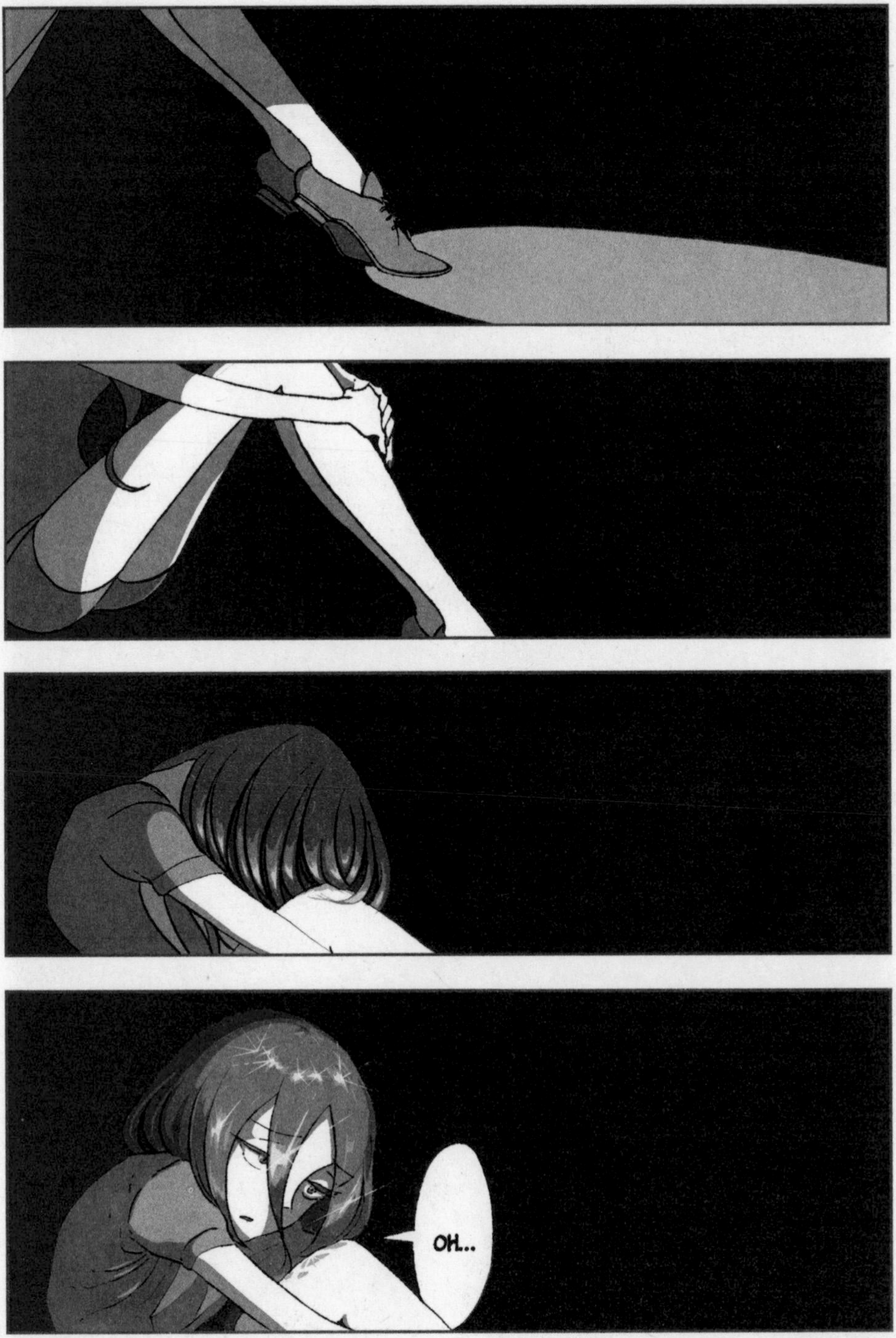
OH...

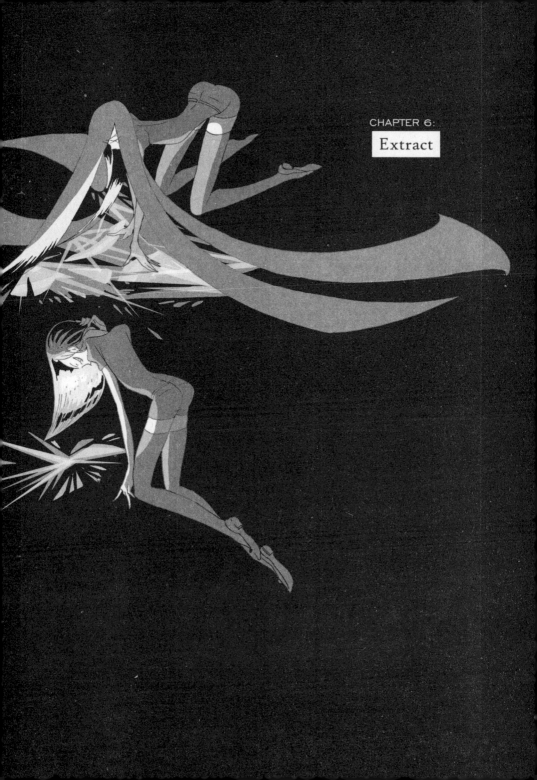

CHAPTER 6:

Extract

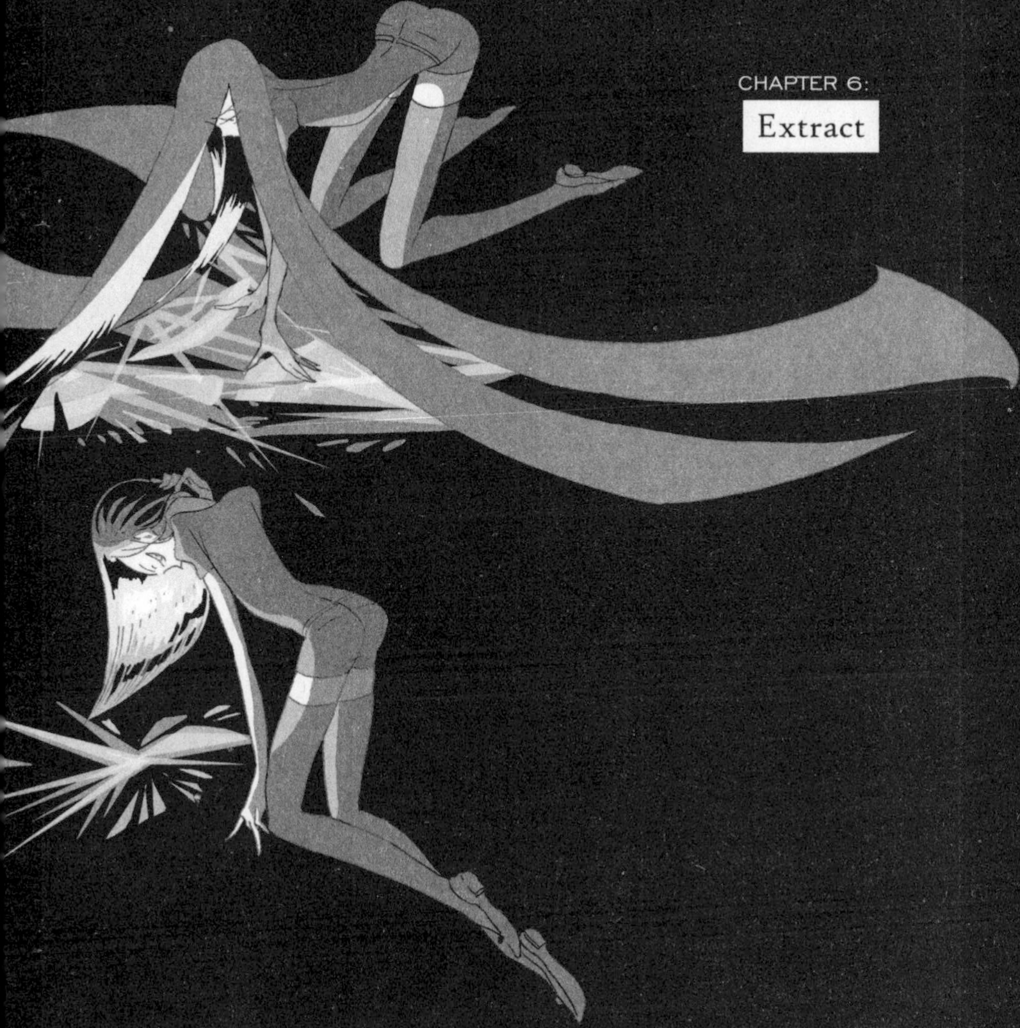

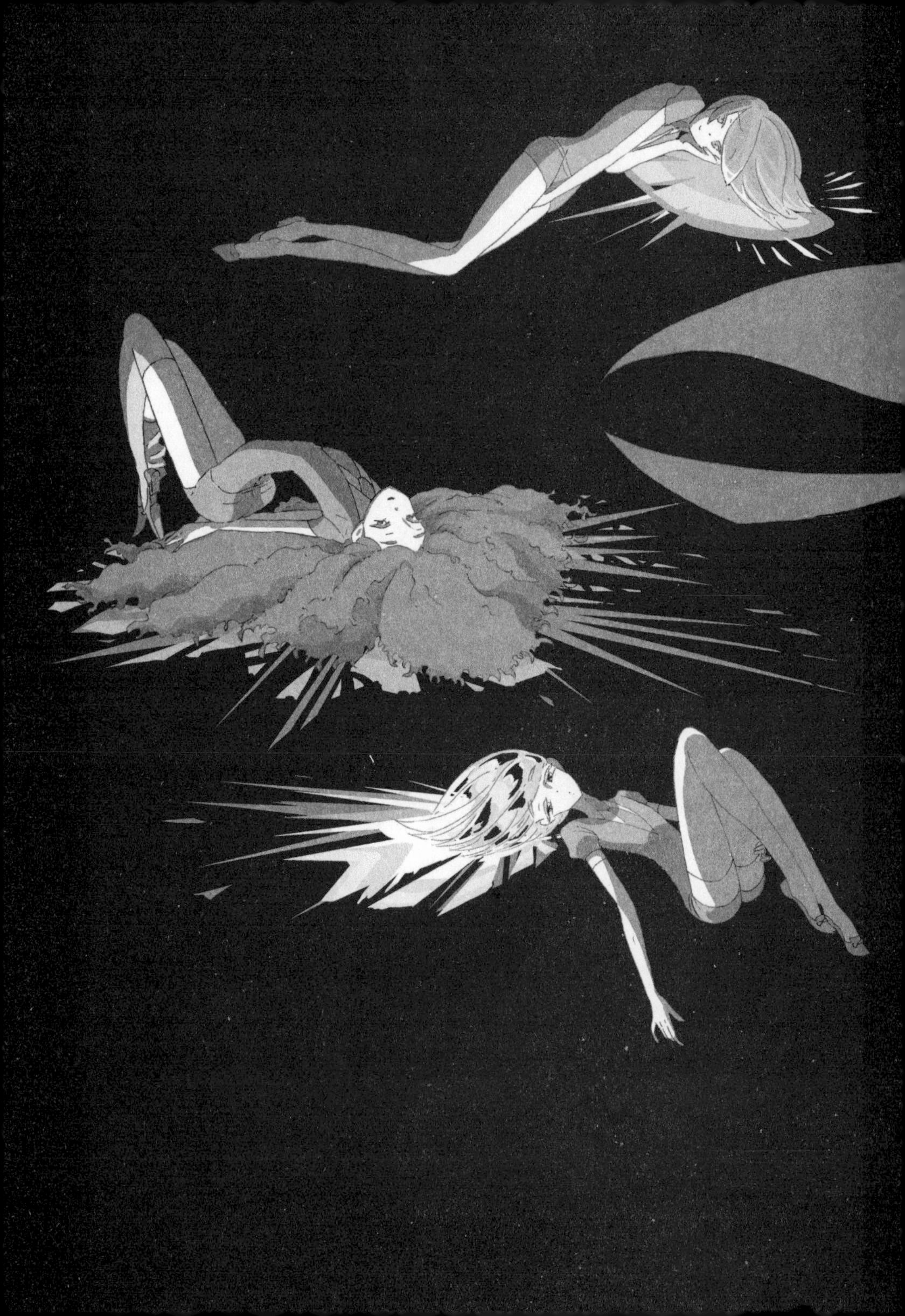

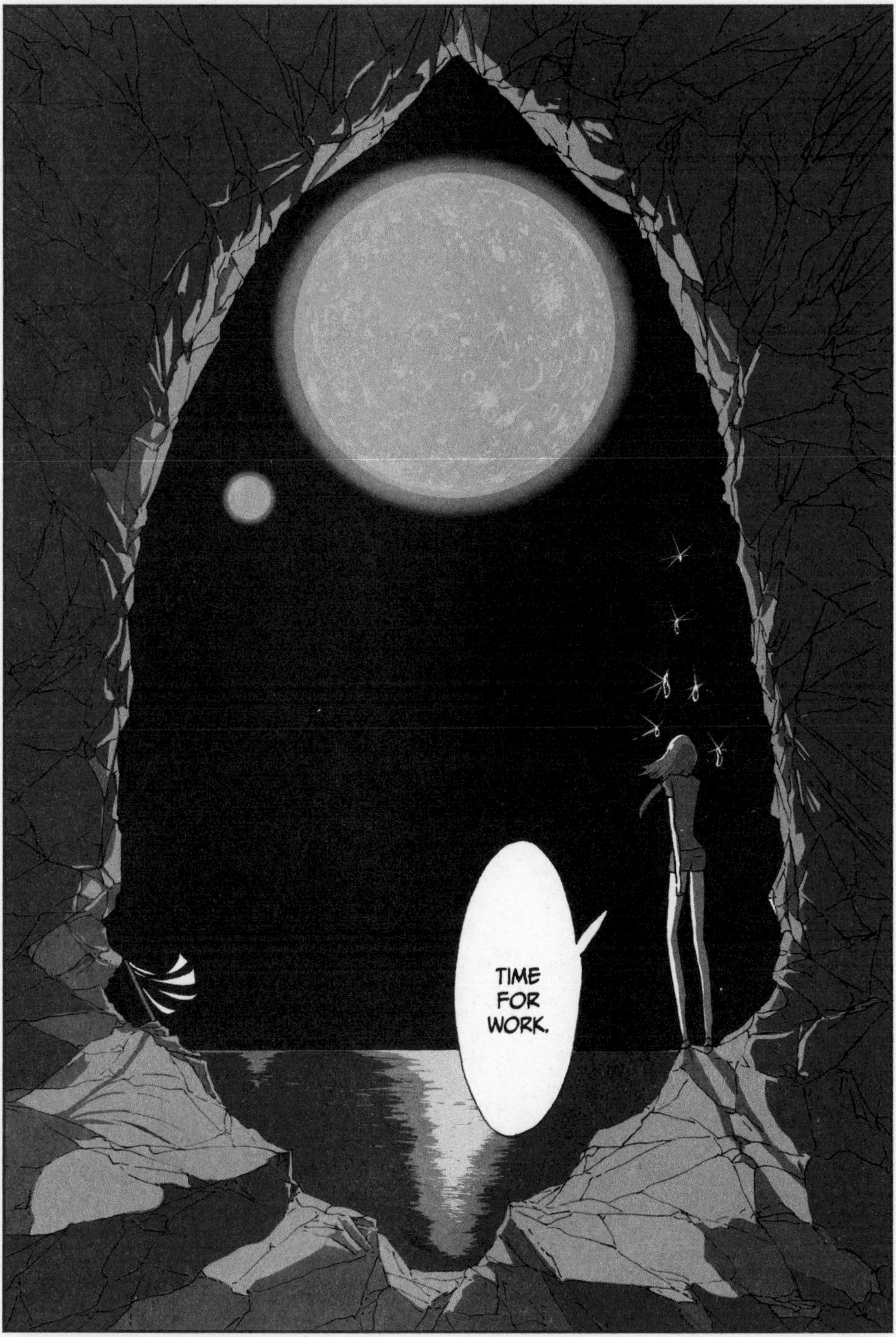
TIME FOR WORK.

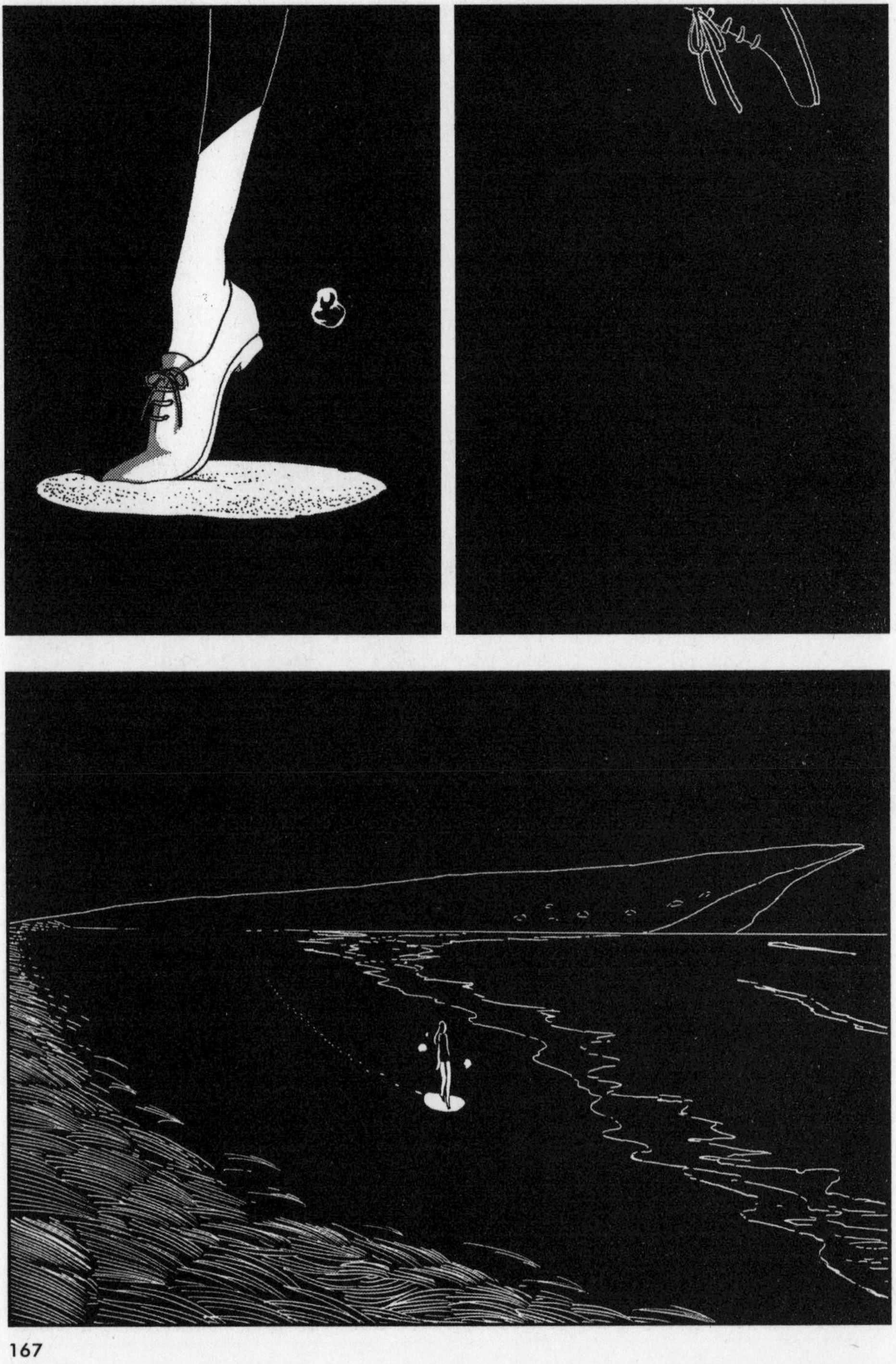

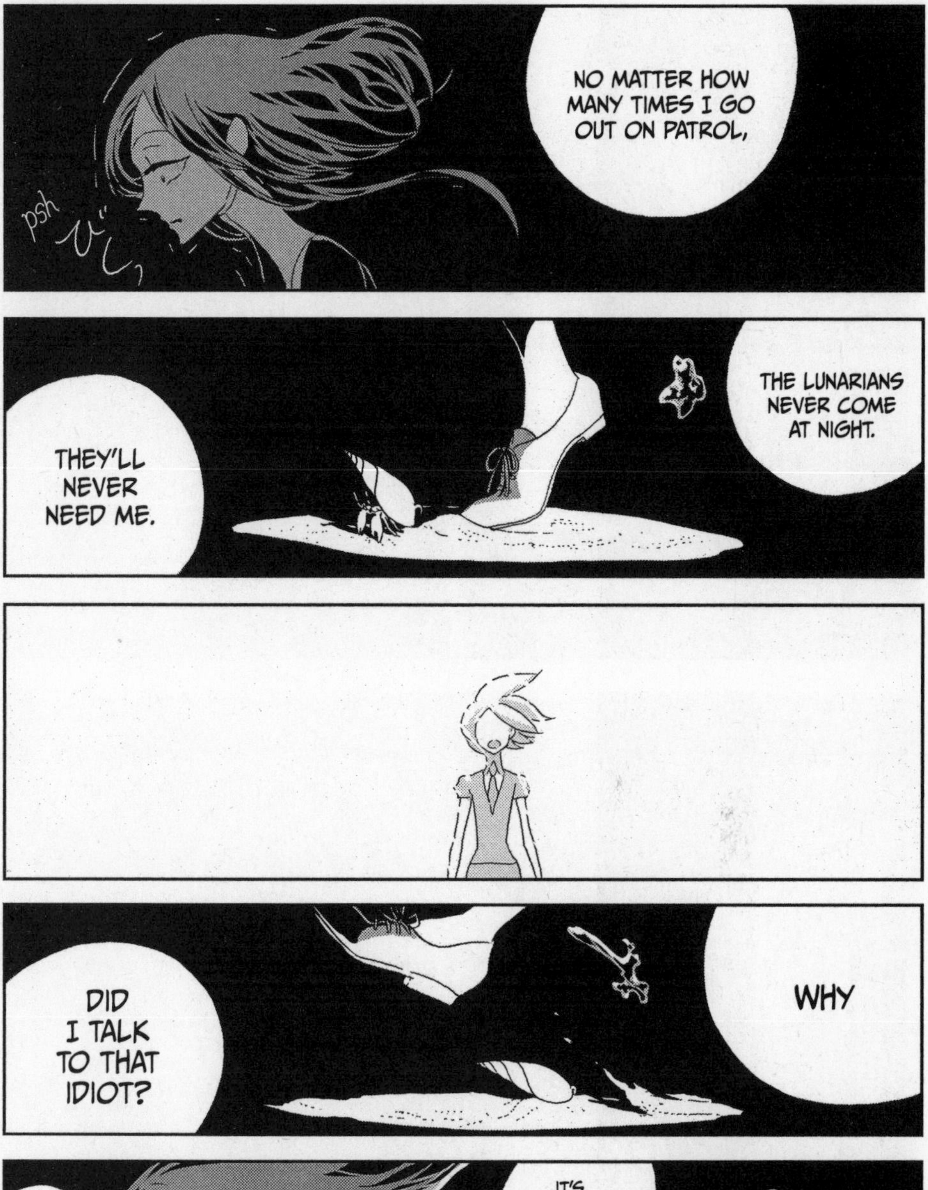
NO MATTER HOW MANY TIMES I GO OUT ON PATROL,
psh
THE LUNARIANS NEVER COME AT NIGHT.
THEY'LL NEVER NEED ME.
WHY
DID I TALK TO THAT IDIOT?
IT'S NOT LIKE ANYTHING IS GOING TO COME OF IT.
DON'T GET YOUR HOPES UP.

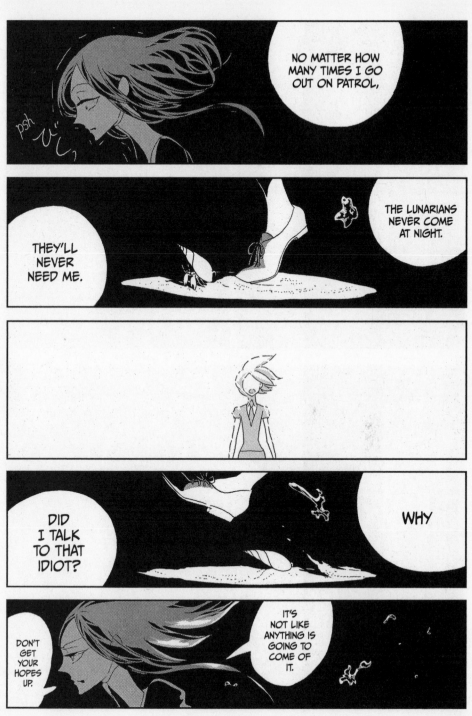

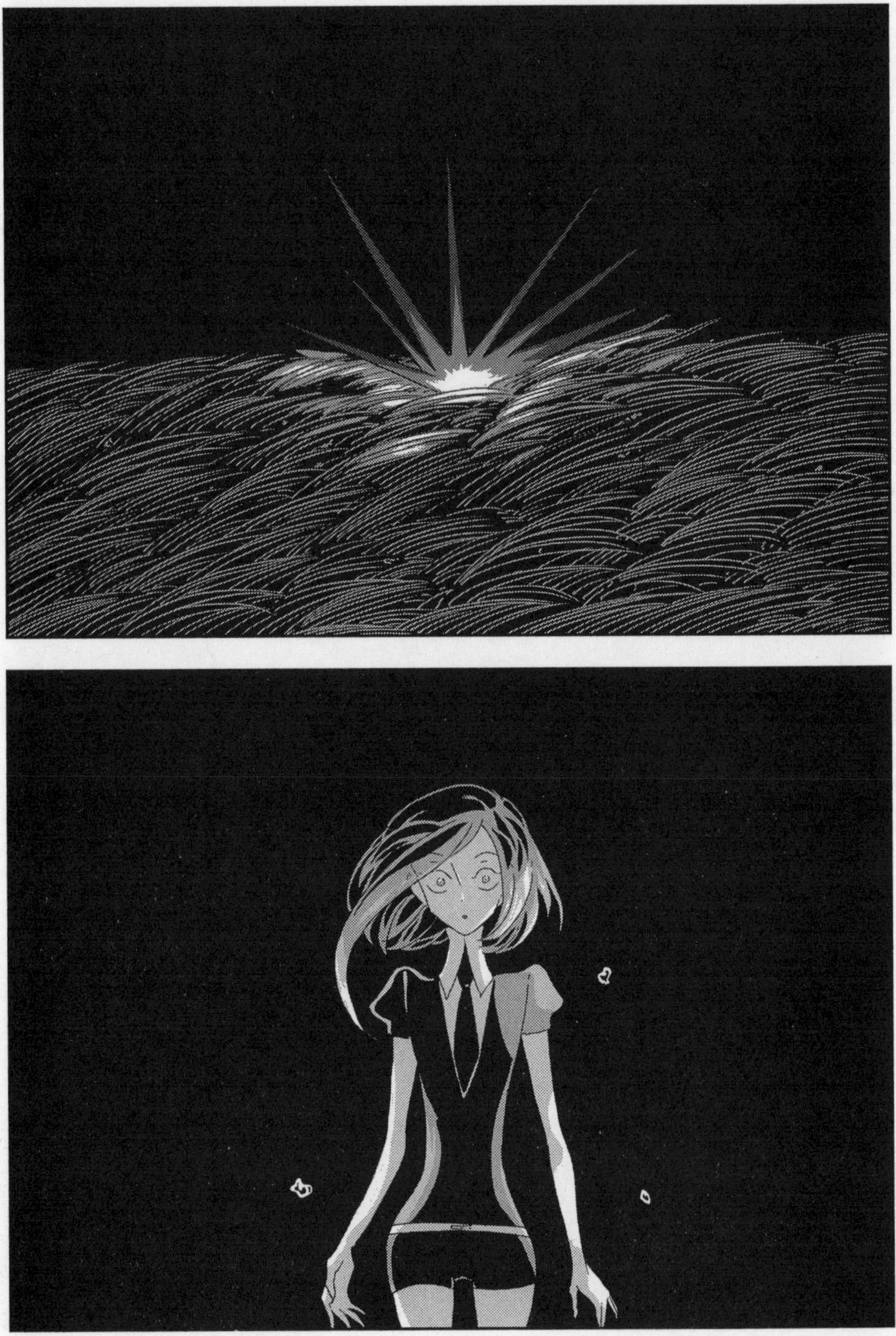

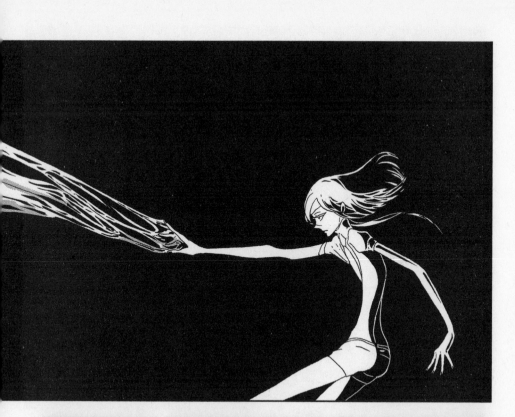

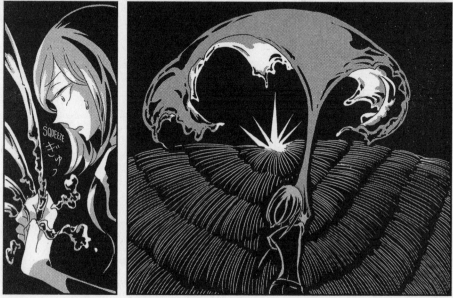

SQUEEZE
ギュッ

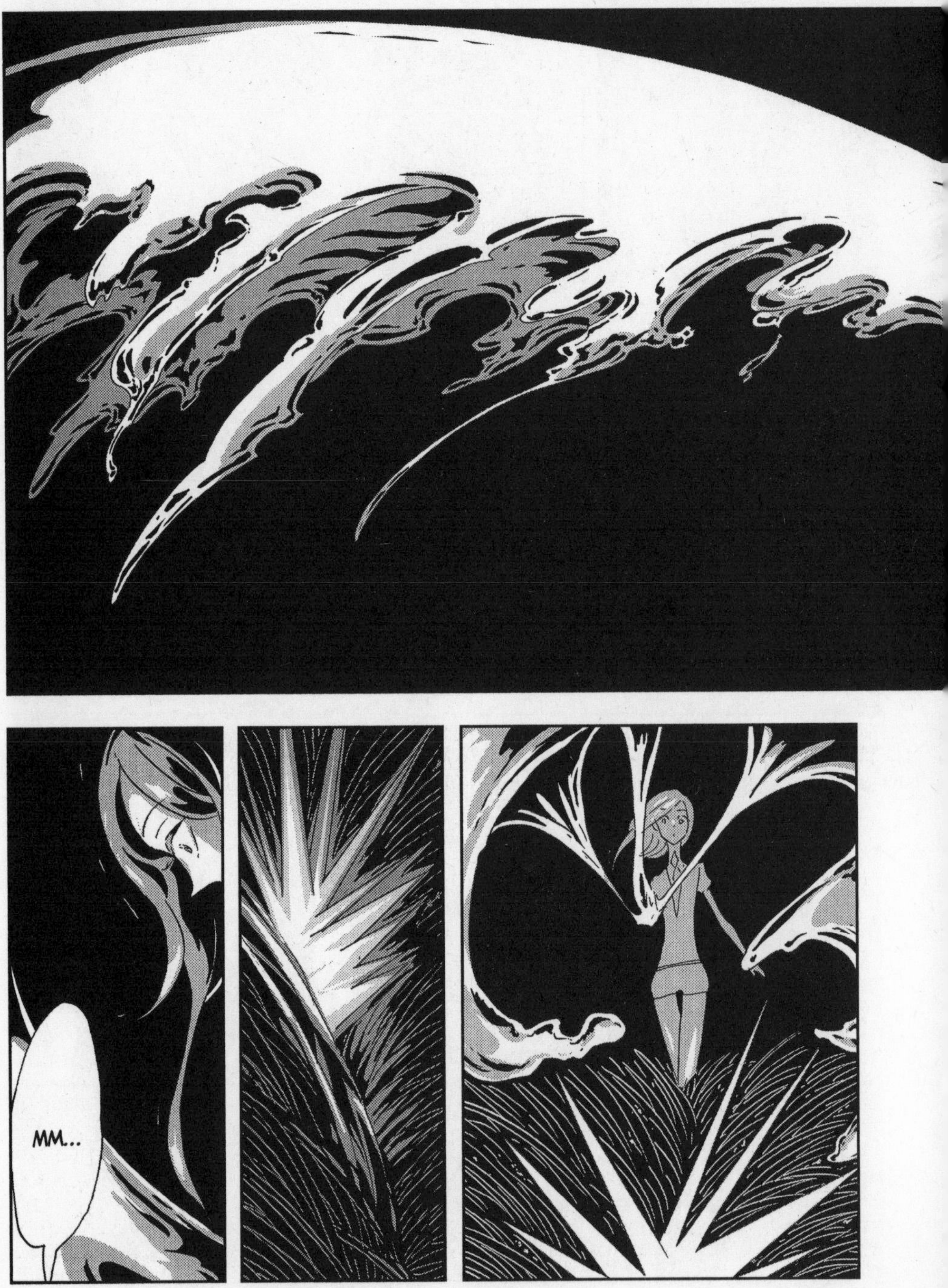
MM...

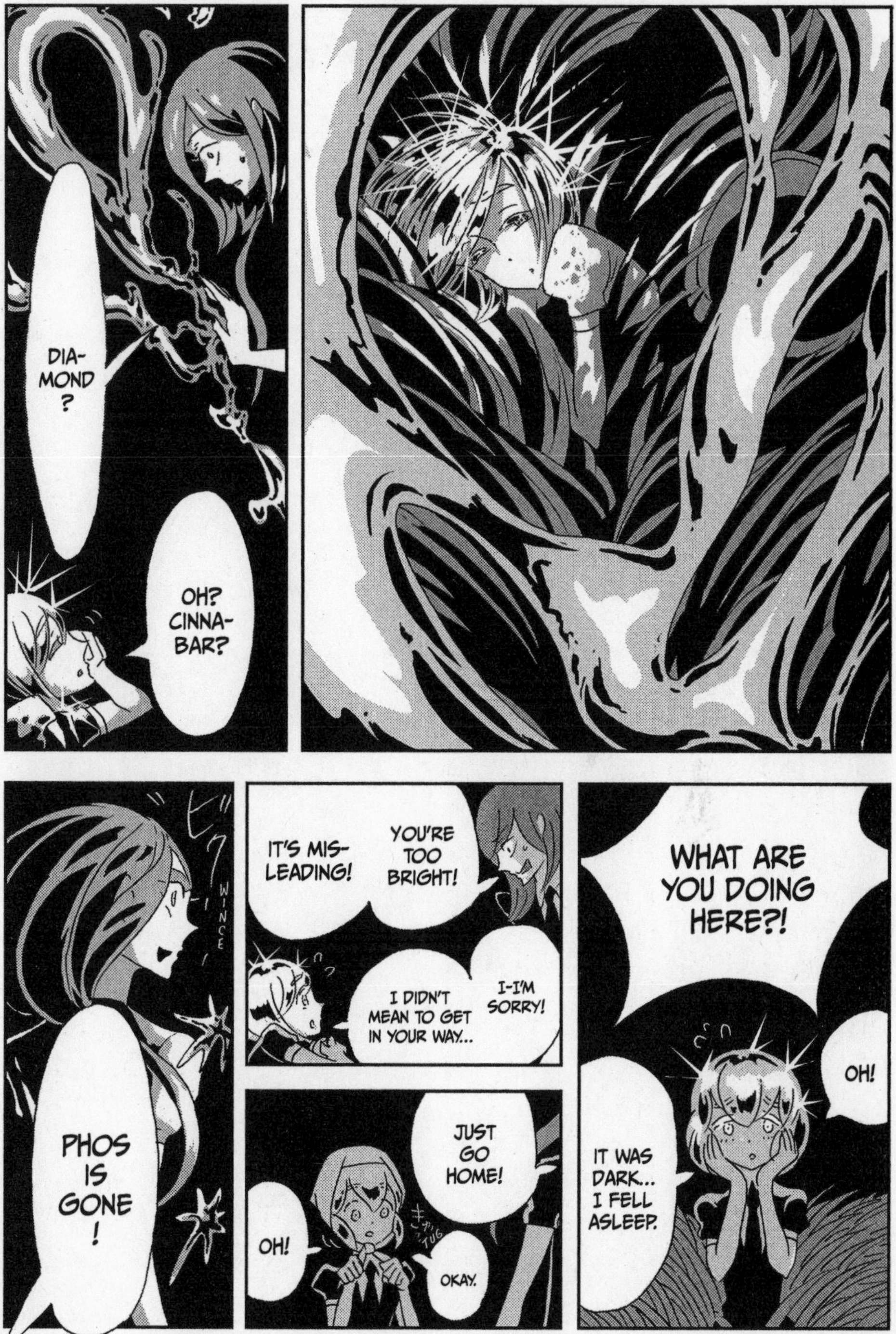
DIA-MOND?
OH? CINNA-BAR?
WHAT ARE YOU DOING HERE?!
OH!
IT WAS DARK... I FELL ASLEEP.
YOU'RE TOO BRIGHT!
IT'S MIS-LEADING!
I-I'M SORRY!
I DIDN'T MEAN TO GET IN YOUR WAY...
JUST GO HOME!
TUG
OH!
OKAY.
WINCE
PHOS IS GONE!

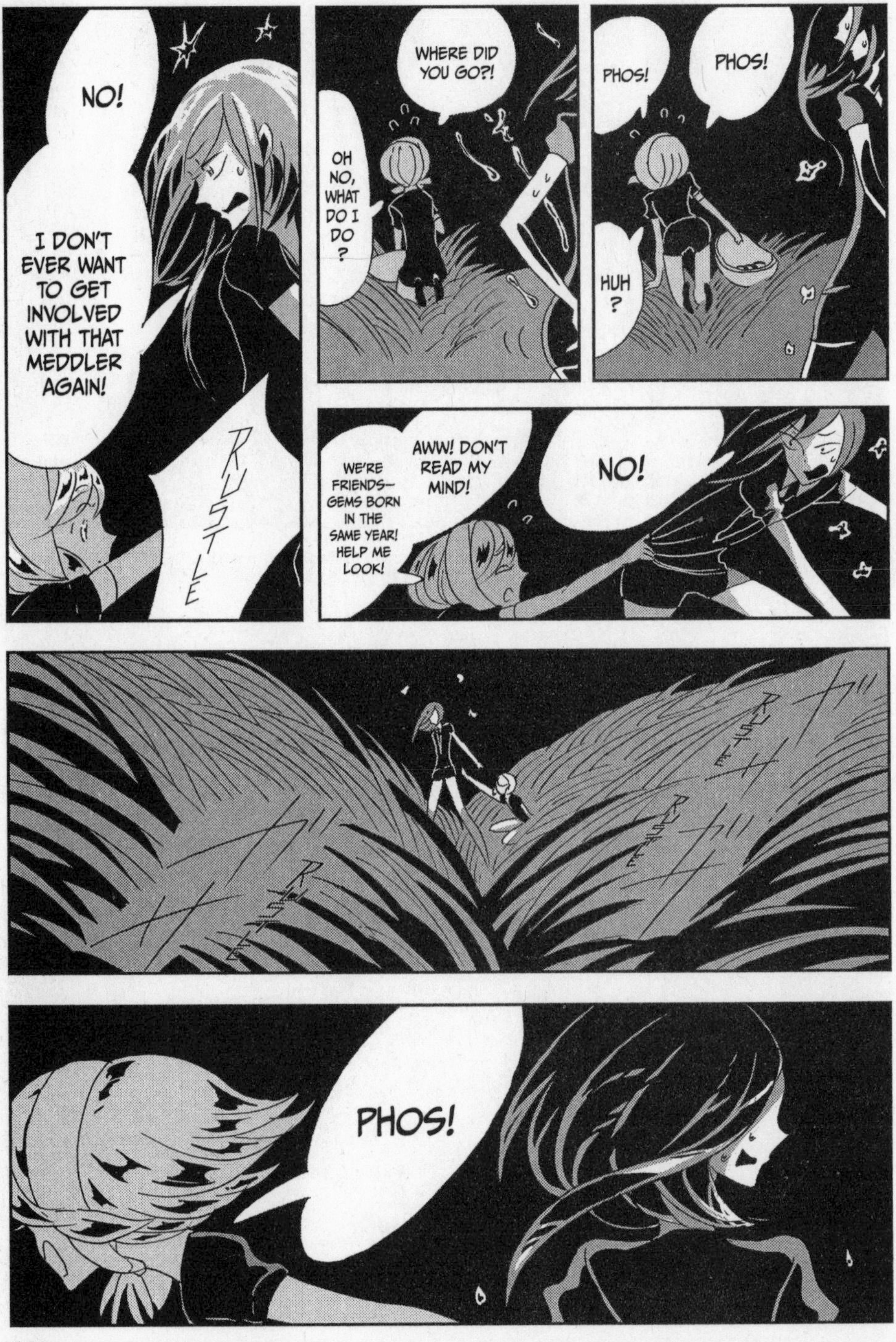
PHOS!
PHOS!
HUH?
WHERE DID YOU GO?!
OH NO, WHAT DO I DO?
NO!
AWW! DON'T READ MY MIND!
WE'RE FRIENDS— GEMS BORN IN THE SAME YEAR! HELP ME LOOK!
NO!
I DON'T EVER WANT TO GET INVOLVED WITH THAT MEDDLER AGAIN!
RUSTLE
RUSTLE
RUSTLE
RUSTLE
PHOS!

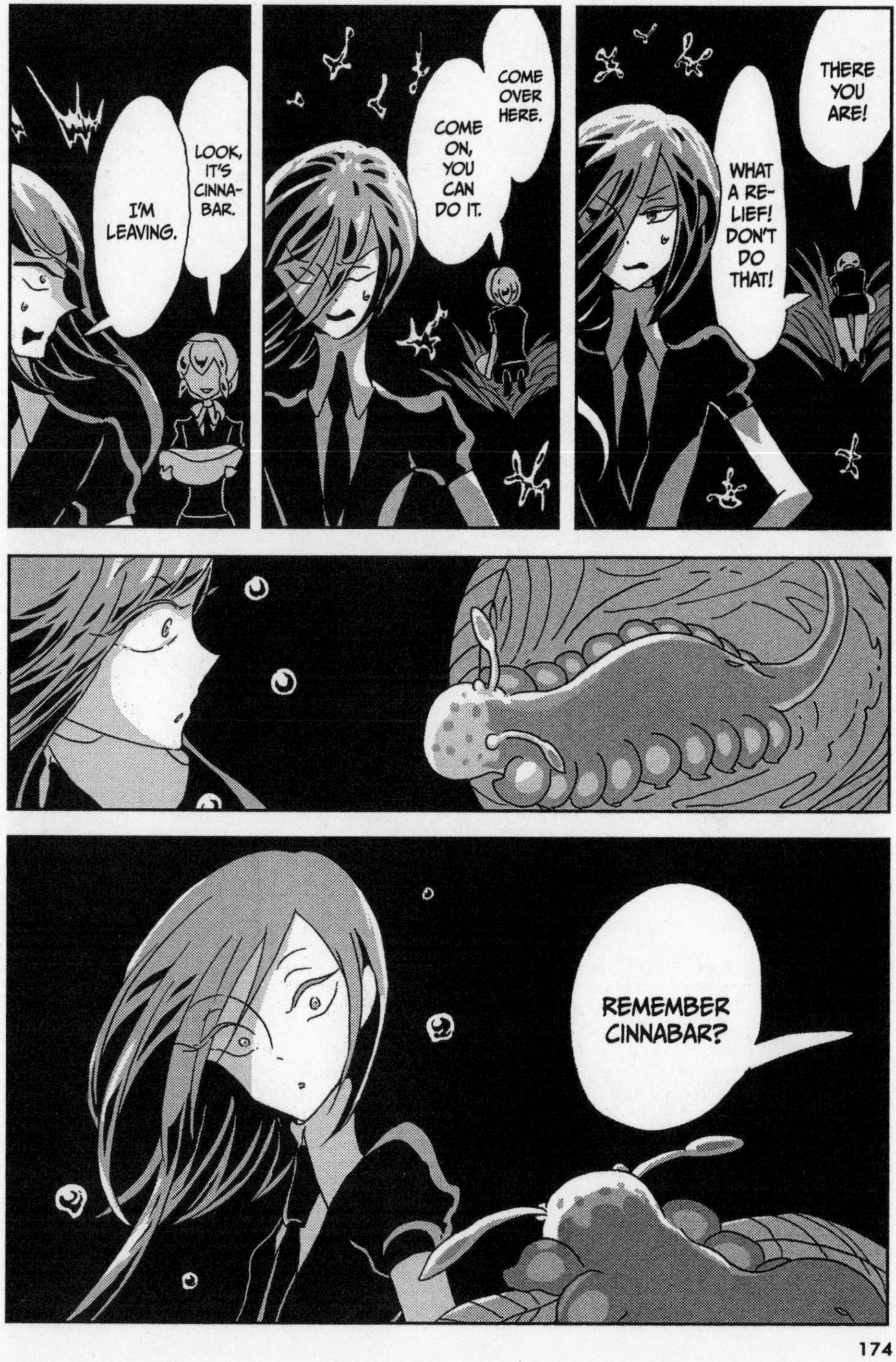
THERE YOU ARE!
WHAT A RELIEF! DON'T DO THAT!
COME OVER HERE.
COME ON, YOU CAN DO IT.
LOOK, IT'S CINNABAR.
I'M LEAVING.
REMEMBER CINNABAR?

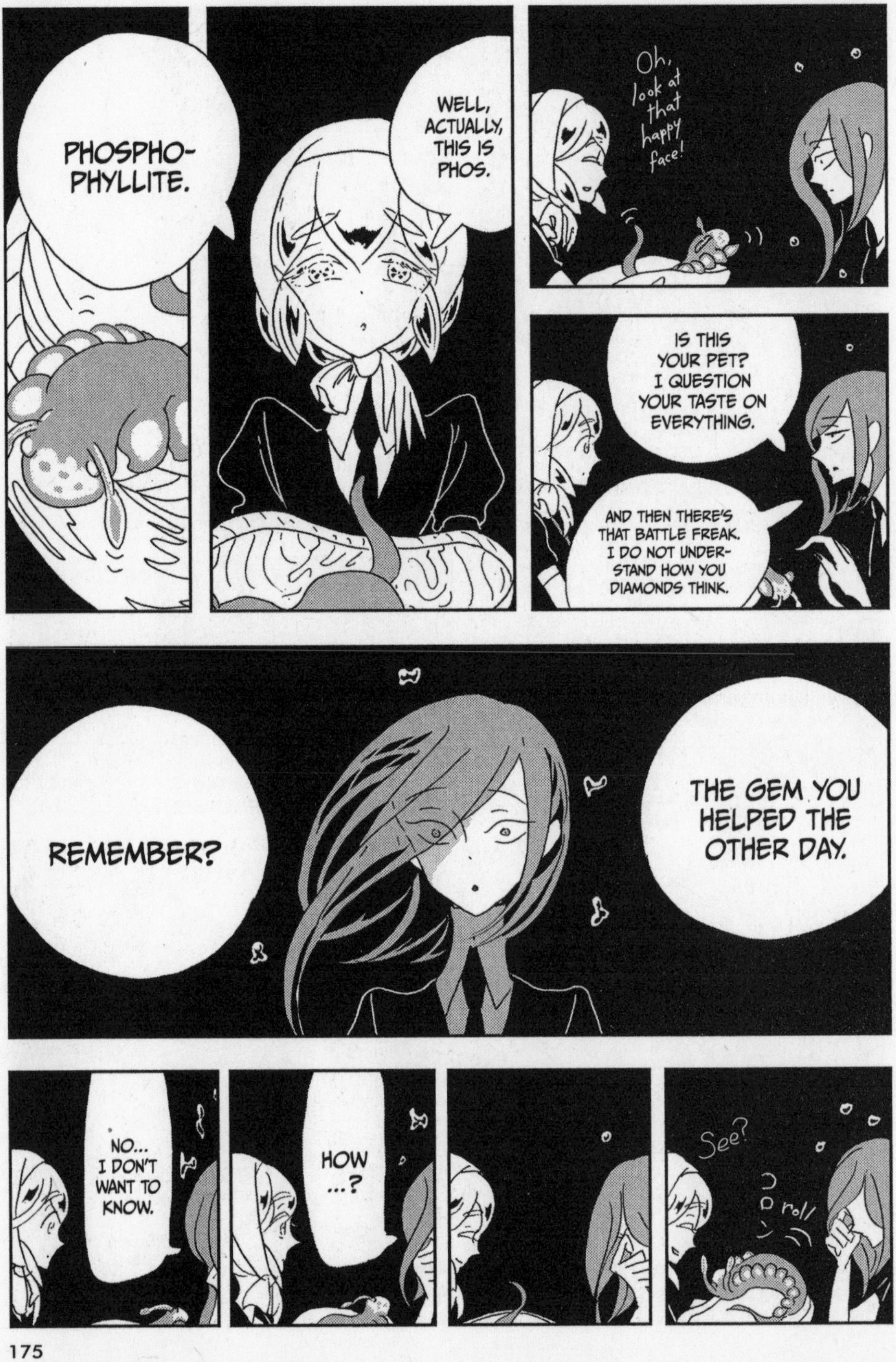
Oh, look at that happy face!
IS THIS YOUR PET? I QUESTION YOUR TASTE ON EVERYTHING.
AND THEN THERE'S THAT BATTLE FREAK. I DO NOT UNDERSTAND HOW YOU DIAMONDS THINK.
WELL, ACTUALLY, THIS IS PHOS.
PHOSPHO-PHYLLITE.
THE GEM YOU HELPED THE OTHER DAY.
REMEMBER?
See?
roll
HOW ...?
NO... I DON'T WANT TO KNOW.

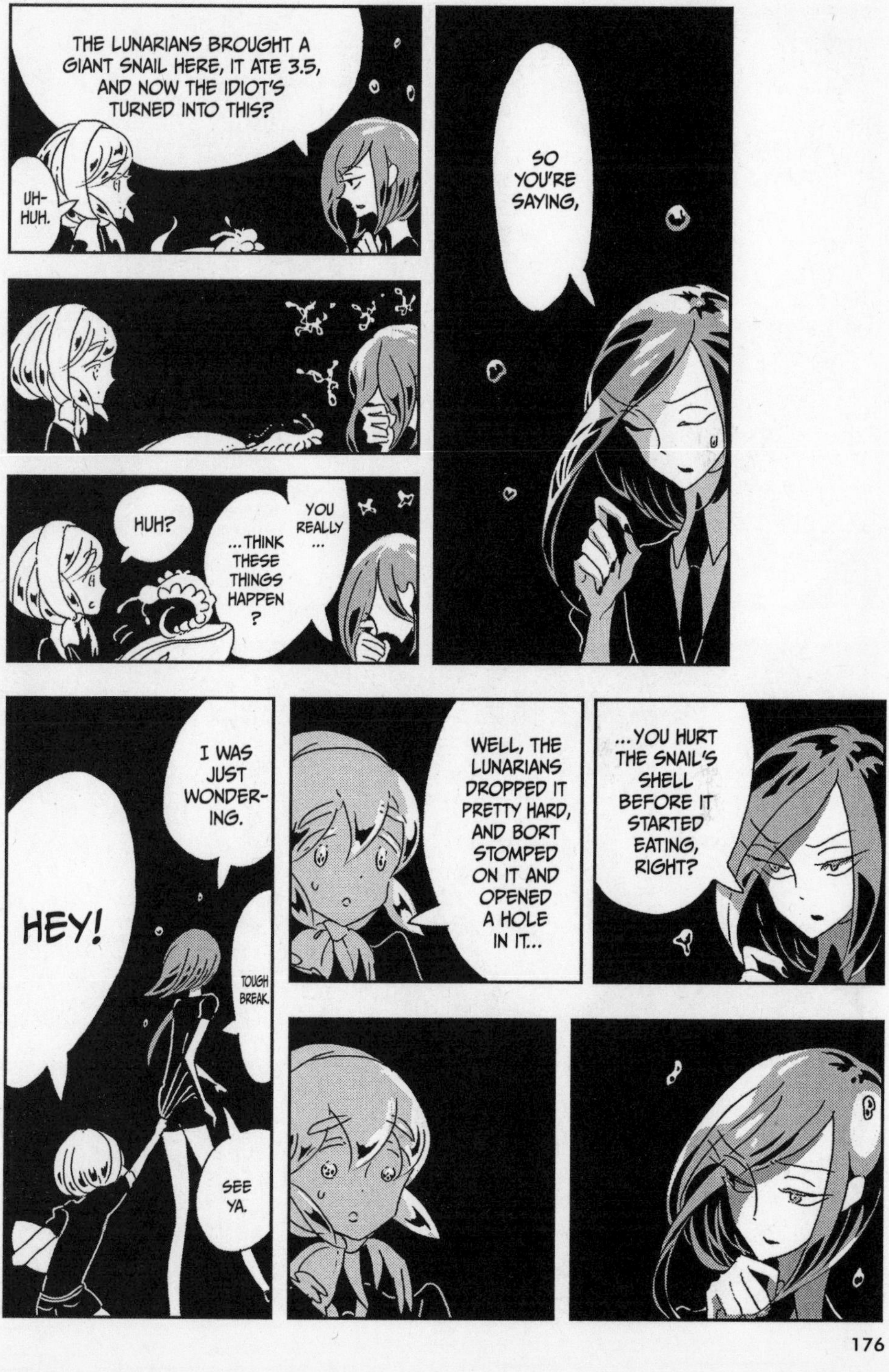
SO YOU'RE SAYING,
THE LUNARIANS BROUGHT A GIANT SNAIL HERE, IT ATE 3.5, AND NOW THE IDIOT'S TURNED INTO THIS?
UH-HUH.
YOU REALLY ...
...THINK THESE THINGS HAPPEN ?
HUH?
...YOU HURT THE SNAIL'S SHELL BEFORE IT STARTED EATING, RIGHT?
WELL, THE LUNARIANS DROPPED IT PRETTY HARD, AND BORT STOMPED ON IT AND OPENED A HOLE IN IT...
I WAS JUST WONDERING.
TOUGH BREAK.
SEE YA.
HEY!

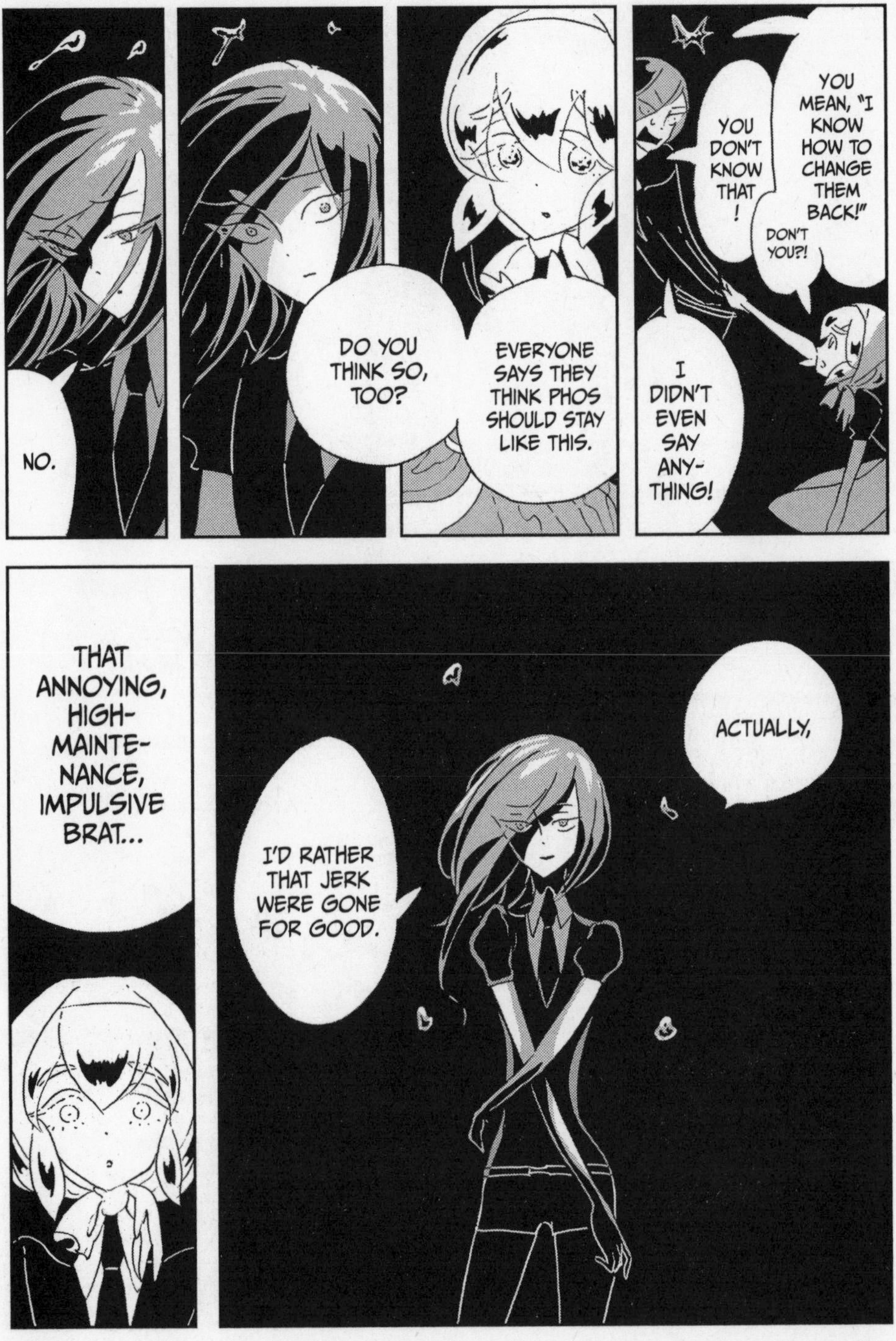
YOU MEAN, "I KNOW HOW TO CHANGE THEM BACK!" DON'T YOU?!
YOU DON'T KNOW THAT!
I DIDN'T EVEN SAY ANY-THING!
EVERYONE SAYS THEY THINK PHOS SHOULD STAY LIKE THIS.
DO YOU THINK SO, TOO?
NO.
ACTUALLY,
I'D RATHER THAT JERK WERE GONE FOR GOOD.
THAT ANNOYING, HIGH-MAINTE-NANCE, IMPULSIVE BRAT...

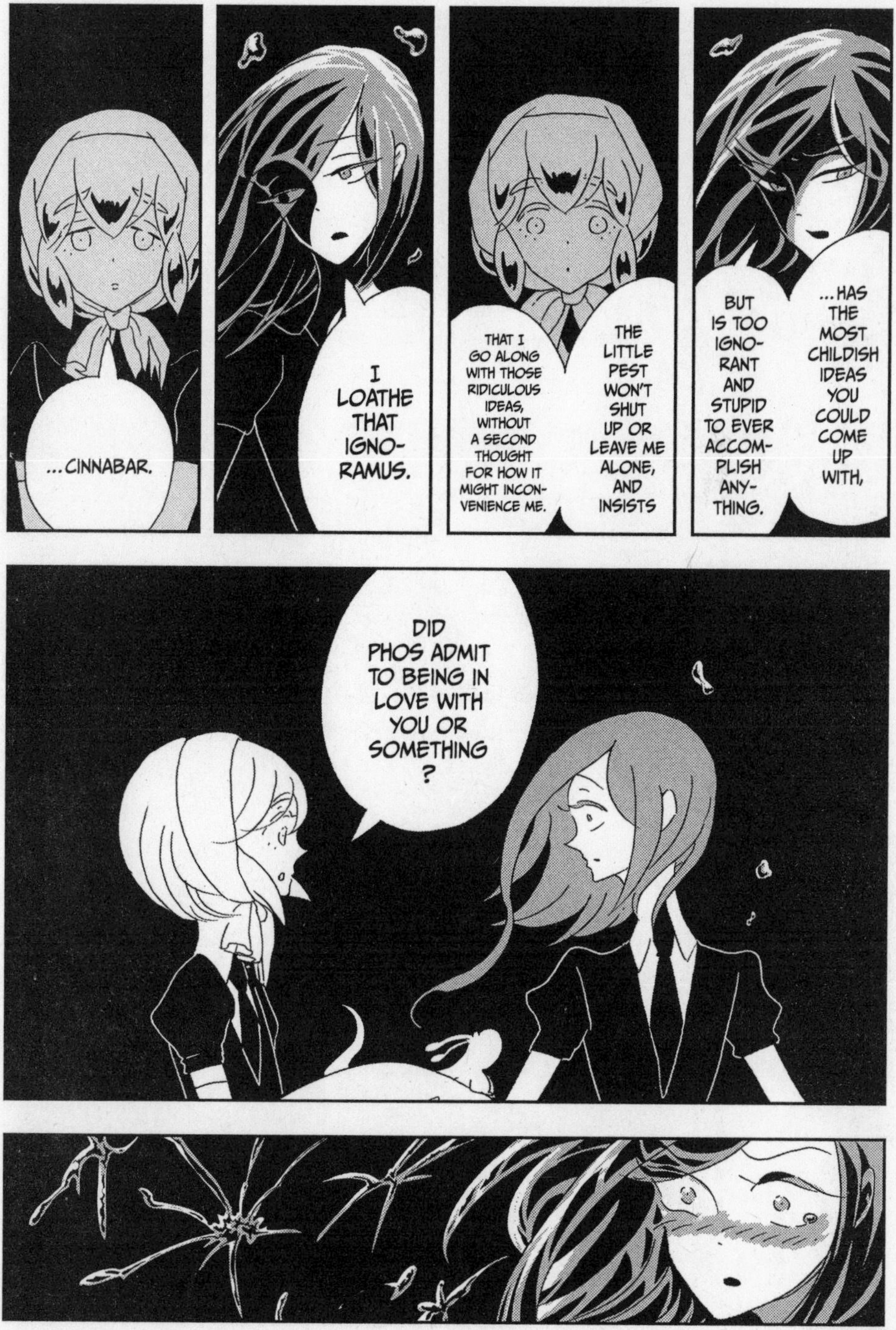
...HAS THE MOST CHILDISH IDEAS YOU COULD COME UP WITH,
BUT IS TOO IGNORANT AND STUPID TO EVER ACCOMPLISH ANYTHING.
THE LITTLE PEST WON'T SHUT UP OR LEAVE ME ALONE, AND INSISTS
THAT I GO ALONG WITH THOSE RIDICULOUS IDEAS, WITHOUT A SECOND THOUGHT FOR HOW IT MIGHT INCONVENIENCE ME.
I LOATHE THAT IGNORAMUS.
...CINNABAR.
DID PHOS ADMIT TO BEING IN LOVE WITH YOU OR SOMETHING?

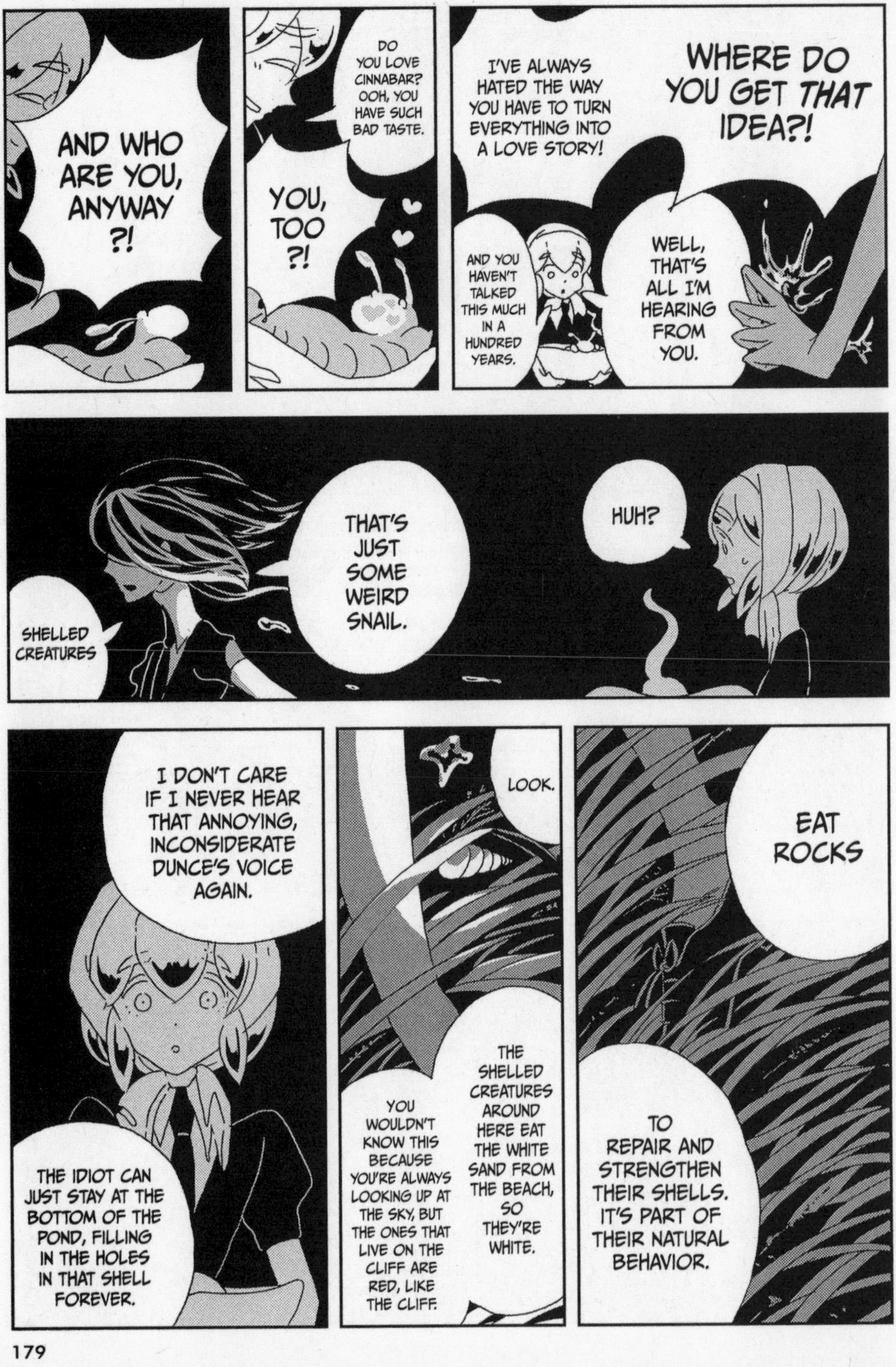
WHERE DO YOU GET THAT IDEA?!
I'VE ALWAYS HATED THE WAY YOU HAVE TO TURN EVERYTHING INTO A LOVE STORY!
WELL, THAT'S ALL I'M HEARING FROM YOU.
AND YOU HAVEN'T TALKED THIS MUCH IN A HUNDRED YEARS.
DO YOU LOVE CINNABAR? OOH, YOU HAVE SUCH BAD TASTE.
YOU, TOO?!
AND WHO ARE YOU, ANYWAY?!
HUH?
THAT'S JUST SOME WEIRD SNAIL.
SHELLED CREATURES
EAT ROCKS
TO REPAIR AND STRENGTHEN THEIR SHELLS. IT'S PART OF THEIR NATURAL BEHAVIOR.
LOOK.
THE SHELLED CREATURES AROUND HERE EAT THE WHITE SAND FROM THE BEACH, SO THEY'RE WHITE.
YOU WOULDN'T KNOW THIS BECAUSE YOU'RE ALWAYS LOOKING UP AT THE SKY, BUT THE ONES THAT LIVE ON THE CLIFF ARE RED, LIKE THE CLIFF.
I DON'T CARE IF I NEVER HEAR THAT ANNOYING, INCONSIDERATE DUNCE'S VOICE AGAIN.
THE IDIOT CAN JUST STAY AT THE BOTTOM OF THE POND, FILLING IN THE HOLES IN THAT SHELL FOREVER.

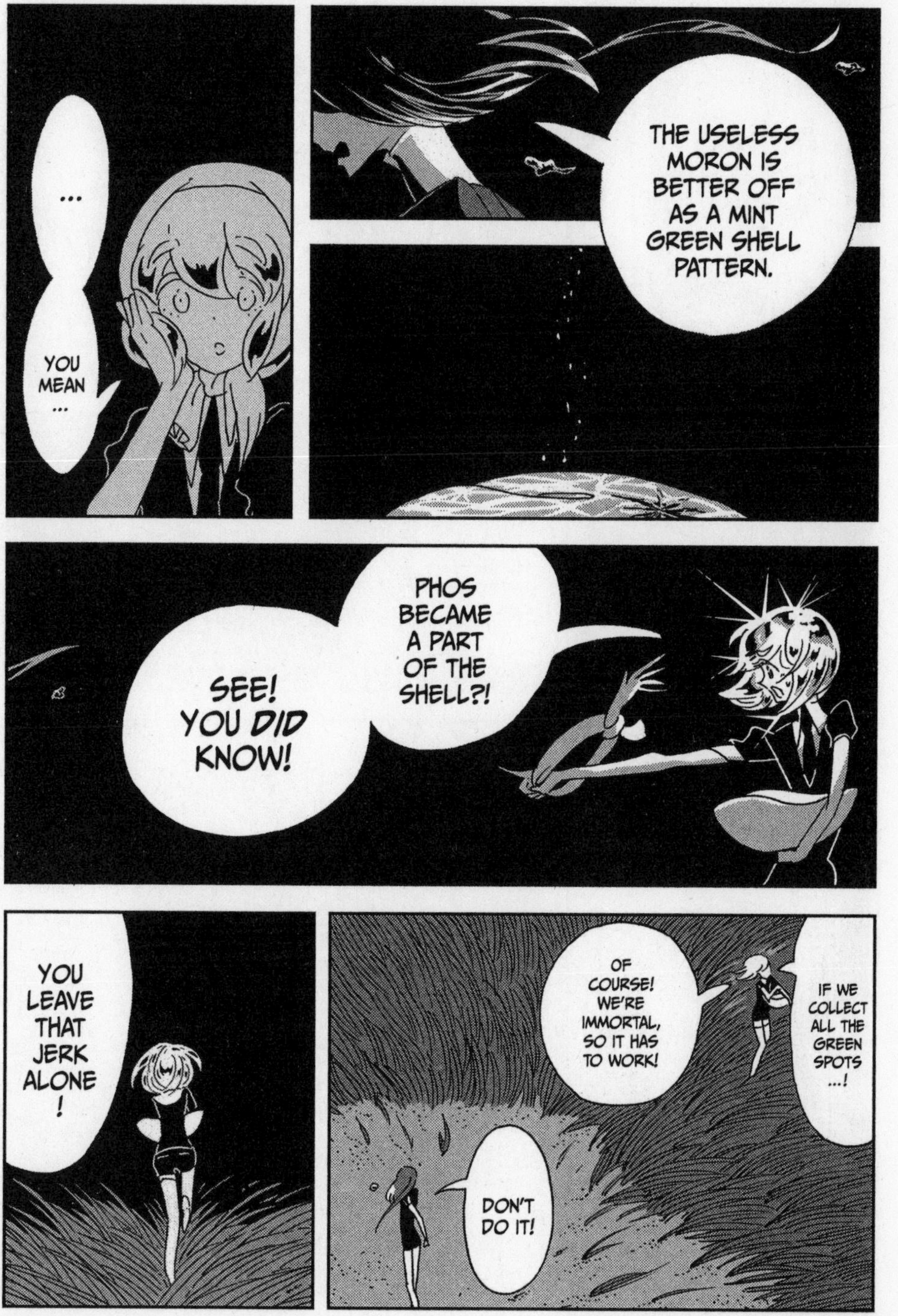
THE USELESS MORON IS BETTER OFF AS A MINT GREEN SHELL PATTERN.
...
YOU MEAN ...
PHOS BECAME A PART OF THE SHELL?!
SEE! YOU *DID* KNOW!
IF WE COLLECT ALL THE GREEN SPOTS ...!
OF COURSE! WE'RE IMMORTAL, SO IT HAS TO WORK!
DON'T DO IT!
YOU LEAVE THAT JERK ALONE!

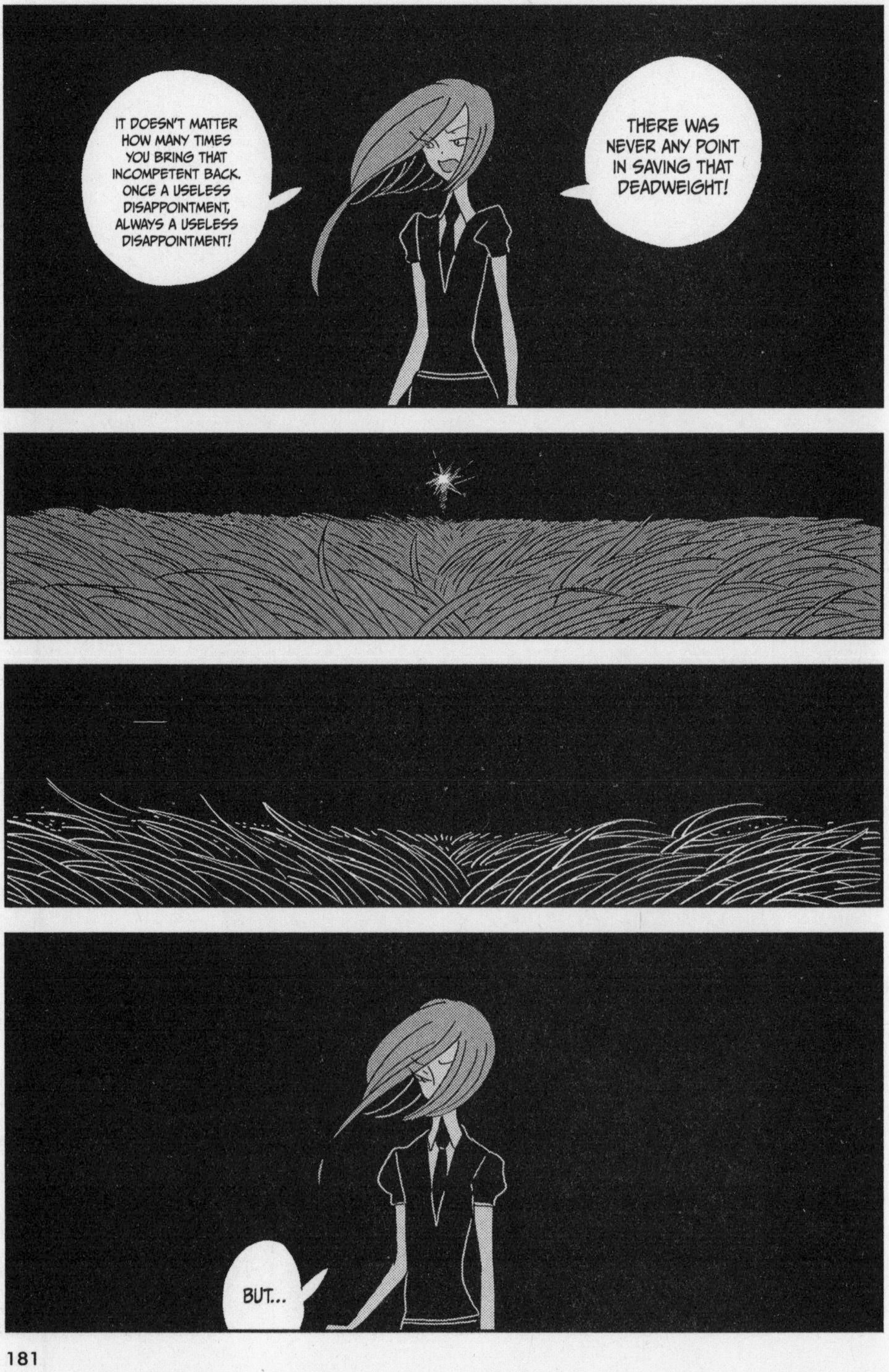
THERE WAS NEVER ANY POINT IN SAVING THAT DEADWEIGHT!
IT DOESN'T MATTER HOW MANY TIMES YOU BRING THAT INCOMPETENT BACK. ONCE A USELESS DISAPPOINTMENT, ALWAYS A USELESS DISAPPOINTMENT!
BUT...

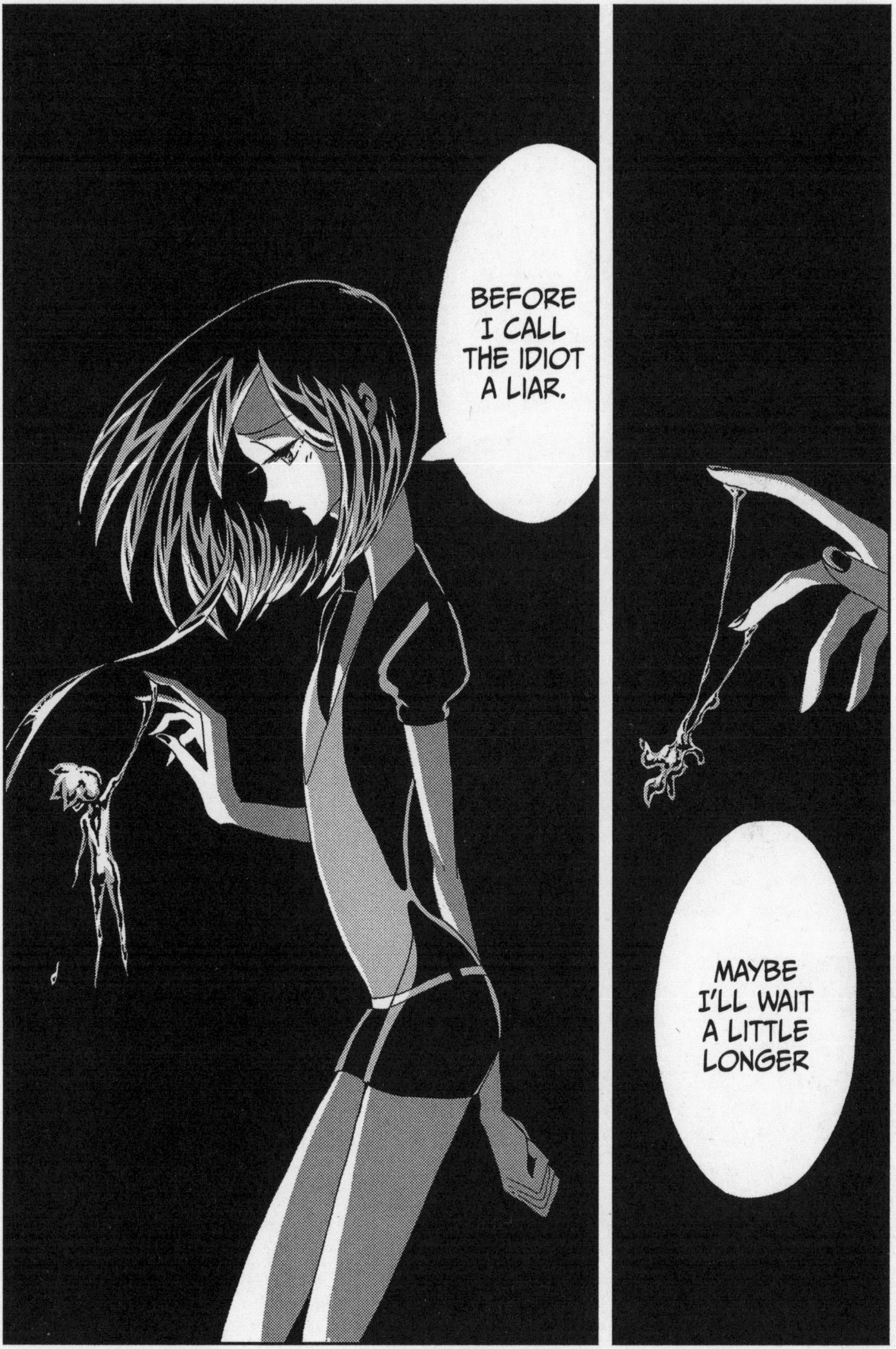
MAYBE I'LL WAIT A LITTLE LONGER
BEFORE I CALL THE IDIOT A LIAR.

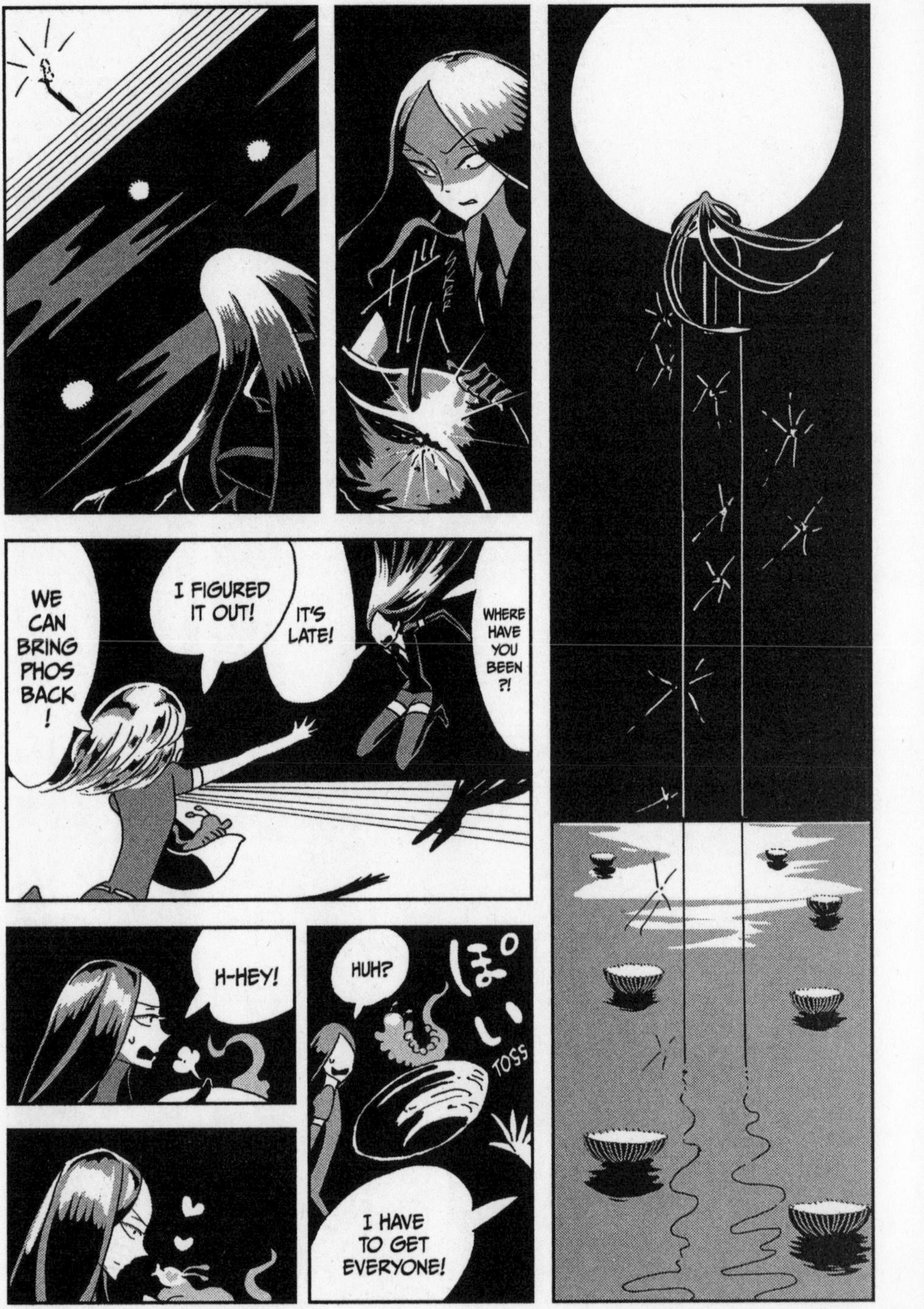
SKRR
WHERE HAVE YOU BEEN ?!
IT'S LATE!
I FIGURED IT OUT!
WE CAN BRING PHOS BACK!
HUH?
ぽい
TOSS
I HAVE TO GET EVERYONE!
H-HEY!

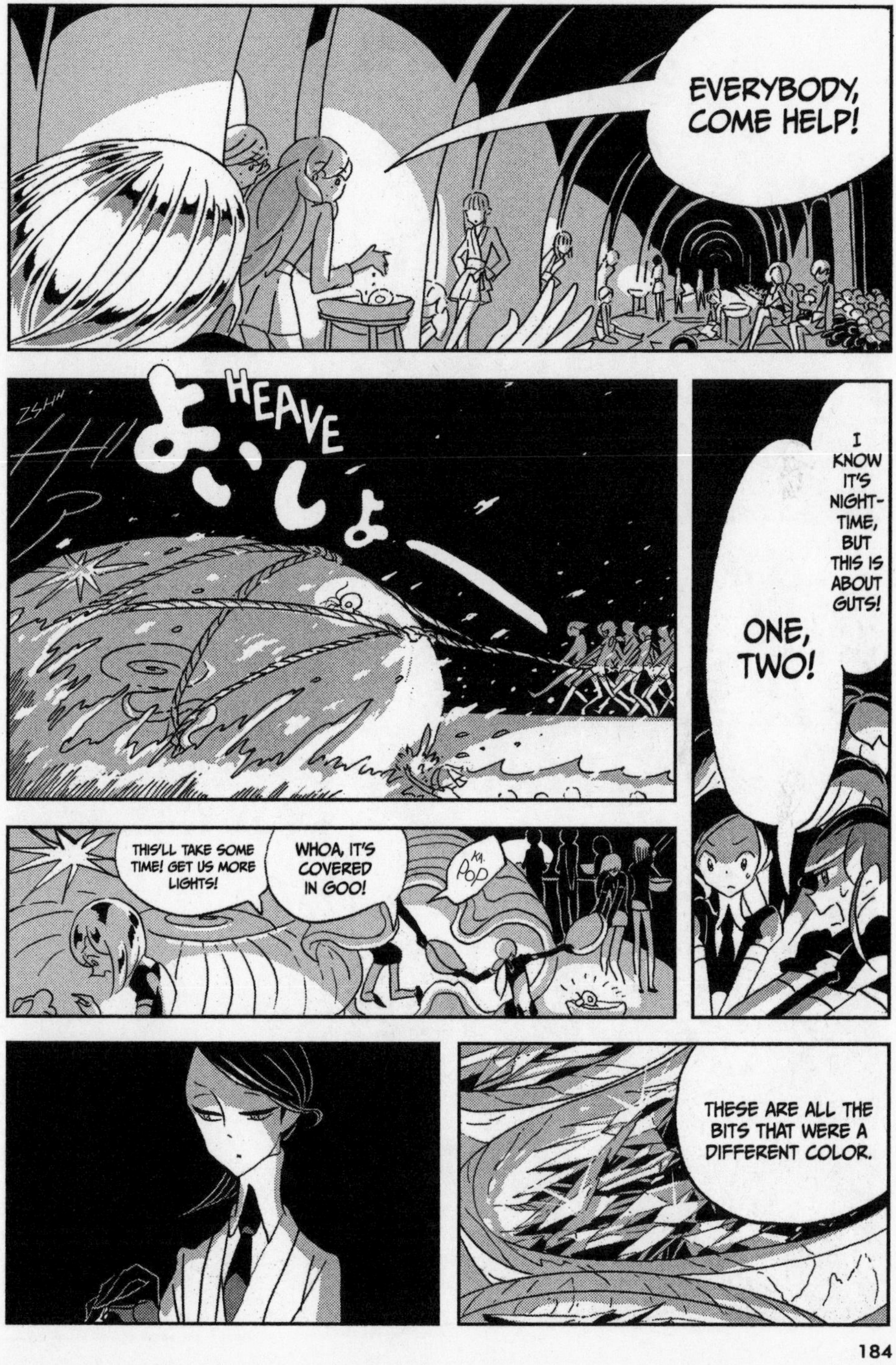
EVERYBODY, COME HELP!
I KNOW IT'S NIGHT-TIME, BUT THIS IS ABOUT GUTS!
ONE, TWO!
ZSHH
よいしょ
HEAVE
KA-POP
WHOA, IT'S COVERED IN GOO!
THIS'LL TAKE SOME TIME! GET US MORE LIGHTS!
THESE ARE ALL THE BITS THAT WERE A DIFFERENT COLOR.

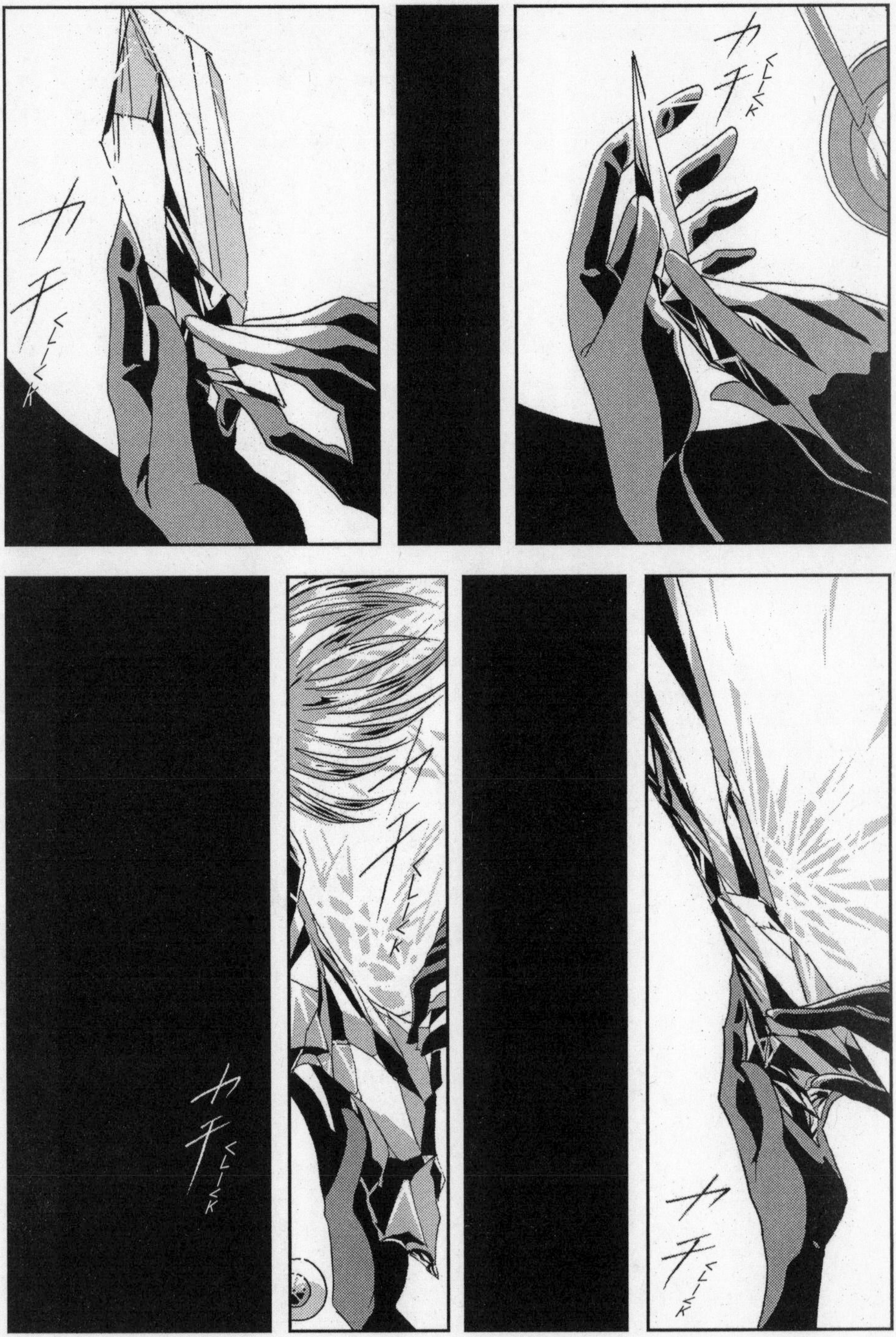
カチ
CLICK
カチ
CLICK
カチ
CLICK
カチ
CLICK
カチ
CLICK

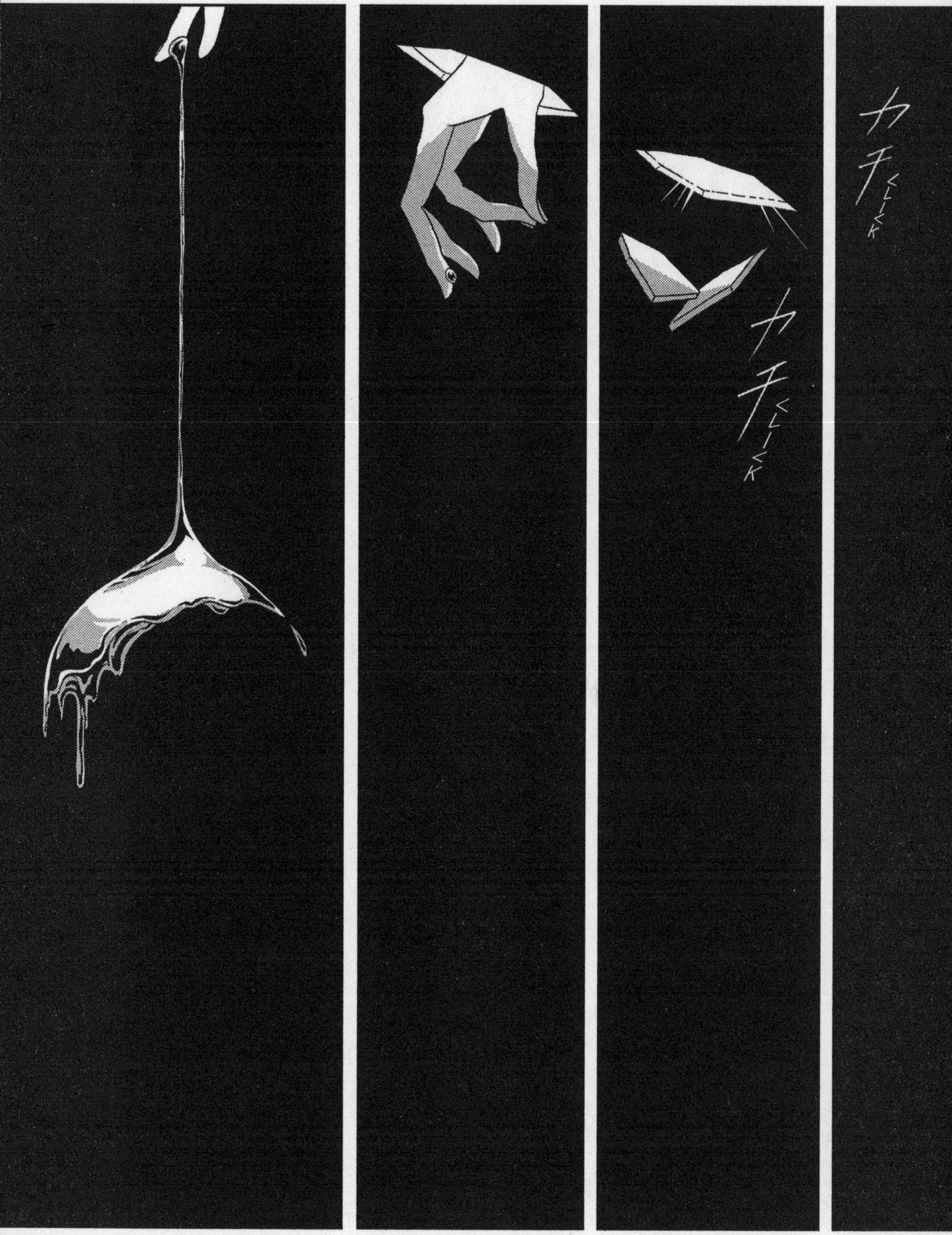
カチ CLICK
カチ CLICK

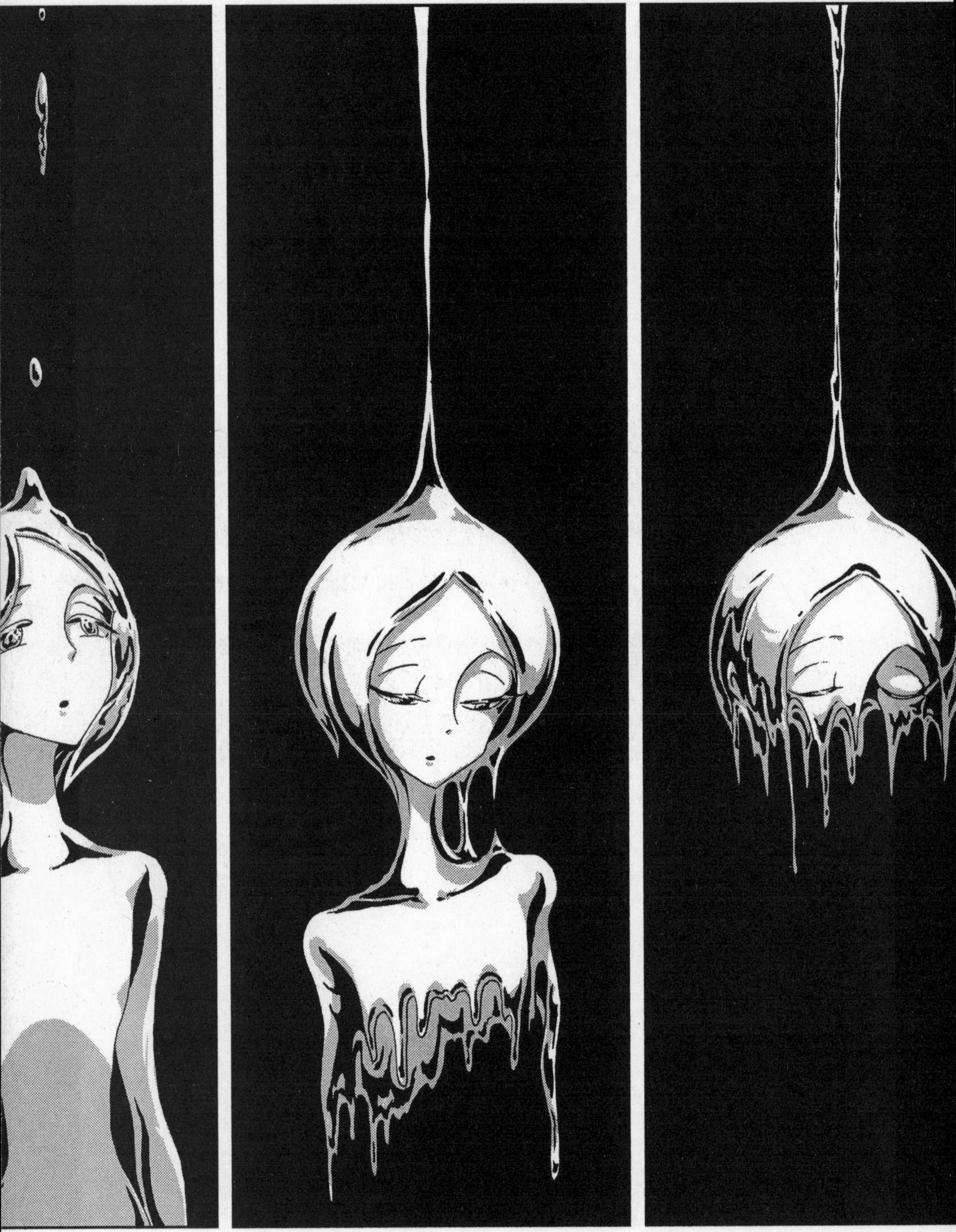

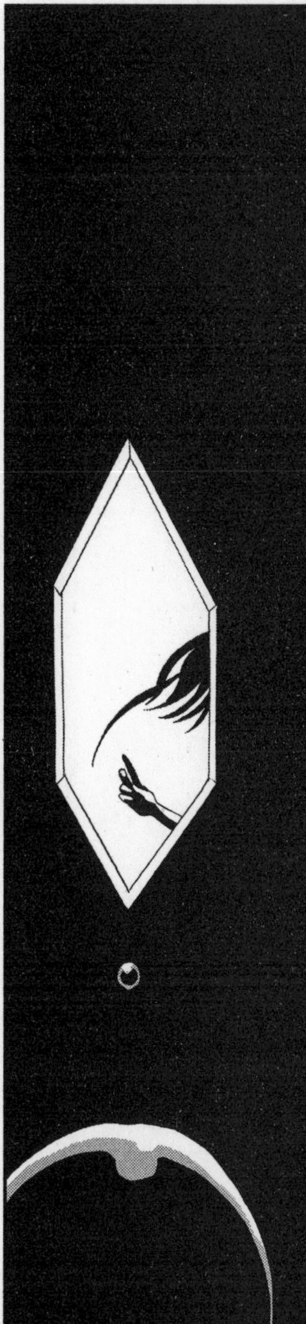
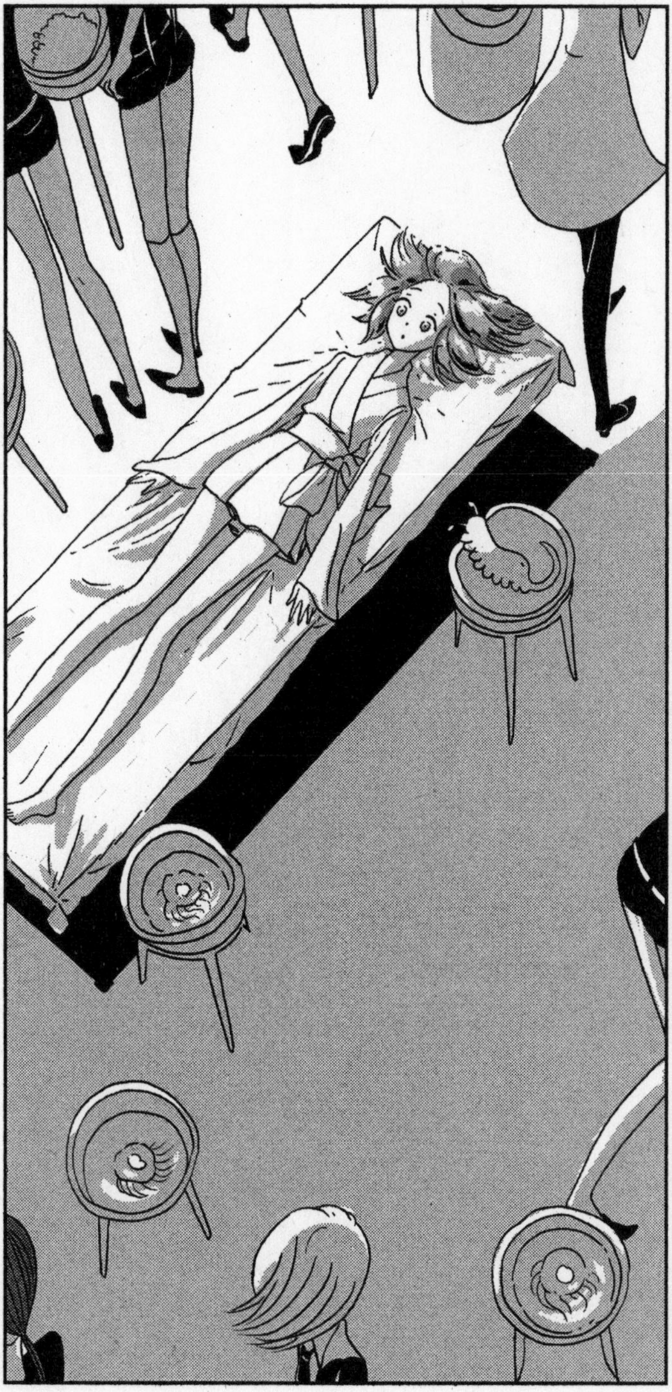

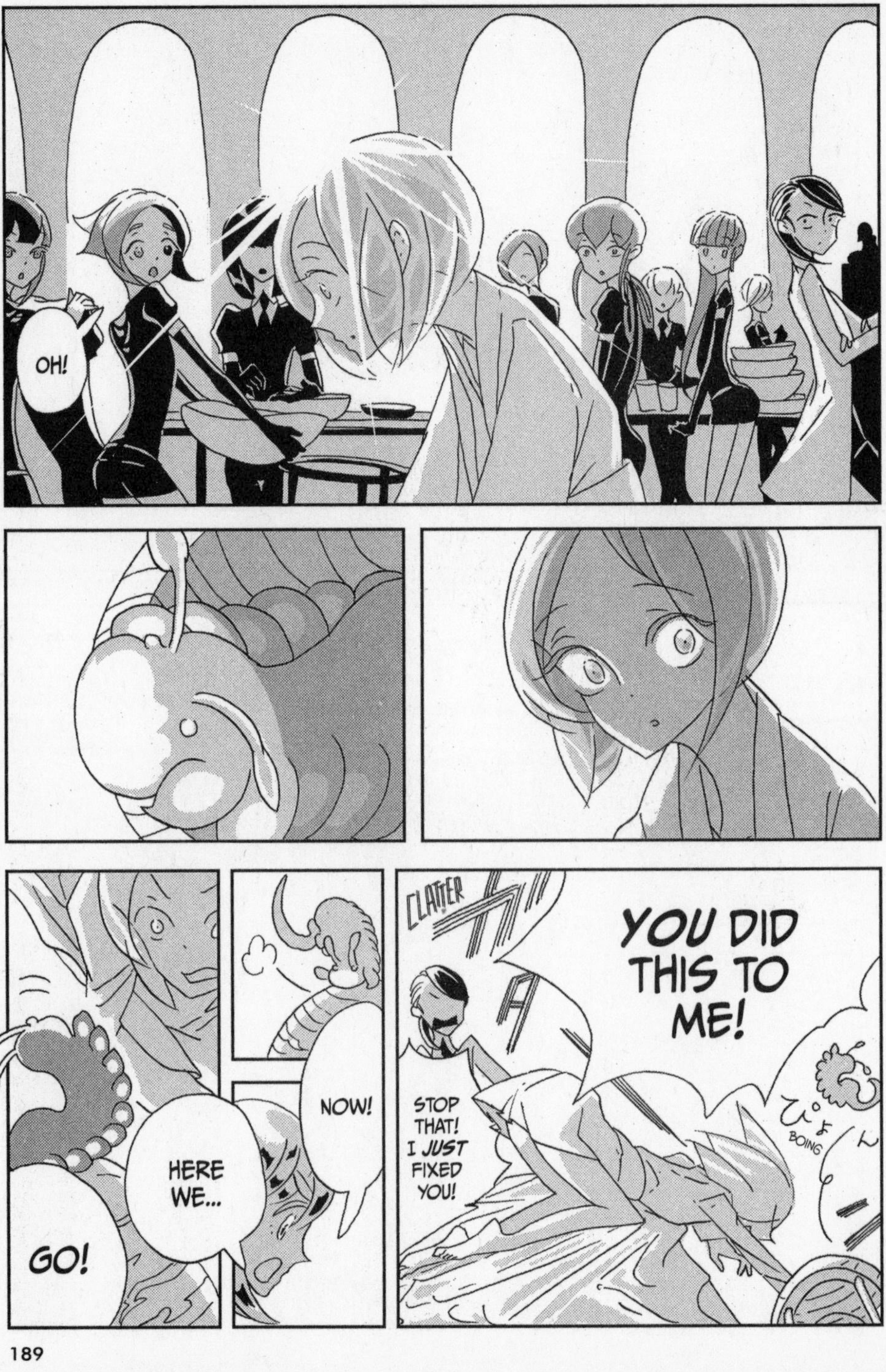

OH!
CLATTER
YOU DID THIS TO ME!
STOP THAT! I JUST FIXED YOU!
ぴょん
BOING
NOW!
HERE WE...
GO!

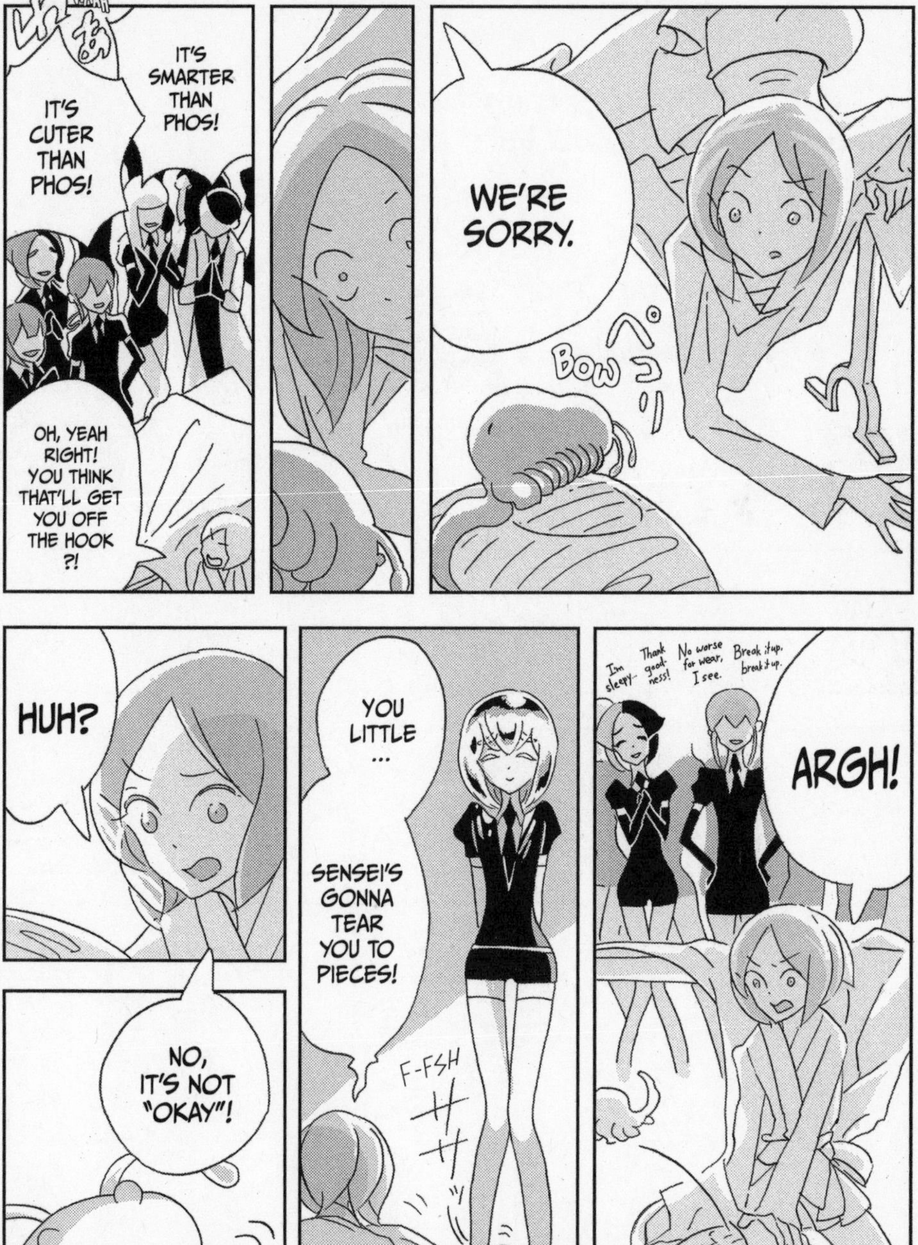
WE'RE SORRY.
BOW
WAAH
IT'S SMARTER THAN PHOS!
IT'S CUTER THAN PHOS!
OH, YEAH RIGHT! YOU THINK THAT'LL GET YOU OFF THE HOOK ?!
Break it up, break it up.
No worse for wear, I see.
Thank goodness!
I'm sleepy...
ARGH!
YOU LITTLE ...
SENSEI'S GONNA TEAR YOU TO PIECES!
F-FSH
HUH?
NO, IT'S NOT "OKAY"!

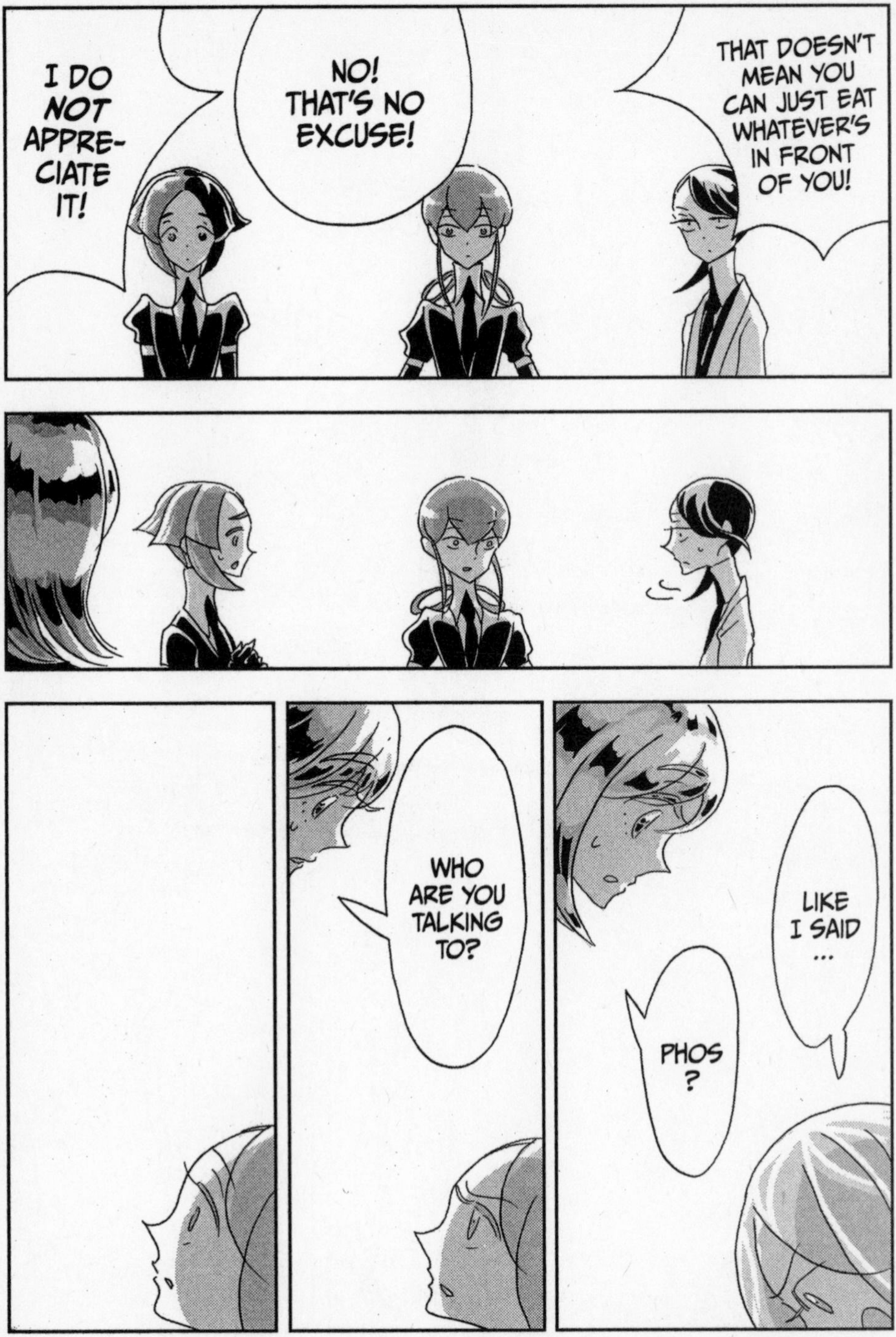
THAT DOESN'T MEAN YOU CAN JUST EAT WHATEVER'S IN FRONT OF YOU!
NO! THAT'S NO EXCUSE!
I DO *NOT* APPRE-CIATE IT!
LIKE I SAID ...
PHOS?
WHO ARE YOU TALKING TO?

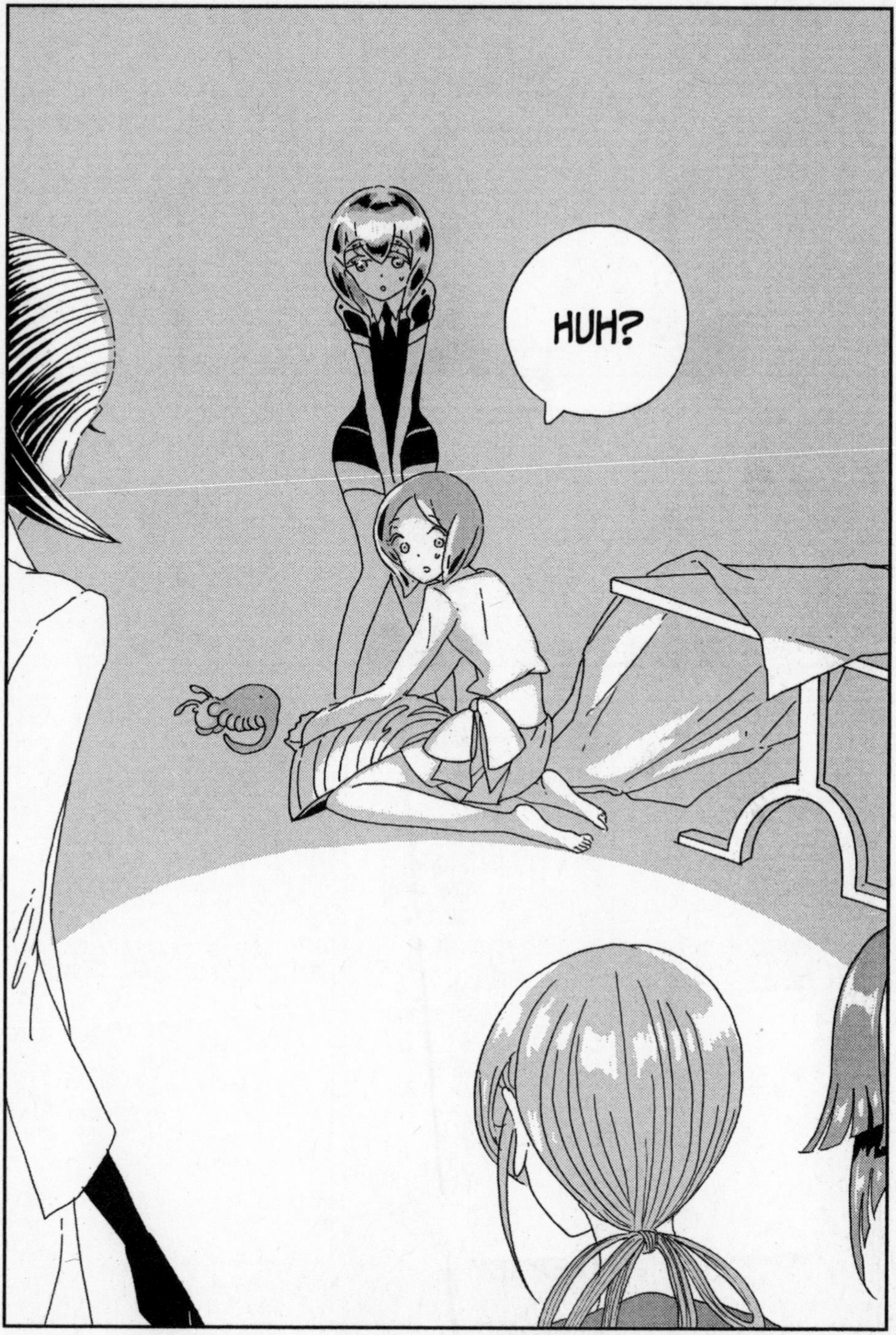
HUH?

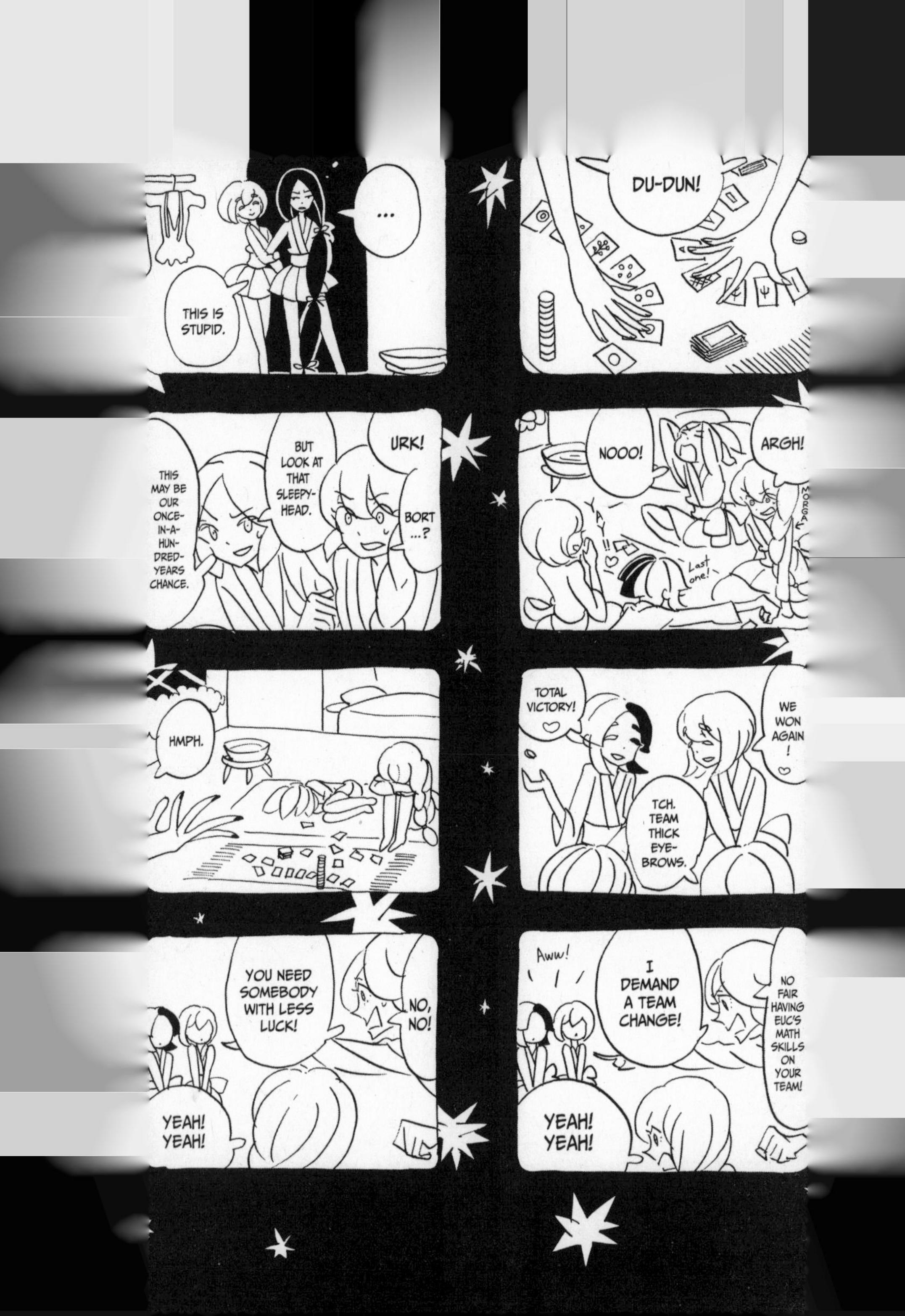
DU-DUN!
...
THIS IS STUPID.
ARGH!
MORGA
NOOO!
Last one!
URK!
BORT ...?
BUT LOOK AT THAT SLEEPY-HEAD.
THIS MAY BE OUR ONCE-IN-A-HUN-DRED-YEARS CHANCE.
WE WON AGAIN!
TOTAL VICTORY!
TCH. TEAM THICK EYE-BROWS.
HMPH.
NO FAIR HAVING EUC'S MATH SKILLS ON YOUR TEAM!
I DEMAND A TEAM CHANGE!
Aww!
YEAH! YEAH!
NO, NO!
YOU NEED SOMEBODY WITH LESS LUCK!
YEAH! YEAH!

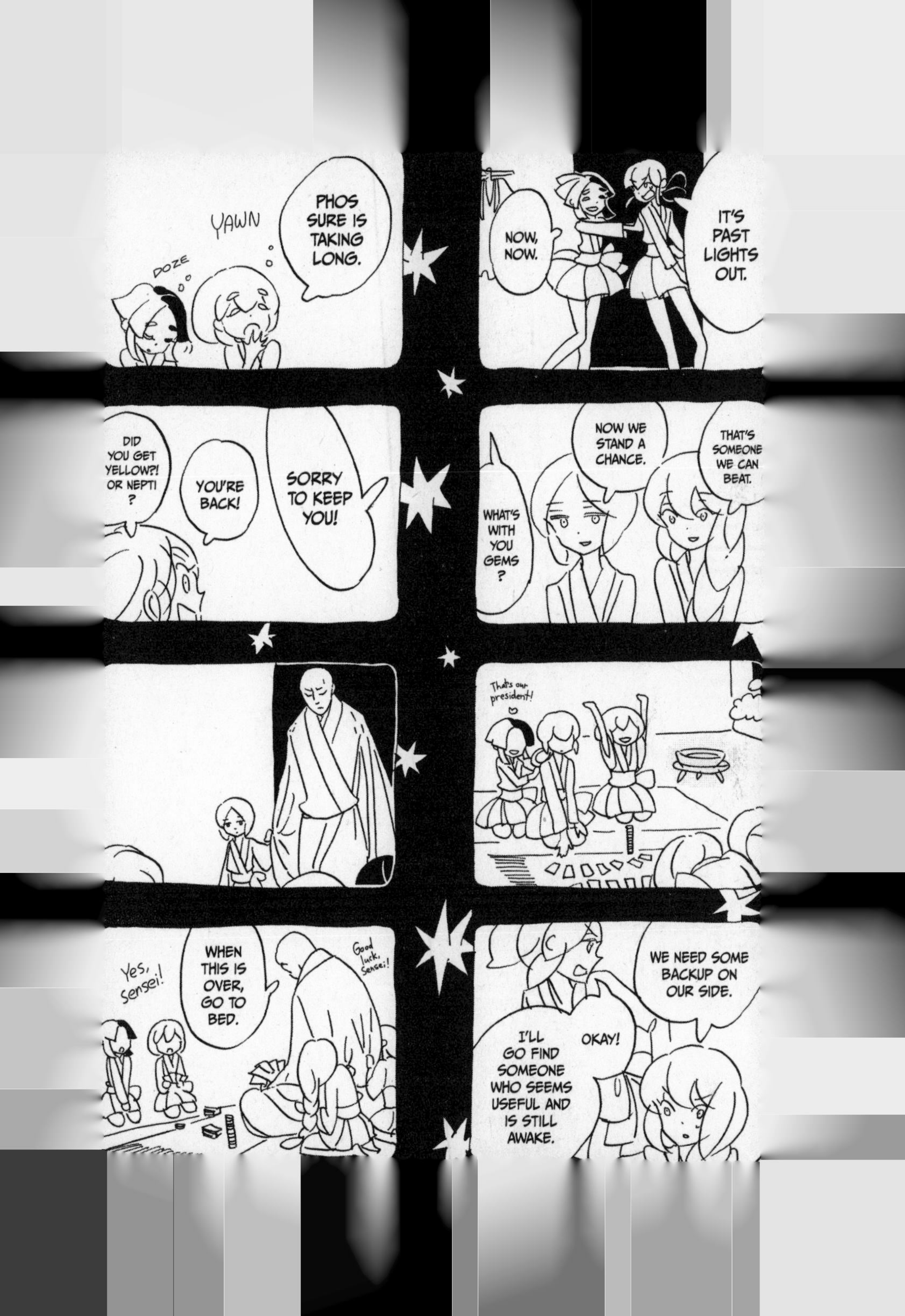
IT'S PAST LIGHTS OUT.
NOW, NOW.
PHOS SURE IS TAKING LONG.
YAWN
DOZE
THAT'S SOMEONE WE CAN BEAT.
NOW WE STAND A CHANCE.
WHAT'S WITH YOU GEMS?
SORRY TO KEEP YOU!
YOU'RE BACK!
DID YOU GET YELLOW?! OR NEPTI?
That's our president!
WE NEED SOME BACKUP ON OUR SIDE.
OKAY!
I'LL GO FIND SOMEONE WHO SEEMS USEFUL AND IS STILL AWAKE.
Good luck, Sensei!
WHEN THIS IS OVER, GO TO BED.
Yes, sensei!

TRANSLATION NOTES

KONGŌ-SENSEI *page 17*

The reader will have noticed that the characters in this series are named after gemstones. The word *kongō* literally means "gold (or metal) hardness," and has significance in Japanese Buddhism. It is related to the Sanskrit word *vajra*, which means both "diamond" and "thunderbolt," and represents indestructibility. Kongō is part of the word for "diamond," but is also used to refer to extremely hard substances, not limited to diamonds, similar to the English word "adamant."

PERV *page 40*

A cliché in anime and manga is that a character will blurt out "White!" while thinking indecent thoughts. The reason for the inappropriate ruminations is that the white is what the character has just seen under a girl's skirt—in other words, her undergarments. In this case, Phos is accusing Morga of looking at something that was not intended for public viewing, but mostly is just being contrary.

HUSK OF A MOLLUSK *page 151*

The translators had Rutile supply the punchline of this unfunny gag, but in the original Japanese it was built into Jade's report that "the shell was empty." The word for both "shell" and "empty" is *kara*, so the sentence was originally, "The *kara* was *kara*." Rutile's response was then, "Because it's a *kara*?"

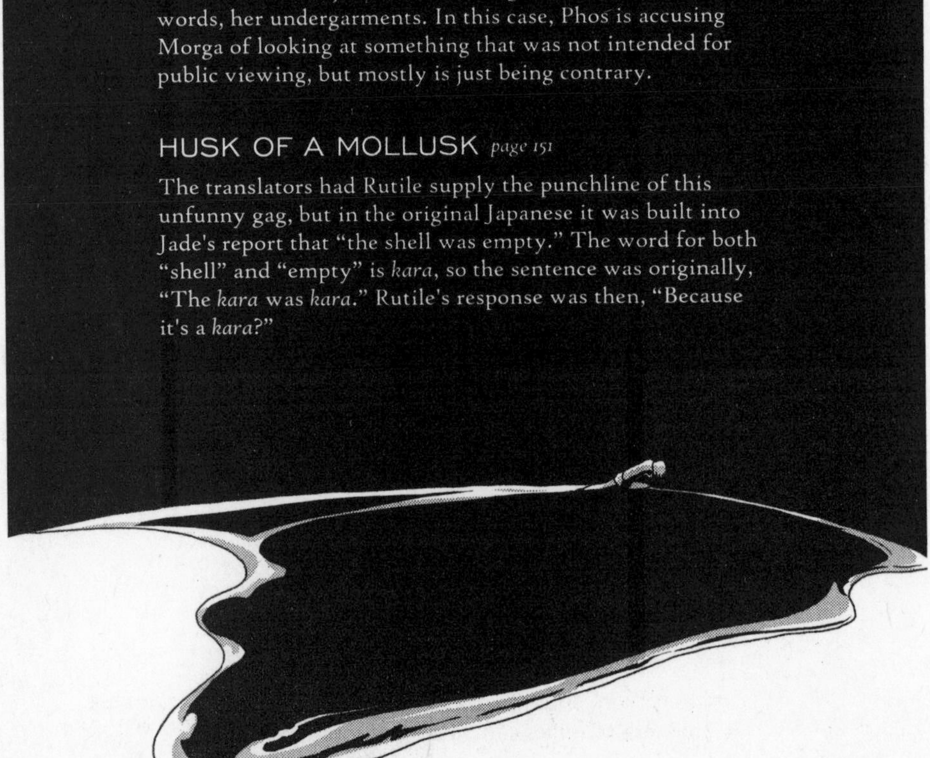

Land of the Lustrous volume 1 is a work of fiction. Names, characters, places, and incidents are the products of the author's imagination or are used fictitiously. Any resemblance to actual events, locales, or persons, living or dead, is entirely coincidental.

A Kodansha Comics Trade Paperback Original.

Land of the Lustrous volume 1 copyright © 2013 Haruko Ichikawa
English translation copyright © 2017 Haruko Ichikawa

All rights reserved.

Published in the United States by Kodansha Comics, an imprint of Kodansha USA Publishing, LLC, New York.

Publication rights for this English edition arranged through Kodansha Ltd., Tokyo.

First published in Japan in 2013 by Kodansha Ltd., Tokyo.

ISBN 978-1-63236-497-5

Printed in the United States of America.

www.kodanshacomics.com

9 8 7 6 5 4 3 2

Translator: Alethea Nibley & Athena Nibley
Lettering: Evan Hayden
Editing: Lauren Scanlan
Kodansha Comics edition cover design: Fawn Lau